Intoxication

The Universal Drive for Mind-Altering Substances

Ronald K. Siegel, Ph.D.

Park Street Press
Rochester, Vermont

For Jane, with love

Park Street Press
One Park Street
Rochester, Vermont 05767
www.InnerTraditions.com

Park Street Press is a division of Inner Traditions International

Library of Congress Cataloging-in-Publication Data
Siegel, Ronald K.
  Intoxication : the universal drive for mind-altering substances / Ronald K. Siegel.
      p. cm.
  Includes bibliographical references and index.
  ISBN 1-59477-069-7 (pbk.)
  1. Animals—Drug use. 2. Substance abuse. I. Title.
  QL756.7.S54 2005
  154.4—dc22

                                                      2005003197

Printed and bound in the United States by Lake Book Manufacturing, Inc.

10 9 8 7 6 5 4 3 2 1

Text design and layout by Rachel Goldenberg
This book was typeset in Sabon with ACaslon as a display typeface

Contents

☀

Preface

There is a silent spring of intoxicants that flows through our lives and bodies. Whether we wake up with a sip of coffee or a sniff of cocaine, take a break with a cigarette or a beer, relax with a cocktail or marijuana, drift to sleep with a pill we purchased at the pharmacy or from our neighborhood dealer, we use drugs to change the way we feel. Nobody wants this to be unhealthy or dangerous. Nobody wants people to live out their lives inside crack houses, to die from tobacco cancer, or to be killed by drunk drivers.

Over the years since I wrote the first edition of this book, most governments of the world have continued to wage a war on drugs. The strategy has been to reduce supply and demand, a policy established by President Richard Nixon when he declared the first war on drugs in 1971. His idea was hardly original but reminiscent of every failed attempt to prohibit intoxicating drugs throughout the history of civilization.

History shows that we have always used drugs. In every age, in every part of this planet, people have pursued intoxication with plant drugs, alcohol, and other mind-altering substances. Surprisingly, we're not the only ones to do this. As you will see in the following pages, almost every species of animal has engaged in the natural pursuit of intoxicants. This behavior has so much force and persistence that it functions like a drive, just like our drives of hunger, thirst, and sex. This "fourth drive" is a natural part of our biology, creating the irrepressible demand for drugs. In a sense, the war on drugs is a war against ourselves, a denial of our very nature.

The inherent futility of this war is illustrated by the very nature of the warfare itself. Our major drugs and medicines were originally produced millions of years ago by plants as chemical defenses against animals and pests that could browse them. Our brains—three pound sacks of sophisticated chemicals with molecular structures and pharmacological actions similar to the substances found in the plants—gave us an affinity for these plant compounds. As intelligent primates we evolved the ability to extract the plant compounds, synthesize their chemical relatives, and develop ways to introduce highly concentrated forms directly into our bodies. It is not surprising that we continue doing so for it is our nature as chemical beings.

All of our wars against drugs, like all our wars against each other, pit enemies using one set of drugs against those using the same or different sets. German and Japanese soldiers used amphetamines for energy and alertness during World War II just as allied soldiers and pilots took them before battle. In recent times pilots flying missions against illegal narcotic operations in South America and Southeast Asia have used amphetamines for staying awake and alert while the targets of their operations fought back with "narcoterrorism" fueled by their own drugs of choice: cocaine or opium. In Hawaii and California marijuana growers high on their own harvest have fought against coffee-guzzling police. Chechen terrorists in the Russian town of Beslan used heroin and morphine as they held more than a thousand hostages in a school for three days while fighting against Russian forces who took their own breaks with tobacco, coffee, and, allegedly, vodka. U.S. jet fighter pilots used amphetamine "go pills" in Operation Desert Storm to fly longer hours as did those responsible for at least ten deadly "friendly fire" accidents in the Afghanistan war. The pilots were then given sedatives or "no-go pills" to help them sleep when they returned to base. Yet invading armies have always been at risk of returning home with local drug habits. American veterans of the Vietnam conflict came back with opium and heroin addictions so it was not surprising that soldiers returning from the war in Afghanistan acquired similar dependencies. And drug trafficking has been used for financial benefit by both sides of armed conflicts in Cambodia, Colombia, Mexico, Nicaragua, Peru, Thailand, and Yemen. It is clear that the fourth drive influences the behavior of nations as well as individuals.

Of course, sometimes this fourth drive runs amok and overshadows the other drives, as when animals and people alike pursue a drug such as cocaine to the exclusion of everything else in their lives. This tells us that we are doing the right thing when we try to curtail the use of certain drugs like cocaine. But the attempt to dam up supplies has never stopped the flow and new sources always emerge to bring the forbidden fruit of intoxicants within our reach.

When I first sat down to write this book the silent spring had become a river of cocaine. Today it has turned into the speeding white water of the methamphetamine epidemic that I predicted would come. Methamphetamine has now become the number one enemy in the war on drugs. More than any target of the war on drugs this one illustrates how the face of the enemy is our own. Unlike most other intoxicants, methamphetamine (also known as crystal or speed) has both medically approved and proven beneficial effects as well as nonmedical uses. It does not stupefy and impair like alcohol or heroin but clarifies and improves. Medical science has discovered that methamphetamine-like drugs are indeed wonder medicines while nonmedical users have discovered they are wonderful euphoriants and empathogens (chemical agents that induce feelings of empathy). In a word, they work. They deliver the benefits of the desired effects but not without costs. Yet, according to the tilted economic scale that governs both medical and nonmedical drug use, when even a few benefits seem almost too good to be true, they tip the balance in favor of continued use despite heavier costs.

Methamphetamine appears in a variety of molecular disguises as prescription drugs to treat fatigue, depression, obesity, and even attention deficit disorders in children. It masquerades as over-the-counter medications promoted to treat asthma and the common cold, or in herbal preparations marketed to boost energy or help weight loss. In less visible yet highly effective forms we find it on athletic fields and battlefields, on long-distance trucking missions and space missions, and in classrooms and work places everywhere. It has been used for fueling the brain with energy and ideas or helping to spill secrets from the brains of POWs who cannot stop talking. And variations on the molecular theme have produced chemical cousins that are used for everything from parties to psychotherapy, from sexual encounters to spiritual quests, from dancing with friends to dancing with the gods. While young people dance and "rave" in a sensual paradise of hip hop music, and hopped up terrorists rant and rave to enter the gates of another paradise, the production, trafficking, and use of methamphetamine and its crystal cousins have created a worldwide epidemic that touches us all. It has changed the war on drugs from one against a specific drug to an absurd war against specific patterns of drug use.

And if that wasn't enough, clandestine designer drug labs are turning out still more intoxicants, some with deadly hallucinogenic properties, while users continually prowl through exotic gardens searching for sources of new chemical delights. When these new drugs become fashionable if not problematic, they, too, will be declared illegal as recently happened to MDMA (Ecstasy) and the Chinese plant *Ephedra* (the source of amphetamine). Prohibition, however, will never work. Users have already developed potent genetic variants of traditional mind-altering plants such as marijuana that are suitable for indoor or backyard cultivation while methods for cultivating homegrown opium poppies, *Ephedra,* the Middle Eastern stimulant khat, hallucinogenic mushrooms, and several other plants are being promoted. New epidemics are looming on the horizon. And so the war on drugs will continue as it has throughout history.

Some people want to stop the war, and put an end to its enormous societal costs, by legalizing drugs such as cocaine or heroin. Legalization is a risky proposal that would cut a major drug-crime connection and reduce many social ills, yet it would invite more use and abuse, thereby increasing treatment costs. Saying "Yes" to a drug and calling it legal doesn't change its basic pharmacology or safety any more than saying "No" changes our basic drive to pursue intoxication. Can you imagine the public health crisis that would ensue if a drug such as cocaine, which ignites the fourth drive better than any substance known, was suddenly stamped with the legal equivalent of the *Good Housekeeping* Seal of Approval? The consequences would be even more severe if cocaine prohibition was totally successful and all cocaine users switched to legal drugs such as alcohol and tobacco.

Outlawing drugs in order to solve drug problems is much like outlawing sex in order to win the war against AIDS. We recognize that people will continue to have sex for nonreproductive reasons despite the laws and mores. Therefore, we try to make sexual practices as safe as possible in order to minimize the spread of the AIDS viruses. In a similar way, we continually try to make our drinking water, foods, and even our pharmaceutical medicines safer.

The ubiquity of chemical intoxicants in our lives is undeniable evidence of the continuing universal need for safer medicines with such applications. While use may not always be for an approved medical purpose, or prudent, or even legal, it is fulfilling the relentless drive we all have to change the way we feel, to alter our behavior and consciousness, and, yes, to intoxicate ourselves. *We must recognize that intoxicants are medicines, treatments for the human condition.* Then we must make them as safe and risk free and as healthy as possible.

Dream with me for a moment. What would be wrong if we had perfectly safe intoxicants? I mean drugs that delivered the same effects as our most popular ones but never caused dependency, disease, dysfunction, or death. Imagine an alcohol-type substance that never caused addiction, liver disease, hangovers, impaired driving, or workplace problems. Would you care to inhale a perfumed mist that is as enjoyable as marijuana or tobacco but as harmless as clean air? How would you like a pain-killer as effective as morphine but safer than aspirin, a mood enhancer that dissolves on your tongue and is more appealing than cocaine and less harmful than caffeine, a tranquilizer less addicting than Valium and more relaxing than a martini, or a safe sleeping pill that allows you to choose to dream or not? Perhaps you would like to munch on a user friendly hallucinogen that is as brief and benign as a good movie?

This is not science fiction. As described in the following pages, there are such intoxicants available right now that are far safer than the ones we currently use. If smokers can switch from tobacco cigarettes to nicotine gum, why can't crack users chew a cocaine gum that has already been tested on animals and found to be relatively safe? Even safer substances may be just around the corner. But we must begin by recognizing that there is a legitimate place in our society for intoxication. Then we must join together in building new, perfectly safe intoxicants for a world that will be ready to discard the old ones like the junk they really are.

This book is your guide to that future. It is a field guide to that silent spring of intoxicants and all the animals and peoples who have sipped its waters. We can no more stop the flow than we can prevent ourselves from drinking. But, by cleaning up the waters we can leave the morass that has been the endless war on drugs and step onto the shores of a healthy tomorrow. Use this book to find the way.

LOS ANGELES, CALIFORNIA
NOVEMBER 2004

Prologue

From the pit I could almost touch the sun. At 3,800 meters in the Andes it seemed more like a hellfire than the benevolent god the Indians worshiped as Giver of Heat, Light, and Life. Layers of sunscreen, sweat, and dust covered my swollen face. Even after weeks in Peru I was not fully adapted to the altitude. The pangs of *soroche* racked my body: shortness of breath, dizziness, nausea, vomiting, diarrhea, blurred vision, and fatigue. My constant headache pounded as I chipped away at dirt and rock. The pit in which I was digging had once been a grave for ancient Peruvian Indians.

The pit was round and approximately three meters in diameter. A previous expedition had removed the pile of stones and dirt that guarded it through the centuries. The interior was lined with clay and limestone and resembled a huge mushroom with a center stem protruding downward. The cap of the mushroom dropped to two and a half meters below the surface, and I was digging near the stem, which ran another meter straight down. I had been working the stem all day and had advanced only a few centimeters. One can't dig quickly with a toothbrush and dental tools, unlikely instruments for solving the puzzle of why we pursue intoxication with drugs. My mind, searching for the missing oxygen, wandered easily. I pretended I was Rodin chipping away at the unfinished *Gates of Hell* to expose a part of our nature that lay hidden in the stone below.

It was almost sundown. Although it was the middle of summer, the cold winds from nearby Lake Titicaca would soon make further digging impossible. There was a faint scratching noise as my pick uncovered a shard from a ceramic pot. I plucked it loose from the dirt with surprising ease. The unique oval shape suggested it was from the pre-Inca Tiahuanaco Empire, perhaps one thousand years old. I brushed the dirt away from the sides to reveal a painted scene. In the center was a cluster of coca branches and leaves. On one side stood a large llama eating the coca. The animal's swollen cheek pouch pictured the ingestion in no uncertain terms. This was Napa, the legendary llama honored in coca ceremonies. On the other side of the coca leaves was an Indian, watching the llama and beginning to reach for the coca with open hands and mouth. Was this the story of coca's discovery in 5000 B.C. by early Andean man? He had apparently observed his pack animals foraging on the plant and perhaps noticed a certain friskiness to their movements. He copied the coca-eating behavior and soon discovered both the stimulating and nutritious properties of the plant. What a surprise that must have been!

No wonder the Indians celebrated coca with ritual and magic. They even burned coca leaves as gifts to the gods. Later that evening, when no one was watching, I threw a few coca leaves on the evening campfire. Thanksgiving had come to the Andes early that year.

I couldn't sleep that night. I was eager to return to Lima and report my find to César at the museum. César was a dark, mustached, pear-shaped man who reminded me of a child's punching toy that always bobs up after you knock it down. César's blood was half Indian, his muscles solid steel, and his luck that of a cat who had survived more than a few falls from the Andean burial sites he uncovered. He had removed the mummies and most of the pottery from this pit and had shared its location with me only when he was satisfied that it was empty save for some odd chips of pottery or small ceremonial stones. He was humoring me. When I told him my theory of how early man learned most of his pharmacology by watching animal reactions to plant drugs, he rolled and tipped in laughter. No proof, he said. The proof would be very old, I argued, and probably recorded by people who lived very close to their animals and plants. It would predate the highly civilized cultural and religious themes depicted on most Indian pottery. Hunting and gathering groups would have been in a good position to observe and record such events. I needed an archaeological site where people had once hunted animals and gathered coca. César graciously permitted me to dig in this pit, which had contained a few pots with animal and plant motifs. He tittered as I left the museum with map in hand. I now pictured a celebration with him at the elegant Hotel Bolívar, where we would toast my find. It would be my secret laughing place.

Dawn came as I was still counting the other bits and pieces of folklore that matched the picture on the shard. According to these tales, animals have guided us to a variety of drugs throughout the ages. In A.D. 900 an Abyssinian herder noticed that his animals were energized after eating the bright red fruit of a tree that would later be named coffee. A shepherd in Yemen discovered the popular Middle Eastern stimulant khat, similar to amphetamine, by watching goats run wild after chewing the leaves. Natives in Australia found powerful anesthetics after observing how fish were stunned and rose to the surface when certain leaves fell into the water. Animals visiting snakeroot plants in tropical Asia were quieted by reserpine, a tranquilizer that, when isolated by an Indian psychiatrist in 1947, would revolutionize the treatment of mental illness.

As I looked at the shard in the morning light, I wondered how many other discoveries of plant drugs had been illuminated by this same sun. Do we thank this Giver of Heat, Light, and Life for the photosynthetic powers of plants and for the tempting drugs those plants release to lure and otherwise enmesh our species? Or, since intoxication was a fact of natural life long before man, do we curse the time when it all started, some 250 million years ago, when the sun was a proud yellow giant and the reptilian giants roamed the earth?

The Mesozoic era began in the black and white of disappearing coal swamps and ice fields. Continents were still close together, volcanoes were building mountains, and the reptiles had only begun their slow evolutionary advance among the ferns and conifers. And so had the angiosperm plants that begat flowering seeds during the Cretaceous period, 135 million years ago. Carried by the winds and rains, these plants spread throughout the land. Under a canopy of sunlight and rising temperatures they started making complex alkaloidal drugs. Ingenious in design, plant alkaloids had the effect of bestowing on hungry animals a bitter taste, dizziness, sickness, or death. As if to signal their unique arrival, angiosperms covered the planet in a Technicolor explosion of tempting fruits and flowers.

Since the land was brimming over with animal life, close encounters between browsing beasts and poisonous plants were inevitable. Some animals, unable to taste the bitterness, probably succumbed to the stress of cumulative toxic effects. With superior sensory skills and hardy livers, birds and mammals survived these bitter lessons. The physiology and behavior of their modern descendants suggest that they survived by developing biochemical mechanisms to detoxify plant drugs and feeding strategies to minimize intake of dangerous amounts. By treating new foods with extreme caution and quickly rejecting specific plants, surviving animals learned to seek out and eat plants rich in nutrients and low in psychoactive drugs. Through trial and error, a number of animals learned to survive the use of plant drugs by ingesting them in only small amounts while preferentially feeding on more familiar and safer foods. Millions of years later, animals behaving in similar ways became man's first teachers.

Wandering in his primordial classroom, early man watched and hunted the teachers. He licked and cleansed his wounds after watching his prey do the same. He sat down in cold rivers to relieve fever after seeing deer do so following the attack of poisonous snakes. He copied the movements of animals in dances of homage and gratitude to greater teachers in the sky. He climbed great mountains while chewing coca just as animals did before him. And there on the mountaintops, closer to the Giver, he offered the smoke of incense and intoxicating plants such as coca.

By the time of the Neolithic revolution, man's brain and tools had allowed him to move to the head of the class, domesticating his former teachers, cultivating his drug plants, and transforming the Giver's garden into a laboratory. Wandering passed into wonderment as further experiences exposed man to the medicinal and intoxicating properties of narcotics. Over the next ten thousand years he learned to sniff, smoke, and inject the drugs. These achievements bypassed the tongue, which would have cried out "no" to the bitterness, and the stomach, which would have rejected an equivalent amount of the plants. Humans abandoned the control that feeding strategies had provided for other surviving species. Equipped with a ferocious curiosity but a fragile physiology, humans faced new experiences with faster, stronger, and more dangerous intoxicants. It was the first day of school.

Sitting on the edge of the pit with my newfound shard, I was as excited as a schoolboy. At sunrise I made a sketch of the shard, then wrapped it in layers of native manta cloth. It went into my pack along with my camping gear. Into my mouth I pushed enormous quantities of coca leaves sprinkled with a sweet-tasting ash to help liberate the cocaine. Although I would not normally use drugs outside of a medical setting or authorized experiment, coca was legal in these highlands. Coca blew like a fresh wind through my tired body. I raced the midday sun down the mountain to the airfield below.

Back in Lima I checked into the Bolívar and soaked in an oversize bath until my skin wrinkled. César didn't answer his telephone, so I took a walk around the city. Coca now seemed mild compared to my body's joy in the oxygen-rich atmosphere of Lima's near sea level location. A tall thin youth with acned skin fell in beside me and matched my gait. It sounded as if he were practicing his English as we exchanged the usual tourist–native pleasantries. He said his name was Roberto and he sold cocaine. So it was a hustle. I quickly explained I was an American scientist studying coca; I would love to talk with him; I didn't want to buy cocaine, but I was willing to buy him dinner. I showed him my passport and assured him the interview would be confidential. His tense face relaxed into a smile only when I deliberately sniffled and started rubbing my nose in a user's gesture of recognition. Roberto led the way to the restaurant.

He claimed cocaine gave him a natural energy and made him feel good. He demonstrated this fact by inhaling some of the sparkling powder from the back of his hand before we entered the restaurant. Did he ever chew coca? No, that was a disgusting Indian habit, he explained, as he twisted his face in mock horror. The Indians in the mountains had told me the same thing about cocaine. They claimed that chewing coca was natural, whereas stuffing your nose with that white powder was an unnatural, disgusting, even dangerous, practice. For the Indians, coca was a natural dietary supplement that supplied needed calories, proteins, and carbohydrates, as well as vitamins and minerals. Coca contained less than 1 percent cocaine, a drug that alleviated hunger and fatigue for human chewers and at the same time repelled most insects and herbivores.

The Indians took things as they were, heeding the bitter warnings of the more concentrated powder, respecting the natural packaging in the leaf. Coca became a useful medicine, and as far as we know no Indian ever died or even had a serious medical problem from eating the leaves.

Could Roberto say the same for cocaine? After all, could anyone survive snorting purified nicotine from the tobacco leaf, a plant that contains a similar percentage of a bitter drug to keep pests away? Chewing, snuffing, or smoking tobacco may be unhealthy, but pure nicotine is lethal. By liberating cocaine from the protective envelope of the leaf, wasn't Roberto concentrating the problems as well as the promises, turning a medicine into a poison?

Roberto answered by pouring another white pile on his hand, snapping it reflexively to his flaring nostrils. To quell my own paranoia about this blatant act, I politely volunteered that the most serious problem with snorting cocaine was getting caught with it. I should have known from his furtive glances that I had said the wrong thing. Roberto bolted upright and excused himself to go to the rest room. He never returned. Nor did the silverware he discreetly rolled in his napkin and took with him.

On the following day I found César standing among the narrow rows of bottles and pottery in the museum, an improbable bull in a china shop. In the shadowy distance his unique frame resembled a large whiskered gourd. We went to his worktable where I took my time unwrapping the shard. He made a squealing sound and slapped my back over and over again. I dared not admit it hurt. We talked for hours and hours, working ourselves up into an ecstasy. We spoke of the thrill of digging into the past, the exhaustion of the Andes, and of science and serendipity. I was hushed when César told me that on the eve of my discovery he saw the bright star Spica in the constellation Virgo. The Incas called the star Mama Coca, a deified name for coca as well as an ancient Inca queen who was its mother. I was almost excited enough to believe there was a connection.

César confirmed that the shard was from a pre-Inca culture but thought it might have been made 4,000 years ago, just as culture was evolving from hunting and gathering activities. A time of innocent use, I said, when coca chewing was acceptable and problem-free. I thought of Roberto and told César that coca never caused the dysfunction that has followed the use of cocaine. César pursed his lips and shook his head so hard I could imagine seeds rattling around in the gourd of his body below. Grabbing my fingers in his, he led me into another section of the museum. His grip tightened as we approached a roped-off room.

An enormous penis saluted as I entered the room. César's face disappeared into a smile and he giggled again. My eyes took in several other erect phalluses, couples in coital positions, scenes of bestiality, sodomy, and homosexuality. A dog was masturbating in the corner, and nearby a parrot wearing a strange headdress held a toad in a compromising position.

The pottery was clearly from the Moche period, far later than my find, dating hundreds of years after coca chewing was established in ancient Peru. Arranged in chronological order, the bottles and vessels reflected an increasingly sexual theme, which César called abnormal. He recounted the opinion of several scholars that constant coca use led to a psychosis affecting the libido centers. Noting that not one single sexual perversion was lacking in the collection, César explained this as evidence of brain damage. I disagreed. Perhaps it was a celebration of reproduction with little or nothing to do with coca. Or perhaps coca, like cocaine, facilitated sexual performance by alleviating fatigue and thus encouraged experimentation But César viewed art with X-rated eyes, and I couldn't change his mind. I remembered that Roberto said he had become disinterested in sex. While I could imagine efforts to rekindle desire with pornography, it was difficult to believe coca chewing was responsible for all these clay follies. Several figurines were playing primitive musical instruments. Sex, drugs, and now rock and roll? César yelped and yawed a yes. Still, long after I left César bobbing among the icons, I was haunted by the image of one particular bottle. It showed death in the form of a living skeleton with a bare head and protruding ribs. The eyes were large dark pits and the teeth, perfectly formed, were clenched in a sinister smile.

I spent the next two days trying to get out of Peru. All flights to Los Angeles were booked for several weeks. I camped out in the Braniff office hoping Elizabeth, the attractive attendant, would take pity and find a seat for me. Peru is a poor country, and despite Elizabeth's Halston-designed airline attire I was sure she could use some extra money. I pushed one thousand *soles* emblazoned with coca leaves and psychedelic patterns across the counter. She looked me straight in the eye as she pushed it back. Her eyes were like wishing wells, the result of pupillary dilation from cocaine.

The money was unnecessary, she said, as there was a cancellation on a flight that night. As she prepared the tickets, I studied her eyes, knowing that their sparkle betrayed the electricity within. Cocaine's primary action is to create a "fire in the brain" of electrical and chemical excitation. Current research suggests that this action occurs in the forebrain, where cocaine prolongs the action of the neurotransmitter dopamine, thus firing reward and euphoria circuits in the brain. Cocaine also appears to increase the effects of the neurotransmitter norepinephrine, thereby stimulating the sympathetic nervous system. The combined effect warms the brain but chills the body. Elizabeth's conversation was spirited as cocaine kindled its subtle fire in the brain. But the words slurred past her perfect teeth and there was a slight tremor in her hand as she passed the tickets over the counter.

My brief expedition was ending, but Elizabeth's eyes showed that the odyssey of life in pursuit of intoxication that began with the shard had never stopped.

Introduction

A poppy flowers in Asia, and a junkie dies in New York. Coca leaves bend in a Peruvian sunshower as bullets hail down on a dealer in Miami. A kitchen chemist brews a designer drug as disease eats away a user's brain. A physician injects himself with a painkiller as a mother gives birth to an addicted baby. At work and at play people use uppers and downers, even drugs that seem to turn them upside down, while governments search for direction in controlling an overwhelming number of chemical recreations that keep flowing through our lives and bodies politic.

These scenes from the modern drug world are neither new nor unique events in history. Old World explorers, medieval herbalists, ancient Greeks, Neolithic shamans, beasts, and bugs everywhere have had accidental or intentional encounters with drugs. Since most drugs are manufactured by chemical processes hidden within "narcotic" plants, these plants have held a universal, almost evolutionary, attraction for humans and other animals throughout history. In every age, animals, including man, have pursued plants that have been designed to defend themselves with narcotic chemicals.

Intoxication has been the inevitable result of these clashes between the animal and plant kingdoms.

The clashes have become drug wars that shake the globe so incessantly that even those who seek intoxication with drugs are beginning to ask the ageless question of the nonuser: Why? Why do people want to do this to themselves? Why do we seek intoxication with drugs? Why are we so uniquely prone to the use and the abuse of intoxicants? Until we answer these questions, *Homo sapiens* will never understand how to deal effectively with the individual and societal problems that have resulted from his status among animals as the king of intoxication.

We're neither the first nor the most experienced species to develop a passion for drugs, yet, in mimicking the behavior of other animals through the millennia, we have become the most eager and reckless explorers of intoxication. Now, like children who have stolen matches from their elders and discovered the magic of fire, we face the puzzling question of why we are drawn to such an endangering enlightenment. This book answers that basic question of why we pursue intoxication. All the animals that fly and crawl and swim through its pages reveal the reasons and rules for this basic and ancient habit.

Recent ethological and laboratory studies with colonies of rodents and islands of primates, and analyses of social and biological history, suggest that the pursuit of intoxication with drugs is a primary motivational force in the behavior of organisms. Our nervous system, like those of rodents and primates, is arranged to respond to chemical intoxicants in much the same way it responds to rewards of food, drink, and sex. Throughout our entire history as a species, intoxication has functioned like the basic drives of hunger, thirst, or sex, sometimes overshadowing all other activities in life. *Intoxication is the fourth drive.* It is as bold and inescapable as the drug stories that dominate today's headlines. Individual and group survival depends on the ability to understand and control this basic motivation to seek out and use intoxicants.

Herein are scores of stories of animals and forgotten human cultures that have been driven by this same pursuit yet managed to distinguish between use and abuse. Most important, ways were established of dealing with intoxicated and abusing individuals. Indeed, these stories will show what intoxication is, why we seek it, its amazing benefits, its destructive consequences when abused, and why we have much to learn from other animals and people who have survived these experiences for generations.

When we watched Dorothy succumb to the magic of opium as she reeled through the poppy fields in *The Wizard of Oz,* we may have been unaware that she was following in the footsteps of other creatures. Like

Dorothy, many animals have accidental encounters with narcotic plants. Some engage in deliberate, even ritualized interactions. Why? For many animals the answer lies in the search for specific effects of stimulation or sedation. In a sense, intoxication allows animals to be in a different state, to act differently and to feel different.

After sampling the numbing nectar of certain orchids, bees drop to the ground in a temporary stupor, then weave back for more. Birds gorge themselves on inebriating berries, then fly with reckless abandon. Cats eagerly sniff aromatic "pleasure" plants, then play with imaginary objects. Cows that browse special range weeds will twitch, shake, and stumble back to the plants for more. Elephants purposely get drunk on fermented fruits. Snacks on "magic mushrooms" cause monkeys to sit with their heads on their hands in a posture reminiscent of Rodin's *Thinker.*

The pursuit of intoxication by animals seems as purposeless as it is passionate. Many animals engage these plants, or their manufactured allies, despite the danger of toxic or poisonous effects. The stupefied bees quickly become victims of predation. The carcasses of "drunken" birds litter the highways. Cats pay for their addiction to pleasure plants with brain damage. Cows poisoned with range weeds may eventually die. Inebriated elephants destroy much property as well as the lives of other animals. Disoriented monkeys ignore their young and wander from the safety of the troop. Human beings are no different.

Experiences with plant drugs have puzzled and fascinated our species for millennia. They have revealed substances powerful enough to heal or to kill. Yet, whether they help or hurt, these plants are also pursued for their power to intoxicate with stimulating, inebriating, tranquilizing, or hallucinogenic properties. We search our planetary garden for these mind-altering delights with a passion so blinding that the garden becomes a labyrinth, the search becomes the goal, and our passion becomes addiction.

Intoxication has also given humans sights to see, voices to listen to, thoughts to ponder, and altered states of consciousness to explore. It has generated conditions that can only be described by such global and imprecise terms as *ecstasy* or *madness.* Some feel closer to an understanding of themselves. Others feel a unity with everything in their environment. Still others look for a rainbow, an Emerald City, a wizard's powers. But for all of us the experience is a rite of passage that takes us *in*to a state of *toxicity,* hence the word *intoxication.*

In this state, we find ourselves playing the hunters and gatherers of plants that fight back by producing defensive narcotic drugs. We consume drugs "to ape the angels," as Baudelaire described life in this *Artificial Paradise,* "only to become animals." When we experience the subsequent intoxication we are touching a part of our being that we share with many other animals who want to steal the powers from the plants but so often become their victims. At these times it seems that the mythical protector of animals, the Roman goddess Fauna, has been seduced by Morpheus, Greek god of sleep and dreams and namesake of morphine. We wander through a waking dream, wondering if we will be kissed by enlightenment or entombed by blackness. In order to ensure that we will find our way through the labyrinth, we must study the roles played by narcotic plants and intoxicated animals and act our own part intelligently and seriously.

Many of the stories presented in this book were uncovered by my research teams studying the drug-using habits of animals, people, and cultures in selected and sometimes previously unvisited areas of the planet. Our own firsthand observations found many entertaining examples, including ducklings who were too busy feeding on narcotic plants to respond to their mother's calls; pigeons who were secretly gobbling behaviorally effective doses of marijuana seeds unknown to their master, psychologist B. F. Skinner; reindeer who fought deer and man over limited supplies of intoxicating mushrooms; and, in a remote Mexican Indian village where no one could afford television, young children who drank hallucinogenic peyote tea, fed the leftovers to their dogs, then curled up with the animals to watch "pretend TV." The children giggled and the dogs twitched.

The research also had a darker side: one of the chimps living on a game preserve became enraged by a powerful stimulant and fought a battle to the death with my team; I was captured and interrogated by marijuana farmers who refused to believe I was a scientist interested only in animals; I became the target of death threats—and one shooting—by patients and prisoners I was trying to study; and team members were often overcome by toxic reactions when they dared to ingest the strange drugs used by their animal and human subjects.

It is easy to view these cases as quirks of animal behavior. After all, animals often engage in bizarre and deviant behaviors. My own initial reactions on finding animals high on natural and man-made drugs was exactly the same. At first the animal stories seemed as rare as the bullets fired by hopped-up patients. Then a consistent pattern of behavior emerged. In every country, in almost every class of animal, I found examples of not only the accidental but the intentional use of drugs. The thousands of cases I investigated convinced me that the action of an animal in seeking out intoxicants was a natural behavior in the animal kingdom.

Over a period of twenty years, from my base as a research psychopharmacologist at UCLA's Department of Psychiatry and Biobehavioral Sciences, I collected thousands of anecdotal accounts that described intoxicated animals who behaved just like the people we studied. I culled other stories from the archival literature, and the major ones are cited in the Bibliography, which includes a complete list of references used in the book. Using a worldwide network of field stations and laboratories, my teams sought further understanding of the most promising cases through systematic observations and experiments. They had at their disposal an arsenal of futuristic techniques, including computerized tracking devices, night-viewing cameras, and biomedical recorders. And to trace the consumption and metabolism of substances, they labeled plant drugs with radioactive markers and performed blood and urine tests for days, weeks, and months after ingestion. In addition, because drug metabolites remain permanently embedded in hair, the researchers obtained samples of animal and human hair. They could thus trace patterns of drug ingestion to within a billionth of a gram for years, even decades, back. Finally, controlled experiments were conducted with both animal and human subjects and the results compared with detailed long-term studies of human users and abusers.

The research often called for innovative designs in order to verify and further explore what I had seen in the field. In a controlled game park I provided an island of monkeys with free access to a garden of psychoactive plants. In the laboratory I taught pigeons how to tell us what they were seeing while under the influence of LSD and gave

monkeys an opportunity to pick and choose their own diet of intoxicants, including cocaine chewing gum. I trained a group of human subjects—the media dubbed them *psychonauts*—to take controlled trips
with LSD and other drugs while making precise psychophysical reports
about their hallucinations. I studied the problems of abuse in the many
clinical patients I saw in hospitals and private settings. Then I went to
the streets and recruited users who were not having problems and studied them to find out why. I learned about the disastrous consequences
of misuse from my forensic practice, where I was called on as an expert
witness in hundreds of murder trials in which defendants were reportedly under the influence. And I was exposed to the war on drugs firsthand as a consultant to two presidential commissions and the World
Health Organization, traveling to many countries, where I interviewed
drug kingpins and pawns.

We begin our examination in Part I in an evolutionary Eden, at the very
dawn of the drug wars, when plants started to produce chemicals as
defenses against herbivores. The chemicals repelled many animals yet
attracted others, who managed to circumvent the poisonous effects by
developing safe feeding strategies. This opened the door for animals to
minimize aversive effects while maximizing desirable effects, turning
poisons into intoxicants and forming the new chemical bond we call
addiction.

Our ancestors learned much about the nature of these chemicals
and bonds by watching animals, an activity that led to the discovery of
many useful substances. The poisons that killed animals were easy to
find. So were strong intoxicants like the hallucinogens, which dramatically altered behavior. Neither the animals nor the humans who
copied them seemed to have difficulty in learning how to use these
intoxicants for specific purposes. For example, monkeys and baboons,
which share our tastes and temperaments, learned to use hallucinogens
and tobacco to relieve boredom with all the shrewdness and zest of
human users.

Next we examine the other major drugs and find that you don't
have to be a primate to appreciate them. Many creatures follow paths
to natural and artificial sources of intoxicants. But alcohol found in fermented fruit, grain, or sap has almost universal appeal. Animals use it

for food, for fun, for medicine; yet they avoid the human problems of abuse because the availability of alcohol is regulated by seasonal fermentations or other acts of nature. Nonetheless, groups of captive animals subjected to humanlike conditions of overcrowding will use it to relieve stress and they develop patterns of alcohol drinking just like our own. And when we look at animal reactions to opium, hashish, marijuana, or cocaine, we can see other reflections of our own behavior. Yet there is little abuse among animals who use the low doses found in the natural plants and who avoid participating in social behavior while they are intoxicated.

In Part II, we look at ourselves, and America itself, as the inheritors of this long natural tradition. The human pursuit of intoxication is motivated by a strong biological drive that pits individual needs against those of society. The struggle to satisfy our psychological and physical demands with drug supplies creates a neurochemical war within our brains, and, outside, a more deadly war on the drugs themselves. The lessons gleaned from the animals show how we can come to peace with this natural force through the education and technology that is our human distinction.

From the flowering of narcotic plants millions of years ago came the seeds of intoxication. The seeds were sown throughout history, in the stomachs of poisoned animals—perhaps dinosaurs—by birds and beasts who carried the seeds across the planet, and in the rain forests and jungles that nurtured them. From accident to addiction; from goats foraging on coffee beans to humans drinking their daily, stimulants; from bees revisiting opium and marijuana flowers to humans looking for their daily "buzz"; from the baboons of South Africa that crave tobacco in imitation of man, to those *Homo sapiens* who smoke cigarettes in order to be more like the Marlboro man; from elephants who seek out fermented fruit to alleviate stress to stressed humans who drink and see pink elephants; from the great herbals of the Middle Ages that described the inventiveness of animals in seeking natural cures for their ailments to the science fiction story by Doris Buck, who envisioned escape from twenty-first-century life with a designer drug that gives the user the illusion of being a dinosaur in the Mesozoic era—the history of life in pursuit of intoxication has repeated itself.

If we can understand intoxication as a universal and totally natural phenomenon, if we can apply the teachings of plants and animals to the questions raised by our own pursuits, then we can free ourselves from repeating past history and move on to design a new future.

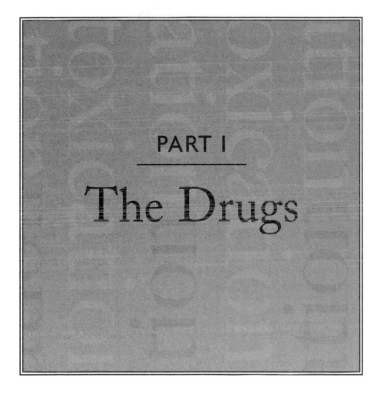

PART I

The Drugs

1

War in Eden

ORIGINS OF
PLANT DRUGS

In the infrared eyes of a Landsat satellite, the giant sequoias and pines of California are thin red hairs. From the perspective of a young man whom I will call Daniel, they were on fire. Daniel and his friends were camping on the edge of a national forest. As they huddled around the evening campfire, he started to tell them about a book he had just read. The book described the adventures of a young anthropologist who had studied the mind-altering plants used by a Yaqui Indian shaman. Daniel decided to prepare one of the shaman's recipes, a tea brewed from wild thorn apple. He gathered a few nearby plants, boiled the leaves, then passed around steaming cups of tea. His friends were hesitant to sip the bitter green syrup, so with a chef's bravado Daniel gulped down the entire pot.

The world was on fire. It began with a fever in his body, quickening the pace of his heart and lungs. It moved up his parched throat, past his dry mouth, over reddened lips, finally erupting into a bloodcurdling scream. Daniel looked to a girlfriend for help, but she changed into a tree. He moved toward the others, but they too changed into trees. Panicked, he ran into the woods. Now the trees were talking to him, warning him to keep running before the demons caught him and turned him into a tree. He ran for eight kilometers, unaware that his bare feet were being shredded by the razor-sharp edges of stinging nettles. A river blocked his escape. He turned. The demons were almost upon him. He tried to light a match. The first one crumbled in his hand. The second one turned into something wiggling and alive. The third one ignited and he managed to start a forest fire that stopped the demons. Then he dove into the cool water.

He was rescued by a forest ranger, hospitalized for several days, then tried for arson. At the trial, he told the judge that it all seemed like a mad dream, but he had learned his lesson and would never again take any drugs. Privately, Daniel told me how the experience changed his view of life. During his hallucinatory delirium, as animals and plants were transformed into one another, he had seen a harmony in nature, a oneness with the experiences of all living things. He felt older and wiser.

Was Daniel just a wayward youth from the 1960s who was looking for a new drug trip? Did he somehow think he was unique in being part of a culture that was searching for meaning in life by freaking out with mind-altering substances? No. Daniel was not thorn apple's first victim but simply part of a continuum of aeons. He had picked a plant to eat that was prepared to fight back with mind-altering chemicals, and he became its victim. He had joined the ranks of countless people and animals throughout time.

Daniel's ordeal with thorn apple was as old as the trees. If those ancient redwoods could really speak, they would tell a history of thorn apple that stretches back to the biblical Eden and the very dawn of creation. Thorn apple, a ubiquitous plant with a green thorny seed capsule resembling a small apple, belongs to the genus *Datura* (pronounced dah´tura). It may not have been the fruit from the tree of knowledge sampled by Adam and Eve, but it is old enough to fit the biblical description. Since Genesis gives no clear botanical identification, artists have shown the tree as an apple, a fig, a pear, and even a banana. And the earliest paintings show Eden as a garden, a paradise watered by rivers, rich in fruitful and flowering trees, and inhabited by angels.

The Eden that spawned Daniel's thorn apples was not the beatific paradise of the Old Testament. Nor was it anything like the divine gardens of life and immortality found in Persian, Hindu, Buddhist, Egyptian, Norse, or countless other mythologies. Rather, the picture of the garden in which apple trees have reddish stems, purple-veined leaves, and green fruits covered with thorns would show a very different landscape. We would see cages full of terrified little boys, altars on which men carve out the beating hearts of other men, women buried alive, strange beasts that are half man and half wolf, children playing with flowers that kill them, animals writhing and dying in grotesque postures, and, overhead, flying through the sky where the angels should be, we see witches on broomsticks. It is a picture that might have been inspired by Hieronymus Bosch's *Garden of Worldly Delights* rather than the Creator's hand. And the story it tells is not just of one man's fall but of a world at war.

The tree in the middle of the Garden of Eden was the tree of the knowledge of good and evil. The ancient Chinese considered *Daturas* sacred and believed that when Buddha spoke the heavens sprinkled them with dew. The Chinese used the flowers and seeds to treat colds and nervous conditions. But in India *Datura* was called the tuft of Shiva, the god of destruction. Liquid extracts were used by Thugs—worshipers of Kali, the goddess of fertility and death—to stupefy sacrificial victims. It was later used to drug young girls and render them powerless to resist a life of prostitution. The girls sometimes drugged customers' wine with *Datura* seeds and whoever drank this potion would lose control of both his will and memory, then his money.

Women of late medieval Europe found another use that earned the plant a more disturbing epithet—devil's weed. These women, dubbed witches, rubbed their naked bodies with a hallucinogenic ointment containing *Datura* and related plants belonging to the so-called nightshade family. The ointment was readily absorbed through the skin and also applied to the vaginal membranes with a staff or handy broomstick. Then, the women straddled the broom and pretended to ride it to the Sabbat party. Some simply smeared themselves with the cream and climbed aboard a large basket for the imaginary trip. There they remained comatose for several hours, only to recover and describe travels to strange lands.

According to experiments carried out in the sixteenth century by Andrés Laguna, physician to Pope Julius III, the young girls anointed with thorn apple fell into an "iron" catatonic state and their journeys were only the dreams produced by the ointment. But they were unable to awaken from the satanic dreams, Snow Whites trapped in a medieval mind. Giovanni Battista Porta, a colleague of Galileo who conducted the experiments with Laguna, described how men would drink a potion made from the same plants in order to create the illusion of being a bird or beast. By covering themselves with a wolf's skin and running about on all fours, the men created their hallucinations of turning into an animal, thereby giving us the basis of our modern were-wolf stories.

Native Indians in the New World found other names and uses for *Daturas*. The Aztecs called it *toloatzin* and valued it as a painkiller. It was one of the drugs given to sacrificial victims to make them drowsy and oblivious to their fate. Most prisoners captured in Aztec wars were kept in wooden cages and fattened. Later, at temple pyramid sacrifices, the priests would tear out the victim's heart and offer it, along with some blood, to the sun-god. Sacrifices were frequent and sometimes endless. In 1487 at the dedication of the main temple in Tenochtitlán, over eighty thousand victims were sacrificed. The line of sacrificial victims stretched for miles, and it took several days for those at the end finally to climb to the top of the pyramid for their turn under the obsidian knife.

Themes of death surrounded other ritual uses of *Datura*. Ancient Colombian Indians offered beer and *Datura* drinks to the wives and slaves of a departed husband or master. In the resulting stupor, the victims were buried alive along with the deceased. In parts of the western Amazon, young boys were given a *Datura* tea for the purpose of gaining wisdom from a near-death experience. If a boy had difficulty swallowing it, the elders inserted a hollow bone or horn into his rectum. The tube was attached to a pouch of the tea which was squeezed until the boy became comatose.

The belief that the *Datura* experience had much to teach the young was widespread throughout the Americas. In Virginia, where the Algonquin Indians called it *wysoccan*, boys were taken into the forest and imprisoned in specially constructed latticework cages, where they were forced to take the drug. The Algonquins believed that the violent intoxications would wipe out all memory of youth and initiate the boys into manhood.

For the very young, a single intoxication could produce a quick end to a short life. Children have been attracted by the sweet scent of *Daturas,* the large flowers that look like toy trumpets, the young fruits that have not yet acquired their defensive thorns, and the small dark seeds that make wonderful objects for play. Many children have inhaled the pollen, swallowed the seeds, or chewed on the leaves; a few have even survived. The intoxications have been dramatic. One five-year-old boy, after playing with the flower and trying to blow it like a trumpet, crushed it against his forehead, chewed on the petals, then began masturbating while barking like a dog.

Adults were not immune to such accidents, especially when traveling in unfamiliar terrain. In 1676, Nathaniel Bacon had just barely left his own youth when he was named to head a militia of Virginia colonists in defiance of British rule and heavy taxes. A group of British soldiers was sent to quell Bacon's rebellion. Bivouacked at Jamestown, the troops made a salad of boiled thorn apple and ate heartily. An account from the time describes how the men made intoxicated fools of themselves for eleven days. Since that time, thorn apple has been known in the United States as "Jamestown weed," commonly shortened to "jimsonweed."

Man is not alone in this landscape of thorns and nightshades. In 1975 I visited a ranch on the idyllic island of Maui where there had been several recent *Datura* deaths in a herd of cattle. Within a few hours after eating the plant, the animals started shaking and wobbling. Then they fell down. Loud noises or sudden movements sent them into seizures. A few could be seen dragging their collapsed hind legs behind them as they "crawled" along on their forelegs. After two days they died.

I walked among the bloated corpses, horribly twisted and contorted in the telltale postures of seizures and convulsions. The bent legs and neck of one corpse made it appear as if it had fallen from a skyscraper rather than knee-high grasses. Another was held in an eerie upright position by several fence posts. The animal had tried to escape to another pasture only to become entangled in the barbed wire. Swarms of flies now filled the cut and rotting flesh. The head was fixed in a mournful bellow at the sky. Something hard and black was coming out of its mouth. This portrait of death in Eden seemed as horrifying as the memorial sculpture of Holocaust victims entangled in barbed wire at Dachau.

I felt I was walking into just such a nightmare when I visited the scene of Daniel's accident a few months after he had recovered. The ground was black and charred. Sections of a hill had turned to mud and slid like some giant primeval slug into the river below. The trees were mere skeletons. Yet the *Datura* was flowering. Unlike its many victims, *Datura* has survived the war on drugs.

As I collected several plant specimens I noticed a few beetles and grubs nibbling the leaves and flowers. Because there were very few other plants emerging from the burned ruins, the insects may not have had a real choice in their diet. Yet the bugs seemed very normal. I suspected that there were other, more disturbed animals in the vicinity. I decided to set up a camp in the burned area where I had a clear view of the *Datura* and the surrounding area.

Several bees made regular visits to the *Datura* flowers. They collected the pollen in the early morning hours and appeared unaffected despite the fact that such close contact could kill a child. I turned my attention to a cluster of seed capsules rotting on the ground. Birds have been known to eat *Datura* seeds, later regurgitating or evacuating them and thereby facilitating dispersal. However, none of the local avians seemed interested. A few ants scurried over the capsules and carried away some of the seeds to their nest. This phenomenon has been observed worldwide, from Africa to the Andes, yet no one knows what the ants do with them. In the Amazon these plants sometimes appear black when covered by swarms of beetles. The beetles, which developed biochemical defenses against the potent chemicals, feed on the seeds. Perhaps the ants have similar mechanisms and use the seeds for food.

I discovered that hawkmoths feed on *Datura* flowers at night. Afterward, these large, sturdy creatures behave as if intoxicated. The moths are normally great flyers but after drinking *Datura* nectar they have difficulty landing on flowers and often miss their target completely, falling into the leaves or onto the ground. They appear to have trouble getting up again, and when they resume flight, their movements are erratic and disoriented.

The next morning a bird arrived in a shower of brilliant jeweled colors, the feathers iridescent like prisms in the morning sun. The violet band separating its black chin from a white collar identified it as a black-chinned hummingbird. Hovering in the air over a *Datura* flower, it extended its long slender bill to feed on the nectar. It sampled two other flowers, then disappeared in a blur. I watched for it to reappear, hoping to see some change in behavior. Sometimes hummingbirds feed on *Datura,* perch, fluff their feathers, then freeze like stiff corpses for several hours. No one knows if this is a drug effect like the iron catatonia of the witches, or simply a way of conserving fuel reserves. But the hummer failed to return, and the question must remain unanswered. I decided to end my vigil and take the plant specimens back to the laboratory for analysis.

I identified Daniel's *Datura* as belonging to the species *stramonium,* although all *Daturas,* some shrubs and some trees, contain the same principal chemicals. From my analysis I calculated that Daniel had ingested ten to fifteen milligrams of a mixture of chemicals, chiefly hyoscyamine and scopolamine with a little atropine. This was a minute amount, but these chemicals, known as alkaloids, were powerful enough to explain Daniel's experience with *Datura*—an experience that traces its history throughout the evolution of plant life.

From the infrared perspective of Landsat, most of the planetary landmasses are flushed with the signs of plant life. The waters of the world appear black, but the satellite's sensors can also see down to a depth of at least ten fathoms and detect evidence of widespread marine life, including the minute plankton, the drifting microorganisms that form the basis of life in the sea. Landsat has even spotted plant life under the Arabian desert in a "fossil river" that some archaeologists believe once fed the real Garden of Eden.

That proposed site for the biblical Eden is now covered by the Persian Gulf, just as the ocean waters once covered the planet before the first algae started to develop in the pre-Cambrian era, about two billion years ago. Even in these simple beginnings, plants were bearing chemical wonders, substances that gradually evolved into sources of drugs.

By the beginning of the Paleozoic era, 600 million years ago, with the appearance of lowlands and mild climates, marine algae were prominent while plant-eating animals and wormlike creatures were starting to evolve. Modern algae include several allegedly intoxicating lichens and seaweeds. The fungi also evolved during this era, and today's fungi contain a number of important intoxicants, including hallucinogenic mushrooms, puffballs, and mold.

Millions of years later, as arid continental areas developed, along with fishes and amphibians, the ferns appeared; the chemicals found in their modern descendants have strong pharmacological actions. The earliest seed-bearing plants, along with reptiles, insects, and spiders, started to appear in the late Paleozoic. The cone-bearing plants, or gymnosperms, which developed 345 million years ago, were hardy survivors and many, such as the conifers, are still with us today. They include several species that yield important drugs such as ephedrine.

It is the flowering of the angiosperms, however, that brought the more numerous plant drugs into the world. They evolved quickly and by the middle of the long Cretaceous period of the Mesozoic era they were dominant. They succeeded by developing a variety of defenses, including an arsenal of chemical weapons and drugs. They represent the source of most intoxications found throughout the animal kingdom as it was forced, and is still being forced, to live in a world in which food and drugs literally grew on the same trees.

The Cretaceous was a time when great swamp deposits were replacing deserts, when the Rocky Mountains and the Andes were born, and when climates started to cool. Some creatures of the Cretaceous could not adapt to the changing climate and rapidly evolving habitat of the planet. Many families of reptiles, including the dinosaurs, disappeared suddenly during this period.

Did the appearance of plant toxins have anything to do with their demise? This possibility has been depicted in several contemporary cartoons, where most scientists feel such notions belong. One drawing depicted a long-necked *Brontosaurus,* a gentle herbivore, happily browsing a bunch of angiosperm flowers, but getting ready to burp and fall. Another showed a flesh-eater, the ferocious *Tyrannosaurus,* which was lying in convulsive seizures after devouring a smaller reptile that had just finished a meal of toxic plants. Still another artist finished the job of cartoon overkill by depicting a group of juvenile dinosaurs slyly sneaking a smoke behind some Cretaceous rocks, with a caption telling the reader this was the real reason dinosaurs became extinct.

Despite the humor in such images, a few geologists and botanists have argued that since the majority of the giant reptiles were herbivores, the appearance of a new class of plants in their diet could have had significant effects. Accordingly, they noted that in the evolutionary race to survive, the angiosperms developed the ability to produce a variety of feeding deterrents, first a group of chemicals called tannins, and later, alkaloids. These chemicals helped the plants survive animal predation. But the dinosaurs, perhaps unable to detect such compounds or to render them physiologically harmless, might have eaten enough to suffer severe disturbances, even death.

These arguments seek to make some sense out of the coincidental rise of the most powerful drugs on the planet and the fall of the most dominant animals. For more than 135 million years the dinosaurs were enormously successful in adapting to and dominating the Earth. However, these and other herbivorous reptiles did not survive the Cretaceous. The Mediterranean tortoise is one of the few remaining plant-eating reptiles, and feeding studies have found that this creature will not be deterred by the taste of certain plant chemicals and will continue eating even as the chemicals approach toxic concentrations. When the tortoise's ancestors were overlords of the planet, they may not have been able to detect the taste of such incipient poisoning.

Such arguments do not prove drugs were responsible for the wholesale cold-blooded murder in the Cretaceous. The more plausible explanations mention a massive meteorite impact that propelled tons of the Earth's crust into the upper atmosphere in the form of a sun-blocking cloud of dust. As day became night, photosynthetic plants starved to death. Left without a food supply, many plant-eating reptiles would have died, as well as those meat-eaters dependent on them.

However, the poison argument emphasizes that plants are powerful enough to cause an accidental overdose. As dinosaurs plodded through antediluvian swamps and shallow coastal waters, they succumbed to many hazards; getting stuck with a bad meal may have been just as deadly as falling into a tar pit. However cartoonlike the notion of even one dinosaur becoming intoxicated and dying may seem, it is no more impossible than a creature that existed millions of years ago, walked on seven pairs of pointed stilts, and had seven tentacles rising about its body, dubbed by paleontologists the "Hallucingenia." Whether behemoths such as these were betrayed by their palates or their planet, many were just too large (up to the one hundred-ton *Brachiosaurus*) or too long-lived (some lived a century or more) to evolve fast enough to escape extinction.

Then, as now, there was just no place where hungry animal life could avoid bumping into struggling plant life. Consequently, the plants developed an elaborate system of physical and chemical defenses in the war for survival. These physical defenses include stiff tough leaves, spines, thistles, bristles, and barbs. Some plants just make themselves difficult to find by using shade, mimicking the appearance of pebbles or stones, or growing in ecological niches where they are unlikely to be found and eaten. A few plants may even band together into defensive guilds. For example, many unprotected grasses grow intermingled with noxious-smelling weeds that mask their presence.

By far the most formidable plant defenses are chemical weapons. Chemical defenses are found throughout the plant kingdom, from fungi to flowers, and these pose different types of barriers. These chemicals are called *secondary substances* or *secondary compounds* because most do not have a primary role in plant metabolism. A few secondary substances are storage compounds and regulators of plant growth, but the great majority have no known metabolic function. The adaptive significance of these substances lies in their repellent properties to insects and other herbivores.

Plants that are easy for herbivores to find are defended by tannins. Tannins are the most ancient defensive compounds and they are present in the leaves, bark, wood, and fruit of certain ferns, gymnosperms, and angiosperms. When animal skins and hides are soaked in water extracts of tannins, they are transformed into leathers that are resistant to bacterial disease, heat, or abrasion. In a similar way, the major role of tannins is to protect plants against fungal and bacterial attack. They also defend plants by making them taste bad. Tannins impart astringency to the mouth, and most animals will pucker and spit after a single unpleasant taste. Once ingested, tannins continue to have a cost for herbivores. Along with lignins, unpalatable secondary substances that provide strength and support in wood tissues, tannins reduce the availability of carbohydrates and proteins, interfere with enzyme activity, and have an overall deleterious effect on digestion. Not surprisingly, plants with high tannin concentrations are rejected by most animals as well as insects.

If tannins don't deter you, there are flavonoids. These two-faced secondary substances attract pollinators and repel pests. Together with carotenoids, which appear with the ripening of fruit, they have a role in providing attractive colors to flowers in order to promote pollination and seed dispersal. But some colorless flavonoids aid plant defenses with astringent and bitter tastes. They are also effective natural insecticides for the plants. A commercial contact insecticide, rotenone, is obtained from one of them. Other flavonoids inhibit enzymes, interfere with vital processes within the cells of animals, and disturb the reproductive capacity of birds and mammals, lowering their fertility and fitness to survive.

A similar group of chemicals, terpenoids, is so effective at keeping away unwanted insects that it is used as a fast-acting knockdown agent in commercial insect sprays. These substances also deter mammals by giving them allergic dermatitis or causing them to vomit. In hungry east Africa, where there never seems to be enough to eat, plant terpenoids can check the voracious appetite of armyworms, desert locusts, or starving humans.

For some creatures, eating even a tomato or potato can be problematic. The leaves of these plants contain proteinase inhibitors, chemicals that defend against insects by inhibiting their digestive enzymes. After a single severe wound, these inhibitors start concentrating in the leaf and stay at high levels for about five hours. A second wound releases a hormone that tells the plant to triple the concentration of the inhibitors. But several insects have developed ways to handle these defenses. When ladybug beetles feed on Mexican squash, they will rapidly cut a circular trench in a leaf. The leaf is almost completely cut through and only a few bits of tissue hold the encircled leaf section in place. The beetle then feeds on the encircled material. Chemical deterrents will be mobilized by the plant but cannot cross the trench to get to the site of the insect feeding. Since the chemicals show up in a widespread region surrounding the trench, when the ladybug finishes eating a section of leaf, it has learned to move at least six meters away to take its next meal.

Lush green pasturelands may be equally unsafe. Forage plants like alfalfa and clover have to defend against grazing animals as well as insect pests. Such plants utilize secondary chemicals called saponins. In water solutions, saponins form a soaplike foam, but inside animals they will break down red blood cells. Small amounts deter insects and kill their larvae. When taken in great quantities by sheep and other grazing animals, saponins cause bloat, decrease food consumption, and depress growth.

Many plants that rely on animals to disperse their seeds must limit feeding rather than kill the animal directly because it might lose a valuable seed carrier. Lipids, found in plant seed oils and some leaves, perform this function. The most interesting lipids are terpenes, which have a strong aromatic flavor. For example, myristicin, found in nutmeg and many other spices, prevents animals from seasoning their diet too heavily with these plants. If taken in sufficient quantities, myristicin causes dizziness and loss of motor coordination.

In the ceaseless war between plants and pests, plants' defensive chemicals and animals' counterdefenses have become ingenious. Plants such as wild parsnips and daisies contain naturally occurring photosensitizers. When ingested by insects that are then exposed to light, these chemicals become highly reactive and literally burn up insect tissues. In hard-bodied insects like boll weevils, they interact directly with the insect's DNA and form lethal chromosomal abnormalities. A few insects have evolved defenses for even these penultimate weapons. Certain larvae, for example, have learned to roll themselves in the leaves while they are eating the plant. The plants fight back in subtle ways. Pulps and saps from several trees contain juvenile hormones that prevent caterpillars from maturing. Like Peter Pan, these creatures never reach adulthood and never reproduce.

Equally ingenious are a group of palatability agents known as *taste-distorting factors*. Whereas other secondary substances affect palatability by just tasting bad, taste-distorting factors modify the perceived taste of whatever the animal eats with them. Many of these factors are saponins, which can suppress the perceived sweetness of sugars, thus enabling plants to camouflage themselves against mammalian herbivores. Gymnemic acid in tropical *Gymnema sylvestre* does more than simply depress the perceived sweetness of its sugary leaves, it distorts as well. After a human chews *Gymnema* leaves, an orange will taste like a lime. Similar effects keep browsing herbivores away from the plant. Another factor, miraculin, works in the opposite way. In the berries of an African shrub, *Synsepalum dulcificum*, miraculin causes acidic substances that ordinarily would taste sour to seem sweet. Chew a *Synsepalum* berry, for example, and a lemon tastes like an orange. For plants that depend on fruit eaters for seed dispersal, it is clearly adaptive to provide sweet-tasting fruit even if it is only an illusion.

The best illusions are created by the secondary substances known as alkaloids. Alkaloids, which include the major hallucinogens and mind-altering drugs, are synthesized in the plants from other chemicals such as amino acids and terpenoids. Nearly one-third of the angiosperm families contain alkaloids. They are by-products of primary metabolic pathways and tend to accumulate in the peripheral parts of the plant such as the bark, leaves, and fruit.

Alkaloid accumulation may be useless for plant metabolism and growth but it confers a selective advantage for survival in the war against insects and herbivores. Caffeine literally knocks out mosquito larvae by disrupting their nervous systems. In the laboratory, water-borne mosquito larvae that ingested caffeine became so confused that they drowned. Other alkaloids protect plants by reducing insect populations, not by deterring individual predators. For example, tomatine will not deter the grasshopper from tomatoes but the grasshopper may eventually die as a result of long-term feeding. In small amounts, several alkaloids, such as nicotine, have marked pathological effects on insects as demonstrated by retardation of growth, development, and reproduction. Higher dosages will paralyze and kill.

Some insects developed the ability to take alkaloids from the plants and sequester them in their body tissues. Thus they could acquire toxic properties that provide a passive defense against their own predators. For example, the tiger moth feeds on yellow *Senecio* flowers found in western grasslands and stores the toxic alkaloids, a defensive practice that renders the moth unacceptable to a variety of potential predators. Even the voracious larva will gorge itself on toxic plants, ensuring that it will be able to turn into a little tiger. Yet most insects and other herbivores were forced to develop different mechanisms for survival.

Because feeding is a necessity for herbivores, they expose themselves to the hazard of being poisoned by every meal. Most survive their meals, thrive, and reproduce because of two successful developments: biochemical adaptations to plant chemicals and feeding strategies that minimize risks of toxicity.

After a toxic chemical has found its way into an animal, a sufficiently large fraction of it has to get to a critical target site such as a key junction in the nervous system or life-support system. Biology and chemistry have provided many obstacles along this path. The compound may be stopped by special barriers, such as the type surrounding the brains of higher mammals, which blocks or slows down the passage of many compounds. It may be channeled away for storage into specialized tissues or body parts as in the tiger moth. The toxin may also undergo rapid metabolic degradations by an arsenal of enzymes. These enzymes change the chemicals into products that can be rapidly excreted. Such enzyme systems have been found in organisms throughout the animal kingdom from the house cricket to humans. They are so efficient that many animals can survive the small amounts of cyanide produced by over one thousand plants as they break up in the body. If deactivation doesn't work, repeated exposures to a toxin may give animals protection in the form of an acquired resistance, a state known as tolerance. Despite the advantages of these biochemical systems, herbivores must be careful not to overload them.

Survival depends not only on the detoxification mechanisms but also on feeding strategies. Therefore, it is of vital importance that animals be able to perceive the presence of alkaloids and other secondary compounds. Perception is the process by which an organism receives or extracts information from the environment. The perception of secondary substances is usually handled by the chemical senses of olfaction and gustation. Some secondary substances, such as the urticating compounds from stinging nettles, can be detected by pain and irritation. Many insects and herbivores have sense cells that respond to these chemicals, resulting in acceptance or avoidance. Several alkaloids, such as quinine in *Cinchona* bark, function as repellents for certain insect species and limit their food consumption by stimulating insect taste receptors that tell the insect the plant is bitter and unpalatable. Although such sensory and behavioral responses are often innate, they can also be modified by experience. Accordingly, as a result of earlier experiences, many animals learn to avoid ingesting secondary substances. The learning can be surprisingly rapid and robust.

Herbivores who are faced with the problem of assessing both nutritional value and potential toxicity of foods almost have to be fast learners. Terrestrial snails and slugs may be slow movers, but they are quick to recognize potentially toxic plants and learn to avoid them. It is not unusual to find garden snails traveling a distance of six meters or more from poisonous plants to areas with more suitable vegetables, although the journey may take two hours. Slugs have the ability to sense unsafe dishes on the basis of a single exposure, an experience they can remember for several weeks. Other animals with more advanced nervous systems can do even better.

When especially dangerous plants are recognized, sometimes animals will risk starvation rather than potential toxicity. The common English garden snail, a close cousin to the edible snail, feasts on almost everything the gardener tries to grow. Yet when confined to boxes with only toxic plants such as tobacco, it will withdraw into its shell and close off the opening by secreting a crusty membrane of hard minerals. The snail can remain behind this closed door in a state of estivation, or hibernation, for as long as six months.

But snails cannot hide forever and they will eventually emerge to resume a search for more palatable food. I decided to test their resolve against the bitter-tasting leaves of Daniel's thorn apple. Although snails often damage drug plants such as coffee, they tend to favor the leaves and avoid the beans and other parts where alkaloids are most concentrated. However, all parts of *Datura,* including the leaves, are rich in the bitter alkaloids. What would happen if snails lived in a world full of *Datura* leaves?

Because garden snails use chemical receptors, I first had to determine how they might react to bitterness. Snails will normally climb up plants in order to eat the younger and less bitter leaves at the top. When placed against a vertical glass rod in the laboratory, these snails automatically creep to the top. They use their foot, which is like a pad that moves along under the shell. The climbing is facilitated by a copious secretion of slime that spreads out a smooth bed of lubricating fluid, along which the snail glides. A series of rippling waves of muscular contraction along the bottom of their foot sends them on their way. When I tied a small cotton thread soaked in bitter quinine solution at the top of the glass rod, snails would taste the quinine with their tentacles or foot, then retreat down the rod. After a few more trials, the snails refused to climb at all.

When placed in boxes containing *Datura* leaves, the snails started their automatic ascents. As they began to eat, a few reacted as if they had just tasted quinine: they retracted into their shells or reversed direction and searched for other food. After several days of searching in vain, some curled up in their shells and estivated. But others ingested the *Datura*. Later, these same animals, carrying numbers painted on their shells for easy identification, appeared markedly sedated. Several fell off leaves and rolled onto their shells. They twisted and struggled to right themselves, waving their tentacles and feet. They were able to get back onto their feet, and most survived despite persistent falling and flip-flopping. The snails were well armed for battle with *Datura*. The shells protected them from falls, and their biochemistry protected them from poisoning. Would their nervous systems also permit them to learn from bitter experiences?

I decided to offer another group of snails, reared on a diet of ivy, a choice of three new foods: regular garden lettuce, *Datura*, and *Lactuca virosa*, or wild lettuce. The leaves of *L. virosa* contain a bitter milky juice called lactucarium, which has the odor and effects of opium.

The snails displayed a remarkable feeding strategy. They treated the new foods with extreme caution and initially ingested only minute amounts. The animals quickly rejected both the *Datura* and the *L. virosa* while concentrating on the lettuce. As they fed on the lettuce, they simultaneously indulged in a sampling of the other choices. They continued to eat the lettuce for as long as possible. Once lettuce supplies were depleted, they fed on their next choice, *L. virosa*, which contained fewer bitter secondary compounds than *Datura* but enough to slow them down. Only when the *Datura* was the sole remaining food source did snails ingest enough to start showing the characteristic signs of molluskan intoxication—falling.

This feeding strategy undoubtedly helped the ancestors of these snails crawl out of the sea during the Paleozoic and survive the land battles with the angiosperms of the Cretaceous. It is precisely this strategy that also enabled the herbivorous mammals to survive in a garden where food and drugs grew on the same trees. While such herbivores as man are capable of detoxifying and eliminating many secondary compounds, limitations on these mechanisms forced the adoption of a careful searching and feeding strategy. By consuming a variety of plant foods, treating new foods with caution, ingesting small amounts on the first encounter, and sampling continuously, the snails developed a successful strategy. Selection of plant foods was guided to a limited degree by sensory cues such as smell or taste, but it became primarily based on learning in response to physiological changes.

The very fact that many herbivores can learn to avoid toxic foods suggests that toxic plants are also *knowingly ingested.* When insects become resistant to secondary plant substances they are frequently described as being "hooked" on them. One American Indian tale describes hawkmoths, like the ones I observed feeding on *Datura,* as being crazy for the plant. They become so passionately fond of the nectar that when they have exhausted the flowers, they will try to pry open the buds, falling all over the place. That, the Indians say, is the mad craving of addiction. Such a colloquial analogy may be only slightly misleading. Animals might be able to learn to select plant compounds for nutritional benefits, medicinal effects, or even for the falls themselves.

The Daniel who tripped on *Datura* had a choice of many plants. He could have selected any number of other greens for his tea—even ones closely related to thorn apple—and had a completely different experience. There are at least forty species of *Datura* alone and they represent many differences in the distribution and concentration of alkaloids and other chemicals. Furthermore, *Datura*'s immediate family includes such diverse intoxicants as tobacco, henbane, mandrake, and the infamous deadly nightshade itself *(Atropa belladonna).* But it also includes such relatively innocent members as eggplant, peppers, even petunias. Not only are there many species in this family—over 2,400—but there are hundreds of thousands in other families. Botanists have not explored all of the plant kingdom, but thus far there may be more than 700,000 species on Earth.

Daniel may have appeared unlucky when he picked the *Datura* out of this planetary pile of leaves, but the odds were that any plant he picked would have contained some chemical surprise. His choice and its resulting experience were representative of what happens when animals and people deliberately ignore the chemical defenses of the plants and, in effect, bite their bullets. The animal kingdom, all 1,125,000 species of us, have been challenged to learn about the bullets, those both magical and deadly. There were many lessons to be learned from the inevitable encounters with drugs in evolution's slow crawl out of Eden. The first lessons we will examine are the ones learned from observing other animals, observations that led us to the discovery of the major plant poisons and intoxicants.

2

A Trip of Goats

DISCOVERY OF POISONS
AND INTOXICANTS

1

Herbalists of the Middle Ages believed that while Satan may have caused man to fall from the Garden of Eden into a jungle of wild animals and plants, God had mercy on man's predicament and gave each plant a particular sign. According to this "Doctrine of Signatures," man could read the marks on each plant and know its use. This notion, which dates back to Babylonian times and probably into prehistory, is both simple and logical. Thus yellow flowers were thought to be good for jaundice, spotted plants for skin defects, and red roses for blood problems. Because a nutmeg cut in half resembles the human brain, it was judged useful for mental disorders. The roots of ginseng resemble the human body, so in the Orient the plant was considered a panacea for everything that ails man. Tiny glowworms feed on the ginseng leaves at night but they extinguish their lights when approached. Such mysterious behavior was thought to confirm the magic of this treasured plant. The Chinese ginseng hunters learned to shoot arrows at the glowing lights and return the next morning to recover the arrows and the plants.

Sometimes our ancestors combined plant signs with myth and superstition. The serpent, the original guardian of the Tree of Life, was alleged to be the first one to crawl out of Eden. As it writhed its way along the ground, twisted plants supposedly grew in its wake, and all such plants were believed to be antidotes for poisons. Man harvested them for snake oil preparations and some useful medicines were actually discovered in this way. The snake plant of the Quileute Indians of western Washington is a twisted stalk that when chewed and swallowed has been found helpful in quickening the onset of labor. The snakeroot plants of India and Africa contain a number of medically useful alkaloids, one appropriately named serpentine, and another, reserpine, which has been found to be an important tranquilizer. The serpent was so trusted it became the mythological master of the healing arts and the emblem of modern medicine.

Animals proved to be more reliable guides than even these mythological signs. Because even a nibble can be dangerous, having lower animals around to taste the food enabled our species to learn from the mistakes of others. A United States Army survival guide states that if you are in doubt about which plants are poisonous, observe the animals that usually select food that is also safe for humans. Early man did the same.

Humans started their long march to civilization as hunters and gatherers who depended entirely on the capture of wild animals and the harvesting of wild-growing plants. Through a long association with animals and plants, choices in foods and drugs were greatly influenced by the interactions humans observed between these two kingdoms. Since man has had a relationship with goats for at least seven thousand years, it is not surprising to find stories about goats leading man to some of his most ancient drugs such as coffee and khat. The legends of these discoveries originate in the ancient land of Abyssinia, not far from where the Garden of Eden may have been, and they are illustrative of folklore from all corners of the world.

Kaldi knew that something was wrong with the goats. During the hot days on the Ethiopian highlands they leaped around the rocks, climbing impossible slopes, then descending in controlled slides and falls. At sunset they usually slept, lying with outstretched limbs, motionless as the mountain itself. Tonight they gamboled uncontrollably, bleating and chasing one another, as their eyes darted in all directions. At first Kaldi thought that birds were pestering the goats and exciting them to near riot. The owlish nightjar feeds near grazing goats at twilight and occasionally startles the animals. Tonight there were no birds. Kaldi noticed that the goats paused only to nibble the red berries from a nearby shrub, then continued to prance in the moonlight. The goats often behaved in unexpected ways, hence their flighty or capricious reputation, but Kaldi had never seen them approach this plant. He knew that the goats always test their food by scent and taste and prefer familiar foods. They especially like leaves; but strange berries? The jasmine scent of the plant's flowers was inviting. He had to try some of the berries himself.

Kaldi was wide awake. His hunger was gone. He felt alert and excited. He brought a few of the berries to the imam of the local monastery. After drinking a tea made from the berries, the imam felt that he had been strengthened by heavenly food, a gift from the angels of Paradise. He would never have to sleep again. He proclaimed that this would be used to keep the faithful awake during the evening prayer services. They called it *kahveh*, "the stimulating and invigorating." In the province of Kaffa, Kaldi had found coffee.

In the nearby land now called Yemen, a story about a stimulating "flower of paradise"—actually leaves from a tree known as khat or qat—relates its discovery to the inquisitive goats. Awzulkernayien, a legendary Yemenite herder, noticed that one of his goats had left the small flock, or "trip." Then he saw the goat, some distance away, running with extraordinary speed to join the others. The herder discovered the source of the animal's excessive stimulation when he later saw the same goat leave the group to eat some leaves from a rather plain-looking tree. When the goat once again repeated its high-speed run, Awzulkernayien tried the leaves for himself and found them stimulating and reviving after a day's work. He began using these leaves on a daily basis and later introduced them into his village. Since that apocryphal time, the chewing of these leaves spread throughout the whole country.

It is likely that these stories about goats were based on actual behavior. Goats frequently browse coffee and were originally responsible for dispersing the plant seeds in their droppings. And if any animal actually guided man to khat it would have been the goat. Khat, more formally known as *Catha edulis,* contains cathine and other astringent amphetamine-like alkaloids that deter most animals—even hungry locusts—but not the goats. If goats can get the leaves, they will quickly develop habits of daily use that change the normally affectionate animals into aggressive and provoking creatures, charging and butting any human within range. Not surprisingly, the khat fields outside of Sana, today's capital of Yemen, are heavily guarded against these bearded intruders. After all, these flowers of paradise that contain the "elixir of life" are far too precious to share with beasts.

While often maligned by contemporary folklore as smelly because the males urinate on themselves, goats were much appreciated by the ancients for showing the way to a variety of other useful plants, including black hellebore, a plant with digitalis-like chemicals used by the ancient Greeks to treat madness but considered too poisonous for modern medicinal use. Over the centuries, goats became known for their remarkable ability to eat anything, and it was speculated that they had a natural resistance to most toxins. In the Middle Ages it was believed that the source of this immunity lay in bezoars—small stones found in goats' stomachs as well as in those of other ruminants. Many goats were sacrificed in order to obtain these stones, which people ingested for their alleged antipoison effects or wore as good-luck amulets. During the Renaissance the highly prized stones were sold for ten times their weight in gold. Bezoars are actually round, tightly matted balls of hair that the animals lick off their coats. Because they are not digestible, they remain in the stomach and gradually take on the appearance of hard, smooth rocks. They are ineffective against poisons. Goats are not invulnerable; they simply have strong investigatory drives and will inspect and chew a variety of novel food sources. They survive their browsing of plants such as black hellebore by following a generalized feeding strategy and nibbling only small amounts.

The names given by early man to plants reveal much about the observed effects on animals. Many plants were named for the attraction that animals displayed toward them. Catnip attracted the cats that eagerly ingested it. Hare's-lettuce was allegedly used by rabbits for stimulant and medicinal effects. Dog grass, swine's grass, pigeon grass, and goose grass all attracted their respective namesakes. Goat's joy was the Sanskrit name for a nightshade plant, *Hyoscyamus niger,* or henbane, which was said to be a delight to the animals who used it sparingly.

Humans copied the behavior and discovered the plant had intoxicating effects when used in small amounts. Overdoses were marked by drowsy and clumsy behaviors, thus generating another common name: Insana. The consequences were often embarrassing. After eating too many Insana roots, a group of monks in nineteenth-century England turned a pious convent into a madhouse when they insisted on chanting drinking songs rather than their prayers.

Many plants were named for their apparent aversive properties. When the seeds of Insana were fed to poultry, it killed them and earned the now-popular name of henbane. Similarly, leopard's bane caused the death of leopards who ate it. Sheep's bane poisoned sheep. Dogbane kept dogs at bay. Cowbane killed cattle and other grazing animals. Many of these unwanted plants still had practical uses for man. When the Iroquois observed animals dying after eating cowbane (also called water hemlock) they used the roots of the plant for their own ritual suicides.

The animals that accompanied man out of Eden did more than simply accept or reject food plants. Like the goats, many animals displayed a remarkable ability to learn from the exploration of their environment. Of particular importance to us were those things animals did when they were wounded or sick. The actual practice of copying animal behavior for purposes of healing dates far back into prehistory, yet can be seen in contemporary practices worldwide. Observations of animals healing themselves by licking led to the custom of lapping a wound with the tongue, a technique still used by shamans in the St. Lawrence Islands who modeled the behavior from their dogs. This mimicking was carried to extremes in the Middle Ages when many recipes for healing wounds included the tongues of puppies. When deer were seen to rub their wounded flanks against the sap of sweet gum trees, Indians found that the sap provided a useful antiseptic for their own wounds.

Useful plant remedies were also discovered through observation of animal feeding behavior. Pumas in ancient Peru were observed to eat the bark from *Cinchona* trees when they were ill. Native Indians learned the value of *Cinchona* from observing this behavior. Although its use was recorded in a 1639 Spanish text, no one believed the stories until 1820 when the alkaloid quinine was isolated from the bark and used successfully to fight malaria.

But animal behavior was often misinterpreted, thus giving rise to more folklore and superstition. In many cases, observers ascribed human motivations to the animals. For example, an Australian story claims that the mistletoe bird becomes so intoxicated on mistletoe berries that it tries to make love to the tree by rubbing vigorously against the branches. While such a tale might suggest that the amorous powers invented by humans for this plant extend to avians as well, the story-tellers were only describing the normal behavior by which the birds wipe off the gluey seeds that become stuck to their feathers. Such mis-interpretations of behavior have also occurred when the diet included animal prey. This happened when birds were observed eating Spanish fly, a beetle with a heart-shaped head and an iridescent emerald body. The birds immediately began a frenzied writhing and rubbing on the ground. Since mating behavior among the beetles lasts for as long as twenty hours, and it is so rapid it actually appears blurred, the link between this creature and sexual prowess was inevitable. The pelvic squirming and thrusting behavior seen in birds and other animals, including people, who have eaten the beetles is not love but irritation. The beetles contain irritating cantharides that raise blisters on the skin or, if eaten, inflame the bladder and urethra.

One native Hawaiian story went so far as to claim that *Bufo mari-nus* toads periodically commit suicide by eating flowers of the strych-nine tree, which cause them to go into convulsions and die. The natives watched these events and thus learned that all parts of the plant were highly poisonous. I found that the suicide is accidental and occurs just after the tree blooms. It is a colorful flowering with fruits that resemble mandarin oranges, seeds that look like gray velvet nickels, and blos-soms that carry the odor of curry. But it is neither the sights nor the smells that attract the toads. The toads ingest the falling blossoms because they will instinctively snap at small, irregularly moving objects that have a configuration similar to that of their insect prey. I found they would even snap at inedible bits of red cloth or paper that I tossed at them.

When sick or wounded animals seek out botanical cures, the behav-ior is even more open to misunderstanding. In India a folktale describes how the mongoose, when bitten by a cobra, retires to the jungle to look for a plant known as mungo root, which it eats as an antidote to the venom. Mongooses have also been reported to pretreat or anoint themselves by rubbing the root over the head and body parts that the snake might attack. This behavior is similar to that of hedgehogs, who will anoint their spines with toad venoms or even tobacco juice as a chemical defense against would-be predators. After anointment, the mongooses fall into a drugged stupor from which they quickly recover.

While conducting field studies in Hawaii, I provided captured mongooses with samples of Indian mungo, which they ate without hesitation. I observed that the eating of the root was followed by typical grooming behavior: the mongoose would use its paws to clean pieces of root adhering to the face and use its mouth to clean other body parts, nibbling and combing the fur with its incisors. This behavior could be easily mistaken for anointment. Mungo root is unnecessary protection for the mongoose, but natives still believed it could be worn to charm away cobras and infections. People also found a strange use for the mongoose itself. The animals have anal scent glands that open in a pouch outside the anus and are used to mark territory. In India, natives scrape the inside of the anal pouch, remove the musky secretion, and use it to flavor their smoking tobacco.

If the habits of goats, mongooses, and tobacco users in India seem less than lovable, the Australian koala has enough universal appeal to compensate for all of them. The big round ears, soft fur, and childish cries combine to give this marsupial a reputation as a cute and cuddly teddy bear. After watching koalas become sleepy from eating eucalyptus leaves, Australian aborigines adopted the custom of using the leaves to soothe and heal wounds. Although the sleepy behavior may be more easily explained by the normal biological rhythms of this nocturnal animal, the koalas do feed exclusively on eucalyptus leaves. They will die without them, even if given other nutritious foods.

This has given support to a native belief that koalas are true drug addicts with a dependency on this potentially dangerous plant. What appears to be a severe drug dependency is the result of a habit gradually acquired during infancy. The learning mechanisms are the same for humans.

It is dangerous to eat eucalyptus, and the pungent bitter leaves almost say so; a variety of essential oils are mixed with toxic prussic and hydrocyanic acids. For man, some of these oils have local anesthetic and germicidal effects, useful in a wide assortment of topical medicines that evolved from native beliefs in the soothing properties. Koalas smell like giant peppermint cough drops and seem literally to have rolled in the leaves. But their bodies are saturated with the aromatic oils from the inside; some oils escape through the skin and fur to deter ectoparasites; others decrease blood pressure, lower body temperature, and relax the muscles. Nonchalantly breaking twigs and leisurely chewing the eucalyptus leaves, the koala is as cool and relaxed as it looks. It is also stubborn, if not actually addicted: of the 350 different species of eucalyptus, it will eat only twenty, preferring five favorite species.

Koalas select the mature leaves, which have less hydrocyanic acid than the tender and juicy younger shoots. In cold climates they choose leaves with phellandrene, a compound that increases body temperature, but in warmer environments they pick leaves with cineole, the oil that decreases temperature. Still, because the koalas do not drink but get their water from the leaves, they had to learn, under pressure of survival, to constrain natural tendencies and endure the bitterness, keep away from juicy leaves, and pick out a few plants from a stack of similar species.

The infant koala is first exposed to the bitter diet when nursing on the mother's milk, which is flavored by eucalyptus. The nursing infant, carried in the mother's pouch and then on her back for a whole year, gradually habituates to the eucalyptus, which serves the dual function of providing nutrition through the milk and at the same time making the flesh of the mother unpalatable to predators. At weaning time the normal feces of the mother are purged from her intestinal tract and she starts eliminating predigested eucalyptus leaves. Since the mother's anus is close to the pouch, the infant koala can start feeding on this eucalyptus pulp. The first samplings give the infant an opportunity to acquire the intestinal flora and fauna required to produce nutrients from the eucalyptus. Subsequent samplings reduce the natural aversion to bitterness and increase the palatability of the leaves. By the time the infant koala leaves the pouch, it is irrevocably programmed to a diet of eucalyptus leaves. Although the koala has become addicted to the plant as a food, the acquisition of plant drug habits can follow a similar course of gradual habituation.

If the koala is reared as a eucalyptus addict, it should be possible to condition an infant koala to another diet. Small koalas have been raised successfully on diets of cow's milk, bread, and honey. However, if the koala has already been programmed with the eucalyptus diet, even milk and honey will be refused. Many captive koalas have died for want of their native leaves. It is this tenacious dependency, once established, that defines a true addiction. In the wild, koalas have proved to be intelligent and resourceful addicts, finding adequate supplies of specific eucalyptus leaves and succumbing in large numbers only to epidemics, forest fires, or the human passion for their hides.

We have seen that the behavior of animals seeking food or botanical medicines is often easy to misinterpret. Whether or not an animal is sated or healed are questions that may not be easily settled through simple observation. The koala's behavior would have been the same whether it was addicted to a food or a drug. But the consequences from eating a plant and living or dying are clearly different. Primitive man learned that there is nothing more obvious than immobilization, nothing more certain than death. Death speaks louder than the color of a leaf and more convincingly than the habits of a goat or koala. Deadly drugs were easy to find.

2

When an animal is incapacitated or dies following ingestion of a particular plant, the lesson is hard and fast. Even if the animal doesn't learn from the experience, we can. The observations of our fellow animals who fell victim alerted us to the powers of plant poisons and the absolute necessity of either leaving them alone or learning how to use them safely.

In the hardship of life for the aborigines in Australia, there were valuable teachings from such poisoned animals. These seminomadic peoples knew of *pituri,* a shrub with bell-shaped flowers and black berries. When the leaves were thrown into watering holes, it killed both the fish and emu in the area. The natives found that they could eat these animals without ill effects. They also learned that chewing small amounts of the plant could ward off hunger and fatigue, yet higher doses might kill. Further tinkering with the plant led to the discovery that smoking the leaves would throw one into a dreamy state. We now know the reason for the effects: *pituri* contains the alkaloid scopolamine, the same ingredient found in *Datura*.

Plants thrown into ponds and lakes provided a natural test tube for the evaluation of such toxins. The principal ingredients from the plant parts were readily dissolved, leached into the waters, or ingested by aquatic life. Natives in the East Indies threw the berries from a local climbing shrub onto the surface of the water. These fingernail-size "fish berries" were devoured by the fish, who were then stunned and rose to the surface for easy capture. When eaten by man, the picrotoxin in fish berry seeds gives rise to a gripping pain followed by a stupor in which there is awareness of passing events but an inability to exercise any voluntary control, a waking nightmare employed by robbers who "hocused" their victims with the seeds.

Insects and birds that suddenly fall from the sky and die on the ground are at least as dramatic as fish rising from the water's depths. The Shamatari tribe in the Amazon valley of Brazil reportedly saw birds and bees drop dead after sucking the nectar from the *piripirioca* plant. The Indians learned to prepare scrapings from the plant's potatoes, place the powder in hollow bamboo canes, and blow the deadly particles at their enemies. The *upas* trees of Malaya were supposedly stronger: they gave off fumes powerful enough to kill a man. According to the first voyagers to the Malay archipelago, the emanations from *upas* killed all animal and plant life in the vicinity.

The powers of *upas* were so fascinating that the Dutch East India Company dispatched a physician in 1783 to verify these claims. In Java he was shown widespread death among animals in the vicinity of *upas*, and he wrote back that the tales were true. The physician had actually seen the aftermath of poisonous gases that had escaped from nearby volcanoes. Furthermore, the physician had misunderstood the Javanese word *upas,* which can refer to any type of poison. However, the mistake went unnoticed even by Charles Darwin, who wrote about this "hydra tree of death." The *upas* were actually *Antiaris toxicaria,* gigantic trees that attain heights of over seventy-five meters and have a creamy sap with the odor of sourdough bread. The sap contains a secondary substance that is harmless when taken orally but if injected, it produces sudden paralysis, then death. The natives utilize it for dart and arrow poisons, and experiments have managed to produce some of the fabled reactions: pigeons die in seconds, monkeys within minutes, and elephants darted in the morning will succumb by nightfall.

The Dutch physician had observed a scene not unlike that which resulted from the silent plumes of carbon dioxide that shot up from the depths of Cameroon's Lake Nios in 1986. Entire herds of cattle, as well as other animals, were struck down in their tracks, flash-frozen in the still frames of everyday life. According to one observer, it appeared as if the area had been hit by a deadly neutron bomb. On the volcanic islands of Hawaii, I found evidence of such a bomb—and it was still ticking.

Although nature's play of poisoned animals can be found on many continents, there is no place where the death scenes seem more dramatic and more out-of-character than on the otherwise paradisiacal islands of Hawaii. With feathery clouds, perpetual rainbows, fog-shrouded forests, and luxuriant beaches, Hawaii could have been the Eden that modern travel posters assure us it still is. From volcanoes that continually bubble lava, to waves curling over ancient coral reefs far below, the land seems ageless.

Growing midway between fire and sea on the lower slopes of Mauna Kea, where animals graze spacious pastures, is a pestiferous fern with the ominous name of bracken. It seems to be a mistake in these pastures when the island's other lush green ferns occupy niches around cascading waterfalls. But bracken is an aggressive plant, invading any area with creeping roots, fighting any foe with draining chemicals. Bracken contains an enzyme that inactivates the important vitamin thiamine and opens the body to vitamin deficiency diseases. It also contains a radiomimetic factor that invades the bone marrow of grazing animals, thus causing the bomblike damage of aplastic anemia, cancer, and death.

It is sometimes difficult to convince animals or ranchers that the fern is a time bomb, since ingestion produces a cumulative type of poisoning that may require weeks or months to develop. During this period, animals such as swine and horses may acquire a taste for bracken and feed primarily on any roots and fronds they can find. Horses become nervous, lose equilibrium, crouch and rock in a display of "fern staggers," a macabre dance that usually signals death. The horses die in clonic spasms with arched neck, feet wide apart, the spine and extremities bent in postures typical of sudden deaths from poison gases. Affected cattle cannot produce sufficient numbers of leukocytes and blood platelets; they hemorrhage and bleed nonstop from all body orifices as well as from the frequent bites of horseflies. Numerous streaks of blood mark their doomed bodies as they run off to hide. They are seldom found alive.

The images of poisoned animals haunt not only the gardens of Hawaii but plains and fields around the world. They continually remind us of the chemical powers in plants and the vital need to learn how to deal with them. Green lily grows in the mountainous fields of Central America where the explosive lethality of its seeds rivals even the *upas* and bracken ferns. The few range animals that browse the lily-seed capsules will soon collapse as if gassed to death. The plant contains sabadilla, once used in the manufacture of an asphyxiating and tear-producing gas that had a similar effect on humans during World War I.

Death from toxic plants can be quiet if not sudden. Orange larkspur kills gently, coaxing cattle into a lethal repose. The Calpella Indians in California observed these effects and gave this "sleep root" to gambling opponents in order to render them stupid. *Zygadenus,* or death camas, is the last word in poisons. But like the larkspurs, it is one of the first plants on the ranges of North America to appear after the snow melts. The grasslike leaves lure grazing livestock to a rapid and deadly coma that bypasses the labored asphyxiation caused by other poisons. This earns the plant its more fitting name of "sweet death." The pink flowers on the plant mark the quiet graves.

However natural death from toxic plants may seem for grazing animals, it is not always a matter of gently lying down and dying. Fitweed sends sheep and cattle into torturous convulsions. Buttercups are full of deceit, and, when eaten by livestock, cause inflammation of the mouth and throat, a painful gastritis, then death. Whorled milkweed will send sheep on a death dance, ending with the animals beating their heads on the ground in violent convulsions.

By contrast, the initial signs of poisoning from *Senecio* plants found throughout temperate climates seem all too quiet, too innocent. At first affected cattle start yawning and gaping. Horses tend to remain solitary while grazing. The animals appear dejected because they have difficulty holding their heads up and may try to support themselves on fence posts or other objects. They wander without direction, stumbling against fences or pushing headlong into them. The gait gradually becomes uncertain, the hind legs and hoofs begin to drag. This "walking disease" turns normally graceful creatures into beastly versions of the living dead, unable to stand without swaying or move without stumbling. Animals may pass bloodstained stools, then start feeding on dirt and clay. In the final stages, the blood seethes with ammonia and the animals hide from sunlight. From time to time one can find the carcasses of such poisoned animals on the savannas of Africa. In the stern economy of nature, where nothing is wasted, vultures and other carrion birds feed on their bloated remains. The natives believe that the vultures are able to eat the poisoned flesh because the birds also feed on another plant, boophone, which they think drives out evil spirits. Inspired by this belief, the natives eventually learned how to apply boophone as a safe and effective topical ointment for cuts and infections.

3

It is obvious that animals eat poisonous plants, often with fatal consequences. Why do they? Among livestock who are not always free to select a natural diet, the poisoning may be accidental. Pastures are often littered with toxic plants that grow in close proximity to forage plants. When animals are grazing they will generally select more palatable and desirable forage and avoid the toxic varieties. However, the most frequent accidental poisonings occur when fenced-in pastures and ranges are overgrazed, thus causing the animals to eat less-preferred plants. When confined to barns, animals have even less choice. Poisonous plants are sometimes harvested with hay or their seeds become mixed with grain, and animals have difficulty in separating good feed from toxic foods. Unable to pick at their food, they die.

Accidental poisonings also occur when animals are moved into new and unfamiliar forage areas. Sometimes weather conditions can so drastically change the landscape that the animal is virtually in a new environment with all the risks of poisoning encountered by traveling creatures. When conditions of drought prevail in the western Colorado areas of North America, and forage grasses are nowhere to be found, it is odd to see horses chewing on absolutely nothing. This "chewing disease" is not the product of a starving brain conjuring some mirage of fresh greens, but of a brain that has literally gone soft. Two plants prosper in the drought—yellow star thistle and Russian knapweed—and, in lieu of other foliage, horses will eat them. A neurotoxin in the plants attacks the nigropallidal portions of the brain, destroys nerve pathways, softens brain tissue, and causes the involuntary motor movements of chewing. Ironically, these movements immobilize the muzzle and prevent normal drinking and feeding. Animals eventually die from starvation or thirst.

Conditions of crowding can also force animals to graze on unpreferred toxic plants. Like the great herds of wildebeest and other grazers on the African plains, herds provide domestic animals with safety from predation. But as a consequence of gregariousness, there is intensive grazing of particular areas. When domestic herds or flocks are massed together they experience a jealous competitive urge to eat almost every available plant. Cattle under such social stress and high competition for food space tend to eat very rapidly. Patches of larkspur or death camas will disappear in a single gluttonous meal. If animals are kept in less dense groups and spread out over ranges, they are less likely to eat any poisonous plant.

On ranches in Hawaii and on the prairies of North America I observed these forces in operation. One year I noticed that a herd of eight hundred cattle suffered only one accidental death from the wild tobacco that spotted their range. The next year the herd had grown to fourteen hundred but no additional range area was provided for them and there were twenty-two unprecedented deaths from tobacco and other toxic plants. Grazing time also affected food choices. In an adjacent field containing good forage grasses as well as bracken and other toxic plants, a herd of cattle was moved through the field quickly and suffered only one loss. When another herd was permitted to over-browse this field, sixteen head were lost.

In nearly all the cases of poisoning, I observed that the sick and dying animals behaved in strange and socially inappropriate ways. They ended up by either leaving the herd or being segregated by the rest of the animals. Even during the initial stages of poisoning, when physical symptoms were not yet visible, the affected animals tended to isolate themselves from the others. Similar observations have been made on animals from Africa to Alaska. Whether they are elephants or reindeer, social animals tend to become asocial when stricken by toxic plants. The behavior might be explained by the tendency of some social animals to reject the strange, whether strange behavior or the actual stranger.

Perhaps strangest of all were the individual animals I observed that revisited toxic plants again and again despite the effects of poisoning. Many stories are told by country veterinarians and ranchers about animals that, having recovered from acute poisoning, return to gorge themselves on toxic plants like nightshade. The ranchers think that the animals are dumb because they go right back to the poison. Actually, much like the koala, they are able to acquire tastes for the particular plants. The relationship that animals establish with these plants has been described as a passion, a fondness, even a craving or habit. It is all of these things; the relationship is addiction.

I found many examples of these addictions, and, despite the presence of nearby herds, individual animals that acquired these toxic tastes were usually found alone. Even highly gregarious and sedentary animals will modify their routine social and feeding behavior when a special chemical taste is acquired. In the Canadian Rockies the wild bighorn sheep do not roam far for food and stay close to bedding spots they may use for years. Yet they will negotiate narrow ledges, knife-edged outcrops, and dangerous talus slides to feed on a mysterious lichen. This particular lichen is a highly colored, crusty vegetation that looks like thick yellow or green paint splashed on the exposed surfaces of rocks and boulders. It is a slow-growing plant, taking as much as a century to spread over a single square inch of rock. But it is also known as a pioneer plant, willing to grow where other plants will not furnish competition. Small ewes have been observed repeatedly leaving the group to scrape this lichen off the rocks with their teeth. The habit becomes so tenacious that the animals wear down their teeth to the level of the gums. Their young skulls are often found without the nipping teeth. The puzzling and crazy behavior was called "sick." A likely explanation for the acquired taste was discovered by local Indians who found the lichen to be a narcotic. Perhaps the strangely behaving and isolated sheep were not sick, but under the influence.

It was on the prairies of the American Southwest that early settlers first noticed animals acting *loco,* a Spanish word meaning "crazy" or "mad," and so concluded that they were sick. There were locoed mules, horses, cattle, sheep, antelopes, pigs, rabbits, hens, bees, and even an insect grub or two. The cause of this widespread madness was an unusual hairy weed with long erect spikes of white flowers so dense that a field can appear covered with patches of snow in the middle of summer. The plant was named *locoweed.*

The animals first approached locoweed with suspicion, but after the initial nibbles they searched for more. After greedily devouring the more accessible flowers and leaves, horses would dig for hidden roots. In 1873, O. B. Ormsby, a rancher in Bakersfield, California, wrote the first description of this locoweed disease in a letter to the Commissioner of Agriculture: he described hallucinations and uncontrollable maniacal fits in his horses. He foresaw an epidemic among horses and cattle, blaming older animals who passed on the loco habit to the young.

It was found that young calves *would* imitate their mothers or other older animals, acting very much like baby koalas or the children of human drug users. Once the locoweed habit was established and animals became confirmed "loco eaters," there were massive losses of livestock. Locoweeds and loco eaters grew in escalating numbers. At least thirty-five different plants found throughout the plains of North America were identified as locoweeds. By 1883, a loss of 25,000 cattle to locoism was reported in a small area of Kansas that was only 5 by 217 kilometers. A national epidemic of locoweed disease was proclaimed in 1905. Research was started but it was not until 1982 that the cause was identified—the suspect plants contained a rare group of indolizidine alkaloids that produced the strong neurological and physiological effects. Despite eradication and other control efforts, including separating younger animals from older locoed ones that might teach them the habit, the plants still survive as does locoweed disease itself. The disease is addiction.

A characteristic of addiction to locoweed, and most other plant drugs, is the tenacity with which animals pursue the plants. When ranchers try taking the plants from fields, some animals try to steal them back from collection sacks or out of wagons. Once animals become addicted to the locoweed alkaloids, they stubbornly refuse to eat normal feed, even if survival is at stake. Locoed animals also develop solitary habits, partly because of a generalized stupor but mostly because they are preoccupied with hunting locoweeds to the exclusion of all other activities. In fields where there are locoed cattle, it is not unusual to see a steer standing off by itself, sometimes remaining in one position for days, moving only when it is time to hunt for locoweed. While locoweeds can kill directly, most deaths occur from starvation and thirst, as the animals seem to ignore bodily needs in favor of the plant's excitement. The animals behave with the same stubborn preoccupation that we see in human alcoholics and cocaine addicts.

Because humans are not so fascinated by locoweed, it is hard for us to understand the exact appeal of the plant but it is easy to spot the addicted animals. They tend to walk with a peculiar stiff gait, staggering a little from side to side as if the legs were partially paralyzed, while the head shakes. They remind one of a pair of Charlie Chaplins in a horse suit. Frequently they will go into paroxysms of rage and attack everything in sight. Sometimes they appear to attack or avoid things that are not in sight. A locoed horse will run through a barbed-wire fence as if it were not there, and then balk and rear at empty ground as if it were alive with snakes. Several accounts by people who have ingested locoweed teas suggest that the main effect is tranquilization and a feeling of mild detachment. Higher doses produce excitement and hallucinations.

One hundred years after Ormsby wrote his letter, I visited the site of his observations in grasslands near Bakersfield. It was the middle of July and the area was dry and sandy. The tumbleweeds rolled about in a hot, blasting wind. As I brushed by the white loco, the seed pods rattled as they may have done for those early settlers who named it rattleweed. This was not the same species that Ormsby had sent samples of with his letter, but with huge taproots that penetrated to a depth of more than two meters, it had survived all the same. Nothing else was growing. The area had long since been abandoned by ranchers. All their animals had died.

Those animals that failed to survive their addictions to locoweed and other plants provided valuable lessons to humankind by settling any debate about plant toxicity. The creatures that survived their encounters with toxic plants and returned to engage in deliberate feeding raised new questions. Why? For many animals, like Kaldi's goats, the answer was in the search for specific effects, such as stimulation from the coffee plant. For locoed cattle that were more likely than horses to survive the habit, even if it went on for years, the question was as puzzling as the mystery narcotic in the lichen pursued by the bighorn sheep. Why did animals continue using toxic plants, enduring the effects of incipient poisoning, entering *into* a state of toxicity, becoming *in*toxicated? If animals knew enough to avoid toxicity in plants, or to utilize medicinal properties, did they also learn how to pursue intoxication with plants?

When physical needs for food or healing overrule the costs of using toxic plants, animals repeat the experience and go back to the plants. Hunger produced by scarcity of food initiated much of the loco eating. But what kept it going when other food became available? It appears to have been an acquired taste, not unlike what happened to the infant koala exposed to partially digested eucalyptus from the mother. Indeed, while young animals may imitate their loco-eating elders, locoweeds also contain flavorful substances ingested by the young through mother's milk, substances that adapt the young to the taste of the plant. If the costs of this feeding are noticed by the mother, she doesn't seem to mind. The contaminated milk also carries plant osteolathyrogens that cause unusual flexing of the joints and contractions of the tendons. Consequently, some young locoed animals take on the appearance of standing on their toes but the mothers continue eating locoweed and feeding the young. Likewise, pregnant animals who are addicted to other toxic plants do not seem bothered by the birth defects produced by their addictions. The animals may quickly discard aborted or malformed fetuses so that they can return to satisfying their acquired tastes. They leave behind a horror show of fetuses with twisted limbs and missing toes and eyes.

Is it possible that animals acquire a taste for the state of intoxication itself? There is no evidence that locoweeds or other similar toxic plants are physically addicting but they might provide a psychological appeal. The question can be more easily answered when the plants are ones that provide little or no nutritional value and no obvious medicinal effects, but that still produce intoxicated behaviors with risks of poisoning. I investigated such a plant, the red bean, which I found on the limestone hills at the edge of the Sonoran Desert in Texas.

A bean that is only a centimeter long seems relatively benign when compared to its Sonoran neighbors, which include Crucifixion thorns, sulphur flowers, gila monsters, tarantulas, ghost-faced bats, and giant scorpions. Yet a single red bean from *Sophora secundiflora,* a beautiful evergreen shrub with violet flowers, will kill a child within a few hours. The bean, also known as mescal bean, contains cytisine and related alkaloids similar to nicotine. It is not useful as a food although archaeological finds in this area have recovered them from early human shelters dating back to the ninth millennium B.C. There is evidence that they were used as ceremonial hallucinogens just as they are today by Plains Indians. The intoxication from half of a bean has been described as an exhilarating delirium during which one experiences visions. A deep sleep lasting several days follows. There is little margin for error. A whole bean can produce nausea, vomiting, headache, sweating, salivation, diarrhea, convulsions, and paralysis of the respiratory muscles. Death is by asphyxiation.

Anthropologists have speculated that the Indians observed the toxic effects on local animals, since the animals eat the plant and traces have been found in their stomachs. When I borrowed several goats from a nearby ranch and allowed them to graze near the red bean shrubs, I observed that a few goats were doing the same thing—trembling, falling, rising, and later browsing the plant again. They continued to fall and rise throughout the day, Mexican jumping beans in the hot Texas sun. Later I found that the hard-coated red beans that passed into their droppings were bruised sufficiently to allow for a partial release of the alkaloids.

It seems plausible that the Indians observed similar effects. After all, they watched and learned much of their pharmacology from the activities of the animals. The Wichita Indians would even use the red bean trance to hold conversations with wild animals and to receive instructions useful in healing. While the Indians respected and modeled animal behaviors, they also may have experimented on themselves with plants such as red bean when animal models were lacking or provided insufficient information on the plant effects.

After watching the goats literally tripping and falling, although they appeared unharmed by the experience, I was uncertain about trying the red bean myself. It was getting dark and time for the animals to rest when I saw that the affected goats isolated themselves from the others. Meanwhile, my packhorses had already discovered the shrubs and were busily tearing into them. I rushed to pull them away. They reared and bucked with excitement. I managed to tie all but one of them to a safe tree. He ran to a nearby hill where he stayed all night, continually walking and tossing his head.

At daybreak I awoke to find him back at the red bean shrub. I chased him away and he trotted stiffly back to the hill where he continued his circling and tossing. I was astonished by this persistence for intoxication. I could understand animals benefiting from stimulating plants such as coffee or healing plants such as quinine. But what possible good was derived from the hallucinogenic red beans? How many other creatures experienced accidents with plant hallucinogens and returned to repeat the behavior? Why?

In the distance the horse reared on his hind legs, a giant question mark in the morning sun.

3

Falling Birds
and Flying Cats
ACCIDENTS WITH
HALLUCINOGENS

1

High noon. A large flock of robins moved across the sky, bracketing the sun in parentheses of spring and hunger. It was February and the annual migration of the American robin, *Turdus migratorius,* was coming to the little California town of Pleasant Hill. The loud rich caroling signaled that it was almost time for the roost to feed on the ripening fruits in the field below. The field provided an assortment of small trees with berries the Indians called *toyon* and we now call "California holly" or "Christmas berry." These vivid ornamental plants with bright scarlet berries and glistening green leaves wrapped a canopy of quiet beauty over unseen dangers.

My jeep was parked under the trees and I was camouflaged in a blind nearby. A series of annual newspaper stories that appeared as regularly as the birds had drawn me to this hiding place. According to an Associated Press story the robins would become intoxicated after eating too many of the berries, which contained a mild toxin. Another article told of a seasonal three-week binge during which robins and other birds would become disoriented and confused, play silly games, or wan-

56

der into cars and windows. Everyone agreed that in human terms the birds were drunk. A "drunk tank" was established at the local museum in neighboring Walnut Creek, where intoxicated birds were brought to recover overnight. I had set up a hot line to receive calls about the location of any disabled or oddly behaving avians. The sites were plotted on a large map of the region with robin-red thumbtacks. The tacks outlined a giant needle stretching throughout the valley. Now I was sitting in its eye as I awaited the birds. A light drizzle started to fall as I began dictating notes into my field tape recorder.

12:10 P.M. There are two or three thousand birds swooping down from the sky. They dive directly toward my jeep, buzz the camera tripods, and start mobbing the trees. The thin branches start bending under the weight of fifty to one hundred birds on each tree. They are eating the berries on the top, working their way down through a labyrinth of crisscrossing branches. Others target the bottom berries with low-level flights or hop to them from the ground.

12:17 P.M. Berries are disappearing into beaks that seem to have no bottom. Ordinarily, four or five berries might be a good meal. Here, individual birds are gorging on as many as thirty. They quickly work their way to the outermost branches, which begin to sag under their collective weight. As the branches wobble, so do the birds and they start falling. Four birds are staggering on the ground, unable to fly.

12:35 P.M. The tree directly in front of me is denuded. Flocks that were mobbing other trees now seem to be resting. There are eighteen birds on the ground. Several are still grasping berries in their beaks. A lone starling pilfers a berry right out of the locked beak of a robin, a characteristic behavior known as robbing.

12:38 P.M. I exit my blind and step into a Hitchcock movie. I walk down aisles lined with trees where hungry birds are perched. They are resting quietly between courses. I try not to startle them as I step around other birds still wobbling on the ground among the bits of leaves, twigs, and half-eaten berries. The tipsy birds can be easily approached and handled. They are almost tame. My hand-operated counters are clicking the numbers as a group of birds on the start of another feeding frenzy flies directly into my head and body. I duck into the jeep.

12:45 P.M. I am driving in low gear to the edge of the field. There are thumps against the roof, then a robin smashes into the windshield. I retrieve it and discover it has a broken wing. I'll take it back to the museum to be splinted.

12:55 P.M. I am on the outer perimeter of the field, just a meter below a highway that completely encircles it. Private houses with white picket fences line the far side. Birds mob the perimeter trees.

1:03 P.M. A passing car startles a group of birds feeding on a perimeter tree. They scatter but one flies across the road at bumper level and is killed.

1:05 P.M. Several birds are stunned momentarily when they fly into the windows and sides of the houses. On the side of the road I find four more birds that have been killed in collisions with cars moving at high speed. The flocks are starting to leave. Lunch on Pleasant Hill is over.

I returned to the museum where I performed autopsies on the dead birds. The autopsies revealed that the stomach, and sometimes the throat, of *every* bird was full of toyon berries, accounting for approximately 5 percent of their total body weight. Neither the stomach contents nor the berries themselves showed evidence of fermentation or alcohol, thus dispelling a popular belief that these birds were drunk. Death was caused by massive trauma inflicted by the collisions, secondary to an unknown intoxication.

The calls to my hot line identified another local source of intoxication—the *Pyracantha* shrub, a member of the rose family. A rose with the common name of firethorn is not as sweet and innocent as its family name suggests. Firethorns have coral red berries on long, prostrate thorny branches. The plant sprouts vigorously after fire or cutting and its showy fruits are popular decorations in gardens around the world. Ripening firethorns often mean intoxication to visiting birds and an early spring circus for the human residents of Pleasant Hill. Dozens of callers described the birds acting like winged clowns: flying, falling, and hopping about in the most erratic, albeit entertaining, ways. Some were found fluttering in the dirt with wings awry, teasing backyard cats. Other teetered on window ledges and pecked at their reflections. Because firethorns were often planted near homes and roads, collisions with windows and cars were reported more frequently than with toyon. On a 1.3-kilometer stretch of roadway bordered by firethorns I recorded thirty-six dead robins over a three-day period. There were no deaths on two control roads that were of equal length but did not have berry bushes.

In addition to the robins, I found the carcass of a cedar waxwing stuffed with firethorn berries. Smaller than a robin, this elegant bird has a brown back, yellow belly, and black mask. The name comes from a red dot on the wings that resembles a spot of red sealing wax. Despite their reputation for sleek plumage, never seeming to have a feather out of place, the waxwings were left rumpled and tipsy by the intoxications. Yet they still had the ability to engage in an unique courtship display. The male fluffed his feathers and turned his head away from the female, who did the same. Then the male passed a firethorn berry as a "present." He offered it to his partner at the tip of the beak and she accepted it. The berry was passed back and forth several times and, eventually, it was eaten by one of the birds at the end of the display.

A courtship present stirs the romantic imagination. After all, love and addiction are often viewed as two sides of the same coin, or, for birds, the same berry. Although descriptions such as these make addiction to a berry seem as innocent as a love affair, there were more practical advantages to toyon for California Indians and early American settlers. The bark of the tree was used for tanning and the berries were roasted and eaten, or made into a pleasant and inebriating cider. So many of these California hollies grew in the suburban hills near Los Angeles that the area was given the name Hollywood.

The secondary substances that cause the theatrical behaviors among avians and inebriating effects in humans have not been identified. There is evidence for a hallucinogen that causes some people to experience delirium and visions. Saponins—those soaplike secondary compounds—may account for some of the "drunkenness" as they do for avian binges on the Tartarian honeysuckle in the eastern part of the continent. Whatever the chemical, it appears to be more concentrated in early spring when the fruits are ripening and the colorful carotenoids increase. The carotenoids may invite attack by birds who then suffer the side effects of intoxication.

Birds are prone to overdoses. Since birds have high metabolic rates and high feeding rates, their intake of great quantities of food increases the likelihood of a larger dose of a secondary chemical being ingested. For birds feeding in flocks, this almost guarantees at least a few over-doses. Group feeding allows members to collect food at a faster and more gluttonous rate than when alone. The flocks of robins sweep patches of toyon like a giant mower, easily distinguishing between trimmed and untouched areas until the berries or their bodies are exhausted. As the berries disappear, birds returning for second helpings eat decreasing amounts and the incidence of intoxications is reduced.

It is unknown if the birds enjoy their intoxication as much as the Indians liked their toyon cider. However, it is clear that even after repeated feedings the birds do not find it unpleasant. While intoxication may be a side effect of feeding in birds, it is generally a low-risk behavior. No birds were directly poisoned by the berries and none seemed deterred by the disorientation or loss of coordination. The most dramatic behaviors were also the most infrequent: birds not noticing where they were going and flying into cars and houses. Human folklore has referred to such phenomena as avian suicides, yet the intoxicated birds are only scapegoats for our own misguided behavior. Death is primarily caused by the actions of humans, usually accidental, sometimes intentional. I saw one driver deliberately veer into a fallen robin and I watched through my field telescope in silent horror as a schoolboy crushed two helpless birds with a rock.

The berry intoxication is just one example of reactions to plants that may be eaten as food but alter the mind. The delirious behaviors are tolerated because they are simply too infrequent and too short to leave lasting impressions. Even the few kills by cats, like those from cars and people, do not threaten the birds sufficiently to stop their intoxicating feedings. The seasonal migrations and patterns of feedings are too instinctively fixed to be changed by the chance deaths of a few individuals.

This regular pattern of intoxication does not mean addiction for the birds. If the birds were flocking to the berries for reasons of pure chemical pleasure, we might expect that the accidental encounters would become more frequent and the birds would hang around the bushes longer. If the intoxication activated some drive that was stronger than hunger in the birds, then we might expect them to leave their migratory flyways and follow the highways of berry bushes instead. In a word, we would expect to see addiction. One example of a powerful addiction resulting from an initial intoxication is provided by cats.

Cats are attracted to catnip purely for reasons of chemical pleasure. Catnip *(Nepeta cataria)* is a perennial herb with downy leaves and a strong mint odor. It is native to such diverse locales as Scandinavia, Kashmir, Canada, and New Jersey. Today it is widely cultivated throughout the world. Surprisingly, there is no overlap in the distribution of the catnip plant and its namesake. Yet when placed near catnip, cats will seek the plant and return to it each day. The behavior is illustrative of our own attraction to drugs that may be alien to our immediate environment but that, once introduced, evoke strong natural feelings. Unlike the birds seeking berries, the cats are exhibiting deliberate intoxications.

When cats encounter the plant, their first reaction is to sniff. To humans, fresh catnip has the odor of mint mixed with fresh-cut grass or alfalfa. In the dried plant, or in commercial cat toys, the alfalfa odor predominates. Upon reaching the plant source, the cat commences to lick and sometimes chew the leaves, in the second stage of the response. The chewing is often interrupted when the cat momentarily stares into space with a blank expression, then quickly shakes its head from side to side. In the third stage the cat will usually rub against the plant with its chin and cheek. Last, there is a "head over" roll with rubbing of the entire body. Extremely sensitive cats may also flip from side to side by rolling over on their backs. The four-stage reaction runs its fixed course in approximately ten minutes.

Biologists have referred to this intoxication as an example of animal addiction to pleasure behavior. The nature of the pleasurable intoxication becomes increasingly evident when high doses of catnip in the form of concentrated extracts are offered to the animals. The subsequent reactions are intense: cats head-twitch violently, salivate profusely, and show other signs of central nervous system excitation. One sign is sexual stimulation. Males have spontaneous erections while females adopt mating stances, complete with vocalization and "love-biting" of any available object.

The similarity of the catnip response to the normal sexual behavior of cats is striking. The presentation of catnip results in a rolling pattern of behavior that is exhibited by estrous females during the course of normal sexual displays. These displays have prompted naturalists to speculate that catnip once served the evolutionary function in the wild of preparing cats for sex, a natural springtime aphrodisiac. This notion does not explain why some cats do not react to catnip or why cats should mate and reproduce so well without the plant. Indeed, only 70 percent of domestic cats respond to catnip. Wild cats include both responders and nonresponders, although the relative percentages are unknown. The intensity of reactions may vary considerably. Civet cats show only mild curiosity—they sniff, sneeze, and rub their chins. A young tiger, however, took one sniff and leaped several feet into the air, urinating in the process, then fell flat on his back. He scrambled to his feet and dashed head-first into the wall of his cage.

The reason for the failure of some cats to become even the least bit excited about catnip and for the exaggerated reactions of others is genetic. Cats can inherit a dominant gene that guides the reaction to catnip. Breeding experiments have confirmed this genetic factor, although even young kittens with the gene invariably show an initial fear-avoidance response and withdraw from the plant. As they get older, those kittens destined to become responders show an ever increasing curiosity toward the plant. Nonresponders become indifferent to it. Supersensitive responders, like the head-smashing young tiger, may be so frightened by their experiences that they develop a conditioned fear reaction. Like humans running away from a bad trip, the tiger may never again trust even a catnip toy that smells like trouble.

The reaction to catnip is based solely on volatile terpenoids called nepetalactones. Although terpenoids can be toxic, curiosity about catnip will not kill the cat. The normal concentration of nepetalactones in the plant is not dangerous (although they repel insect pests). It is the presence of catniplike chemicals in male cat urine that accounts for the similarity of the catnip response and sexual behavior. In a sense, nepetalactones coincidentally mimic a natural courtship pheromone produced by the tomcat, thus giving catnip reactions their sexual appearance.

Matatabi, which the Japanese call a pleasure plant, does the same trick for cats even better. This plant contains secondary compounds closely related in chemical structure and behavioral activity to nepetalactones. Concentrated matatabi chemicals, in doses unavailable to the cats in the natural plant, were placed on cotton balls and presented to the large cats at the Osaka Zoo. After an initial exposure, the cats became so eager for more that they would ignore whatever else they were doing—eating, drinking, or even having sexual intercourse—whenever the chemicals were made available. They displayed a very intense "catnip" response, then rolled on their backs where they stayed for some time "in complete ecstasy." One observer noted that the animals were truly addicted because they continued to approach and react despite damage to the olfactory centers that spread into the stem of the brain itself.

Intoxicated cats are still happy cats, according to every behavioral index. The stronger the dose or concentration of terpenoids, the more intense the reaction and the more tenacious the affinity for the intoxication. It is this affinity, passion, fondness, attraction, or love that defines a psychological addiction. Humans also react to changing doses of catnip with a progression of effects and affections for the experiences. Weak teas were once used in the United States for pain, but catnip is now left out of medical dispensatories. Higher doses of nepetalactones can be delivered via the smoking of catnip leaves, which gives people a pleasant hallucinogenic experience.

Do cats also hallucinate on the plant? It could be argued that we have no way of knowing whether another animal is hallucinating. But animals might confirm the presence of hallucinations by responding to them, trying to grasp them, track them, avoid them, or in some other way behaving as if things were actually there. Much of the behavior of cats under the influence of catnip suggests that they are having such false perceptions. When cats gaze vacantly in no particular direction, their accompanying actions indicate that they are seeing things. Some cats will paw and play with "phantom butterflies" in the air; others lower their ears and pounce on "invisible mice"; still others show fear and hiss in the absence of any other animal or object.

Similar things happened when other animals used plant hallucinogens. People were usually around to witness the animals' reactions, then try the plant for themselves. These events took place in every part of the planet and everywhere people and animals shared similar reactions. In the forests of Gabon and the northern Congo, natives observed boars digging up and eating the roots of the *iboga* shrub. The boars went into wild frenzies, jumping around, and displaying fear and flight reactions. When porcupines and gorillas did the same thing with the plant, the natives concluded that the animals were fleeing from frightening visions and started using the root to produce their own fantastic images. In later experiments, the plant's major alkaloid, ibogaine, was injected into dogs and cats, causing them to act as if they were seeing frightening things.

In the emerald forests of the Amazon, the Tukano Indians say that jaguars not only claw and gnaw the nauseating bark of *yaje* but also chew the vines and leaves, a most uncharacteristic behavior for carnivores who normally prey on an assortment of rodents and small animals. The reactions of jaguars to this vine are unknown, but when the *yaje* alkaloid, harmine, was given to a dog, the animal stared at a point in front of it, suddenly jumped back, then went on staring again. Injection of related alkaloids into laboratory cats produced similar behaviors of jumping and staring. The natives believe the vine sends the cats on flights to another world. Their shamans teach them that by using the vine they too will be transformed into a jaguar with "jaguar eyes" capable of seeing in the dark, an effect explained by the pupillary dilation that often accompanies hallucinogenic intoxications. Hunters utilize this effect and take low doses of *yaje* to increase visual acuity and enhance sensory awareness. In a similar way, a predator like the jaguar might have learned that the *yaje* heightened sensory abilities such as smell, thus facilitating survival.

Other American Indian cultures believe there is an intimate connection between plant hallucinogens and animals. In the forbidding mountains of the Sierra Madre the Huichol Indians will often use the same word for deer and peyote. The union is symbolized by an ancient piece of Mexican pottery that depicts a deer holding a peyote cactus in its mouth, a prehistoric Bambi who shared not only the emotions of humans but also their choice in mind-altering substances. According to Huichol mythology, the great god of peyote first appeared as a deer and every one of his tracks became a peyote plant.

While dispersal of peyote by deer ingesting and eliminating cactus buttons might provide a basis for this myth, no one has been able to catch a deer in the act of nibbling this spineless cactus. Yet the Indians' dogs and goats will readily eat any unguarded peyote they find. Once three goats knocked over a container of forty-three fresh peyote and quickly gobbled them up. For the remainder of the day the goats displayed unusual energy, charging and butting each other and humans as well. When not running amok, the animals would stare into space and twitch their heads, a characteristic sign of hallucinations.

The native tribesmen of Siberia often see such head-twitching in their reindeer. In the Siberian summer, reindeer feast on a variety of mushrooms. Under the birch trees, they seek out their favorite: the *Amanita muscaria*. This red-capped and white-flecked mushroom is also called fly agaric because flies attracted to it will become stunned and fall into a helpless stupor after drinking its juices. Domesticated reindeer become unmanageable in their greed for this mushroom and act as if they are drunk: running aimlessly about, making noise, head-twitching, and isolating themselves from the herds. They may be no different from the Norse Vikings who ate the fly agaric to produce the ecstatic reckless rage for which they earned the nickname "Berserkers."

The active principle is ibotenic acid, a secondary substance that is transformed by the body into an equally intoxicating chemical, muscimole. The tribesmen noticed that the reindeer display an equally intense passion for human urine that contains the muscimole metabolite. Whenever they smell urine in the vicinity, reindeer scamper to the source and start fighting with each other for access to the clumps of yellow-stained snow. The urine has the same intoxicating effect on the reindeer as the fly agaric mushrooms. The reindeer's pursuit of urine, with or without muscimole, is so aggressive that travelers to the area have been warned about the danger of urinating in the open tundra when there are reindeer around. The Chukchee tribesmen utilize this passion by saving the muscimole-spiked urine in sealskin or sheet-metal containers for use in rounding up the reindeer or extending their own intoxications for another day. While they value the reindeer, the mushrooms are more precious. The barter price for a single fly agaric can be two or three reindeer. The reindeer may feed and clothe the body, but the mushrooms nourish the soul with ecstastic visions and this is worth more to the natives.

The mushroom chemicals are so potent that the smallest bite can produce a great deal of bizarre behavior. Head-twitching is a common sight when fly agaric is nibbled by deer, squirrels, or chipmunks. Herds of Canadian caribou, close relatives of the reindeer, show the biggest effects. During their migrations, the wild caribou move in a long single file column, as precisely spaced as pearls on a string. Occasionally the route will pass clusters of fly agaric, and adult females have been seen nibbling them. Within an hour or two, these caribou leave the column and run with an awkward side-to-side shaking of their hindquarters. If it were not for the accompanying head-twitching, this movement would be virtually identical to the "dance of death" the mother caribou will use to lure wolves or other enemies away from their young. Since the intoxicated and disoriented caribou may lag behind the column, leaving the young unprotected as well, the results may still be the same. Either mother or young may be lost to the wolves, not unlike the intoxicated robins preyed upon by cats.

While fly agaric may not kill animals directly, it can kill people, although the consequences of the intoxications are minimized for the tribes who sun-dry or toast the mushrooms, processes that seem to weaken the toxins. Nonetheless, eating even one mushroom will induce twitching, trembling, slight convulsions, and numbness in the limbs. As uncomfortable as these effects may seem to an outside observer, the users are happy and often experience a desire to dance and sing along with their hallucinations. Clinical observations have revealed a jovial, almost drunken disposition, flushing of the skin, and a slight tearing of the eyes. This picture of intoxication reminds one of American cartoonist Thomas Nast's famous portrayal of Santa Claus with twinkling eyes and cherry nose, driving a sleigh pulled by reindeer flying over the treetops.

Hallucinogenic mushrooms such as the fly agaric have been dispersed throughout the world as widely as the image of Santa himself. And magic or sacred mushrooms, as some varieties are called, have appeared around the world, popping up from the Kamchatka peninsula of Siberia to the highlands of Mexico. The sacred mushrooms vary in many botanical characteristics but all contain derivatives of a powerful hallucinogenic substance, psilocybin.

These psilocybin derivatives are less intoxicating than the secondary chemicals in fly agaric and cause little disruption in the behavior of cattle, sheep, and goats that have been observed browsing them. Smaller animals receive proportionately larger doses and exhibit more dramatic effects. On ranches in Hawaii and Mexico, I saw dogs deliberately nipping the caps off psilocybin mushrooms and swallowing them. A few minutes later the dogs were running about in circles, head-twitching, yelping, and refusing to respond to human commands. Such behavior is similar to that recorded in *Innocent Killers* by Jane Goodall, who observed a jackal cub, Rufus, eating a mysterious mushroom:

> Ten minutes later he seemed to go mad. He rushed around in circles and then charged, flatout, first at a Thompson's gazelle and then at a bull wildebeest. Both animals, possibly as surprised as I was, hurried out of his way. Could the mushroom have caused hallucinations? Had Rufus been on a trip? The question must remain unanswered as I could not find another for identification.

Despite the nibbling and browsing, most animals appear to have a natural indifference to mushrooms. Primates, however, seem to love them or hate them. We offered some grocery store mushrooms to the residents in the UCLA primate center. Our laboratory-reared monkeys seemed to like them. But monkeys captured from the wild were reluctant to taste them. Several displayed alarm and fear at the mere sight of them. One stump-tailed macaque became so panicked, banging itself against the cage walls, that it had to be tranquilized so as to avoid injuring itself. It is inviting to speculate about previous experiences that these animals may have had with more potent mushrooms in their natural habitats. When one of our laboratory rhesus monkeys was given a psilocybin mushroom that caused it to become disoriented and confused, the original indifference to mushrooms was replaced by an intractable refusal to accept any future offerings of mushrooms, harmless or psychoactive. Perhaps some primates in the wild learn similar lessons.

Cultures of *Homo sapiens* also seem divided into groups with differing attitudes regarding the eating of wild mushrooms; most are indifferent but there are also mycophiles and mycophobes. So it is hard to understand the universal esteem granted to the truffle, a fungus that lives out its life in the dark, dank underground of oak forests. The truffle, like catnip, illustrates how a plant can evoke a powerful attraction because it excites a basic biological drive in animals.

Truffles exist in a subterranean world that seems a most unfitting habitat for an aphrodisiac. These fungi resemble crispy, jet black sea sponges; most are the size of Ping-Pong balls but, at depths of up to one meter, some have been as large as giant potatoes and weigh in at almost a kilogram. One of the most expensive foods in the world, truffles have been referred to as "black diamonds," although Italian and Arctic varieties are white. Field mice and rabbits burrow into them and destroy them. Even chickens will try to get to them by scratching the surface soil. But pigs are the best truffle hunters, capable of detecting the musky odor from great distances.

The pig's passion for truffles is the same as our own, according to Etruscan and Roman myths that attribute aphrodisiac qualities to the fungi. Even contemporary folktales claim that particularly odorous truffles will encourage sex by making women more tender and men more agreeable. There is a strong chemical basis for the stories.

Truffles contain a steroid, androstenol, which gives them the pronounced musklike scent and a nutty taste. This same steroid is synthesized in the testes of the boar and transferred to the salivary gland from which it is secreted during premating behavior. Androstenol makes boars more aggressive and tends to immobilize the sow in a mating stance. The concentration of the steroid in truffles is about twice the concentration found in boars, hence the vigorous interest shown by pigs in search of this delicacy. Androstenol is also synthesized by human males in the testes and secreted by axillary sweat glands, giving male sweat a musky odor that plays a preparatory role in human sexual behavior.

All this may have been appreciated by the early Spaniards, who called the truffle *trufa,* meaning "testicles of earth itself," and used it to facilitate sexual behavior. And it may be an old story to Northern flying squirrels, which have been seen feeding on truffles that lie just below the surface of the Alaskan soil. In northern California, a flying squirrel was observed gliding to a slightly exposed truffle lying on the ground. After eating for a few minutes, it left carrying a small piece of the truffle. The squirrel was followed to its nest in an abandoned woodpecker's hole. It took the truffle inside to where its mate awaited. One can only imagine the characteristic mating behavior of flying squirrels that followed: the sexual partners wrap their arms around each other and the male uses his flight skin like a cloak to surround the female.

Mystery and superstition have always shielded the effects of another fungus, ergot, from full view. Ergot is a parasitic fungus that infects rye, wheat, and other grasses. The fungus forms *sclerotia*—hard, dark purple bodies that secretly replace the grains and seeds in the cereals. The sclerotium itself is a veritable laboratory of potent chemicals known as ergot alkaloids, whose effects are foretold by their purple color—an ominous color that Homeric hymns have linked with the awesome powers of Lord Hades and the underworld.

Ergot alkaloids are structurally similar to neurochemicals present in the nervous tissue of warm-blooded animals. They can interfere with the flow of blood through the body as well as seriously alter the perceptions and movements of the animals. Grazing animals were probably the first to encounter this fungus, which is still a hazard to livestock. A large single meal of contaminated grasses may produce agitation and muscle spasms. The animals stagger in stiff, bounding movements, their eyes jerk back and forth, and eventually they fall. They sit with dazed appearance, isolated from the flock or herd, but as the intoxication subsides they rejoin the group. The effects from chronic feeding are not noticeable for several weeks or longer, the length of time depending on the concentration of ergot alkaloids in the grasses. Lameness appears first, then limbs become numb and necrotic. Gangrene finally erupts. Cattle stricken with gangrenous ergotism tend to segregate themselves but still remain with the herd when it starts moving. The herd leaves behind 5 percent who are prostrate, starving, and dying.

Grazing animals are not alone in their ergot intoxications. Some adventurous farmers have been tempted to taste the ergot-spotted grains after observing unusual behavior in their animals; but the first human use was probably an accident experienced by ancient agriculturists. When the infected grains found their way into breads that were then eaten, mass intoxications and poisonings resulted. The first intentional use followed shortly after the first accidents when the ancient Athenians conducted secret ceremonies in the temple at Eleusis. There, during these nocturnal "mysteries," individuals drank *kykeon,* a mixture of barley with ergot, water, and mint. For two millennia, until suppression of these rites by Christianity in the fourth century A.D., thousands of people were given this unique experience annually. Participants included Aristotle, Sophocles, Plato, Aeschylus, Pindar, and several Roman emperors. It was a blissful experience, according to Homer, one that could lift men out of a gloomy darkness and give them what Cicero called "a reason to live in joy." Confronted by a profoundly religious experience, the initiates surrendered to the visions with awe and wonderment.

The intentional uses of hallucinogenic plants by both animals and native peoples have been events just as infrequent and structured as the passage through the portals at Eleusis. The picture of animals chewing on *yaje* vines, *iboga* roots, or fly agaric mushrooms is something that is seen only intermittently. Similarly, the participants at Eleusis came only once a year; *Datura* ceremonies may happen only once in a lifetime; and the modern use of magic mushrooms is as intermittent in native cultures as it is at high school parties.

Ritual and recreational intoxications from hallucinogens do not occur continually with humans. A major reason for this controlled use is tolerance, which can develop quickly and block most effects. In order to overcome tolerance, increasingly larger doses have to be used. But such large doses are not always easy to come by in nature and they still may fail to break through the massive tolerance that develops to drugs such as ergot alkaloids. Humans have learned that a better way to handle the drugs is to space the doses over time, thus allowing for many weeks—even months—between intoxications. This prevents tolerance and gives people an opportunity to reflect on the experience and assimilate it into their lives. Since some animals, such as rats, also take only intermittent samples of hallucinogens in the wild, perhaps they are doing the same thing.

Periodic intoxications are seen in several animals that seem to know much about hallucinogenic plants and generally avoid the strong psychoactive parts. There is a suggestion that they also know what they are doing when they depart from their usual feeding to eat the psychoactive portions. For example, morning glories, which contain the same alkaloids as ergot, are eaten by rats, which feed regularly on the plant's vines and fruits. The rodents tend to avoid the larger concentration of alkaloids in the seeds. Yet, when disturbed by severe weather conditions, a rat will occasionally snack on a single seed, then display the characteristic head-twitches of intoxication.

I once observed two Hawaiian mongooses depart from their regular diet of meat, eggs, and juicy fruits to chew the highly potent seeds of a silver morning glory that had been planted in their spacious outdoor pen. The mongooses twitched and circled their pen, then appeared calmed for several hours. During the next few months, the mongooses ignored the seeds. Then I observed one mongoose eating the seeds again, but it was on a special occasion: its mate had just died and a tropical storm had reduced much of the pen to a field of mud. Morning glory seeds are used by modern Mexican Indians to console themselves in times of trouble; perhaps the animals are doing the same.

It is clear that many animals are attracted to elements of intoxicating and hallucinogenic experiences. The real danger is when their natural infrequent intoxications are repeated, when the pursuit is so passionate that a life-threatening pattern of behavior is established. Birds do this with berries but they are protected by seasonal ripening. Bees do it with the stupefying nectars of specialized Umbelliferae flowers, but are also protected from frequent use by seasonal flowering. However, industrious ants can do it all the time inside their colonies. They provide a powerful example of a severe addiction to a disorienting intoxicant.

A variety of ants lives in symbiotic relationship with special beetles. The ants, playing the role of hosts, provide food and care for their beetle guests. In return, the beetles produce secretions from their abdominal areas and allow the ants to lick them. The ants may become so overwhelmed by the intoxicating nature of these secretions that they become temporarily disoriented and less sure of their footing.

Entomologists have labeled the ants' passion both a love and an addiction. Love is seen in the care and feeding the ant extends to the beetle larvae, which are accepted as part of the ant's own brood. Consider the example of the yellow ant, *Lasius flavus,* and the *Lomechusa* beetle, named after an ancient Roman poisoner. In times of danger, the ants will even move the beetle larvae to safety before they tend to their own eggs. The addiction is manifested by the worker ants, which seem totally disinterested in anything but the intoxicating secretion produced by the beetle. Consequently, the ants allow more *Lomechusa* beetles to move into the colony, resulting in a corresponding dwindling of the ant population. Excessive intake of the intoxicant can cause such mania in the colony that female ant larvae become damaged in such a way that they develop into useless cripples rather than reproductive queens. Accordingly, "*Lomechusa*-mania," a case of severe addiction, can contribute to the decline and fall of the ant society. The case provides a true fable for our species to contemplate regarding the presence of hallucinogenic drugs in the modern workplace.

2

There is no question that behavior under the influence of hallucinogens is dysfunctional to many activities. The very word *hallucination* is from the Latin *alucinari,* meaning "to wander in mind or attention," or "to dream." Preoccupation with the experiential aspects of hallucinogenic intoxication is always done at the expense of the ability to deal with the demands of perceptual-motor behaviors in the real world. Even animals without advanced nervous systems can be readily distracted by these drugs.

In order to spin successful webs, spiders need good control and attention. The usual regularity of the web patterns is determined by the spider taking the shortest path that demands the least effort in spinning. The slight irregularities that occur in a normal web are usually due to distracting external stimuli that cause the spider to swerve from the shortest path.

Treatment with mescaline from peyote or psilocybin from the sacred mushrooms disrupts the web-spinning behavior, causing marked distortions and irregularities in the construction of the web. Low doses of

LSD actually improve the steering ability of spiders, allowing them to build a web that is more regular in central angle and spiral spacing, and has a larger catching area. But high doses of LSD can radically change the geometry, creating asymmetric webs that are longer and narrower than usual and have irregular angles. The surreal LSD webs are striking departures from the conventional designs. Artistic interpretations aside, these webs may stretch to new dimensions but they have a reduced catching area that is simply below survival standards. When spiders spun their webs in the weightlessness of *Skylab,* they also produced asymmetrical and irregular structures. Whether the disturbance is from "inner" or outer space, even automatic genetic guidance systems can be overridden. The effects are found not only with animals that stay suspended in the air, but in those found swimming in the seas.

The swimming behavior of Siamese fighting fish is rigidly controlled and guided by visual and olfactory cues in the water. Their movements are deliberate and well coordinated. If faced with an attacking fish, they display a lateral fighting stance complete with expanded fins and darkened pigmentation. When exposed to LSD or related hallucinogens, they display their famous fighting stance in an empty tank, acting as if they were seeing another fish. These drugged fish, like the spiders, have difficulty in orienting themselves; they posture vertically in the water, with their heads turned up to the surface. They even execute unusual vertical barrel rolls. Such upsets may prevent fish from noticing things that are actually there. Guppies treated with LSD rapidly swam into the wall of their tank and kept on swimming, unaware that they were not making any progress.

Land-based animals, especially those with advanced nervous systems, seem even more confused by these drugs. When hallucinogen-treated rodents are not twitching their heads, they may be too busy scratching and grooming themselves to engage in other activities. In one experiment, researchers gave mice and rats powdered *yopo* beans, a hallucinogen used by Guahibo Indians in South America, and found the animals staggering and constantly looking around as if they were orienting themselves to hallucinations. Similar behavior was seen when mice were injected with LSD: they would directly attack any object placed in front of them, sometimes attacking nothing at all. Rabbits, cats, and dogs respond to derivatives of plant hallucinogens with similar behaviors, including chasing unseen objects and ignoring objects that are present in their environment.

It has been a simple matter to administer a hallucinogenic drug to a laboratory animal and study the effects on learning, performance, memory, and other tasks. In general, these studies have shown that sufficient doses of hallucinogens can impair accuracy, disrupt control, and produce shifts in the attention of animals trying to concentrate on solving problems. Their abilities to discriminate between colored lights or react to a buzzer quickly enough to avoid a mild electric shock are often compromised. Behaviors important in natural habitats are also changed for the worse.

From the bottom of the phylogenetic scale to the top, animals cannot effectively do other things when they are doing hallucinogens. Earthworms become disorganized after receiving LSD and aimlessly crawl and burrow through the topsoil. Even late-arriving birds would have little difficulty getting one of these confused worms. The mystery snail, a favorite for aquarium keepers, cannot hang on to any surface or leaf while under the influence of LSD. The rippling waves of its foot are so violent that the snail slides to the bottom of the tank or plant. In its native habitat in the South American tropics, there are no glass walls to protect the snail from the reach of predators.

Mice and rats can still run in exercise wheels or climb ropes after injections of hallucinogens, although they are somewhat slower than normal, but they will be easily distracted by lights or sounds and may freeze in their tracks. If the distraction is a predator in the wild, the rodent could fail to escape and be killed. One exception would be a cat under the influence—such animals have been known to fondle mice rather than eat them. In one study, a female cat treated with ergot alkaloids allowed a mouse to nurse from it. However, the LSD-treated rat would be a poor mother: it still collects bits of paper to be used in a nest but is unable to carry out the more complex activities of nest construction. It doesn't seem to know what to do with the paper and places it in useless piles.

Hallucinogenic drugs may also prevent the animal from knowing how to survive. In nature as well as in city environments, rats often have to swim in order to escape danger, and they rapidly learn the way out of underwater mazes in the laboratory. Yet even under survival motivation, rats treated with LSD or mescaline cannot successfully negotiate the mazes and will drown. A chilling experiment with squir-rel monkeys suggested that the same is true for primates. Pairs of these small monkeys were placed in a tank filled with water, forcing them to swim and to fight to climb on top of each other in order to survive. In such situations, a dominant monkey will usually emerge over a submis-sive one. When the pairs were treated with LSD, there were no winners.

Hallucinogens tend to make animals more fearful for the short period they are under the influence of the drugs. Mice and rats are not only fearful of new stimuli but they also exhibit a generalized fear of open spaces. They defecate more, a sign of emotional stress; run from strange events; and back into corners to hide.

This state of intoxication produced by hallucinogens does not appear to be one that can be permitted to happen too frequently and still allow for survival in the wild. Infrequent and low-dose exposures might be handled, as they seem to be, but excessive use is not wise. Fortunately, excessive use is not the rule. Why, then, do animals even bother with the occasional nibble or chew? Why would any animal want such an experience? Why take a drug only to back into a dark cor-ner? The answer can be found in the corner in which the rat is hiding, in the darkness of the brain itself.

3

When morning glories or related plant hallucinogens are ingested, humans will frequently describe a pleasant delirium wherein they soar through thousands of colorful visions. The nature of these visions is suggested by the modern names given to the horticultural varieties of morning glories: Heavenly Blue, Pearly Gates, Flying Saucers, Wedding Bells, Blue Star, and Summer Skies. While some names were inspired by the physical appearances of the ornamental flowers, they are apt descriptors of the intoxication itself—a generally beautiful and uplifting experience, but one so intense that it cannot be quickly followed by another. Whether the hallucinogens are used for magic, ritual, healing, entertainment, or simple amusement, people do not engage in such experiences often. And no matter what the cultural context is, users all tell of sights to see, voices to listen to, thoughts to ponder, and altered states of consciousness to explore. If it is this subjective experience that so distracts and captivates people, would animals seek out such experiences in conditions that parallel our own use?

Darkness, solitude, and the silence of night are the most common times for humans to use hallucinogens. All primitive societies prefer these drugs under conditions when there is little else to see or hear in the environment. In dark settings, users report attenuation of unpleasant reactions and a heightening of pleasant effects. Repeated use of hallucinogens is generally motivated by a desire to experience these novel states, which are interpreted as stimulating and rewarding.

In dark and isolated settings, monkeys also find exploring visual stimuli exciting and rewarding. In a classic demonstration of this motivation to explore, rhesus monkeys were confined, one at a time, to a dimly lighted wire cage that was covered with an opaque box. Two small windows were located on one wall of the box and, if either of these was unlatched, the monkey could push it open and peek into the surrounding laboratory world. When the windows were painted blue and yellow— and the blue one was always unlocked—the monkeys learned to open the blue window in order to look out for about thirty seconds. The door-pushing behavior was persistent and most monkeys were willing to do it for hours. The longer they were visually deprived in the opaque box, the more they pushed the window open when allowed to do so.

What would happen if the only window to the world was a "window" provided by a hallucinogenic drug? Would monkeys self-administer the drug under such conditions? There is good evidence to suggest that they would. Many hallucinogenic alkaloids produce electrical excitation in the brain and nervous system that mimics the effects produced by light when it strikes the retina of the eye. It is this type of electrical excitation that is responsible for creating visual effects in people and other primates. When the visual areas of human surgical patients are electrically stimulated, or when human subjects are given drugs like LSD, they often report seeing things in their mind's eye. One unanesthetized patient was electrically stimulated in the occipital lobe and reached out quickly from the operating table to catch a hallucinated butterfly. Stimulation in the same area of a rhesus monkey's brain caused the monkey to attempt catching flies in the air. Because animals and people under the influence of hallucinogens often act in the same way, the drugs are probably triggering similar mechanisms. And because monkeys need visual stimulation as much as we do, I was certain they would accept an enlightening hallucinogen rather than darkness. I designed an experiment in my laboratory to test this hypothesis.

The drug I selected was derived from *yopo* and *epena,* two hallucinogens used in South America. *Yopo,* prepared from the ground beans used by the Guahibo, is inhaled as a snuff through hollow bird-bone or bamboo tubes. Users display characteristic gesticulating postures, then fall into hallucinatory trances. *Epena,* a similar snuff, is prepared from the bark of *Virola* trees and used by tribes in the northwestern Amazon region. Both plants contain dimethyltryptamine (DMT) that has been produced synthetically and is usually smoked or injected. North American users report that DMT produces a short "retinal circus" of colorful geometric and memory images that lasts for thirty minutes.

Alex, Claude, and Lucy were the subjects. They were three adult rhesus monkeys, born and raised in captivity, with no previous experience with hallucinogens. All were veterans of my laboratory, where they had spent many years taking daily trips to the smoking box. The box was a large metal cage that provided free access to a food bin and a water dispenser. A hollow stainless steel tube protruded through one wall of the box. It was connected to a smoking machine that delivered the smoke from burning cigarettes. The monkeys had been trained to puff on the tube in order to inhale tobacco smoke so that the effects of this behavior could be studied. Tobacco smoking was something that all three of these monkeys did to varying degrees without any additional rewards. They were so familiar with the box that they could find the smoking tube in the dark.

The box was placed inside a lightproof and soundproof chamber that effectively isolated it from all visual and auditory contact with the outside world. The chamber was outfitted with an infrared video monitoring system so that an animal in the box could still be observed in the dark. Initially, each monkey was given the opportunity to live alone in the dark chamber for ten consecutive days and nights. The smoking machine was filled with cigarettes made from ordinary garden lettuce. The cigarettes were made available to the animals at the rate of one per hour, for a total of twenty-four each day. Over the ten days that they lived in this totally deprived environment, the animals smoked very few lettuce cigarettes: Alex hardly puffed at all; Claude puffed on a cigarette once every day, but not enough to finish any of them; and Lucy refused to puff on any of the 240 cigarettes made available to her.

Six months later, after a rest in the monkey colony, the animals were once again placed in isolation. This time the lettuce cigarettes were laced with DMT, enough so that a whole cigarette would deliver a monkey-size hallucinogenic dose. Previous trials with other rhesus monkeys in the regular laboratory environment had already determined that after the initial puffs of DMT, they would refuse to go near the smoking tube again.

Alex was the first to enter the chamber where he would live for the next twenty days without any outside stimulation except for that available every hour from the DMT cigarettes. On the second day, he approached the tube and started puffing. He got carried away and within a few minutes of staccato puffing he had smoked an entire cigarette! Immediately he went prone on the cage floor, then started bumping and groping at the cage walls. He spasmed and vomited, but within twenty minutes he had fully recovered. Even though it was pitch-black, Alex put on an aggressive display to the smoking tube—threatening it with facial expressions and loud barks—and never went near the tube again. I concluded that Alex had had a bad trip, not unlike a poisoned meal. He would never become a DMT user.

Now it was Claude's turn. Strong and healthy, Claude had ruled the monkey colony as the dominant male for years. He never refused a challenge and never got sick. He had made it through the boredom of the earlier ten-day experiment by sleeping or sitting in stoic resolve. On Day 3 he approached the DMT tube, took five quick puffs, and sat down. He stared and turned his head quickly about for several minutes. This orienting behavior became more obvious on Day 4 when Claude puffed enough to finish off almost an entire DMT cigarette. By Day 8 he had worked up to smoking almost two whole cigarettes each day. He was intoxicated every day. If Claude's trips were not good, they certainly seemed to amuse him. Sometimes he would reach out and attempt to grasp imaginary objects. He slapped and swatted at things in the air. During one particular intoxication, he started a fight with his left foot. Claude kept up a daily pattern of DMT smoking and intoxicated antics until Day 20, when the experiment ended.

Finally, it was time for little Lucy to enter the box. Lucy was the smallest female in the colony and also the brightest. If rewarded with an orange or a chocolate candy, she could solve the most difficult puzzles and problems; she became a stubborn statue if denied a treat. She didn't smoke the lettuce cigarettes when there were no other rewards, and I was predicting Lucy wouldn't fall for DMT. The first five days seemed like a replay of the earlier test. Lucy ignored the tube and seemed comfortable in her dark, quiet surroundings. There is no night or day in the box and Lucy started sleeping during most of my daytime watch. The electronic sensors, on guard all the time, recorded a single puff on Day 6; however, Lucy showed no change in behavior. When she totally ignored the tube on Day 7, I was betting she had experienced an unpleasant reaction to that puff and, like Alex, would forever after keep her distance from the tube. When nothing happened on Day 8, I wrote in my log that the rest of the days promised to be the same.

Day 9. 6:00 P.M. Lucy approached the tube and ran off a cluster of puffs on a DMT cigarette. She immediately crouched in a corner, rubbed her eyes, shook her head, and looked up with an expression of disbelief. I didn't believe it either. She used her hands and eyes to track "movements" in the box, then relaxed. Thirty minutes later, when the next cigarette became available, she smoked most of it. After some more tracking and rubbing, Lucy yawned and went to sleep.

Day 10. 9:00 A.M. Lucy smoked another cigarette and spread out on her stomach, moving her hands over the cage floor and following them with her eyes—movements virtually identical with those observed in the tracking of real objects.

Day 11. 2:00 P.M. Another cigarette was smoked and Lucy circled the cage, trying to catch something. She tumbled and rolled, then stood for several minutes with her head on the floor between her feet and her hindquarters up in the air.

Day 12. 12:30 P.M. Lucy was startled after smoking part of a cigarette. She backed into a corner and grimaced in fear.

Day 19. 11:00 P.M. Lucy has recovered from her startle reaction and has been smoking almost two DMT cigarettes a day for the past several days. She has become extremely proficient at catching whatever she has been chasing: she now brings "it" to her mouth, chews and lip-smacks with delight.

Day 20. 12:00 A.M. Lucy has just finished another cigarette as the experiment ends. I slowly fade in the room lights, enter the chamber, and open the cage door to take her back to the monkey colony. Lucy jumps into my heavily-gloved hands, chattering away, happily picking at butterflies from the brain.

Little Lucy and her big pal Claude have clearly demonstrated an acceptance of DMT intoxication in order to see through the same hallucinogenic window we do. Under the right conditions it was as useful to a monkey as it is to a human. We share the same motivation to light up our lives with chemical glimpses of another world.

4

A Shrewdness of Apes

LEARNING TO USE TOBACCO
AND OTHER DRUGS

1

It is a landscape of dread. Waterways snake their way through forbidding swamps. The air is hot and saturated. Columns of smoke and mist coil around the trees, then rise to escape through the canopy above. Pencil-thin shafts of sunlight cut through the haze, dappling the jungle floor with specks of light. In this twilight world of the Orinoco Delta of Venezuela, the puffed eyes of the Warao, dimmed by the effects of tobacco, see only terror. Poisoning from tobacco renders them color-blind and they tend to see life in the black and white of good and evil. They are preyed upon by surrounding tribes, at the mercy of ruthless gods who are said to eat their children, and incessantly agitated by the incredible amounts of nicotine that saturate their bodies. The nervousness is palpable to any visitor who dares trek to their villages.

The Warao believe that the Earth is a saucer and they inhabit the very center of it. Surrounding the saucer is an ocean where the giant Snake of Being lives. Another monster, a four-headed serpent, lives beneath the Earth itself. Much of a Warao's life is spent in pleasing the spirits who rule this land and in trying to transcend its boundaries. Their only escape, their only window to another world, their only hallucinogen, is tobacco.

A Warao shaman will select a slender two-foot tube of cane filled with the malodorous leaves of black tobacco, perfumed with a fragrant resin to make it attractive to the gods. Smoking ten to thirty of these cigars, the shaman "eats" and swallows the smoke, allowing the fumes to suffuse his entire body. Buoyed by this smoke, he enters an ecstatic trance and ascends on a "celestial bridge" over "a rainbow of colors" to a supernatural world. There he feeds the spirits with tobacco smoke and is rewarded with blessings of health and happiness.

Tobacco shamanism is a relatively old pattern of drug use for our species, dating back eight thousand years. Although Paleolithic settlers arrived on the American continents with their shamanistic traditions long before that time, and tobacco was already widely dispersed, it was not until the development of slash-and-burn farming in South America that tobacco was cultivated for drug purposes. Wild species of tobacco had a propensity to grow on newly disturbed soil—even soil covered with ashes—literally right under the noses of early human farmers.

The habit of tobacco smoking probably developed from the custom of burning incense during religious and secular ceremonies. The fires would be fueled by dry twigs, leaves, and resins from aromatic plants such as tobacco. As fire-keepers blew on the embers, they would also inhale the smoke and within six seconds—the time it takes the nicotine alkaloid to reach the brain—would have discovered that the effect of this plant was to induce a form of trance.

Nicotine is found throughout the plant, but it is concentrated in the leaves. Although this alkaloid can explain most of the effects from tobacco, the smoke of tobacco contains nine hundred other constituents. Several of these compounds, including carbon dioxide, myristicin, and nitrous oxide, have known hallucinogenic effects. Harman, an alkaloid similar to the harmine found in *yaje*, is produced in tobacco smoke as are many chemical deliriants. Consequently, tobacco smoking can produce an intoxication that shares all the qualities ascribed to a hallucinatory experience.

By freeing users from the dread of physical or mental landscapes, tobacco became an ideal drug for primitive magic and religion. It was readily consumed by the cleansing power of fire. The smoke, which could conceal the movements of shamans and was inherently evocative of changing shapes and mysterious images, rose like clouds to the abode of the gods themselves. Indeed, the gods of many American Indians, like those of the Mayans before them, were thought to smoke tobacco cigars, like corporate chieftains of an ancient world. Shamans believe that the gods will enter into beneficial relationships with us only if we continue to sacrifice the drug to them. Tobacco nourishment is considered the food of the gods and proper for man as well. Therefore South American shamans will take this nourishment into their bodies in any number of ways: by drinking, licking, chewing, and snuffing different preparations of the plant. And because they are tool-using primates, these cultures have developed a variety of devices to assist the feasts. Bowls for the drinking of tobacco in the form of a syrupy infusion are among the oldest artifacts that have been discovered. Snuffing tubes, pipes, and equipment for making cigars and cigarettes came later. The most recent advance in technology, dating to Mayan times, was the use of rectal syringes for the rapid absorption of tobacco juice from enemas.

Although humans discovered for themselves how to use tobacco, folklore and mythology attribute similar discoveries to animals. One story claims that insects are fond of tobacco leaves and the speed with which they devour the plant suggested the stimulant properties to the early settlers of South America. Tobacco was magical because one of these insects, a worm, would change into a small hawk. The story may be based upon observations of the hornworm, a natural insect pest of tobacco.

The hornworm, like tobacco budworms and other insects that feed on the plant, has an extremely efficient excretory system that passes the tobacco through the gut so fast that toxic doses of nicotine cannot accumulate. A few other insects have developed ways to survive tobacco meals by selectively feeding on plant tissue that does not contain nicotine, detoxifying nicotine with enzymes, or using neural sheaths to block nicotine from penetrating into the nervous system where it can kill. Once the nicotine problem has been managed, insects can enjoy the cellulose, starches, sugars, and other nutritional elements of the tobacco leaf. Unlike many of these other insects, the hornworm is unique in that it metamorphoses from the larval stage to become a large hawkmoth, which has no mechanisms for handling nicotine but, of course, can simply fly away.

Tobacco pests are exceptional because most insects cannot survive the poisonous effects of nicotine when they come into contact with the plant. South American Indians took advantage of these properties and employed tobacco as a natural insecticide for preserving or fumigating seeds and foods, cleansing the skin of insects and parasites, fumigating virgins prior to marriage, as well as purging the bodies and souls of patients.

Were humans also exceptional animals in their ability to survive the use of this plant? The evidence is that some primates, in addition to man, mastered a semblance of control over tobacco. The development of that control required intelligence, good feeding strategies, and the right environment where the drug was both available and useful. These were the same requirements for the safe use of our other plant intoxicants. But unlike such drugs as marijuana, tobacco's toxicity presented special problems.

There is a scene in an old Laurel and Hardy movie in which a dog smokes a cigar, rears up, spins around, and falls over in a state of death-like collapse. Although the scene is a product of clever film editing, the effects of tobacco have not been misrepresented. Ingestion of a single tobacco seed is certain death to young birds. The mere browsing of wild tobacco has poisoned cattle, sheep, and rabbits from the plains of Africa and Australia to the highlands of the Andes. Death occurs within minutes. The flightless ostriches are particularly sensitive. Before dying on the sandy plains of Africa, the birds exhibit a spasmodic jumping coupled with an awkward beating of their useless wings, turning them into giant stick figures on a desert hot plate. Their convulsed and bent bodies are later found isolated from the rest of the flock.

If a dog smoking a cigar seems suitable material for a classic comedy, then one of the first actual medical experiments done with an animal might pass for a science fiction horror story were it not for the fact that it is true. The story begins in New York City. It is night and the patients inside Bellevue Hospital are unusually agitated. On the upper floors the women are screaming and the men are throwing their shoes out the window at a large black cat that is howling on the streets below. This continues for several nights, until a medical student finally traps the cat and takes it to his laboratory for an impromptu experiment. He soaks some tobacco, equivalent to the amount in a standard cigarette, draws up the fluid into a hypodermic syringe, then slowly injects it under the cat's skin. In a few minutes the cat begins to quiver, then tremble. It dies in violent convulsions twenty minutes later. The student, who went on to become a famous Chicago physician and researcher, concluded that "the poison destroyed the nine lives a cat is popularly supposed to possess."

Crude experiments in the early days of tobacco research seemed to suggest that this food of gods and shamans was also the fulfillment of an ancient Turkish prophecy. According to the legend, a snake, perhaps the same one evicted from Eden, bit the prophet Muhammad on the wrist. Muhammad sucked the poison from the wound and spat it upon the earth. From these drops sprang tobacco, a "wondrous weed" that promised to have the bitterness of the serpent's tooth mixed with the sweet saliva of the prophet.

Organisms from bacteria to baboons were tested by early researchers. Infusion of tobacco smoke into a colony of luminous marine bacteria caused the microorganisms to turn off their lights. Not only were bees, flies, and other insects quickly killed by the smoke, but leeches feeding on the blood of human tobacco smokers also perished. Frogs, pigeons, mice, rats, guinea pigs, rabbits, and dogs were placed in enclosed chambers and forced to breathe tobacco smoke. They died slowly over weeks, sometimes months. Some dogs were forced to inhale smoke from a cigarette fitted to a face mask or passively breathe the smoke via tracheal tubes. Hundreds of beagles and other animals died in these experiments.

A rabbit was shaved and a drop of nicotine was applied to its skin; it died quickly. Pure nicotine was now recognized as a more potent drug for use in the experiments. One-sixth of a drop would kill a cat and one-half drop would kill a dog. One drop of nicotine was applied to the eye of a white mouse and the eye of a sparrow. Both animals died instantly. An exceptionally potent nicotine spray was tested on ten turkeys, who instantly stiffened and died like so many wooden Indians caught in the grip of tobacco.

Despite this toxicity, animals in the wild still had a fighting chance to survive nicotine poisoning because tobacco is generally not found near animals that will feed on it. Even man had to learn to cultivate the plant in order to have accessible supplies. Therefore, it is not surprising that most instances of tobacco use among animals have occurred in situations where humans provided it. What is surprising, however, is that animal use is so much like our own once they get hold of the drug.

The primates described by Darwin exhibited the most inventive uses of tobacco. Darwin noted that monkeys acquire a strong taste for smoking tobacco without previous training and he correctly concluded that the "nerves" of taste must be very similar in monkeys and man. A smoking monkey, who had probably mimicked the behavior of a trainer, was first displayed at a fair in The Hague in 1635. Since that time, smoking monkeys and apes have appeared in shows and circuses throughout the world, providing an amusing fun-house mirror for human spectators.

Captive monkeys have copied other patterns of human tobacco use. Tame capuchin monkeys have acquired habits of placing tobacco snuff in their cheeks, then chewing and sucking just like their owners. Many will learn tricks for rewards of snuff. Other monkeys display adverse reactions. While on a voyage with a tobacco-chewing sailor, a monkey named Jocko helped himself to a quid and started chewing and spitting. Soon afterward the monkey became sick, moaning and holding his stomach, but ultimately he recovered. Thereafter, Jocko ran away whenever he saw or smelled tobacco. For primates that have acquired a liking for tobacco, recurrent approach behavior is more the rule.

Laboratory primates can be trained to smoke tobacco, despite their initial annoyance at the irritating smoke. At first the primates may cough and close their eyes, but experimenters can gradually get them to inhale deeply for as long as five seconds. Studies utilizing radioactively labeled tobacco have confirmed that the smoke is penetrating deep into the lungs, where it is quickly absorbed by the blood. Sometimes the animals have to be bribed with food or water rewards in order to start smoking, but once established, tobacco smoking may continue without additional incentives.

Research has confirmed that monkeys smoke for the same reason we do: nicotine. It is also the reason many pets such as hamsters will eat tobacco. When golden Syrian hamsters are provided free access to chewing tobacco, they rapidly escalate their intake. In a series of laboratory studies, the hamsters voluntarily consumed some every day even though food and water were always available. Intake increased gradually over a period of four months until the animals were chewing daily doses equivalent to 2.6 percent of their body weights. When denicotinized tobacco was substituted, the hamsters turned away, thereby pointing to nicotine as the object of the craving.

In a test of nicotine craving in primates, two rhesus monkeys voluntarily smoked cigarettes every day for two years without additional rewards. The animals were provided with Long Peace, a Japanese brand of cigarettes, each of which contained 1.9 milligrams of nicotine. They were given access to the cigarettes for twenty hours each day, but most smoking occurred at the start of each daily session and again in the late evening. The maximum smoking for any single session was forty-seven cigarettes. When given Just brand cigarettes, containing only 0.3 milligrams of nicotine, the number of cigarettes smoked decreased. But one monkey puffed harder in order to get more nicotine. The monkeys smoked even less when special nicotine-free cigarettes were used in the tests. The role of nicotine in providing the principal pharmacological reward for tobacco use has been further demonstrated by studies in which rhesus monkeys and baboons learned to press a lever in order to earn small intravenous injections of nicotine itself. When monkeys who had learned to press a lever as fast as two times per second in order to get the injections of nicotine were given mecamylamine, which blocks the effects of nicotine, their rate of lever-pressing dropped to almost zero.

The frequency of tobacco use by primates in the wild is not exactly zero, but it's low. When it does occur, the animals go for weak doses of nicotine. In Africa, young baboons, like the young native children, seem to be particularly fond of sucking the flowers of wild tobacco plants. Both baboons and children seem to be engaging in a familiar game of investigation and exploration. The game is called "plant-eating" and it is a popular children's game in central Turkey and in many other areas of the world. In Turkey, children between the ages of six and nine make a game out of eating various parts of plants in order to experience pleasant sensations or discover new effects. The game is often played with henbane, which grows wild throughout the region. As a consequence, 1 out of 4 children becomes severely intoxicated, and 1 out of

10 dies. In Africa, the baboons and children playing with tobacco flowers have allowed for intoxication but circumvented lethal reactions by
using the weakest part of the plant. Of the total nicotine in the tobacco
plant, the leaves contain 64 percent; the stems, 18 percent; the roots,
13 percent; and the flowers chosen by the young primates, a small but
still psychoactive 5 percent.

After the initial experimental trials with flowers, baboons may, under
special conditions, seek out other parts of the plant. In 1903 the South
African naturalist Eugene Marais began living with a troop of three
hundred wild chacma baboons and soon discovered some of those conditions. He stayed with them for three years until he felt he had understood their *soul,* a term best explained as "mind." While his
interpretation of the baboon's use of tobacco and other plant drugs
may have been colored by his own addiction to morphine, Marais's
observations provide important clues to primate behavior. Marais
found that the wild baboons had many opportunities to eat tobacco as
the troop passed through tobacco fields on their forays to orchards.
However, unlike other observers, he never saw them make use of it.
Tobacco also grew around Marais's hut, which the baboons frequently
visited without touching the plants. Yet all the *captive* baboons he
observed "beg for tobacco and eat or chew it with all the zest of a
long-established habit." He even described tool using in a captive male
baboon who had learned to scratch the oil out of a pipe stem with a
blade of grass, which he then cleaned onto a piece of paper, rolled up,
and chewed.

Marais believed that the difference between the wild and captive
baboon was the mental state of depression and suffering brought on by
confinement. In this state the captive baboon expressed a "powerful psychological predisposition" to the use of an intoxicant such as tobacco,
which promised to relieve the depression by producing a state of mental
exhilaration or happiness. Like the Warao trapped in a dreaded environment, the captive baboon reached out for escape to tobaccoland.

Although Marais's own chronic depression, which lead to suicide in
1935, undoubtedly influenced his theory, it is in agreement with studies suggesting that captured and caged primates are willing to ingest
plant drugs that they might otherwise walk away from in the wild. For

example, squirrel monkeys will normally ignore nicotine solutions offered to them in a test cage. But if the monkeys are stressed with a mild electric shock to their tails, they will voluntarily drink the nicotine in preference to water.

In natural habitats, primates may ignore the psychological benefits of plants because they don't need them, but they excel at utilizing the medicinal properties when necessary. Marais's baboons sparingly chewed and sucked the roots of a semiaquatic poisonous plant, the same thing the local natives did to achieve emetic effects with the plant. Elsewhere in South Africa, monkeys have been observed digging for the roots of *kameroo*, a plant used by natives as a refreshing stimulant. There a newly captured gibbon was found to have a severely swollen wound. When the wound was lanced it was found to contain the finely masticated leaves of a medicinal plant that the natives used for their own treatment of wounds. The gibbon's wound had healed over the mass of chewed leaf, which he had applied himself.

Primates have excelled over all other animals in discovering uses of plants for specific pharmacological purposes. For example, *Aspilia* leaves are used by chimpanzees at Tanzania's Gombe National Park. Native east Africans used the plant to relieve stomach troubles and intestinal worms; still, the discovery of use by chimps was a surprise. Jane Goodall pioneered the investigation by noting that chimp dung often contained one species of leaf that invariably had not been chewed. The leaves were later identified as *Aspilia,* a bushy shrub that grows over three meters high. As soon as the chimps wake up in the morning they seek out the leaves. Even before the usual breakfasting at nearby forage areas, some chimps walk for twenty minutes to the open grasslands where *Aspilia* bushes grow.

There, instead of tearing the leaves off the bush and eating them as they might do with other forage plants, the chimpanzee will gingerly close its lips over the unplucked leaf and hold it there for a few seconds. Several leaves may be tried in this way before the animal selects one to pluck and places it in its mouth. However, the leaf is not chewed but rolled in the mouth and swallowed whole. In a ten-minute feeding period, the chimp will select and swallow as many as thirty small leaves. The surface cells of the leaves are ruptured as they pass through the gut, thus releasing thiarubrine A, an extremely powerful antibiotic that can kill common disease-causing bacteria. In this way the chimps are medicating themselves for the same intestinal parasites that local natives treat with *Aspilia*.

The selectivity manifested by the chimpanzee is seen in the dietary habits of other primates who choose to avoid rather than use plant chemicals. Japanese monkeys in the Boso Mountains have an extremely flexible diet. When favored plants are not in season, rather than use the remaining toxic ones, the monkeys feed on fail-safe insects or even pebbles and soils. Gorillas in west Africa eat a species of *Lobelia*, which contains a nicotinelike alkaloid and is known as Indian tobacco, but they avoid the stems, which contain most of the drug. My team watched spider monkeys feeding on *Strychnos* fruit, which grows to the size of gray-green tennis balls in the Malayan jungles. The hard, brittle rind encases a number of seeds that resemble silver bullets packed in a greenish-black pulp. Each bullet contains strychnine and brucine, alkaloids that are used by the jungle tribes for poisoning their darts. Yet the monkeys would break open the rind, eat the appetite-stimulating pulp, and throw away the seeds. The only deaths occurred when they were hit by the native darts.

Since primates excel at learning to control their own diets and medicines, it is not surprising that they should also be capable of seeking out their own intoxicants when the effects are either needed or desired. Thus tobacco's unique effects may appeal to captive baboons' needs to medicate depression. Similarly, the baboons may use other intoxicants not so much out of need but out of desire.

In times of plenty, Marais reported that wild baboons will go out of their way to eat the red plumlike fruit of a tree belonging to the Cycadaceae family, a rare plant with a very limited habitat. The fruit has an unpleasant odor and is known to be poisonous to humans, yet the baboons strip the trees and feast on it. When food is scarce, we would expect baboons to act the way monkeys do, devouring all the fruit they come across. But eating such unpleasant fruit when much tastier ones are available is unusual. Subsequently the baboons appear intoxicated or "drunk": "The drunkenness manifested itself in staggering gait, inability to move quickly, and in utter carelessness of danger, all of which rendered them, at such time, an easy prey to the hunters' dogs and rifles." Marais never saw a baboon die from a direct overdose of the fruit, but he observed its deadly convulsive effects in young children who had each eaten a couple of the plums. Why would baboons in the wild consume such an intoxicant? Marais speculated that the fruit produced some pleasant feeling or euphoria in the wild animals, which had developed a tolerance to the nastier effects.

Previous exposure to a particular plant is one way in which primates as well as other mammals reduce the aversiveness of a plant's odor, taste, or other unpleasant effect. We share with the baboons a suspicion of new foods. Putting aside the young children and baboons who eat tobacco flowers, we are generally reluctant to eat strange foods, whether we are foraging for a living or traveling abroad. Yet mere exposure to a plant in one's environment will enhance its acceptability, or at least encourage investigatory behaviors. Any remaining resistance can be overcome if hunger or accident induces one actually to try the food. In a sense, familiarity breeds experimentation.

2

On a small island in a California game preserve, I found examples of such experimentation and safe-feeding strategies. The island consisted of approximately two hectares of lush foliage surrounded by a small lake that prevented the monkeys from escaping. The island inhabitants included many species of tropical birds, several capybaras, and a troop of twenty-three squirrel monkeys. The facial coloring of this monkey makes it look like a bony skull that has dipped its mouth too deeply into a jar of blackberry jam. Large appealing eyes, a long tail that can be wrapped over its sleeping body like a furry security blanket, and a frequent peeping sound all combine to make the monkey a cute and lovable animal. Only its habit of grooming with urine prevents the squirrel monkey from becoming a more popular pet. In the wild, these monkeys live in an aerial world where they forage among the treetops as individuals. Here they gathered each morning on the island beach in rolling balls of fur to feed on provisions of monkey chow, fruits, and vegetables that were delivered by their keepers. The monkeys seemed happy and thrived in a world full of play and exploration, free from hunger and predation. I called their island "Pala" after the fictional garden paradise described by Aldous Huxley in *Island*.

Under the cover of darkness, I transplanted a fully grown garden of tobacco plants to a clearing near the beach. Dawn and the arrival of the daily food shipment was still an hour away as I positioned my observers and cameras. The monkeys were certain to notice their new garden, yet the harmonious conditions on Pala did not seem to require any need for a drug plant. I expected a few curious juveniles might investigate the plants but I also predicted that the island residents were safe from developing any addiction.

The morning feeding took place as usual. And as usual it was over in a few minutes. It didn't take Skippy, a young male with a distinctive limp, much longer to find the garden. He simply walked through without stopping. A few others did the same. It was a disappointing first encounter. For the first week nothing unusual happened. A few monkeys visited the garden and tore at the yellow tobacco flowers but left the rest of the plant alone. Each day I watered and inspected the garden for evidence of foraging, repaired any trampled or uprooted plants, and collected droppings from around the island. But I found no evidence of plant consumption.

When two weeks had gone by and the garden remained uneaten, I had the daily fruit and vegetable provisions stopped for two days. The monkeys still got their chow but they twittered and chirped and held long vigils on the beach. Rather than go to the garden, the monkeys foraged for insects and other more edible leaves. I also learned they were begging the observers for candy bars and other treats, so we resumed the provisions. By the fourth week the garden was dying and I replaced several plants, leaving the dead leaves and stalks in a pile near the garden's edge. I also added a berry tree made out of real firethorn branches mounted on an old wooden coatrack. While a few animals nibbled a berry only to spit it out, they seemed more interested in playing "king on the coatrack." Playfulness is regarded as one strong indication of animal intelligence, refusal to eat firethorns may be another.

As the garden became a more frequent site of monkey activity, the tobacco plants were investigated more intensely. Familiarity was breeding experimentation. Sidecar, a female whose infant rode on her back, discovered the pile of old leaves and tasted a dry tobacco leaf, then dropped it. Several other monkeys explored the pile, smelling or tasting various leaves, but they generally ignored the growing plants. By the end of the sixth week, the garden was completely dead and no efforts were made to replant it. Over the next several weeks I observed several monkeys holding the dry tobacco leaves and I finally caught Aunt Bertha, who frequently huddled with Sidecar, nibbling one. Daily inspections of the garden revealed that pieces of the now yellowed tobacco leaves were slowly disappearing.

When I had discarded the dead tobacco leaves in the pile, the process of curing was initiated. The hot summer sun removed much of the moisture from the leaves and permitted the chemical changes known as curing to begin: starches were reduced, sugars were increased, and other changes rendered the leaves more palatable. The monkeys seemed more willing to taste these sweetened leaves, but they didn't seem to eat harmful amounts.

I could not identify any excessive tobacco eating or nicotine-induced behaviors. Skippy was observed to be playing in the tobacco more frequently than the others, yet even his occasional chaws resulted in no unusual behavior. He, together with other monkeys, had demonstrated a typical primate drive to explore new plant foods, adopting a pattern of drug use that *Homo sapiens* has termed experimental. Perhaps conditions on Pala simply did not favor the production of other patterns of use. Perhaps I had provided an unappetizing selection of drugs. After ten weeks, I retrieved all remaining plant fragments from the garden and departed the island. I still wonder what happened to the tobacco seeds and gardening trowel I had left behind.

3

Whether or not experimental drug use leads to more frequent patterns of use depends on the ability of the animal to detect the physical and psychological effects. These effects must then be evaluated in terms of the animal's needs.

Once the drug enters the body, animals with good sensory equipment and learning abilities can evaluate the metabolic consequences. For many animals eating plant drugs, the results are often a learned taste aversion. The negative consequences of bitterness or sickness act to punish the animal for its choice and it will subsequently reject future opportunities based on certain cues. These cues are the ones originally associated with the sensory basis of food selection. Thus, visually dominant feeders, such as birds, may learn to associate sights with the visceral events that occur as a result of feeding. Species such as mice and rats rely more on flavor. This type of learning occurs reliably and rapidly, and it is retained for long periods of time. We may never forget a particular episode of food poisoning and we may find it hard to approach a meal with similar sights and smells and flavors, just as the seafaring monkey Jocko ran away from anything that even remotely resembled tobacco. Taste aversion learning becomes a lifesaving mechanism for animals faced with nature's botanical cafeteria.

The amount of a particular secondary substance delivered by plant ingestion is an important factor in taste aversion learning. Tobacco flowers have minor amounts of nicotine, and ingestion never causes sickness in the baboons or children who nibble them. But many people have experienced the initial nausea and malaise that caused Jocko to reject a concentrated amount of tobacco leaves. The ability voluntarily to regulate the intake of the drug is also important. Animals forced to eat or smoke tobacco don't like it. Yet when allowed to self-administer their own amounts, animals will not only volunteer to smoke tobacco but to drink concentrated solutions of nicotine.

Availability plays an equally critical role. Wild tobaccos and baboons do not usually occur together so there are limited opportunities for the overuse of the plant that would result in either taste aversion or toxicity and dependency. In laboratory studies, experimenters have been more generous with tobacco or nicotine and have found it relatively easy to addict their animal subjects. Forced exposure to nicotine can readily reduce taste aversions and open the door to subsequent use.

In the human world of plant drug use, the practices of preparing, mixing, and flavoring foods may help overcome taste aversion. The Warao mixes aromatic resins with black tobacco as much for his own pleasure as for the gods. Humans have developed these practices into culturally transmitted cuisines. Indian tribes in North and South America once mixed tobacco with a wide variety of substances, including cloves, crude brown sugar, and anise oil. Commercial tobaccos are also heavily adulterated and diluted with both natural and artificial additives. Without such modifications, many humans might reject initial use. Likewise, Marais's captive baboons might have preferred the sweetened flavor of cured tobacco more than the harsh uncured tobacco rejected by their wild cousins. The monkeys on Pala initially ignored the bad-tasting tobacco, but once it was cured they approached it with the same sweet tooth that we seem to have.

After the initial taste aversion is overcome, repeated use acquaints the animal with more important metabolic consequences: the psychoactive properties themselves. Until the animal becomes tolerant, the effects of nicotine on the peripheral and central nervous system are most unpleasant: nausea, pallor, weakness, abdominal pain, headache, and dizziness. Tolerance to these unpleasant effects develops very rapidly, starting immediately after the first exposure. Then the animal will experience fewer negative effects and more stimulating effects that make the drug increasingly attractive.

Nicotine will increase the general locomotor activity and vigilance of animals and allow for more rapid and efficient learning. When a rat is tested in an experimental situation where a tone signals that an electric shock will soon follow, the rats often freeze when the tone comes on rather than press a lever that will prevent the shock. Nicotine facilitates the rat's ability to overcome the disruptive effects of freezing in such a stressful situation. The drug enables them to press the lever more often and receive fewer shocks. Similar effects have been found with squirrel monkeys. Nicotine also decreases aggressive behavior in laboratory animals, reducing the number of bite attacks that rats, cats, and monkeys will carry out in fighting situations. While nicotine is a stimulant, it has this selective calming or relaxing effect as testified to by many human smokers.

When these nicotine effects wear off, there appears another cluster of effects that seem to go in the opposite direction of the intoxication. This withdrawal syndrome is transient but still noticeable in its tension, restlessness, irritability, increased hunger, inability to concentrate, lightheadedness, and insomnia. Taken together, these symptoms portray a state of dysphoria marked by a craving for more tobacco. Additional tobacco seems to reduce if not altogether dispel the withdrawal. Cycling between intoxication and withdrawal defines a state of physical addiction or dependence. Physical addiction is somewhat different from the psychological addiction or craving we have seen with locoweed and other toxic plants that do not produce physical withdrawal syndromes. But both types of addiction can be serious matters for the animal. Many people feel they will die without a cigarette, and withdrawal symptoms from other physically addicting drugs such as morphine have killed their addicted users. Psychological cravings can be just as potent. It may take time for locoed animals to recover, if at all, and the survival of addicted animals like koalas may still be threatened if their acquired tastes cannot be satisfied.

Can animals know about such things as addiction and withdrawal if they do not experience it themselves? As far as we know, other animals have nothing approximating our human abilities to communicate information gathered from other generations. The various cultures of man are unique in transmitting information on good and bad foods or drugs based on the previous experiences of individuals. Still, the same extremely acute sensory systems and malleable learning mechanisms used by man have endowed many animals with the means for communicating information to others in their immediate space and time. Many animals inherit altruistic behaviors such as danger warning calls to alert others to particularly aversive situations. After rejecting the bitter firethorn berries, some of the monkeys on Pala gave yap calls that told others in the troop to keep away. Animal communication can also function as a source of information about more attractive prey or feeding sites. From the dances of the bees that signal the precise location of sweet nectar to the burial of noxious foods by rats, animals communicate much dietary information.

Omnivores such as rats have developed a number of strategies for determining the safe or harmful value of foods or drugs they encounter. Some strategies result in transmission of information from individuals to others in the social group. Weanling rat pups, like infant koalas, learn about safe foods from the flavor of the mother's milk or by following her to food caches. Adult animals can also benefit from social influences during feeding. Adult rats, for example, will avoid consuming a novel flavor that was first experienced in the presence of a sick rat. This is known as the poisoned-partner effect and explains how rats can learn to avoid poisons even if they themselves escape toxic effects, so long as they can observe the poisoning in a familiar partner. The poisoned-partner effect is clearly adaptive. Members of a colony can learn about the toxic consequences of a particular plant as a result of the acute poisoning of only one member. For social omnivores like rats, this strategy has a great advantage for survival.

Primates have had to make use of similar strategies. Infant monkeys and baboons observe and imitate the feeding patterns of their mothers. Chimpanzees not only observe the feeding patterns of others but are capable of discriminating by social communication the nature and amount of foods that are hidden from sight. Communication can take the form of gestures or sounds that can be perceived by other chimps. These strategies have been extremely helpful in transmitting information about edible foods.

Information about inedible foods and both toxic and intoxicating plants must also be learned and remembered, otherwise each group member would have to reassess continually the quality of foods. Such an individual-oriented feeding strategy would result in considerable risk in sampling new foods and would reduce foraging efficiency. Although juvenile primates are notoriously adventurous in sampling novel plants and foods, most primates remember to follow the rules for safe feeding: keeping to familiar foods and minimizing intake of new ones while adjusting the diet to its needs. The monkeys on Pala yapped about fresh tobacco, but when it cured they called to others with location trills and play peeps, calls that may have identified it as an acceptable "recreational" drug.

Common sense tells us that the needs of caged primates are very different from those of the primate in the wild or in a preserve environment such as Pala. Marais described the captive baboon in a state of depression with an overpowering need to relieve its suffering. He found evidence, later supported by other primate studies, that baboons have the ability to avoid plant intoxicants when they are not needed and to approach and consume them when the needs and opportunities come together. This capacity was expressed by the captive chacma in its willingness to ingest both tobacco and alcohol when offered by Marais.

The baboons, like humans, developed cravings and addictions to these intoxicants.

Captive primates will show a remarkable drive to intoxicate themselves even in a roomy laboratory cage. Whether for reasons of exploration, curiosity, stimulation, tranquilization, dispelling boredom, or depression, laboratory primates have willingly pursued a vast array of intoxicants when given the opportunity. In a sense, they appear to medicate mental needs just as in wild habitats they use *Aspilia* or other plants to treat physical needs. Marais attributed this "mental mischief" to a consciousness or awareness shared by baboon and man. Not surprisingly, primates share a pursuit of the exact same drugs.

An experimental model has been developed to observe and measure this drug-taking behavior in primates and other animals. Animals are given access to a small lever or panel to press in order to produce delivery of the drug. The delivery might be in the form of something to eat or drink or even an automatic injection of drug solution into a catheter running directly into the animal's veins or muscles. Responses on the lever might also produce fixed exposures to fumes to inhale, such as those from ether or glue, or it might result in drugs being pumped directly into the animal's stomach via an intragastric tube. Researchers have even developed a "pill popper," a clever device that dispenses drug capsules directly into a monkey's mouth.

The types of drugs administered by animals in these situations are the same types taken by humans. They include the major drug groups represented by alcohol, opium, marijuana, and cocaine. We shall examine each of these in the following chapters. Animals also self-administer other types of drugs popular among our species and these include nitrous oxide (laughing gas), ether, and phencyclidine (PCP). Since this model is useful for predicting those drugs that will be abused by man, it is equally important to note drugs that will not be taken by the animals.

Most major psychiatric drugs, including chlorpromazine (Thorazine), are not abused by man and they are not self-administered by animals. Despite widespread clinical use of analgesics such as aspirin, these are rarely abused by people and they are not pursued by the animals tested in these models.

The self-administration model has proved valuable in demonstrating that drug seeking and drug taking are biologically normal behaviors. It has shown that drugs that are readily pursued by animals are commonly abused by humans. While selections of drugs by baboons and monkeys are closer to our own, most of these drugs are also self-administered by a wide variety of mammals, including rats, cats, and dogs. The ability of a drug to serve as a reward or reinforcer for behavior is not dependent on any abnormalities in the brain. Rather, those drugs that animals select to use are those capable of interacting with the normal brain mechanisms developed through evolution to mediate biologically essential behaviors directed toward food, water, and sex. In a sense, pursuit of intoxicating drugs is the rule rather than an aberration.

Since primates are the result of evolution's last days in Eden, it is understandable that the pursuit of drugs in the Orinoco Delta, on Pala, or among Marais's baboons should be more than similar to us: they are close enough to win the proverbial cigar. Not only do our tastes and reactions coincide, but so do our emotional needs and moods that govern the selection of specific drugs. Marais believed that the use of alcohol—which we explore in the next chapter—was perhaps the single most important intoxicant selected by primates, creatures plagued with the pain of consciousness.

Nowhere was this more evident than among his baboons who huddled together at the end of the day and gazed at the setting sun. The light in their world was about to go out. As darkness moved across the sky, they observed a period of silence and evening melancholy. Then, from all sides, the group would let out a sound of mourning, a sound never uttered other than on occasions of great sorrow.

5

Ark on the Rocks

ALCOHOL AS THE
UNIVERSAL INTOXICANT

1

Noah was six hundred years old when the Flood began. As the waters receded, so goes the Hebrew story, the inhabitants of the Ark spread out across the land and multiplied. Of all these animals, Noah loved the goats best and he enjoyed watching them as they scampered freely over the rocky hillsides. One goat acted unusually playful and Noah followed him to a tree. There he saw the goat eat some grapes that caused the animal to jump and frolic about. Hot and thirsty, Noah followed the example of the goat and drank the sweet juice from the grapes. He fell into a merry mood and started singing a song. On the way home, Noah somehow lost his clothes and fell fast asleep outside his house. He awoke the next morning, told the story to his sons, and retrieved the vine to be planted in their garden.

A Romanian version of the story adds that when Noah started planting the vine, the Devil appeared and assisted him. The Devil killed the goat and poured its blood on the roots of the vine in remembrance of the discovery. Next the Devil watered the roots with the blood of a lion, and then with the blood of a swine. Thus, whenever man drinks a little wine, he gets merry and frolics like a young kid. If he drinks a little more, he becomes flushed and roars like a lion. Overindulgence will cause him to wallow in the mire like a pig. For alcohol will surely turn a man into a beast.

Some believe that other animals led man to alcohol. An ancient Greek legend credits apes with being the first grape eaters, displaying a special fondness for the fermented ones. Whether discovered by man or beast, intoxication with alcohol has attracted many creatures throughout history. They have utilized the natural sources, such as fermented fruits and grains, and the man-made beers, wines, and distilled spirits. The accidental and intentional use of these substances is of great antiquity.

Many cultures—such as the Palestinian, which considered *yayin,* the sweet wine of Noah, a divine gift—place the origins of this drug close to the origins of man himself. In Sumerian, the language of mankind's first medical text, the original "tree of life" was none other than the vine that intoxicates. A Persian myth tells of its discovery by a woman who first drank the fermented juices from grapes that had been stored in a pottery jar. It is likely that the Persian story is closer to what may have actually happened.

The use of wine probably started well before 4241 B.C., the year when man started numbering his days with the introduction of the calendar in ancient Egypt. The storage of either fresh or dried grapes in jars, stone bowls, or even in cavities in rocks would have allowed accidental fermentation to occur with changes in moisture and temperature. Often the bubbling juice must have been thrown away, as it was no longer sweet, but the first drinker certainly would have discovered the effects.

It seems likely that *Homo sapiens* in the land of the Old Testament was neither the first nor the only visitor who reached for the grapes from the vine. The vine itself had been around for a long time since the Tertiary period. The historical wines of the Middle East were made from the *Vitis vinifera,* a famous but more recent species that has existed for approximately a million years. Early man had access to these grapes as well as other natural sources of alcohol.

Many of the wild fruits and foods that were collected by hunter-gatherers had a high enough sugar content to be fermented into an intoxicating drink. Prehistoric cave paintings show that honey was sought after, collected, and probably stored. As honey is almost pure sugar and ferments readily, it formed the basis for intoxicating drinks in many early groups of humans. Mead, prepared from fermented honey and water, was widely used in the Mediterranean region and was a standard offering to the ancient gods. Elsewhere, cultures produced fermented drinks out of their own native plants. Natives in Siberia used red alga; North American Indians made a liquor from maple syrup; those in Central America made pulque from agave and cactus; South American Indians used jungle fruits; South Africans used the sap from palm stems; and early Oriental man learned to make an alcoholic beverage from rice.

Many other fruits and grains provided natural starting materials for fermentation to alcohol. Beer, known to early Neolithic agriculturists, is probably the oldest alcoholic drink. Wild wheat and barley were soaked in water to make gruel. If left out in the open, the grain did not spoil. Instead, natural yeast in the air converted it to a dark, bubbling brew that made whoever drank it feel good. The ancient Egyptians probably developed techniques for brewing beer from barley and emmer wheat before they learned how to make bread.

The Egyptians had discovered the basic process of brewing and learned to excel in the art of making wine as well as beer. While they may not have understood the scientific principles of fermentation— first explained by Louis Pasteur and others in the nineteenth century— the Egyptians produced highly popular drinks. Barley beer is still made today by the same methods they pioneered. The grain is first steeped in water to start a germination that renders the starches soluble, a process known as malting. The malt is then treated with hot water in a vessel, forming a porridgelike mash. This process converts the starches of the malt into fermentable sugars. The mash is boiled, cooled, and put into a fermentation vessel. Similar vessels were used for the making of grape wine, but the Egyptians never seemed to have enough grapes to satisfy the growing demands of their people. They had to learn how to make wine from figs, pomegranates, and dates. They also learned to flavor the wines with juices of a variety of plants such as rue and wormwood.

Beer and wine became national drinks for the living and, according to pyramid writings, were used by the dead in the afterlife. Alcoholic drinks were also reputed to be favored by the gods, a theme we have seen expressed with man's celebration of other intoxicants such as tobacco. The Egyptians had their own divinities that ruled over the use of beer and wine. Menquet, goddess of beer, was pictured as a woman holding two jars of beer. Hathor, represented as a sacred bull, was the divinity of the grapevine and was duly honored on a monthly "Day of Intoxication."

The discovery of distilled spirits may have occurred independently in various parts of the world but the earliest appearance was in ninth-century Arabia. Since that time distilled preparations became as widespread as beer and wine; instances of alcoholism were commonplace. Public drunkenness was a regular feature of daily life in almost every society touched by alcohol, from the early dynasties of Egypt to Renaissance Europe.

The Elizabethan writer Thomas Nashe described different kinds of drunkenness that humans might display. Ape drunk is a state in which one leaps and yells like an ape. A man is lion drunk when he roars and fights; fox drunk when crafty; swine drunk when heavy and lethargic; sheep drunk when unable to speak; and goat drunk when "he hath no minde but on Lecherie." Not surprisingly, Old and New World drinking establishments adopted the names and images of an animal kingdom full of love for alcohol. Some read like a Nashe prophecy: Blue Monkey, Drunken Fish, Blind Pig, Dead Rat.

If alcohol turns a man into a beast, what does it do to the animals? The notion of drunk animals conjures up images such as Dumbo, the flying elephant who accidentally drank some alcohol and started seeing dancing pink elephants. Dozens of animated cartoon characters entertained us with similar alcoholic antics. And almost every pet owner or animal keeper has an equally dramatic story to tell about accidental or deliberate intoxication with alcohol in their animals. These intoxications occur with both natural and artificial sources of alcohol. They affect all insects and animals from aphids to zebras; and all animals show similar reactions.

Insects, despite their highly evolved mechanisms of detoxification, are as vulnerable to alcohol as the rest of us. Many insects attack wine grapes and rapidly destroy vineyards, while becoming accidentally intoxicated on the odd fermenting grape. In 1545 a legal complaint against the insects was made by the wine growers of St. Julien, a small hamlet in France. The insects were actually brought to trial. The prosecution argued that lower animals should be subject to the laws of man. The insects were appointed an advocate who argued that they were only exercising their biblical rights to be fruitful and multiply, thereby obeying a divine law. The archival records indicate that a judge deliberated for a long period, but the final decision is unknown—the last page of the surviving records was destroyed by weevils!

The defense had argued that the insects were only doing what came naturally. Therefore, they could not be denied their rights to adequate means of subsistence suited to their natural impulses. The defense could have raised an equally valid and more universal argument that the entire animal kingdom is driven by the same pursuit of intoxication. It is part of our nature.

For many flying insects, that nature would include drinking fermented juices and mashes. Bumblebees, hornets, and wasps become uncoordinated and temporarily grounded after sipping from fermented fruits. Insects also get drunk on mash, as do many animals. While mash intoxication is usually unintentional, a few animals will go out of their way to get the fermenting mixtures. In rural America illegal stills were often traced by the trail of tipsy livestock and wildlife that managed to find the mash. The pigs and chickens kept by the Sedang Moi in Southeast Asia will pursue rice-beer mash to the point of insensibility. By the next morning, the animals are waddling with "hangovers." In West Bengal, a herd of 150 elephants broke into an illegal still and drank copious quantities of the moonshine mash. Intoxicated, they rampaged across the land, killing five people, injuring a dozen, demolishing seven concrete buildings, and trampling twenty village huts.

The tendency to follow the scent of alcohol has been used to lure insects and animals into traps. The insect's natural attraction to sweet drinks has been utilized by the well-known method of "sugaring" for moths and butterflies. Sugaring is used by field collectors who spread a mixture of sugar, beer, and rum on the trunks of trees. The sweet, intoxicating mixture rapidly attracts swarms of insects that can be gathered easily after they feed. In Africa natives leave bowls of milk and beer out overnight in order to trap rodents. They pick up the drunk animals the next morning. Darwin cited a report from northeastern Africa where natives would catch wild baboons with bowls of strong beer. The drunk animals were observed the next morning to be "very cross and dismal; they held their aching heads with both hands, and wore a pitiable expression; when beer or wine was offered them, they turned away with disgust."

Birds fall for alcohol and many have been captured and murdered in traps baited with alcohol. Many ingenious devices were developed for the mass hunting of the North American passenger pigeon. One trap lured the birds with a decoy—a live pigeon with its eyes sewn shut—tied to a perch called a stool. As they approached the decoy, the inquisitive birds could be netted and their heads crushed with a pair of pincers. This original "stool pigeon" approach proved to be less effective than feeding the pigeons grain soaked in alcohol, a feed that made them literally dead drunk.

Many people who have kept starlings for pets have observed their attraction to wines and other alcoholic drinks. They appear to be one of the few birds capable of adjusting their intake so as to avoid toxic effects. They also cannot help vocalizing about it. Parrots feel the same. When Shakespeare wrote in *Othello* that a sensible man when drunk will "speak parrot and squabble," he was probably unaware of the similarities. Parrots eat fermented fruits or drink alcoholic beverages that make them more talkative, according to their owners. The birds stop talking and drinking only after they fall over. In 1976 a dealer of rare birds took advantage of this by overdosing his parrots on tequila so they would be silent as he smuggled them across the Mexican border. He succeeded in getting them through U.S. Customs, but was arrested when he sold them to an undercover agent. Equally unlucky was the intoxicated California owner of a trained parrot who forcefed her bird a drink of 151-proof rum. The bird allegedly cackled "Good-night, Mama" and died! An autopsy confirmed death by alcohol poisoning.

But capturing or killing animals with alcohol is illustrative of human intentions, not the animal's desire to experience intoxication per se. Spiking a bowl of milk with beer shows us that animals get inebriated, but they do not have a real choice. Sugaring by any other name is still deliberate poisoning by man. And while the animal world is clearly willing to accept alcohol, will they intentionally seek the intoxication?

Raccoons have been known to seek out the alcohol readily and eagerly if only provided with the opportunity to do so. They will even open bottles and pull out corks for themselves. This behavior is not particularly difficult for the raccoon, which has the most sensitive forepaws in the animal kingdom. Indeed, each finger has its own compartment in the raccoon's brain, a brain that is all the more remarkable because it will allow the animal to drink some alcohol but stops it before it gets drunk.

Nineteenth-century writers enjoyed commenting on the presence of such human behaviors in lower animals. Many observers did not approve of alcohol intoxication in man or beast and referred to the behavior as "intemperance." Some, like George Beard, a leading neurologist of the day, echoed the belief that intemperance was a disease that only man's brain can appreciate.

In 1879 W. Lauder Lindsay, a physician and naturalist, published a two-volume work, *Mind in the Lower Animals*, which started to change opinions. Lindsay documented many reports of animal intoxication, illustrating the universal pursuit of alcohol. The reports went beyond mere descriptions of behavior and interpreted the actions of the animals with a Victorian anthropomorphism.

Lindsay graded the animal reactions on a rudimentary list that we might call a scale of 1 to 10, 1 being simple excitement, as in the case of intoxicated horses that kick and bite to the point of becoming unmanageable, and 10 being death, as when an orangutan "died through drinking up a bottle of rum which he had stolen, uncorked and emptied." Lindsay awarded a score of 2 for intense excitement to the elephants who were rendered so furious by wine that they would trample to death their human victims in the ancient hippodrome at Alexandria. Depression rated a 3, as in baboons who appeared to slip from initial excitement into a dismal mood. A 4 was given when an animal showed stupidity—a diminished capacity to function safely or appreciate danger—as in the case of a drunk monkey who rashly attacked a shark.

Most animals qualified for the middle score of 5 by showing "eccentricities of motion," including reeling and staggering gaits. Animals captured with alcohol bait got a 6 for their stupor; those with patterns of chronic use leading to alcoholism deserved a 7; while animals suffering physical damage warranted an 8. Insane animals were 9s, but they were sometimes better off being a dead 10. One insane dog lived at a brewery and "was so passionately fond of drinks" that he turned away with disdain from life-sustaining biscuits and food.

Lindsay's work popularized the notion that there was some force present throughout the animal kingdom that drove creatures to intoxication. For the first time people started to realize that man was not alone in his appetite for inebriation. Thus, by the twilight of the century, when Leo Tolstoy published his essay "Why Do Men Stupefy Themselves?" his answer to the question succinctly encapsulated the new prevailing logic. It blended the ideas of Lindsay with George Beard and a future Eugene Marais:

> The cause of the worldwide consumption of hashish, opium, wine, and tobacco lies not in the taste, nor in any pleasure, recreation, or mirth they afford, but simply in man's need to hide from himself the demands of conscience. . . . For man is a spiritual as well as animal being. He may be moved by things that influence his spiritual nature, or by things that influence his animal nature.

Undoubtedly, Lindsay would have been amused by the scorekeeping that continued in newspapers and magazines throughout most of the twentieth century. Tapper, a wine-loving chimpanzee, escaped from an animal show in Saint Augustine, Florida, and made national news when he was captured with a bribe of wine. After drinking a full bottle, the drowsy chimp, probably a stuporous 6 on the Lindsay scale, went quietly back to his quarters. For racehorse Firey Noon, a bottle of beer before each meal would have earned him a 1 as it also made him first across the finish line at Miami's Calder Race Course. A female monkey developed a craving for white rum and earned a 5 as she staggered, missed a leap, and fell from her perch.

The journalists who wrote these accounts gave human names,

motivations, and personalities to the intoxicated animals. Clay Henry, a black mountain goat from Texas, was labeled the "six-pack kid" by *Time* because of his ability to grab a bottle or can of beer between his teeth and drink it, a habit that littered Henry's yard with empties. The Associated Press ran a wire story about Roger, a two-year-old sheep who lapped up a quart of vodka every evening for a year "without weaving, staggering or slurring his baaaaas." However, a story headlined "Screwdrivers a Threat in the Pig Pen" told of a study by the U.S. Department of Agriculture in which pigs drank a quart of vodka a day with dire results. The heavy-drinking dominant "king pig" lost his status to a light-drinking piglet.

Other animals have frightened rather than amused us. A beer-drinking horse in Romania terrorized a neighborhood with loud neighing, kicking, and biting; its owner was finally brought to court. Scrumpy, a squirrel drunk on cider, must have been at level 2 when it attacked its human owner. The owner was probably somewhat higher than that when he escaped from Scrumpy by jumping from his bedroom window. Only when this comedy of intoxication turned into human tragedies did people stop laughing and begin the first serious animal experiments to find the reasons why.

2

The scene was Paris in 1860 at the start of the absinthe epidemic. Absinthe was a popular blue-green liquor that was prepared from a distillate of wormwood and aromatic herbs and spices. The alcohol content was high and varied between 45 and 75 percent. The absinthes also contained thujone, a wormwood chemical similar to the active ingredient in marijuana. In addition to producing all the symptoms of alcohol intoxication, absinthe was strong enough to cause hallucinations, convulsions, and seizures. One absinthe drinker became so obsessed that it was impossible for him to see a blue silk dress without attempting to set it on fire. During one day alone he used his cigar to set thirty-seven dresses on fire before he was arrested. Another absinthe victim suffered from a delusion that he was being persecuted by invisible enemies who used electricity to torment him. He lived for several months in a deep ditch, covering himself with dirt every evening for added protection.

Another *absintheur,* under the pretense of kissing his dearest friends, bit pieces out of their faces.

The absinthe drinkers provided subjects for study by artists Pablo Picasso, Henri de Toulouse-Lautrec, Edouard Manet, and Edgar Degas. The swirling delirium and colorful hallucinations inspired the work of heavy drinkers including Vincent Van Gogh, Paul Verlaine, and Amedeo Modigliani. Their work illustrated the widespread acceptance of what French author Henri Balesta described as "an artificial paradise, removed from the bonds of reality, where [the drinker's] craziest, most frenzied thoughts, are garbed in poetic form." Unfortunately, the drinker was destined to be disappointed when the depression of withdrawal hit the next day. But paradise lost could be regained with another absinthe.

Like the captive baboons medicating their pain and depression, human absinthe drinkers could look beyond their immediate withdrawal pains and remember how to recapture the pleasantness. They could even instruct their young in overcoming initial taste aversions. Children as young as six would accompany their fathers to cabarets where they were initiated into the absinthe habit. Once accustomed to the taste and the intoxication, they were like those young bovine loco eaters who followed their parents down the road to dependency, premature sickness, and eventual death. The epidemic brought a parade of patients to Bicêtre, the leading psychiatric hospital in Paris. Alarmed by the progressive damage caused by absinthe, especially among the young, and anxious to free *absintheurs* from the bonds of their beastly condition, the psychiatrists initiated the first controlled animal experiments on alcohol.

Jacques-Joseph Valentin Magnan, an intern at Bicêtre, developed the techniques for studying alcohol addiction in animals. The subjects were taken from barns or backyards and included dogs, pigs, roosters, and hens. The animals were force-fed gelatin capsules containing absinthe. Since the animals kept vomiting, the trick was to keep enough absinthe in the animal for a sufficient period of time to see an effect. The researchers introduced a new method that is still in use today: intragastric administration. Absinthe was pumped into the stomachs of the animals until something happened. Usually the animal displayed poor coordination and unsteady balance, then violent muscular tremors. After a few minutes, a dog with bloodshot and glassy eyes appeared to be seized by a Dionysian hysteria: he barked furiously, snapped his jaws, and, with clenched teeth, shook his head from side to side as though he were tearing apart his prey. The attack lasted for almost two hours.

Cats, rabbits, and birds were also used, but these animals always seemed to be fighting the effects. Fish did not survive long enough to permit detailed observation. A few concentrated drops of absinthe in a tank of fish killed them faster than prussic acid, the favorite of nineteenth-century poisoners. Finally, it was decided to use guinea pigs. Because these animals do not vomit readily, they could hold down more absinthe. To ensure that the guinea pigs would not reject it, the researchers placed them in glass cases filled with absinthe vapors. The vapors alone were powerful enough to send the animals into states of excitation and epileptiform convulsions. Between convulsive jerks, the frightened guinea pigs would sit up in the glass case, motionless and breathless. A serous liquid would discharge from their nostrils. They actually cried. Another convulsion would seize them and they would stretch out, paws scratching the ground and beating the air. The convulsions caused them to bite the sides of the case and look around plaintively for a way to escape. The experimenters described guinea pigs in this state as "stupid," meaning stuporous.

Fowls were considered stupid in another sense of the word. At least one rooster developed a liking for absinthe and learned to drink it voluntarily. After each dose, the rooster fell and lay motionless for a moment. He beat his wings and scraped the ground until he finally stood up, only to drink and fall again "just as though he were as stupid as a man." At last some similarities across species were recognized. Later experimenters found many more.

Modern investigators have employed the methods developed by the absinthe researchers to induce alcohol dependence in animals. There have been many improvements, such as techniques for intravenous administration, but the basic procedures still involve inhalation of alcohol vapors as well as oral and intragastric feeding. Forced alcohol administration has been effective in producing addiction in many animals. The addiction is manifested by withdrawal symptoms that occur on cessation of alcohol intake and are solely a function of alcohol clearing from the blood. For most animals these signs reflect a continuum of increasing central nervous system hyperexcitability leading to seizures, convulsions, and death.

Some species have their own unique variations on this general theme of withdrawal. Mice become easily startled, coiling and beating their tails. Rats shiver like wet dogs (the "wet-dog" shakes) and may fly into running convulsions if one simply jingles a ring of keys over their cage. Dogs tremble and attend to nonexistent visual stimuli. Monkeys become irritable, retch and vomit, and exhibit intense scratching. Chimpanzees shy away from the light, develop sweaty palms and feet, and pay little attention to sounds.

Laboratory-induced alcoholic animals have enabled investigators to study the underlying physiology and biochemistry of the disorder. In addition to dependence, animals develop tolerance along with chronic liver damage, the universal characteristics of human alcoholism. Female alcoholic macaques even develop the same reproductive system failures as alcoholic women. Using techniques whereby animals can self-administer their own alcohol, rather than having it literally forced down their throats, researchers have been able to study a key prerequisite for human alcoholism: self-intoxication. They have discovered that alcohol is a strong reward, or reinforcer, and animals will self-administer it to the point of intoxication. As do humans, animals differ in their tastes, times, and places for drinking. Yet all of us seem to drink for the same basic reasons and according to the same rules.

Several animals simply like alcohol and will voluntarily drink without additional incentives. Syrian hamsters, those golden rodents who chew tobacco, readily drink a 10 percent alcohol solution—the same strength as hard cider—and prefer it to water. Male hamsters can drink stronger solutions than females but switch back to water when the alcohol concentration starts to exceed 25 percent, the amount found in fruit brandies. Female hamsters seem to have the same instincts regarding drinking as human females. Pregnant hamsters greatly decrease their alcohol consumption shortly before delivery and while they are nursing.

Chimpanzees are even closer to humans in their alcohol preferences, amounts, and patterns of drinking behavior. They prefer flavored alcohols like vodka to plain ethanol and they will drink beer and wine, although they prefer the sweeter sherries and ports. Some individual chimpanzees appear to become intoxicated as they guzzle as much as 20 ounces of 40 percent alcohol in a few minutes. This is equal to 20 glasses of a strong liqueur. The intoxication is manifested by impaired coordination, stupor, and sleep. Males drink more than female chimps and consequently become intoxicated at least twice as often. The heavier animals of either sex drink substantially more than their lighter peers. Like baboons exposed to tobacco, chimps with previous exposure to alcohol use significantly more than those animals without previous experience.

The intoxication sets its own limits on a primate's propensity to take alcohol. If an experimental "bar" is open daily for limited times, a monkey initially drinks eagerly. As the monkey becomes inebriated, it takes less. If the bar is open around the clock, the monkey stays intoxicated on a continual basis except for brief periods of abstinence. This cyclical pattern of drinking is much like the human alcoholic who goes on binges. For both monkey and man, the self-administration of alcohol is a self-administration of intoxication.

These natural preferences and limits for alcohol can be altered by the gradual exposures that lead rodents and chimps to drink more. They can also be influenced by physiological needs that render alcohol intoxication beneficial to the animal. Tame domesticated laboratory rats can be *forced* to drink extremely high concentrations of alcohol continually over long periods of time, but at the end of the experiment they will usually return to their normal preferences for low alcohol concentrations or water. Wild Norway rats, however, may become increasingly partial to strong alcohol and continue to drink it. One explanation that has been proposed for the difference is that the wild ones, unaccustomed to captivity, are under greater stress than the tame rats. Alcohol reduces the stress, thus benefiting the animal.

If alcohol appeals to stressed animals, then the domesticated house cat, the quintessential relaxed pet, would be expected to shun offers of alcohol. Laboratory studies have confirmed that cats refuse to take alcohol in any appreciable amounts, even if low concentrations are mixed with milk. Cats rendered neurotic and fearful behave quite differently. When given mild electric shocks, cats show more dramatic physiological signs of tension: the hair stands on end, the pupils dilate, the paws sweat, the heart races, and the muscles tremble. The cats may exhibit other disturbances, including regressive kittenish behaviors and repetitive compulsive movements. Alcohol dissolves such behaviors.

Animal studies have found that the shock need not be so crude. Sometimes all that is needed is a noisy place, a disturbing alarm clock, some food deprivation, or a sexually frustrating situation. Many types of conflict and stress can be partially eliminated by alcohol but a few seem impervious. Continuous low doses of amphetamines will make both rats and people tense. Both show increased alcohol consumption to reduce the tension. Yet anxious rats lost in a labyrinth are not helped by alcohol and wander without direction. The task is too complex to be executed by an intoxicated, albeit relaxed, rat.

Stress is not the only factor that controls the amount of alcohol consumed by laboratory animals. The genetic strain can influence alcohol intake for animals, just as genes are thought to do for humans. For example, alcohol-preferring rats, known as AA rats, belong to a genetic line that prefers alcohol because they have a more active basal metabolic rate, higher food intake, and a higher energy requirement than rats that do not drink as much.

Social rearing conditions can dramatically alter even this biological predisposition. Consider strains of mice that have been specifically bred for preference (drinker mice) or aversion (nondrinker mice) to alcohol. When nondrinker weanling mice are housed for seven weeks with adult drinker mice, the nondrinkers voluntarily increase their alcohol consumption. Conversely, when drinker weanling mice are housed with adult nondrinkers, the youngsters drink less. Here the use of alcohol is altered as a result of peer pressure and example rather than housing conditions. Since colonies of rodents tend to feed and drink at sites frequented by adults, the weanling mice "learn" to drink whatever the adult model is drinking, not unlike the French children who accompanied their parents to absinthe bars.

Previous exposure and experience with alcohol seem to whet the appetite for more. When both alcohol and water are made available to mice, the amount of alcohol consumed will gradually increase as a function of this exposure. If monkeys are trained to inject themselves with alcohol, the next time they are required to do the same experiment they will inject substantially greater amounts. They do this now because they are more experienced with alcohol, not because they are tolerant to its effects. Once again we see how familiarity breeds experimentation.

Housing conditions can also motivate animals to seek alcohol's effects. The lighting is one of the more important factors. When there is constant darkness, young rats drink more than normal. Older rats drink more in conditions of continuous light. The environmental temperature is also important. When rats are chilled, they may drink more alcohol. Since rats and mice huddle together for warmth, among other reasons, it is not surprising that living with another animal reduces alcohol intake.

In the larger social world of a rat colony, alcohol consumption follows patterns that are familiar to human communities. Psychologist Gaylord Ellison and his coworkers at the University of California at Los Angeles have conducted a series of novel studies that illustrates how social environment facilitates alcoholism. Ellison studied colonies of rats living for as long as seven months in large and spacious environments. Each colony consisted of a burrow area for housing, a behavioral arena with activity wheels and climbing ropes, and a feeding area. Stable colonies of rats raised with unlimited access to water and 10 percent alcohol consumed less alcohol than rats reared in isolation cages. But the colony rats developed some uncannily familiar patterns. They congregated at the fluid spouts where social drinking was facilitated. Peak drinking of alcohol occurred in the hours just before feeding—the "cocktail hour" effect—and just before sleeping—the "nightcap" effect. Furthermore, the investigators observed days of considerable alcohol consumption separated by days of less alcohol and more water intake. While cyclical intake has been noted in studies with individual animals, this cycling in unison by colony members suggested a "party" phenomenon was occurring every three or four days.

Ellison found that a unique subgroup of animals developed in the colony. Animals in this subgroup were extreme consumers of alcohol. Several rats were almost exclusive drinkers of alcohol, and there were a number that almost always drank water. The researchers dyed the fur of the heavy drinkers and studied videotapes of their behavior over the following weeks. They discovered that the high-consumers drank alcohol early in the morning, in addition to the cocktail and nightcap hours, a pattern of use that is also seen among human alcoholics. The high-consumers also ate less food, remained generally inactive, and stayed in their burrows much of the time. They became less dominant in colony life and began losing minor wrestling matches and aggressive bouts. Did the rats also become alcoholic? There was evidence that they did. When alcohol was removed from the colony, transient withdrawal effects were noticed. The high-consumers displayed the typical syndrome of hyperactivity within a few hours. Weeks later the alcoholic rats had recovered. They no longer stayed in their burrows.

The conditions in the colony that led some animals to become extreme alcohol consumers and others to behave like abstainers were primarily social. Unlike the uniform conditions forced on laboratory rats in isolated cages, the spacious and complex colony permitted wide variations in behavior to be exhibited. Genetic predispositions to drink alcohol may have been expressed more readily, but the enriched social environment dictated that social behaviors would become increasingly more important.

Some animals in the colonies may have found it difficult to interact socially and then learned that alcohol increased their ability to engage in such social behaviors as grooming, mounting, or even drinking at the communal spouts. Other rats may have felt pressure from the king rat, a distinctively large and dominant animal that feeds first and takes the best burrow. A king rat developed in each of the colonies and each king was an extreme nonconsumer of alcohol. Ellison speculated that "the stress of being at the bottom of a dominance hierarchy, and failing at competition for food, leads some animals to develop extreme alcohol-consumption habits." Still other rats may have found intoxication a novel change, or altered state, especially after seven months in the same colony in the basement of the psychology building.

Alcohol use in colony cages, however spacious and enriched, is still unnatural. Although these studies reflect conditions in some human communities such as crowded cities, neither the animals used nor the forms of alcohol available represent events in natural habitats. Intoxication with ethanol solutions, beer, wine, and distilled spirits is dramatic but not typical of what happens in nature, as we shall see next.

3

In wild habitats most intoxications occur with the ingestion of fermented fruits, grains, or saps. Field teams have investigated dozens of cases, from Sumatra to the Sudan, involving creatures from bumblebees to bull elephants. The results? In natural habitats, most animals seek alcohol-laden food for the smells, tastes, calories, or nutrients they provide. The intoxications are side effects but not serious enough to deter future use.

One type of accidental intoxication occurs when tree sap is exposed to the proper temperature and ferments. The North American sapsuckers, a type of woodpecker, drill pitlike holes in trees that then fill with sap. The birds feed on the sap and the insects attracted to the sap pits. They move on to other trees, literally "leaving the doors open" for the sap to ferment and intoxicate other animals before the tree heals over. The drinking of fermented sap has been responsible for an array of abnormal behaviors observed in hummingbirds, squirrels, and unsuspecting sapsuckers.

Inadvertent intoxications can also follow feeding on fermented and rotting fruits. Repeated ingestion of fermented foods by fruit bats, civet cats, or squirrels may eventually expose the animals to acquired tastes for alcohol. For example, many Indonesian animals learn to pursue the fermented durian fruit, a twenty-five-centimeter ball of thorns and offensive odors with a nutritious custard filling. The smell is similar to onions and coal gas; the taste is like cream caramel and strawberries. Natives love the fruit but foreign visitors have described it as "French custard passed through a sewer pipe" and usually refuse to taste it. Once visitors start eating it, however, they find it difficult to stop.

Durian may be the most prized fruit in the world and also one of the most dangerous. In Malaysia people and animals alike have been killed by a falling durian, which can weigh as much as five kilograms, yet they risk their lives to get one. This heavily armored fruit splits slightly when ripe, then crashes to the ground where it rots and ferments in only a day or two. A menagerie of jungle beasts, alerted by the ripening odor, parade to the fallen fruit. They are led by Asian elephants, who generally avoid the competition and intoxication by arriving early and picking the ripening fruit from the trees before it falls into the reach of other animals. Monkeys, orangutans, honey bears, and squirrels also eat the fruit in the trees. What falls, rots, and ferments is left for the pigs, deer, tapirs, rhinoceros, and humans. The large seeds are eaten and dispersed by hornbills and tortoises. The remains are consumed by ants and beetles.

Everyone keeps a watchful eye for tigers, who are the most passionate eaters of all; a local custom in Sumatra is to wait to see if a tiger is in the vicinity before retrieving a durian. Tigers have been known to attack native children carrying baskets of durian, playing wolf to the little native Red Riding Hoods. If necessary, tigers will kill, but they are less interested in eating their victims than carrying off the fruit. The durian is often used for tiger bait in traps, although more than one native has lost his life fighting for the bait.

Despite this widespread appreciation for durian, the only animals that become intoxicated are late-arriving elephants, monkeys, and the flying foxes (bats) of Borneo. Elephants that may have migrated from great distances sometimes gorge themselves on the fermented fruit remaining on the ground; they start swaying in a lethargic manner. The monkeys frequently lose motor coordination, have difficulty climbing, and start head-shaking. The flying foxes, which are the largest bats in the world and have the same tastes as humans, feed at night on mostly fermented and rotten fruit. Durian is not only foul smelling but fouls the bat's sonar, thus causing navigational difficulties; the bats keep falling down and waddling on the ground. Yet the high-energy food supply, if not the intoxication itself, makes addicts out of the bats as well as the elephants and monkeys who repeatedly seek out the fermented durians.

In Africa, the pursuit of fermented fruits is even more deliberate and the intoxication more noticeable. African elephants join other beasts in a march across the savannas to ripening fruit from the doum, marula, mgongo, and palmyra *(Borassus)* palm trees. These fruits tend to ferment quickly—sometimes while still attached to the trees—generating odorous molecules that attract more animal migrations. In his 1857 travels, missionary David Livingstone first recorded the passionate fondness that elephants show for *Borassus* fruits. He found that after eating the fruits on the ground, the animals would shake the trees for more.

The elephants spend most of their day feeding and eating in order to supply their daily requirement of fifty thousand calories. This is a full-time job, and the elephants normally do not travel any farther or faster than necessary to satisfy these energy needs. In heavily forested areas they may travel only a few kilometers a day at a leisurely pace of 4 to 6 kilometers per hour. However, when the fruits ripen, the adult elephants, led by the matriarch, follow rivers and paths to the fruits, sometimes traveling 30 kilometers or more in a single day. By the time the elephants arrive, some of the fruit has fermented into mash. After eating the mash, continuing fermentation in the elephants' intestines produces additional ethanol, thus increasing the total amount of alcohol ingested.

Elephants do not eat enough to get intoxicated if they arrive alone or in small groups. But late-arriving elephants or those in herds are sometimes faced with competition from animals that are already feeding on the fruits. The elephants gorge themselves into drunkenness just as their Asian cousins do with durian. They become hyperexcitable and easily startled by unusual sounds or sudden movements. A fleeting encounter with another animal or an unexpected bump can cause them to attack or flee at speeds of 30 kilometers per hour, like a bat out of Borneo.

Occasionally a young elephant will put its trunk into the mother's mouth and sample what she is eating, pulling some of it out, and then chewing and swallowing. This is probably how they learn what to eat. As they imitate their mothers or other adults, they start feeding and calling out with squeaks and peeps. The adults answer with reassuring rumbling sounds, then everybody feeds. Only the very small calves seem slightly unsteady and intoxicated, but the experience can be important.

The learning experiences of the young elephants establish the mechanisms by which elephants always seem to find their favorite foods, including the fruit. A young calf will learn from its mother where the choice feeding grounds are, where to find water in the dry season, where to go on seasonal migrations, and, presumably, what to do with the fermented fruit when it finds some. This information is retained and used when a female calf grows up and becomes the new matriarch. Then younger animals learn from her, and a local tradition is established. The collective wisdom of centuries can be carried by these animals unless a matriarch is killed by poachers and the chain is broken. Thus the seasonal binges on alcohol become part of elephant behavior.

The initial reasons for feeding on the fruit were for food. Do elephants still find alcohol attractive if they are not hungry? To help answer the question I used three Asiatic elephants that were born and raised in North America and had never tasted alcohol. The elephants, part of a trained animal show, were housed between performances in a small barn. Although they were chained by one foreleg and one hind leg to the barn wall, they had free access to alfalfa, grain, fruit, and water. I gave them a fifth choice: alcohol. The alcohol was provided in large calibrated buckets containing ethanol solutions in concentrations ranging from 0 percent to 50 percent in order to reflect the amount of alcohol in various beverages. All three elephants preferred the 7 percent solution, equal to the alcohol content of strong ale. This is the same concentration of alcohol found in the fermented fruits and grains eaten by the elephants in Asia and Africa.

The elephants readily took to drinking the 7 percent alcohol without any food or water deprivation. Since the solutions were unflavored and unsweetened, only the normal pleasant odor of the ethanol was present. In strong solutions ethanol can produce a burning taste. This made higher concentrations unpleasant and caused the elephants to twist their trunks in distaste. Even when one of their favorite flavors, mint, was added to the buckets, elephants would drink nothing stronger than the 10 percent solution.

When the elephants were provided with unlimited access to the 7 percent solution, they adjusted their daily intake to 7 liters, equivalent to 35 cans of beer. The massive weights of these animals, however, shrink the dosage to the equivalent of only 1.5 cans of beer for an average adult man. Nevertheless, these naïve elephants, like many beginning human drinkers, displayed dramatic effects. They started growling—a vocalization pattern associated with arousal—and flapping their ears more than usual. Elephants do not have sweat glands in their skin, but they do have numerous veins close to the surface of their ears, so flapping them is a handy way to regulate temperature. They began swaying rapidly for an hour or two, then slowed down and leaned against their chains, which prevented them from falling over.

Subsequent tests with unchained elephants provided convincing evidence that they never refused the alcohol and almost always drank enough to appear inebriated. Several elephants acted drunk, for they kept leaning, staggering, or inappropriately wrapped their trunks about themselves. One actually slipped and fell, but quickly got up again. Flapping their ears like a frustrated Dumbo, they had difficulty responding to commands from their handler. They kept dropping their trunkhold on each other's tails—the trained elephant's version of walking a straight line. Their intoxication was obvious.

Studying elephants in a barn may be a little like Marais's studies of captive baboons. If we apply the principle that captivity may predispose an intelligent creature like the elephant to seek the comfort of intoxication, then we must consider the tranquilizing and sedating properties of alcohol to be the real attraction of the intoxication. Stress from increased herd density or competition for food may also lead elephants to drunken binges on fermented foods. If this is the case, under the right conditions, can the intoxication from pure alcohol itself become a reason for use? While the intoxication from fermented fruit may be an accidental side effect, will elephants with access to undisguised alcohol intentionally get drunk?

I conducted a series of studies with an elephant herd in a spacious California game park in order to answer these questions. The herd consisted of seven African elephants including one bull, Congo, and six cows. They ranged in weight from Congo at 3,000 kilograms to Rafiki, a mere 1,600 kilos. The elephants were restricted to two hectares with free access to a large freshwater stream, and their diet was maintained with hay, alfalfa, grain, and fruit. I, together with my team, made observations of the herd from roving jeeps. The elephants had accepted our presence over a period of several months while we became familiar with their behavior.

The elephants spent most of the time in a tightly compacted herd grouping. Their major activities were feeding and drinking. They also engaged in many forms of social interaction; trunk-to-trunk contacts and group bathing were frequent events. Pushing, shoving, and aggressive vocalizations were almost nonexistent. The entire scene was one of family unity, a fitting landscape for the human families that drove through the park.

If the elephants were having a peaceful Sunday picnic, then alcohol certainly caused it to rain. Each elephant was given the opportunity to drink from a large drum kept in the back of one of the jeeps. The drum contained the 7 percent unflavored ethanol solution and the elephant could drink all it wanted in a thirty-minute period while the other elephants were kept away by park rangers. Some took as much as 75 liters, swallowing some solution but also spraying much of it about. After the drinking session, the jeep withdrew and the elephant was allowed to regroup with the herd. They rarely made it.

The intoxicated elephant, rocking and swaying, would usually go its separate way and spend most of the first three hours away from the remaining herd. Everything was the complete reverse of normal behavior. Feeding and drinking decreased, as did bathing and physical contacts with the others. Ear flapping increased and several times the elephant would lie down on the ground for relatively prolonged periods. Alcohol also seemed to bring out the individual personality of each animal. Both Congo the bull and Nyla the dominant cow became more domineering showing increased aggression and threatening vocalizations to the rest of the herd. Congo even tried to pursue the jeep with the alcohol drum and attacked me when I wouldn't let him have any more. The submissive elephants became even meeker, shying away from most physical and vocal encounters.

When the entire herd was given access to the alcohol drum, the more dominant animals prevented the submissive ones from drinking more than 6 or 7 liters each, resulting in decreased alcohol intake for these elephants. The herd pressed against the jeep, crushing the steel sides and threatening to do the same to little Rafiki. When I tried to rescue her, Nyla pinned me to the jeep until I squeezed my way under her and ducked to escape. The elephants continued to fight, yet each ingested enough alcohol to cause a major disruptive effect: individuals separated themselves over the preserve area, causing the entire herd to dissolve. If they been able had to crawl into a burrow, as Ellison's rats were, I was sure they would have used it.

More dramatic effects were achieved when the herd was given access to alcohol but confined to a smaller area that forced them to interact. Alcohol intake increased when the elephants were crammed into less than one hectare with other savanna animals including rhinos, gazelles, zebras, and ostriches. Individual elephants displayed the same range of reactions shown by people: some became boisterous and aggressive, trumpeting and attacking nearby animals, including the researchers; others became passive and lethargic; still others appeared amorous.

There was also a hint of the murderous behavior exhibited by intoxicated elephants in the wild. After drinking his fill, Congo went to his favorite wallow near the stream. He was confronted by one of the rhinos with whom he usually shared the spot. Congo was not in the mood for sharing. He cocked his tail, raised his head, threw dirt in the air, and growled. As the growl slowly changed from a low rumble to a motorcycle-like roar, I knew a life-threatening clash was imminent. I drove my jeep between the two animals. I should have known better. The motorcycle became a snort, then a boom, then a trumpet. Congo charged. I jumped to safety, but at the last moment Congo decided to swerve around the jeep, then chase the rhino, which tactfully retreated. I found myself knee-deep in the wallow, which I had all to myself.

When the preserve was enlarged to its normal size, and bothersome rhinos and other animals were evicted, alcohol drinking returned to normal levels. Several months later, when the preserve was rattled by construction crews, elephants congregated in the area where alcohol was once available. If elephants never forget, then why do they drink? Certainly they were not addicted to alcohol; they were denied continuous exposures that could have led to alcoholism, just as seasonal ripening of the fruit prevents alcoholism in the wild. In the preserve, the elephants seem to seek the periodic intoxication in order to escape the external environmental stresses by altering their internal environment, thereby reducing the discomfort. In the wild, stressed from poaching and deforestation, perhaps they accept intoxication for the same reason. Marais would have argued that alcohol helped them ease the "pain of consciousness." In a sense, a contemporary quip was correct when it claimed that elephants drink to forget.

The lesson should always be remembered. Under the right conditions, the intoxication itself can become a reason for use and animals with access to alcohol will intentionally get drunk by consuming more than their usual amounts. For laboratory animals the stress of captivity, confinement, or conflict will persuade many to become alcoholic. When similar conditions occur in social colonies, herds, or natural habitats, they drive animals to alcohol. The most convincing examples have been the two animals that have life expectancies of approximately seventy years, select mates for life, provide collective care for their young, suffer death from heart disease, bury their dead, and kill for love of drink: people and pachyderms.

Some of the earliest artistic conceptions of Eden depicted elephants among the animals that once shared Paradise with man. In Theodore de Bry's 1563 engraving of the biblical scene in which animals leave Noah's Ark to search for a new paradise, a pair of elephants is leading the long file. Somewhere in the shadow of those beasts do we not see our own emerging figure?

6

Milk of Paradise

ROMANCE AND
ADDICTION WITH OPIUM

1

Opium is as old as tobacco, as universally recognized as alcohol, and as rooted in tradition as the plant hallucinogens. And like all these sources of intoxication, the accidental and deliberate use of opium is widespread throughout the animal kingdom. Yet opium is unique in that the intoxication is almost always pleasurable. The drive to opium's pleasure is manifested in patterns of use and addiction found across time and species. Not surprisingly, opium is the most celebrated drug in literature.

A sultan's palace, clashing cymbals, flashing scimitars, dancing girls strewing flowers, and an infinite number of white elephants, caparisoned in countless gorgeous colors—these are the opening images of *The Mystery of Edwin Drood* by Charles Dickens. Odd things to find in the bleakness of a London opium den where the central character of the novel lies dimly illuminated by a flickering lamp. The pictures, however, are all in the mind's eye of the opium dreamer.

Opium took many people out of the darkness of their dens, slums, factory towns, and class tensions in nineteenth-century England. Unlike alcohol with its unpredictable effects, opium was appealing because it *always* soothed the body while romancing the imagination. It was widely used as an everyday remedy for common ailments, much as aspirin is today. The Romantic writers and poets discovered that it opened the mind to a stream of visions. Thomas De Quincey proclaimed that this "just, subtle, and mighty" drug relieved the suffering he witnessed in London and gave him the keys to paradise. Psychic and physical discomfort was replaced with hope and a halcyon calm. In a word, the opium dreamer was happy. But the architecture of De Quincey's visionary paradise, full of cathedrals and palaces and shining lights, had a dark side as well. De Quincey's mental landscape was haunted by ugly birds, snakes, and crocodiles.

From De Quincey's confessions of opium's pleasures to Elizabeth Barrett Browning's letters describing the pain of withdrawal, literary figures gave us glimpses of what lay beyond the gates. At the end of "Kubla Khan," Samuel Taylor Coleridge tells us that Xanadu was only a vision born in an opium dream. Like a mirage that shows a magnificent city on a desolate expanse of ocean or desert, the images induced by opium are actually reflected images of real things located elsewhere, of stored memories and images in the brain itself. Coleridge had only to drink "the milk of Paradise" for his mind's eye to focus on them.

John Keats never wanted to admit taking opium, although as a doctor he was well acquainted with it. His early poems seem unrelated to opium, but the images of Asian poppies, domineering potions, and paradise gardens in "The Fall of Hyperion," written in 1819, are more suggestive. During the winter of that year it was suspected that he had been secretly taking laudanum (a tincture of opium). He turned out some of his most lyrical poems but grew progressively more indolent. He died of tuberculosis in 1821 and no one ever knew with medical certainty if this truly great poet who penned such classics as "Ode on a Grecian Urn" had used opium all along.

Unlike the Drood mystery, the Keats puzzle has now been solved by no less a Sherlockian clue than a strand of human hair. In 1816 Keats met Leigh Hunt, an influential editor who published one of his sonnets and introduced the budding poet to Shelley and Wordsworth. Hunt also snipped a lock of Keats's hair for his famous hair collection. Part of that lock is now at the University of Iowa, but I secured several strands of it for analysis. Sherlock Holmes might have commented on the striking color of the hair—like a red sunset—and divined that such glorious hair must have belonged to an extremely striking man, perhaps one who wore his hair long and thick, as indeed Keats did. I, together with colleagues in the nuclear medicine laboratory, looked for something not visible to the naked eye: molecules of morphine, a telltale metabolite of opium. Using a sensitive chemical procedure known as radioimmunoassay, we found morphine in massive amounts. Keats was not only a user, he was probably dependent on the drug as well.

Opium was obtained then, as now, from the poppy, a plant that has received more attention than any other in history. Its power is legendary. In Homer's *Odyssey,* Helen of Troy used an opium-based elixir called *nepenthe* to banish grief and sorrow. And throughout Greek mythology the poppy was dedicated to the nocturnal gods: to Nyx, goddess of night; to Hypnos, god of sleep; to Morpheus, god of dreams; and to Thanatos, god of death.

When Keats sang praises to a Grecian urn he was probably unaware that small clay vases, called juglets, were used by ancient Greek merchants in a flourishing opium trade throughout the Mediterranean. Opium juglets made in Cyprus and dating from 1600 B.C. have been unearthed at sites in Egypt and Syria. These juglets have a distinctive shape resembling an upside-down poppyhead. Some even have vertical strips in relief on the body imitating the incisions that are made in the poppy capsule to allow the milk to ooze out. The milk is actually a white latex or juice the Greeks named *opion.* The opium poppy *(Papaver somniferum)* is named after Somnus, the Roman god of sleep; and morphine, the most important of the fifty alkaloids in the plant, is named after the Greek god of dreams. The ancient Israelites called it *rôsh,* or gall, and it may have been given to Jesus to drink before the Crucifixion. The original use, however, is far older than even the Greek, Roman, or Christian gods.

The archaeological evidence suggests that opium poppies were cultivated and used by Stone Age lake-dwellers in areas of central Europe and present-day Switzerland. From there they were deliberately spread and traded to the eastern Mediterranean in the late Bronze Age. Masses of well-preserved poppy seeds have been found among the remains of Neolithic lakeshore settlements indicating their use as a reserve or famine food.

The poppy produces a large number of small, oily seeds that are edible without heating or refining. As many as thirty thousand of these tiny seeds can be found in a single capsule. The tasty seeds are rich in nutrients and they can be eaten raw, pressed for their oil, baked into cakes, ground into flour, or made into a porridge. Poppyseed oil cakes produce enough digestible protein to make them useful as a food for animals, and Neolithic farmers probably fed them to their domesticated animals.

Livestock generally dislike foraging on the poppies if there is better feed available. Eating too many poppies violates the rules for safe feeding. The stems of field poppies—including the variety used as an emblem by the American Legion—contain traces of morphine but toxic amounts of rhoeadine; both alkaloids are also present in the flowers, and they have caused poisoning in cattle and horses who like to nibble them. Some varieties of poppies contain little or no morphine but a lot of thebaine, which kills animals with strychninelike convulsions.

The opium poppy is less toxic than these field varieties; some parts can be eaten with relative safety by animals. High-calorie poppyseed cakes have been fed to a number of animals in order to cause them to gain weight. Tortoises apparently crave the cakes, even though they keep them in a half-sleep. Similar effects were achieved with poultry when they were fattened with a mixture of gin and opium-poppy latex for the London market of Dickens's time.

But access to the entire opium poppy plant has caused problems for livestock. Farmers have dried the plants like hay and used this poppy straw as bedding material for their stables. Sometimes the dried plants become mixed with cattle feed and are unknowingly consumed by the animals. The drying destroys 30 percent of the alkaloids but enough remain so that the animals can nibble their way to intoxication. The characteristic aroma of such a stable evokes memories of an opium den; the behavior recalls scenes from locoweed poisoning.

The animals become agitated within two hours after eating the poppies. They paw the ground with their front legs while stamping from one hind leg to the other. These steps are interrupted by rapid turning and circling. The dance continues, to the accompaniment of loud bellowing, for as long as fifty-six hours. Gradually, the stimulation is replaced by signs of disorientation, staggering, and poor coordination. The animals have obvious difficulty with vision as they bump into objects. They become more and more listless, then lie down on what is left of their "opium dens" and sleep deeply for several days.

If cows dream of a bovine paradise to which they become addicted, it is hard to determine from their behavior. Farmers are quick to recognize the cause of the intoxication and remove the poppies, thus preventing future relapses for the animals. Those few animals that die usually show symptoms of gastroenteritis rather than an opium overdose. The poppy debris causes a prolonged and fatal indigestion.

However, the *occasional* browsing of cultivated opium poppies by oxen and water buffalo working near the opium fields in southeast Asia may produce intoxications without fatal consequences because the animals can dilute their intake with other food. Poppies are often planted side by side with food grains such as wheat, and it is not uncommon for stray or hungry animals to infiltrate these areas. But, unlike cows trapped in stables of poppy straw, the grazers usually follow safe feeding strategies and mix their intake of poppies with other forage.

For some animals the intoxications may not be fatal, but they can be addicting. The water buffalo only looks fearsome, with its huge bulk, sweeping horns, and beady eyes. These lumbering beasts are naturally timid and startle easily; they must be handled quietly and gently. Those that had browsed the opium poppies became as docile as lambs and surprised their owners, who had to use rough handling and loud shouting to get them to work. Although the buffalo typically stay together in small herds, those that used opium became loners. At the end of the opium harvest behavior returned to normal but not before the animals displayed restlessness, tremors, and convulsions—behavioral proof of their withdrawal from addiction.

During the fighting waged by *Homo sapiens* in Cambodia and Vietnam, water buffalo within earshot of combat zones were once again observed browsing opium poppies, showing signs of addiction and withdrawal. If these animals were simply reacting to the stress of noise in their environment, they were no different from the game park elephants that reacted to stress by seeking out alcohol. If the buffalo were motivated to seek new food supplies due to wartime shortages and ravages of their habitat, they remind us of how flexible animals like tigers have been when battling for survival. In Vietnam, tigers learned to go toward the sound of gunfire in order to feed on the human casualties.

In war or peace the opium fields are favorite hunting grounds for a variety of insects, birds, and rodents. These creatures have no difficulty in finding the fields because the opium poppy, even if it is not deliberately planted, tends to sow itself in the same general area each year. The seeds are located in capsules that sit on top of tall stalks. They are dispersed at the end of their annual lives by jactitation, a process that involves the shaking of the capsules and the subsequent release of the seeds. The seeds scatter no farther than fifteen meters unless carried away by animals. Unlike their refined drugs, which are traded around the globe, poppy fields tend to stay in fixed locations, usually in warm and moderately humid climates.

While finding the opium poppy is relatively easy, finding opium in the poppy is all a matter of timing. Only the most experienced mammals and birds can figure out when to attack the plant. The golden capsules, which ripen to the size of pigeon eggs, produce almost all of the opium within a two-week period. Once peak morphine levels are achieved, they remain high for only a day. A harvest delay of even four hours can mean the loss of a good crop. This limited period of activity probably accounts for the paucity of serious intoxications among browsing animals in the wild. As with ripening and fermenting fruits, we see once again how nature's seasons control the frequency of intoxication.

Humans excel in the ability to calculate this two-week period and take advantage of the alkaloidal production. The pods are lanced by hand; tears of white latex ooze out and coagulate into a gum, gradually turning brown upon exposure to air. The gum is left to seep overnight and is then collected the next morning by scraping the capsules and allowing the scrapings to harden. Each pod yields a morsel of opium the size of a small pea; ten to fifteen of these constitute an adult human dose.

Birds also excel in the ability to puncture the pods but they are seeking the seeds, not the capsule latex. Unlike the capsules, which contain raw opium for only a short period of time, the seeds are time-resistant vaults of morphine and related alkaloids. When the seed coats are macerated in the bird's bill or crop, or chewed and ground by humans, digestive enzymes release the alkaloids. The amounts, however, are small; ingestion of poppy seeds, called "maw" seeds when found in commercial birdseed mixtures, do not result in dramatic intoxications for birds. Likewise, the small amounts of poppy seeds on breads and rolls may affect human palates but not behavior, despite the detectable presence of morphine in subsequent blood or urine samples.

The central nervous system effects are all related to the amount of seeds and the weight of the individual, the same parameters that dictate behaviorally effective dosages for most drugs. Poppy seeds have been found in the remains of mammoths, but we would not expect such giants to be affected by the tiny amounts. A diet of concentrated poppy seeds for a small bird or child, however, will generally influence behavior. Some birds seem to love them. The pet bird belonging to Ovid's mistress Corinna was allegedly given poppy seeds to make it sleep. And a sixteenth-century recipe called for "powder of white Poppie seede given to children in milke" to cause them to sleep. This concoction was first invented by the ancient Greeks and is still given to infants in some rural areas of Europe. American Indians prepared a syrup of poppy flowers and seeds, sweetened with honey, as an unfailing remedy for quieting children and inducing sleep. Perhaps the only safe, nonpsychoactive way to lure a child to sleep with poppy seeds was pioneered by the Lisu of southeast Asia. These tribal people use the dried seed pods as rattles for their restless babies.

Birds are such avid poppy-seed eaters that they have become a real pest to opium growers. The poppies are plagued by attacks from finches who peck holes in the base of the capsules before they can be harvested. It is unknown if any of these birds become intoxicated; the rich oil content of the seeds might be sufficient to maintain feeding behavior. Similarly, bees visit the poppy flowers but they seek the pollen, which is rich in unsaturated fatty acids, and seem unconcerned about the alkaloids despite reports of their "violent cravings" for opium.

Our teams conducted detailed observations on opium fields in southeast Asia, Mexico, and California. In California we observed sparrows and lazuli buntings feeding on the poppies. Both types of birds have strong bills that can crush the seeds, and they did so with enthusiasm. Yet neither appeared affected by their diet, even when provided with bird feeders filled to capacity with the poppy seeds. Since the buntings were nesting nearby, I had hoped to comment on the use of poppy seeds in quieting baby buntings, but the adult buntings never shared the seeds with their young.

Growers have employed an arsenal of acoustical devices that effectively scare the birds from the fields but do nothing to stop invasions by rodents. Mice and rats tear at the capsules and destroy them as they forage for the seeds. Small mice will occasionally die from apparent overdoses but the larger rats seem relatively immune. Yao villagers in Laos spread poisoned rice to prevent the rats from eating stored seeds or newly planted opium crops. Still, the plants come under continuous assault from insects.

Various parts of the poppy are eaten by insects. We watched them very carefully and found most were only hungry. The parts they selected to eat were not even very rich in alkaloids. The nematodes stay in the roots. Leaf miners lay their eggs at the base of the roots; when hatched, the minute larvae move to the leaves, where they cut out tunnels within the green spongy tissue and eat. The miners follow a winding course through the leaves for several days, then chew their way to the outside and return to the roots. Poppy seeds are the favorite food of some ant species but the sticky latex that oozes from their bite marks keeps many away. They can enter the capsule after the opium latex has been harvested, although we have still found a number of their bodies stuck forever inside this gummy paradise.

Beetles and weevils do the most damage. These insects favor vegetable debris of all kinds and are infamous for their ability to survive on groceries and drugs that have been processed by man. They have invaded and adapted to every habitat from the Namib Desert in southeastern Africa to the remote and inhospitable islands beyond the polar circles. Nothing keeps them away from the opium poppy. Their voracious appetite for the poppies illustrates that a strong addiction to a plant is much the same whether it is for food or for drugs, just as we have seen with koalas eating eucalyptus.

These insects even have a folklore to match their behavior. Opium beetle larvae make fast food out of the seeds, a habit that seems to slow them down, according to a fanciful story told by one Mexican opium grower. He claimed that when the larvae grew into beetles, they flew so slowly he was able to grab them out of the air with his hands, despite his own constant intoxication with opium. He also claimed that the ones that got away were addicted and would return. While opium beetles are not very good flyers, barely achieving speeds of 8 kilometers per hour, their flight speeds are determined by their wing structure, not their fuel. By contrast, the tobacco hawkmoth can reach speeds of 54 kilometers per hour; the speed comes from good wing muscles, not nicotine.

The grower's other notion, that the beetles were addicted and would return to eat the plant, might seem equally fantastic if not for the fact that the diet of beetle grubs can influence their food preferences when they turn into adults. Adult beetles have a keen sense of smell and use it to find preferred foods, but preferences are based on familiarity, not dependency. Yet the possibility of developing a strain of poppy-seeking bugs that could be used for detecting illegal supplies attracted the U.S. Army Land Warfare Laboratory. The army researchers tried without success to raise insect larvae on diets of opiates so that their progeny would seek out the plants. The experiments might have been more successful if the grubs had been reared on the plants themselves rather than on the purified drugs, which lack the smells and tastes of the natural products.

Poppy weevils do not appear to fall under the influence of opium any more than beetles do, but they would make better soldiers in the war on drugs. The weevils develop ravenous appetites for the plant. The infestation of poppy fields by these insects is so great that the latex production is reduced by 30 percent and seed production is cut almost entirely. These figures so impressed the United Nations Division of Narcotic Drugs that they once considered drafting an army of weevils to control illegal opium production. Of all the insects that pester the poppy, only these poppy weevils appear willing to die rather than switch their feeding to other plants. Although the weevils do not experience intoxication, their preference for the poppies represents the same life-threatening addiction we humans display to the alkaloids inside.

Although the opium poppies still manage to escape total destruction from insects and animals in nature, they do so only by existing in habitats where other potential eaters are conspicuously absent. Once opium is obtained from the plant and dried, it does not remain long in the fields or habitats that produced it. It is distributed almost exclusively to humans. We, in turn, share concentrated preparations of the intoxicant with our animal friends, just as we do with tobacco and alcohol. And like the animal images that decorate our saloons and color our barroom jokes, the chain of opium distribution is linked with icons of intoxicated animals.

In the past opium was sold on the open market, where it was weighed for the buyer on scales with brass weights cast in the shape of animals. The most popular weights were elephants, arranged in graduated sizes from ones the size of a pea to others as big as a fist. Today many of these same animals appear on preweighed packages of opium that are illegally traded around the world. Opium smokers in some cities will ask dealers for the "elephant brand" or "rooster brand" because of the traditional high quality associated with these trademarks.

Humans may need the assurance of such images; other animals are not nearly so particular. Most animals consume the concentrated preparations with relish, like so many poppy weevils. The taste for the pleasant intoxication quickly leads to regular pursuit and addiction. Unlike the low incidence of abuse and addiction found among animals using safe-feeding strategies with the opium poppy, the availability of fist-size balls of concentrated opium was bound to lead to more severe dependencies. Humans pushed the stronger doses at the animals, thereby pushing them into unnatural patterns of addiction.

When opium was in vogue as a medicine for humans, it was also given to animals either in pieces of raw opium, pills containing powdered opium, or opium extracts. Even the smoke seemed to be inhaled readily by animals. The closed space of opium dens provided a convenient cage for observing this phenomenon. The owner of a nineteenth-century opium den in Paris kept two blackbirds in the smoking area. Whenever someone lit a pipe, the birds would perch on the smoker's bed and extend their beaks toward the smoke. The dens were also occupied by mice and rats that came out into the open whenever the pungent, sweet odor filled the air. These rodents frequently nibbled leftover scraps of opium. Jean Cocteau, a twentieth-century writer who was also an opium addict, described the attraction:

> All animals are charmed by opium. Addicts in the colonies know
> the danger of this bait for wild beasts and reptiles. Flies gather

round the tray and dream, the lizards with their little mittens swoon on the ceiling above the lamp and wait for the night, mice come close and nibble the dross. . . . The cockroaches and the spiders form a circle in ecstasy.

Some animals became regular eaters or sniffers. Starting in the seventeenth century and continuing to the early 1900s, horses were fed opium to increase their stamina; the drug relieved the pain of exhausting work and was thus eagerly eaten by the animals. Travelers in Turkey would routinely give as much as two grams of opium to their riding animals before a fatiguing trip. In Afghanistan and Cambodia monkeys and dogs often lived in an atmosphere of opium smoke, where they gradually began to enjoy it and await the hour when their masters would light a pipe. If more than a day or two went by without access to the opium smoke, the animals fell into states of depression that were promptly relieved when opium was provided again. When an addicted opium smoker detoxified successfully in 1960, his equally addicted dog died during the abrupt withdrawal.

True to their trademark, elephants became the most passionate users of all. It started in the same way that was once believed to be the method by which drug pushers entrapped innocent children or pimps won the allegiance of prostitutes: by offering free gifts of the drug. Wild elephants in Burma and India were sometimes captured by giving them gifts of opium balls or baiting fruit with the opium. Once sedated and harnessed with ropes and chains, the elephants were given handouts of opium to manage their temper and help them adapt to a new life of working for humans. While opium could enslave elephants in a new occupation, it could also free them from one of their most violent disorders: musth.

Male Asiatic elephants are particularly prone to musth, a seasonal disorder characterized by aggression and secretions from temporal glands, sweatlike ducts opening between the eye and ear. Their plasma testosterone levels increase and the resulting paroxysms of excitement can become so violent that the elephants go on destructive rampages, killing human handlers and riders. A few decades ago many of these "mad" elephants had their tusks sawed off or they were confined to torturous "crush cages." Some were shackled and hobbled with chains. Most were destroyed. Wally, an elephant on (or in) musth, gored his keeper to death at a zoo in San Francisco and was executed by firing squad. Toto, an elephant that became too unmanageable for circus duty, was hanged.

Working elephants that were too valuable to be destroyed were often saved from insanity, theirs as well as our own, by opium. The drivers of the elephants—the *mahouts* in India and *oozies* in Burma—would give opium to their animals on musth. It cured them. But like humans who medicated themselves too heavily, there were elephants who could not or would not control their use. Some elephants became addicted and took so much opium that they were not only sedated from madness but absent from work. Even when the elephants were used for carrying humans on tiger hunts in Thailand, they would literally lie down on the job, despite the risk of mauling from the cats.

In low, regulated doses, severe addiction was avoided, just as accidental deaths among grazing animals could be circumvented with safe-feeding strategies. Opium became a useful treat in training elephants for logging and hauling operations. Once the training was completed, good work performance was aided by regular rations of opium balls or pills. These practices continue in remote regions of Afghanistan, Burma, and India. The mahout or oozie simply offers the opium pill to the elephant, which can recognize the smell and take it like a peanut from the driver's hand. Elephants are less than eager to accept other medicinal drugs in this manner. Sometimes an elephant gag has to be used. The gag consists of a large wooden muzzle with a large hole in the center. The medicine is passed through the hole by hand and deposited at the back of the throat. The elephant may use its tongue to resist or even try to catch the driver's hand between its grinder teeth. No elephant ever needed to be gagged for a pill of opium.

A handler from India described how one particular trained elephant would beg for opium. The animal would nudge the driver and search his body and clothing with its trunk. If the ration of opium was not forthcoming, the elephant would begin snorting and trumpeting. After eating the opium, the elephant would squeak and chirp, vocalization patterns suggestive of pleasure calls. When deprived of opium for several days, the elephant became restless and showed other signs of displeasure, if not withdrawal. The handler, using a slang expression from the Western world, claimed that the elephant had a "monkey on its back" and was addicted to the opium.

The slang and jargon of opium users always contained references to people acting like animals. But medical scientists did not become interested in studying the effects of opium on animals until many years after human studies began.

2

Opium was worthy of note in many early medical treatises, including recommendations for use by the Greek physician Hippocrates. Human reactions were the ones of interest and even the first experimental investigation into the properties of opium, conducted in 1696 by Gideon Harvey, mentioned only human studies. In 1700, attempts to study animal reactions found that opium killed cats and caused dogs to vomit. For the next hundred years, a handful of experimenters failed to improve on this knowledge. Then A. P. Charvet, a young medical student studying at Grenoble, began a systematic series of opium studies on animals. Charvet gave opium to every conceivable form of life including water beetles, crayfish, snails, fish, salamanders, toads, frogs, sparrows, blackbirds, guinea pigs, rabbits, cats, dogs, and medical students. He even experimented on himself and took copious notes on everything that happened. His 1826 book, *De l'action comparée de l'opium, et de ses principes constituans sur l'économie animale* (The Action of Opium and Its Principal Constituents on Animal Conduct), was the very first book in modern experimental psychopharmacology as well as the first book devoted solely to drugs and animal behavior.

Charvet rigorously ignored the anthropomorphism of previous investigators, as well as the Romantic literary movement that was already sweeping through Europe. Instead he chose to look at animal reactions to opium in terms of their physiological and behavioral changes rather than their passions, dreams, and stupors. He did this by carefully monitoring everything that he could. When he wanted to study the effects of opium on the flying behavior of sparrows, for example, he not only watched their flight patterns but also measured respiration and heart rates at regular intervals following each dose. The experiments could not have happened at a more exciting time. Every medical scientist was talking about opium and the alkaloids morphine and narcotine, which had been recently isolated. These compounds were the magical elixirs for medicine. In his student zeal Charvet experimented on everything from sluggish paramecia to ailing plants.

His experiments revealed that opium affects all animals, including humans, in the same way: it produces a continuum of effects ranging from mild sedation and relaxation to paralysis and death. Charvet made the important discovery that these effects were dependent on several factors, the most important of which were the dose, the method of administration, and the individual's past history and tolerance for the drug. These findings were revolutionary because they suggested that a drug such as opium was not a magical elixir that automatically transported one to Paradise or even soothed the beast that nineteenth-century morality claimed was within us all. Instead opium was simply another chemical substance, much like alcohol, with certain pharmacological properties and behavioral possibilities. It could just as easily calm a nervous rabbit as send it to the hereafter; all you had to do was increase the dose or get a different rabbit, one that was either smaller or less tolerant to opium, and, quick as you could say Morpheus and Thanatos, sleep would turn to death.

Unfortunately, Charvet's work was published as just another required doctoral thesis, and his book was totally ignored among the heaps of obscure theses of the day. It would take another century before other scientists caught up with his findings. So when famed psychiatrist S. Weir Mitchell tried to put pigeons to sleep with a few Black Drops, a liquid opium preparation also favored by Coleridge, the pigeons remained awake and Mitchell wrote that they had a natural immunity. After the announcement in a leading medical journal in 1869, this simple curiosity of nature began to get retold and still finds its way into scientific literature today. Although Mitchell qualified his opinion with more detailed experiments in which the birds died and published them one year later in the same journal, the myth of pigeon immunity survived.

The important point is not how many Black Drops it takes to kill a pigeon, but rather how casual comments and faulty science become transformed into accepted scientific gospel, even in the drug world of the nineteenth century. If you were a nineteenth-century Romantic aspiring to follow in the tradition of De Quincey, it might have been comforting to know that birds, too, can fly on opium with immunity.

The danger is that if you are a twenty-first-century youth exploring LSD-induced visions of Paradise you may panic when an "authority" makes the dishonest claim that you will go blind or fry your brains.

In the early days of research with opium and its alkaloids, as in those early days of LSD exploration, everything was of interest, and publishable, even observations on single animals. Systematic observation and experiment like Charvet's was the exception, not the rule. Another exceptional investigator was Mitchell, who had the intuition to repeat experiments and the integrity to correct his earlier opinions. Mitchell found that concentrates of morphine were much more powerful than opium extracts. Weak oral doses of opium did not affect ducks, for example, but just a few grains of morphine caused them to slip and quack. Heroin had not yet been manufactured, but Mitchell would have found that derivative even more potent.

Mitchell employed the hypodermic syringe and needle in order to inject the drugs directly into the animals, thereby speeding up the onset of action as well as the total amount of the drug that could be given. Changing these two factors allowed for the full force of opium's power to be realized. The injection device itself was relatively new. The first one was a quill outfitted with a small bladder, a primitive but effective device invented by architect Christopher Wren. Wren was intrigued by William Harvey's new ideas concerning the circulation of blood and he used his device to inject opium directly into the veins of dogs. The effects were far more dramatic than those achieved via oral administration. American and Scottish surgeons improved the design, adding a hollow sewing needle here and a syringe there, and by the time of the Civil War in the United States, soldiers could be routinely injected with morphine. This not only relieved the pain of their battlefield wounds but also created a postwar "army disease" of addiction.

The hypodermic permitted one to force a large bolus of the drug directly into an animal or person without waiting for him to eat or drink it. It was fast and the animal couldn't get rid of it. A major obstacle to studies on pigeons was that they would retch and vomit, thereby reducing the amount ingested and creating the appearance of immunity to toxic quantities. Now Mitchell could kill his pigeons by simply pricking them with a modified sewing needle. The animals browsing opium poppies had few problems compared to what was now in store for them—and us—when the alkaloids could be injected directly into the body. The animal kingdom was destined to have problems that Mother Nature never intended.

Armed with this new tool, medical researchers studied the effects of regular daily doses of opium and its alkaloids. The same general symptoms seen in Civil War veterans could be duplicated in animals. In one series of experiments, dogs were given regular injections of morphine. The researchers admitted it was difficult to assess mental or psychological changes but they saw constipation, scratching, changes in temperament, and a gradual decrease in the stupefying or narcotic action of the drug. These were relatively mild effects compared to behavior once the injections stopped; then the battles really started. There were tremors and twitching, howling and whining, gnawing at objects, restlessness, salivation, vomiting, muscular weakness, respiratory distress and panting, sleepiness, diarrhea, and weight loss. Some dogs would start to die during this period, but a quick injection of the morphine would reverse the symptoms of abstinence and reinstate the unremarkable behavior seen before. This, then, was the picture of addiction's most telling scene: withdrawal.

The other scene was the craving or passion for the drug that was obvious from the behavior of these animals prior to their daily injections. Pigeons became tranquil and sedate after injection. They barely moved. As soon as the experimenter approached with the syringe a few hours later, the pigeons came to the front of their cages, wings flapping with excitement, and stood without further protest for their next injection. When cats were used as subjects, it was often necessary for the handlers to use trickery and force to avoid being bitten or scratched during the initial injections. Resistance vanished after a few injections and the cats would run to the experimenter, jump on his lap, and even lick his hand while waiting for the morphine. While the addiction was primarily a relationship between the animal and the drug, that relationship could be expanded to include people, needles, and anything else that became associated with the drug. Even the physical environment could become a conditioned cue. During withdrawal, rats would run to the side of the box where they had previously received their morphine injections. The desire for morphine was almost as clear in these animals as in the behavior of primates.

In 1940, when he was seven years old, Frank had already been at Yale for several years. He was in a group of laboratory chimpanzees that were chosen to receive daily doses of morphine. Frank's initial doses were very small, increasing rapidly over the first weeks. He started getting two injections a day—only one on Sundays—and was soon scratching, picking at his hair and pulling it out, all typical primate reactions to daily doses. By the fourth week, Frank was almost completely denuded. There were few physical changes as dramatic as the hairless body. He lost some of his appetite and weight and had minor constipation, but his metabolic functions seemed normal. He cooperated with daily rectal temperature readings, which registered normal as did his pulse and respiration. His pupils were considerably enlarged, in contrast to the pinpoint pupils of humans—one of the few differences between animal and human addicts.

Frank was clearly desirous of the morphine. He was eager to be taken from his cage to the injection room, tugging at his leash and actually leading the experimenter. Before the injection Frank was excited and would often jump up on the injection box. As soon as he saw the loaded syringe he would voluntarily bend over, waiting for the injection. After the shot, he showed his appreciation by grooming the experimenter's hands, shoes, and clothing. The first signs of addiction were seen when a dose was skipped. Frank became a little restless and irritable, and he gave several deep, prolonged yawns that are characteristic of mild withdrawal. After several weeks of injections, he displayed other symptoms of physical dependency: he would appear in the injection room with drops of perspiration on his face and a watery discharge from his nose.

Morphine was not deleterious to Frank's general health as long as he got his injections. His activity and playfulness were subdued, and he withdrew socially, yet he remained sexually excitable. Immediately after injections, he would get an erection and masturbate. He would also get frustrated if the injection procedure did not happen on time, whimpering and crying like a baby. One of Frank's fellow chimps became so impatient while waiting for the morphine that he opened the box where the syringe was kept and started to pick it up before he was caught.

When the morphine injections were finally stopped, Frank went through the typical physiological signs of withdrawal and became unfriendly and unsociable as well. He resisted being handled and was markedly irritated by the most minor things in the laboratory. Still, his withdrawal was not as severe as that of most chimpanzees, who screamed and threw temper tantrums. One chimp became so unmanageable that the experimenter finally capitulated and led him to the injection room, where the animal was given a placebo injection. The chimp was temporarily quieted and even began picking at his wrist a little.

These tricks did more than momentarily calm the animal; they proved that some behaviors such as the wrist picking and initial quiescence after injection were conditioned behaviors that had become reflexively linked to the drug. Frank did not need such foolery and he managed to endure a less violent withdrawal. He regained his lost weight and his general health remained excellent. Several months later, he mated with a female from the lab colony and became the father of a normal, healthy baby chimp.

Getting into the Yale morphine program had been relatively easy for the chimps; staying there was also painless; getting out through the withdrawal was the difficult part. The cyclical addiction was not only an attempt to recapture a pleasurable state induced by the injections, but an attempt to alleviate the symptoms produced by the delay or omission of the injections.

The chimps had no chance to relapse once the experimenters chose to end the study, just as the seasonal poppy harvest or ripening of marula fruit may act to control bouts of intoxication in the wild. In studies conducted in other laboratories where primates have the opportunity to reinstate morphine injections, they will usually do so. They can maintain the state of addiction with little difficulty as long as adequate supplies are available.

The departure from that state creates a powerful motivation to restore it. After all, no animal wishes to be booted out of Paradise. If restoration is impossible, then some other means of escape from the hellish pains of withdrawal may be appealing. When morphine-dependent mice or rats are abruptly withdrawn, they manifest a rodent version of the abstinence syndrome. This syndrome includes the behaviors of hyperactivity, teeth chattering, "wet-dog" shakes, salivation, nasal discharge, and vocalizations whenever they are touched. The animals usually go through such withdrawal on the floors of their cages. However, if placed in a confined area such as on a platform, they jump!

The mice are jumping to escape the unpleasantness of withdrawal. They look and feel for a way out of the environment in which withdrawal is taking place. If placed in a vertical cylinder, these mice will start jumping to reach the top and escape. But if a cover is placed over the top or the cylinder is made higher, thus preventing the animals from escaping, they will not jump. Jumping is not so much a reflexive action elicited by withdrawal but a goal-directed search for escape from unpleasant feelings. The persistence of this motivation can be simply and reliably measured by the speed and number of jumps; in open cylinders that are just high enough to prevent the animals from going over the top, some addicted mice will jump fifty times in a ten-minute period.

A favored route of escape is known as relapse. But here again the environment can control much of the behavior. After withdrawal from morphine, rats are more likely to take morphine again when they are placed in the same "home" environment where the original addiction occurred than if exposed to morphine in a new environment. Human addicts who are detoxified and then returned to the same city environments are also more likely to relapse than those relocated to new communities. Sometimes the home environment can be a safe one if addiction occurs elsewhere. Soldiers addicted to heroin in Vietnam had low relapse rates when they returned to a different environment in the United States.

Overdose, either accidental or deliberate, provides a more permanent escape from the cycle of addiction and withdrawal, yet the environment can still be important. In cases of accidental overdose, deaths often occur following a dose of the drug that would not be expected to prove fatal in a tolerant addict. Sometimes death follows a dose that was tolerated on the previous day. These idiosyncratic reactions are partially influenced by the environment. Consider what happens with a single dose of heroin that will kill 96 percent of normal rats. When that dose is given to addicted rats in their home cages, tolerance will protect some, while cues previously associated with sublethal doses will reduce effects for others; only 32 percent die. But if the addicted rats receive that same dose in a new environment, they suffer a 64 percent mortality. It can be concluded that fatal overdoses are simply more likely to occur in new environments than in the familiar opium den or chimpanzee injection room.

Changes in preparations, doses, and methods of administration have also accounted for many deaths. For example, there were heartbreaking tragedies when the relatively benign poppy seed and milk drinks were eventually replaced by laudanum syrups to soothe infants in nineteenth-century England. These "quieting" syrups were helpful to mothers and babysitters alike, but the infants, many of whom started receiving the syrups on the first day of life, suffered an alarming mortality rate. The syrups were neither uniformly prepared nor precisely administered, and hundreds of infants died; thousands suffered addiction and withdrawal.

From opium extracts to morphine and heroin; from drinking the milk of Paradise to smoking and injecting its essences; from mammoths eating poppy seeds to new techniques for capturing elephants with darts filled with synthetic opiates more powerful than morphine; from opium eaters seeking to escape from the filthy surroundings of nineteenth-century slums to contemporary addicts looking for a way out from the miseries of withdrawal—the powers, promises, and problems of artificial paradise continue to brew.

In the novel *Twilight,* author Frank Danby tells the tragic story of a highly sensitive woman living under the influence of morphine. While the drug gives her beautiful visions, her perception of reality becomes more and more blurred, like the twilight before a desperate sleep. The tragedy was realized in the real life of Elizabeth Siddal.

Lizzie Siddal had flowing, flaming hair the color of Keats's. Her sensual and spiritual look was immortalized in the paintings by her husband Dante Gabriel Rossetti. It was said that she epitomized the medieval standard of beauty in vogue during the nineteenth century. But her health was poor—she suffered from tuberculosis and a spinal deformity—and she was insecure in her marriage to the famous artist. Rossetti's infidelities caused her great pain and depression. She turned more and more to laudanum, and after their first child was stillborn, she descended into addiction, taking as many as one hundred drops at a time.

At the age of twenty-eight she went to bed with an overdose of laudanum and a suicide note pinned to her nightgown. A few days earlier she had written a poem under the influence of the drug:

Life and night are falling from me,
Death and day are opening on me.
Wherever my footsteps come and go
Life is a stony road of woe.
   Lord, have I long to go?
Hollow hearts are ever near me,
Soulless eyes have ceased to cheer me:
   Lord, may I come to Thee?
Life and youth and summer weather
To my heart no joy can gather:
Lord, lift me from life's stony way.
Loved eyes, long closed in death, watch o'er me—
Holy Death is waiting for me—
   Lord, may I come to-day?
My outward life feels sad and still,
Like lilies in a frozen rill.

I am gazing upwards to the sun,
Lord, Lord, remembering my lost one.
   O Lord, remember me!
How is it in the unknown land?
Do the dead wander hand in hand?
Do we clasp dead hands, and quiver
With an endless joy for ever?
Is the air filled with the sound
Of spirits circling round and round?
Are there lakes, of endless song,
To rest our tired eyes upon?
Do tall white angels gaze and wend
Along the banks where lilies bend?
Lord we know not how this may be;

Good Lord, we put our faith in Thee—
O God, remember me.

After her death, Rossetti painted his wife as Dante's beloved Beatrice in *Beata Beatrix*. In the painting Lizzie is seen with death's messenger, a bird, which drops an opium poppy between her hands. Her face is glowing in the beatific paradise of opium intoxication. As told by her poem, it is a paradise without laughter.

Meanwhile, others of her day felt that a drug that induces both pleasurable visions *and* laughter might be better than opium. They chose hashish and marijuana for their ticket to Paradise.

7

Emerald Laughter

HASHISH AND MARIJUANA

1

"This will be deducted from your share in Paradise."

With these words, the good doctor opened a crystal vase and took a spoonful of greenish paste which he gave to each guest. The paste had the taste of cinnamon and cloves mixed with nutmeg, pistachio, sugar, orange juice, and butter. The coloring came from an "herb" called hashish, the resin from the marijuana plant. The guests had been coming to see the doctor once each month to eat this confection known as *dawamesc*. The name was Arabic. The setting was the elegant Hôtel Pimodan in Paris's Latin Quarter. The time was the middle of nineteenth century. The effects transcended all borders of space and time.

"Today we must die of laughing," proclaimed one guest as he burst into sobs, with tears running down the side of his nose.

Another participant, the novelist Théophile Gautier, saw a bluish haze, then a crowd of cherub heads appeared on the ceiling. They "had such comical expressions, such cheerful, and happy faces," explained Gautier, "that I could not help sharing their hiliarity."

The drawing room filled with visions of extraordinary figures whose antics stirred the maddest laughter. Everything seemed hysterically funny. Gautier's laughs burst out like thunder: "No, it's too funny; that's enough! My God, my God, how I am enjoying myself! More and more! Enough! I can't stand anymore. . . . Ho ho, ha ha, hee hee! What a good joke, what a beautiful play on words! Stop! I'm suffocating! I can't breathe! Don't look at me like that . . . or hold me in, I'm going to burst."

Deafening jeers and peals of laughter from other members of this infamous Club des Haschichins could be overheard in adjoining hotel rooms as the joyous frenzy reached its peak. Charles Baudelaire, who was present during these "paroxysms of mirth," found it useless to resist the silliness that gushed from his hashish brain. Later, as the laughter lost its resonance, the guests could only lie back and surrender to the visions with awe and wonderment. Gautier experienced the floating, ecstatic bliss of an intoxication that took him into heaven and the abyss of delight. He spent what seemed like an eternity in Paradise. For Baudelaire, the uncontrollable laughter gave way to a stupor, then a feeling of calm that was so transcendental it prompted him to conclude: "It will amaze no one that one last, supreme thought comes bursting from the dreamer's brain: 'I have become God!'"

Throughout it all the doctor, psychiatrist Jacques Joseph Moreau, kept careful records. Moreau learned that the subjective effects were directly related to the dosage of hashish. Small doses gave his guests feelings of happiness followed by excitement. Intermediate doses caused ideas to become dissociated as their minds started to wander. Their sense of time was distorted and they claimed minutes seemed like hours. Higher doses made their senses seem more acute, but thoughts and feelings blended together. Still more hashish, and fantastic images flooded their brains.

Moreau found that hashish possessed the characteristics of plunging one into a hallucinatory state while preserving the ability to observe and report events. He described hashish hallucinations as being similar to dreams wherein imagined visual, auditory, and tactile stimuli appear to be part of reality. This artificial world was the gateway between two modes of existence—the objective and the subjective—and by using hashish anyone could pass through the gates. While Moreau proposed using the drug to understand the realms of the mentally ill who were stuck somewhere between the two modes, his guests were more concerned with exploring their own artificial paradises. And when Moreau experimented with hashish himself, despite his scientific dedication, he couldn't stop laughing.

He had first learned about hashish while traveling through Arab countries. At that time, the term "hashish" referred to the entire *Cannabis* plant. It now refers to the resin-covered flowers or bracts of the plant, which are generally the most potent parts. Collecting the gooey resin was once a simple matter of rubbing against the plants, although more modern methods sift and press the resins from the plant. Marijuana is a more recent term derived from the Mexican-Spanish *mariguana,* meaning "intoxicant," and referring to a mixture of leaves, flowers, and stems. Both hashish and marijuana preparations can be eaten, drunk, or smoked, although it was eaten in the places visited by Moreau.

Cannabis is one of the few plants that legends say *was not* discovered by animals. Yet it attracts and affects animals as well as people, although most animals depend on people for their supplies. According to the Arab legend, the plant itself radiated an aura of joy and gaiety. The apocryphal discovery occurred in A.D. 1155. Haydar, an ascetic monk who founded a religious order of Sufis, discovered the plant dancing in the heat of a summer day. He learned to drink a tincture of the plant leaves in wine, a drink that made him laugh. Soon other Sufis were drinking from Haydar's "emerald" cup.

Medieval Muslim society disapproved. They labeled as intoxicated anyone "whose orderly speech is confused and who spills his hidden secret, or someone who does not know heaven from earth or length from width." By this definition, almost everyone who drank from the emerald cup was intoxicated. Floating to heaven in a hashish stupor was bad enough, but laughing riotously about it was unacceptable. Hashish intoxication, like alcohol, was forbidden. The Sufis became the heretics of Arab society.

The Sufis were isolated from society in much the same way hashish was thought to isolate the user from his rational mind. Since the mind is what distinguishes man from irrational animals, the effect of hashish was believed to turn its users into dumb animals. The literature of the Arab world celebrated these themes. In *A Thousand and One Nights,* a collection of tales supposedly told by the harem girl Scheherazade to her sultan, there are stories of people under the influence of hashish acting in dumb ways. For example, one story tells of an intoxicated fisherman who believes a moonlit street is a river and a dog is a big fish that he tries to catch.

Those who continued to use hashish were warned that it would damage them. To illustrate the point, one sage placed a quantity of hashish on a piece of liver and let it stay there for a while. Soon the liver was full of holes like a sponge. This was a silly experiment, but an impressive demonstration that would stick in the minds of the masses, not unlike modern television ads that portray drugs destroying brain cells like so many eggs in a frying pan. Users were also warned that hashish was strong enough to turn a lion into a beetle, and only a beast as dumb as an ox would graze upon such a plant. Accordingly, hashish was fit only as fodder for animals, to increase their appetite and fatten them. Animals were permitted to eat the drug because they were only dumb irrational beasts that did not laugh. But they did get intoxicated.

The stories that we collected about animals becoming intoxicated on hashish, marijuana, or other forms of *Cannabis* could keep Scheherazade spinning her tales for another thousand and one nights. The reports include the expected ones from users who describe the antics of their pets following exposure to marijuana. Cats display an initial catniplike playful excitement followed by sleep. Dogs follow nonexistent objects, fall asleep, then twitch and groan through their "dreams." Cows are more content. And captive iguanas act as marijuana "clocks" for Mexican Indians. The iguana is placed in the center of a circle of smokers. When it falls down under the influence, the participants know it is time to stop.

The higher the phylogenetic status of the animal, the more exaggerated—and suspect—the reports seem to become. One user shared his marijuana smoking with a pet chimpanzee, which reportedly became intoxicated and started "dancing." Another pet chimp matched his human keeper puff for puff until both were too intoxicated to continue. But if a super dose can be consumed, as one owner of a chimp swore in a letter to the editor of *High Times* magazine, the animal may start to utter several discernible English words! The owner was honest enough to admit that his own state of intoxication may have influenced his perception.

We can understand how animals may be fed marijuana or accidentally eat their owner's supplies. But will animals intentionally pursue the intoxicating herb? The question caused me to think of the many cartoons showing animals deliberately mimicking human users. One such cartoon, actually an ad for an electric device that turned marijuana into hashish, showed a cat and several other animals smoking joints and laughing. In 1974 I found myself in a living cartoon with such an animal. I thought it was a rodent although he had no name, not even, as yet, a specific identification. He was only a suspect, accused of taking confiscated marijuana from a police department vault in San Jose, California. Evidence bags of marijuana had been broken into and the contents were scattered or missing. Although the police were baffled as well as irritated about the lost evidence, the method of operation used by this suspect was similar to other cases I had read about. Rats or mice were also suspected of similar activities in the Bexar County Courthouse in San Antonio and in police departments around the country.

Many of these cases were enthusiastically covered by wire services as well as local papers, which made references to "inebriated," "happy," "addicted," "mellow," "stuporous," "spaced-out," "high," "stoned," "dope-crazed," or otherwise intoxicated rodents. The rats in San Antonio were seen "swinging on a flagpole." A mouse was observed staggering after a foray into contraband marijuana stored in the office of the District Attorney of Sequoyah County, Oklahoma, and *Time* published a cartoon of the "happy" and "delirious" rodent.

Most if not all of these descriptions could be dismissed as examples of journalistic hyperbole and good humor. However, since no one had ever caught or studied one of these animals, the San Jose suspect was too close to my laboratories at UCLA to ignore. I wanted to know why the animal was eating such enormous quantities of marijuana. Was it intoxicated? Addicted?

The suspect, a lovable field mouse dubbed "Marty Mouse," had nibbled a destructive path through cartons of evidence before nesting in large bricks of confiscated marijuana. He was snared by a marijuana and peanut butter trap. After the San Jose police caught him, Marty captured headlines around the world. I brought him to my lab at UCLA despite the protests of a "Free Marty" fan club outfitted with T-shirts and bumper stickers. Marty had been sentenced by a San Jose judge to begin a life term as a police mascot after my tests. While fans sought a pardon from President Ford, I began the experiments.

The results? Marty readily ate marijuana seeds, a favorite treat for birds, rodents, livestock, and even fish. Rich in edible oils yet low in psychoactive cannabinoids, the seeds failed to change Marty's behavior as long as he could also eat normal laboratory chow. When restricted to an exclusive diet of marijuana plants, he ate the seeds first and then other parts of the plants. Marty may not have liked the initial taste of marijuana leaves and stems, but it had been the least bitter and most nutritious substance available in the vault, sustaining him with proteins, sugars, amino acids, calories, and a vitamin or two. In the vault it was unnecessary to eat more than a few ounces of marijuana; the bulk of the "grass" he took had been used for bedding material.

Now, in the lab, marijuana provided him with the same nutrition, as well as substantial amounts of psychoactive ingredients. He was following a relatively safe feeding strategy, eating more seeds and stems than leaves. Nonetheless, his behavior started to change. He appeared quieter and less active. The counter on the exercise running wheel attached to his cage recorded a significant drop in daily activity. His mood became erratic: first quiet and withdrawn, then irritable and aggressive. His head twitched frequently—the rodent sign of hallucinations. He slept more and seemed disinterested in breeding with a lab mouse, Mary Jane—so named in order to appease the regular UCLA press conferences held about Marty. When returned to a diet of lab chow and marijuana, Marty continued to feed on the chow and seeds, nibbling infrequently on the other parts of the plant. He was demonstrating the experimental eating of drug plants that so often comes with familiarity. His behavior returned to its normal peppiness, although the odd head-twitch was suggestive of an acquired taste for a psychoactive effect.

I was tempted to conclude that Marty was using marijuana as both a food and drug, but he was only one animal. Pet owners' stories aside, I was uncertain if he was simply exhibiting idiosyncratic behavior or some general appreciation for marijuana's nutritional and pharmacological effects. Although I had to return him to the San Jose police, I was now eager to study other animals to find out more about marijuana's attraction.

Infrequent use of marijuana may be tolerated by animals such as Marty, but chronic use—some call it abuse—was thought to have turned the Hawaiian mongoose into a mad fiend. Mongooses are smelly, unloved carnivores who play havoc with the ecology by eating anything—including each other. Marijuana growers on Maui suspected that these bandits raided the fields, destroyed harvested plants, and invaded homes looking for more. The case against the mongoose was supported by evidence of mongoose scats loaded with marijuana seeds.

The growers invited my team to observe and we set time-lapse cameras to record the action in any field where we found mongoose scats. While the mongoose is active only during the day, the cameras were equipped with light-amplification devices to record nocturnal activity, as a favor to our hosts who suspected there might be human bandits as well. Some plants were reportedly dragged away by mongooses or weaselly humans and never seen again. The actual perpetrators, however, were not on the original list of suspects.

Rattus rattus, or rats! Under the cover of darkness, rats mischievously stripped the plants for the seeds. At sunrise a few stragglers, still feeding or perhaps slowed by intoxication, were quickly dispatched by the stealthy mongooses on their morning patrols. With lightning speed the mongooses would seize a rat by the top of its head and audibly crush the cranium. The mongooses ignored the marijuana; the seeds in their scats came from the breakfast rats.

Not every field investigation worked out the way we planned. The mongooses were not intoxicated. And the slowness of the rats may have been more a function of preoccupation with feeding than intoxication itself. But our cameras also caught a host of sparrows raiding the plants after they had gone to seed, robbing all the seeds from the top branches within minutes. Instead of falling down, the birds appeared excited and stimulated by the seeds.

This avian love for marijuana seeds has endured for thousands of years. Whenever seed-eating birds have been given the opportunity to feast on the marijuana seeds, they have done so with relish. The scientists in Moreau's time reported that birds fed hemp seeds developed amorous inclinations to the point of "erotomania." Modern pigeon breeders call it "pigeon candy" and claim it turns any bird into a successful breeder. But humans have been using hemp seeds as an aphrodisiac since ancient Greek and Roman times, and was this not just another case of exuberant anthropomorphism? Bird owners and marijuana growers insist it is not; they claim that hemp seeds produce a mild intoxication in the birds. Owners report that their parrots and parakeets talk more; lovebirds are more affectionate; and songbirds sing better when the seeds are available.

The birds are singing for some very good nutritional and pharmacological reasons. The seeds are rich in fatty acids and oil that give a gloss and sheen to the bird's feathers as well as an overabundance of calories for their high-energy metabolism. Small quantities of cannabinoids, including tetrahydrocannabinol (THC), the ingredient responsible for the major psychoactive effects in humans, are also present in both the seeds and the green gummy calyx that surrounds the wild seeds. By eating only a teaspoon of seeds, birds can enjoy the nutritional benefits while consuming enough cannabinoids that they become affected by the stimulant properties as well.

I decided to look more carefully at the effects of this pigeon candy and, while still a student, went to see Mr. Nodell. Alan Nodell was the local pigeon breeder who supplied the Psychology Department at Dalhousie University in Halifax, Nova Scotia, with homer pigeons. Some were descended from pigeons that once flew as messengers for the Royal Canadian Air Force. Mr. Nodell was a kind, gray-haired man with a plump chest. His thick glasses barely corrected his nearsightedness and, even after years of acquaintance, I was uncertain whether he recognized me. He always had on four or five tattered coats, each torn just enough to allow one to see the next coat underneath. The heavy coats, which he wore even in the mild Nova Scotia summers, caused him to waddle about the lofts like some giant bespectacled pigeon. Mr. Nodell was the first to acquaint me with the history of pigeon candy, although he was no longer able to get it for his five breeding lofts. When I showed him several sacks of marijuana seeds, courtesy of the United Nations Narcotics Division, his eyes teared and he readily granted me permission to conduct feeding studies on a loft of his domestic pigeons.

In laboratory studies with caged pigeons, I had previously determined that they prefer hemp seeds to all other major seed types. After feeding, the pigeons were routinely placed in small activity cages that electronically monitored their movements. The increased activity was consistent with the predicted stimulant effects. I was worried because the principles of behavior I was studying were established in pigeon experiments conducted by B. F. Skinner, who fed his birds a 10 percent hemp mixture. He was unaware of the psychoactive properties of these seeds and I wondered to what extent the foundations of Skinnerian psychology were made under the influence. Simple tasks such as pecking at a small illuminated panel seemed unaffected, but I *knew* the animals were changing in very subtle ways. Now I wanted to see what would happen in a social environment where complex behaviors are often more sensitive to drug effects.

The loft population totaled 120 pigeons with equal numbers of hens and cocks. There were several pairs incubating eggs or rearing chicks in nesting boxes located throughout the loft. All had access to communal supplies of mixed grain, grit, and water. I positioned myself in a blind within the spacious loft itself and conducted my observations over several cold winter months. I soon discovered the reason for Mr. Nodell's many coats. Forced to wear a gray thermal jumpsuit, as well as a gas mask to filter out the pigeon dust—which could cause a variety of respiratory infections—I looked more like a pigeon than did Mr. Nodell.

Initially, a communal bowl was filled once each day with a precise weight of hemp seeds—and was emptied by the birds in less time than it took me to fill it. I tried giving selected pigeons individual portions in their private boxes, but it became too difficult keeping the other birds away. Finally, I adopted a procedure whereby individual pigeons would be removed from the loft, fed hemp seeds away from the others, then released back into the loft. The hemp-fed birds were certainly easier to handle than the others. They appeared to make more pleasure calls and coos. At the same time they remained alert and perky from the stimulant effects of the small amounts of THC in the seeds. They also flocked to me whenever I appeared from my blind. As I took a selected bird to the special feeding area, several birds would usually try to follow me— I had become a Pied Piper with promises of pigeon candy.

Since the seeds did little else to change behavior and Skinner's data seemed secure, I increased the dosage by injecting the pigeons with a concentrated extract of *Cannabis;* others got a control injection of saline. Low doses are exciting, but high doses tend to quiet behavior. The *Cannabis*-treated pigeons remained docile and easy to handle, perhaps too gentle as they withdrew from social interactions in the loft. They spent less time with their mates and chicks, but more time grooming themselves. They also engaged in less flying and, consequently, got into fewer fights with other pigeons in the public areas. After the injections stopped, these changes gradually disappeared and, in three or four days, the loft was back to normal. If hemp seeds were pleasing candies, then *Cannabis* extracts were sickening syrups—the pigeons had stopped following me. From these studies I concluded that the low doses of marijuana seeds clearly benefited the birds with a nutritious, pleasant stimulation and they seemed to know it. I was equally firm in my belief that the high-dose injections constituted abuse and no pigeon would willingly self-administer such quantities even if it could find them in nature.

2

The *Cannabis* plant has a way of naturally controlling use and preventing abuse by animals. Rabbits, moles, squirrels, groundhogs, and raccoons will forage on the seedlings, much to the chagrin of growers. These animals do not seem to get intoxicated on the small amounts of THC present in the developing plants. As the plants grow, they develop hard, fibrous stems that deter such raiders who might otherwise experience behavioral effects. When fully developed, the plants have other defenses. Mature plants exude a characteristic aroma that is aversive to many animals and keeps them away from the especially intoxicating amounts of THC that develop at that time. The aroma is derived from glandular hairs, which probably developed in the wild to protect the fruit against herbivores. The glands produce most of the THC and other cannabinoids in the form of resins. The resins send at least seventeen chemicals into the air around the plant to yield an odor that is not only distinctive but intoxicating. Farmers working in hemp fields have experienced headaches, vertigo, confusion, and delirium. While such an odor may function to deter some potential herbivores, it attracts many others.

In 1951 a string of horses and mules from a Greek infantry unit followed their leader into a pasture containing wild *Cannabis indica,* a particularly potent species of hemp. After grazing for only a few minutes, the animals were stricken with a sudden malaise. They appeared intoxicated: some were trembling, cold, and covered in sweat; a few were foaming at the mouth; most were falling down. Eight horses and seven mules never got up; they died within thirty minutes. These animals had perished in their first encounter with marijuana.

Those that survive such episodes by following good herbivore feeding strategies may become frequent visitors to the plants and continue use without abuse. Cows and horses in Hawaii selectively feed on the marijuana flowers, which give them a case of mild staggers but are otherwise tolerated because the flowers are not available for more than a few weeks each year. Lambs in eastern European hemp fields will repeatedly browse the plants and become "gay and crazy." They survive because their meals are mixed with other pasturage, thus resulting in low doses. Deer infiltrate marijuana fields in North America and monkeys raid the ones in South America, yet both animals tolerate snacks on the plant by selecting the tender, younger, and relatively less potent top leaves. The marijuana growers are not happy with these hungry visitors and are on a constant vigil for signs of their presence. Yet the most destructive enemies are the armies of ants and the hordes of flying and crawling insects that invade the plants, whether they grow in outdoor fields or in sheltered indoor gardens. We even found them in one of the most protected areas in the world for *Cannabis* cultivation, the Rapti Valley in Nepal.

The Rapti Valley is a dense forest jungle situated high in the Himalayas, where legends claim life survived the biblical deluge. Inhabited by leopards, snakes, and poisonous spiders, the valley is defended by these residents against most intruders. Rich, resinous *Cannabis* has been growing there for as long as anybody remembers. The natives still collect the hashish in the traditional way. Cupping their hands together as if in prayer, they hold the resinous bracts in their palms and gently rub back and forth. Their palms are soon black with hashish, which is then rolled into shiny spheres the size of golf balls.

Our observers purchased these Nepalese "temple balls" in the early 1970s before sales were outlawed. If the valley's lush foliage did not suggest images of Paradise, the names of the accommodations in Kathmandu certainly did. The balls were purchased at the government-registered Eden Hashish Centre, located near the Eden Hotel and Restaurant. The hotel even provided a Heavenly Pleasure Room where the hashish, as well as local forms of marijuana, could be smoked. Instead of smoking, our team carefully dissected several kilos of hashish under a field microscope. The royal temple balls, made from the very "nectar of the gods," were full of bugs!

Bits and pieces of mashed insects had been trapped in the sticky resin before the plant was harvested. The hashish shopkeeper was as reluctant to believe the view through our microscope as the faithful priests had been to look through Galileo's telescope. The gods sent the hemp plant to man so that he might attain delight. One did not need a lens to know that the nectar was pure, any more than one needed proof that the Earth was the center of the universe. The growers were more willing to acknowledge insect problems with their plants, but they claimed that in this Eden, where *Cannabis* grows in such abundance, plants that are obviously infested are simply discarded. They attributed our findings to be the fault of greedy traffickers who sacrificed traditional quality control for fast profits.

Most growers in North and South America cannot afford to throw plants away. They must fight the insects, a fight that has become a series of never-ending battles. Even on the marijuana plantation at the University of Mississippi, a miniature Rapti Valley protected by the U.S. government, red ants destroyed a good part of the plants during one of the early years of the cultivation program.

Journalists and marijuana aficionados have enjoyed speculating about these "intoxicated" insects, elevating them to the status of humans who intentionally pursue the effects. Writers have joked about "bees with a buzz" in reference to bees that are attracted to *Cannabis* pollen, which is rich in cannabinoids. The bee honey, when collected and assayed, has been shown to contain traces of THC but there is no evidence that the bees are disturbed by their feeding. The United Nations studied the habits of marijuana-eating insects and agreed that intoxication was not a problem for these pests. The insects use the plants for food, and, while they may overeat, they seem immune to the pharmacological effects.

Grasshoppers, however, *are* affected by feeding on marijuana. In Czechoslovakia I met an old hemp farmer who told me tales of grasshoppers that could jump to spectacular heights because of marijuana. He showed me a small patch of wild plants where I could camp out and see for myself. As I started spying on the plants with my field microscope and camera, Russian soldiers on a nearby hill began watching my every movement.

I had read that the odor of European hemp is stimulating enough to produce euphoria and this was why the harvesting of hemp was always associated with social festivities, dancing, and even erotic playfulness. The ancestors of my Russian overseers had used a hashishlike candy, *guc-kand,* to put women in a "happy mood," to keep children from crying, and to put young boys in a painless sleep before circumcision. They had also used a "happy porridge" made from hashish as a strong aphrodisiac. Now I almost wished the soldiers—who seemed as nervous as I felt—could catch a whiff of these happy plants that were slowly changing my mood. I found myself mildly intoxicated. But unless I was having negative hallucinations—that is, not seeing things that were really there—I did not see a single grasshopper. Instead I was rapidly discovering another vestigial effect of marijuana: paranoia. I was simply too nervous to work. I waved good-bye to the farmer. The Russian soldiers waved back.

Several years later I found myself in another marijuana patch, this one consisting of two hundred plants hidden between rows of corn in the midwestern United States. It was summertime and the grasshoppers were jumping. And they were eating the marijuana! But if the United Nations ever dreamed of sending Mosaic plagues of grasshoppers to destroy *Cannabis,* they would have to find a more finicky pest. The grasshoppers were eating everything, including the corn and tall grasses. I observed several executing unusual jumps from the marijuana leaves. Although they did not jump to the heights of the Czech tales, they were erratic: jumping repeatedly, quickly, and to no particular place. After netting a few, I discovered the reason was mechanical, not biochemical. The legs of the grasshoppers had acquired some sticky resin from the marijuana leaves, gumming up the jumping mechanism as well as reducing the amount of chirping they could produce by scraping their legs. In the insects' efforts to clean themselves, bits of resin had also adhered to the antennae and abdominal hearing membranes, further confusing their behavior. The grasshoppers were suffering miserable side effects without even the main beneficial effect of a "happy" intoxication.

It was unusual that few other insects visited these outdoor plants. I had seen more insect pests on marijuana growing in greenhouses or even in the protected environment of indoor hydroponic gardens. Further inspection revealed the startling reason why. Assassins! Hidden among the bushy leaves were wide, boat-shaped bugs with little beaks. These hunters, belonging to the Assassin family, prey on other insects by thrusting their beaks forward to pierce the victim's skin. Their bites are quick; sucking the blood from the victim can take longer. Other members of the Assassin family are known as masked hunters. These quiet assassins, camouflaged with pieces of lint, can slip into your bed. If a bedbug isn't available for a quick meal, these hunters can inflict painful bites on your lips as you sleep, hence their other name of "kissing bugs." Some Assassins are referred to as conenoses because their head and mouthparts form conelike protrusions, conjuring up comic images of dunces. The death and diseases they carry are no laughing matter. If ever a group of bugs could embody the love and death and laughter associated with *Cannabis* folklore it would be these Assassins.

The Assassin bugs were no more intoxicated with *Cannabis* than were the killers belonging to a religious sect of the same name in ancient Persia and Syria. The leader of this sect was Hasan-ibn-Sabah, a charismatic Shiite scholar known as the "Old Man of the Mountains." In a mountain stronghold, Hasan trained his terrorist fighters and promised them entry to Paradise in exchange for their service. According to Marco Polo's account and several subsequent interpretations, the stronghold contained a garden paradise where the recruit was drugged with a hashish potion and allowed to savor an artificial paradise complete with sensuous girls. Afterward, he was brought before the Old Man who promised to readmit him to the garden, provided his orders were carried out.

The members of the sect called themselves *fidais*, the "devoted ones." Their enemies called them Assassins, a derogatory name for loud, unruly people and derived from the Arabic word *hashishiyyin,* "the hashishers." But, contrary to continuing myths about their use of hashish, the Assassins were not allowed to take hashish before going out on a mission. Like the Assassin bugs, Hasan's killers would disguise themselves, then slip into the enemy's camp and wait, sometimes for days or months, for the right moment to strike with their daggers into the hearts of the victims.

The Assassins probably knew that the intoxication is a privilege reserved for those who can afford to avoid physical responsibilities. They did not go to work under the influence of the drug for the same reasons that animals in the wild, who must fight for survival, do not overdo their ingestion of intoxicating plants. After all, laughing inside the safety of a hotel room or garden is one thing. But doing it in the middle of an enemy camp is too risky. Hashish may have produced a delightful vision of Paradise, but the mental effects are experienced at the expense of physical capabilities. Low doses may stimulate and excite; higher doses produce visual difficulties, disorientation, and incoordination. Most research shows that *Cannabis* and its ingredients have potent antiaggressive actions. Rats trained to kill mice, for example, will either refuse to kill or else do such a sloppy job that the Old Man would not have been proud of them.

Reactions to *Cannabis* are not all-or-none. As we have seen with the other major intoxicants, the dose is critical. During the 1830s, while the last remnant of the Assassin sect led unsuccessful uprisings against the Shah of Iran, Sir William O'Shaughnessy, a physician serving with the British East India Company in Calcutta, began a series of important studies. O'Shaughnessy was interested in treating patients with *Cannabis,* but first he tested the effects of this new medicine on animals. His pioneering experiments established that the effects of *Cannabis* in animals or people were dependent on the dosages. Low doses produced intoxicating effects. Higher doses, as in alcoholic extracts of the leaves, produced great difficulty in movements and a generalized sedation with insensibility to pain. Dogs could be rendered unconscious for more than a day if only given enough. It was not surprising when subsequent researchers found that animals were reluctant to take doses stronger than those found in the natural products of seeds and plants.

It is relatively easy to get mice such as Marty Mouse to ingest low-dose seeds but almost impossible to coax them into taking high-dose extracts. Rats will readily drink very dilute solutions of hashish extracts, but when offered a choice between a concentrated hashish solution and water, they prefer the water. No amount of experimental manipulation can persuade them to overcome this aversion. When small amounts of *Cannabis* were mixed into food and given to chacma baboons in South Africa, the baboons ate their food, gained weight, and appeared normal. When larger amounts were mixed into the food, baboons ate less, lost weight, and became apathetic. These results have nothing to do with unpleasant tastes; rats and primates find the high-dose intoxications uncomfortable, whether they come from oral doses or from injections.

Injections bypass taste problems, yet rats and monkeys remain reluctant to self-administer THC in this way. When equipped with surgically implanted devices that automatically inject high doses of THC into the veins, the animals generally refuse to press levers that will initiate the injections. Inhaling THC seems no more desirable to these animals than injecting it. Monkeys and apes have been trained to smoke *Cannabis* preparations for food or water rewards, but they stop smoking it as soon as the food or water are no longer available.

There are exceptions. After first being rewarded with food, rhesus monkeys were trained to smoke hashish. This made the monkeys docile and inactive. After the food reward was discontinued, most monkeys stopped smoking, but one continued puffing on the hashish for another sixteen weeks. That monkey was unusual; most animals will not continue taking *Cannabis* when the intoxication starts to compete with the ability to carry out normal behaviors.

Studies with THC have confirmed that intoxication creates postural changes, ataxia, and abnormal movements in a variety of species, similar to the effects we saw with other hallucinogens. Pigeons are perky around hemp seeds but high doses of THC cause them to lie on their ventral surfaces in a state of flaccid paralysis. When aroused, the birds can still move, but in unflattering ways. Instead of their graceful and reliable flights, Mr. Nodell's homing pigeons would dive-bomb to the ground and sit there. At dosages that produce obvious hallucinatory behavior in animals, motor activity is decreased. Dogs spend more time barking at moving objects than chasing them, monkeys stop scratching and grooming themselves, and other animals become transfixed by sensory stimuli of all sorts.

Animals might still be able to escape from dangerous situations, but under the influence of these high THC doses they are not particularly adept at avoiding them. Sometimes they sit and stare until it is too late. If a warning light in an experimental box goes on, signaling to a rat that it must press a lever in order to avoid an upcoming electric shock— a task it has learned to do in a sober state—it may not press the lever when intoxicated.

THC causes animals to misjudge events; pigeons wait too long to respond to buzzers or lights that tell them food is available for brief periods; and rats turn the wrong way in mazes. Monkeys and chimpanzees ignore previous training and press levers or execute other trained tasks at the wrong times or at the wrong speeds. Learning new tasks, particularly complicated ones, is difficult for the intoxicated animals and they sometimes fail to remember how to solve simple puzzles that they had previously mastered.

Throughout these tests, the intoxicated animals often appear distracted and preoccupied as they do when they are tested with doses of hallucinogens like LSD. Some of Mr. Nodell's pigeons treated with high doses of THC seemed almost hypnotized and didn't blink an eye or bat a wing at my approaching hands. When monkeys were given THC, their eyes seemed to follow imaginary objects hovering in the air. If only one could find out what they were "seeing"; would it really be more important than avoiding an electric shock or missing a meal?

I gave a group of rhesus monkeys in the laboratory an opportunity to tell us something about the nature of these perceptions. The monkeys would sit in a special chair at a desk. On the desk would be two M & M chocolate candies. At least that is what it looked like from the monkey's perspective. Actually, only one M & M was real; the other was a three-dimensional projection arranged by parabolic mirrors hidden inside the desk. The illusion was remarkably convincing. The two candies looked much the same in terms of color, size, and shape. When the desk was pushed up to the chair, the monkey could easily reach out and grab the real M & M; if it reached for the illusory M & M, its hand would only go through the projection. Initially, the monkeys—like the children and adults who have played with this illusion device in toy stores and museums—made the mistade of grasping at the projected object as if it were real.

In order to grasp the real candy correctly before the desk was pushed back out of reach, the monkeys had to learn a difficult discrimination. The real and illusory objects differed from each other along very subtle dimensions. Real M & Ms were more vivid, brighter, coherent, and concrete than their unreal counterparts. It is precisely these dimensions that scientists and philosophers have used to distinguish real perceptions from dreams and hallucinations. Real perceptions, like real M & Ms, are more solid and veridical than the artificial paradises of the Club des Haschichins or mirages of chocolate candy.

Our monkeys had a confusing time differentiating between the real and illusory candies. Yet, after several months, they mastered the discrimination and learned to reach quickly for the real treats, which they either ate right away or stuffed into their cheek pouches for a later snack. The test proved to be extremely sensitive to injections of THC. Low doses impaired the ability of the monkeys to pick the real M & M. When their grasp literally went through the projection of the illusory M & M, they would display facial expressions of surprise. It also frustrated the animals; Groucho, a six-month-old male rhesus, would give an alarm bark and kick the desk whenever he missed. As the dose of THC increased, the monkeys took longer and longer to decide which M & M to go for and, increasingly, it would be the wrong choice. At high doses, they seemed to lose interest in the test. They performed only at chance levels and appeared just as interested in the mirage as in the real candy, often playing with the projected image by poking and probing it with their fingers. The frustration also disappeared. Groucho would emit a short series of grunting sounds between 0.5 and 1.5 kilocycles. The sounds are called *girning*, noises associated with pleasure and contentment. Groucho's girning was laughter to my ears.

The laughter vanished when I experimented with more extreme dosages. While most other behavior was also suppressed and I could not use these dosages in the formal tests with the illusion device, I noticed the monkeys adopting a familiar stance. The extreme doses of

THC caused the monkeys to assume a typical crouched posture in the chair: they leaned forward and supported their heads with one hand, a posture reminiscent of Rodin's *Thinker*. If left undisturbed they would remain in this "thinking monkey" position for sixty to ninety minutes; their gaze was fixed and they appeared lost in thought. I, too, wondered what they were seeing and thinking.

Years before I had asked this same question about Mr. Nodell's pigeons when, in the midst of their intoxication from the *Cannabis* extract, they would sit on the bottom of the loft and peck at "things" in the air. Pigeons can fly through these gates of perception, so to speak, and report information on what they see. Because a pigeon's visual system is similar to those of monkeys and people, psychopharmacologists have used this animal to study the effects of drugs on vision. To find out what pigeons might be seeing during a *Cannabis* session, I arranged a series of elaborate experiments with Mr. Nodell's birds. In one of the early preliminary studies, the pigeons were trained to watch a screen on which visual stimuli were rear-projected by a special slide projector. The stimuli might be geometric forms, colors, or even complex patterns. Several response keys were located near the screen and each key displayed a different visual stimulus. One of the keys would always display the same pattern that was shown on the screen, and the pigeon was trained to peck at that key, thus matching its response to the sample projected on the screen. When the pigeon pecked the key that correctly matched the screen's pattern, it was rewarded with some grain.

After learning this "matching-to-sample" procedure, the birds were injected with various drugs and then periodically shown blank screens. They had been trained not to peck a key when the screen was blank. Under the influence of THC or a *Cannabis* extract they pecked certain keys when the screen was blank. In effect, their key pecks were indicating that they saw something on the screen and it looked like the pattern on the particular response key they were pecking. When provided with a vast array of different patterns on the response keys to match to whatever they were seeing on the blank screen, the pigeons pecked out a particular message over and over again: blue geometric patterns.

Now I arranged a similar experiment for Groucho. Instead of pecking the response keys, Groucho could simply tap them with his fingers to earn his reward of fruit juice. During the test with THC, he tapped out his vision: *blue geometric patterns!*

I conducted similar experiments with human volunteers. Instead of pecking or tapping, they were trained in a very precise psychophysical language to describe the colors, forms, and movements they saw in their mind's eye while lying down in a completely dark room. When it came to reporting drug-induced hallucinations, these subjects were reliable observers, called *psychonauts,* and we shall meet them again in a later chapter. Here they were given capsules of THC or marijuana cigarettes. They laughed and called out their measurements of the images: "lattice-tunnels overlaying repeating lines pulsating at 470 millimicrons"—*blue geometric patterns!* And they were moving!

The human subjects were describing the same bluish haze that entertained Gautier and other members of the Club des Haschichins in the salon of the Hôtel Pimodan. Out of that atmosphere arose geometric arrangements and a carnival of images. The images pulsated and changed so quickly that neither Gautier nor the psychonauts could keep pace with them. Their descriptions gave way to feelings and emotions; first laughter, then an experience of floating out of their bodies.

While Gautier and his literary colleagues were exploring the romance of these feelings, another small club of Frenchmen was using dosages of hashish ten times greater to follow the soul's ecstatic journey out of the body into a spiritual world. Under the tutelage of psycho-pharmacologist Louis-Alphonse Cahagnet, these subjects documented visions of death and the afterlife, experiences identical to those known as "near-death experiences." The prototypical experience started with the user being pulled out of time into a sacred stillness. A feeling of peace and a sense of well-being captured the soul as it separated from the body, then flung it into a bright light at a moment of supreme happiness.

Some subjects find it impossible to describe all that happens; others describe a panoramic review of their lives, encounters with departed spirits, celestial music, and profound visions and thoughts. Geometrically sculpted images introduce themes of cosmic importance. The forms parade across the mind's eye so fast that the cherubs melt into gargoyles, then a crypt of one's own body. The blue geometric forms become towering cathedrals filled with the white light of the Universal Being. Man is but a mite here and none of Cahagnet's subjects dared to show the arrogance of Baudelaire when he proclaimed that he had become God.

Cahagnet's subjects recognized the hashish visions for what they were: projections of stored memories and images in the brain, enormously enjoyable and creative, but no more capable of being grasped than an illusory M & M. Nobody really died during these intoxications, and few *Cannabis* users have ever suffered lethal overdoses. The visions evaporated and Cahagnet's subjects returned to their bodies and earthly lives, enriched by the experience and the memories they kept.

When Cahagnet's subjects explored the beyond within, their outward behavior had been identical to that of the animals receiving high doses of hashish or THC—quiet and still, almost mesmerized. While we may never know what else birds and monkeys see besides blue geometric patterns, their *Cannabis* experiences may very well reflect the same joy and happiness that characterizes human intoxications. After all, we share the same drive and pursuit for the drug, as well as similar brain mechanisms, so why shouldn't the experiences created by such common biology be alike? Darwin viewed laughter as a counterpart to discomfort, a way in which the species communicates a state of well-being. Konrad Lorenz saw it as an expression of social unity, a way to thwart aggression. The pursuit of the taming and comforting effects of intoxication from hemp seeds and other mild forms of *Cannabis* might just be the animal kingdom's way of trying to laugh.

8

Forced March

COCA AND COCAINE

1

Coca is a rather plain-looking shrub that has fascinated us for thousands of years. It is different from any other drug plant. We, as well as other species, control it, getting benefits without abuse or death; however, once the cocaine alkaloid is freed from the leaf, attraction turns to abuse and addiction. Sometimes the hunger for cocaine is so great and the supplies so enormous that parts of the planet itself seem blanketed by the drug. That blanket obscures the basic reason for the cocaine fever that grips so many species who like the plant but love the alkaloid. It is simply the nicest chemical gift that the brain can receive. Coca was just as appreciated in Incan society as it is among modern Andean peoples. The alkaloid was just as welcomed at the turn of the century as it is today. The drive to pursue the intoxication from both leaf and powder has been as unchanging as parts of the planet itself.

Consider a scene in Antarctica: Landsat satellite images of Antarctica are so still they are almost boring. Nothing seems to change very quickly. From space, the rifts in the glaciers and ice streams appear like giant sled tracks frozen in time. They have not moved far since 1909. From the perspective of explorers on the ground at that time, marks from sledges were lifesaving trail guides through a world where contours of snow and ice changed with every gust of freezing wind.

In January 1909, Sir Ernest Shackleton was leading an expedition across a glacier to a mountain depot where food had been stockpiled. Having gone without food for forty hours, he and his men were not only hungry, they were also sunburned, frostbitten, and exhausted from the physical strain. They had prepared for such a crisis and proceeded to dose themselves hourly with "Forced March" tablets. The tablets were cocaine. The manufacturer had advertised the tablets as capable of sustaining strength without a subsequent depression. The men kept going, reached the depot, and survived what Shackleton described as the hardest and most trying days of their lives.

Twentieth-century explorers were not the first to experience the stimulation of cocaine. Sir Clements Markham, who was the president of the Royal Geographical Society, had accepted Shackleton for an earlier Antarctic expedition. Markham was intimately familiar with the long history of coca use. Earlier in his career, he chewed coca while he traveled throughout Peru, a land where Indians had been chewing coca and walking the rocky Andean trails with their llamas for thousands of years.

There is archaeological evidence that early man used coca in 3000 B.C. Hunters and gatherers almost certainly found the plant several thousand years earlier. Initial use of coca probably started around 5000 B.C., at about the same time llamas became domesticated. It may have been by watching flocks of llamas that coca's properties were originally discovered. A story told by Peruvian Indians mentions that coca was first used by llamas traveling in the montaña, the high jungle region of the Andean slopes and foothills. The animals were deprived of their normal forage and sampled the coca. The coca leaves sustained the animals, and the humans copied the coca-eating behavior.

Coca is a collective term for over 250 species of plants; some 200 are native to the American tropics. Aided by the chemical defenses of its alkaloids, coca flourished in the continuously moist forest conditions found in the montaña. The major species, Erythroxylum coca, known for its concentrations of cocaine alkaloids, originated as a wild plant in eastern Peru. In the wild, coca takes the form of slender trees or under-story shrubs. The plants are not readily accessible to any but the most hungry of animals.

Besides the llamas, there are legends of hungry sloths and monkeys finding and using coca. But no matter who was the first to find the plant, all would have benefited from a nourishing meal, especially when they ventured to high altitudes where other food was in scant supply. Nutritional analysis has revealed that 100 grams of coca leaves contain 305 calories, 18.9 grams of protein, and 42.6 grams of carbohydrates, and satisfy the human Recommended Dietary Allowance for calcium, iron, phosphorus, riboflavin, and vitamins A and E. The coca leaves could have sustained the Peruvian travelers. Indeed, coca is higher in nutrients than at least fifty other foods common to Latin America. Although the full complement of these nutrients may not be absorbed via the normal practice of chewing and sucking the leaves, other minor alkaloidal ingredients in coca increase blood glucose levels and help combat cold and hunger. Coca also contains a small amount of cocaine, the major alkaloid responsible for the stimulation.

Do the hungry animals experience intoxication along with the nourishment? Birds, those great lovers of hemp seeds, are also fond of coca seeds and they love to pilfer them from newly sown fields. But there are no real changes in avian behavior. Insects attack the sprouting coca plant, and I collected several folktales that told of stimulated ants, beetles, and moth larvae. In an effort to find out the degree to which these pests are stimulated, our teams monitored several clandestine greenhouses and outdoor gardens operated by coca growers in California. The growers told us the expected stories about "coked up" insects, but the aphids, mites, and leafhoppers we found on the coca seemed normal.

In one of the outdoor patches we found several coca plants that had been attacked by garden snails, a common pest in California backyards. By now I was very familiar with snail behavior and I immediately recognized that these were no ordinary snails. They *seemed* stimulated and were feeding on the coca leaves in broad daylight, a most brazen act for these nocturnal creatures. I rescued several dozen snails and brought them to the laboratory for continued observations. I found that the coca-fed snails would climb a glass rod in about 90 seconds, whereas those snails fed on ordinary garden ivy did it in about 120 seconds. Reducing traveling time by 25 percent might not be important to snails, but when the distances are measured in kilometers rather than centimeters, it is significant. Uncontrolled experiments conducted during the nineteenth century suggested that chewing coca quickened both the pulse and the pace of trekkers, reducing by 30 percent the elapsed time of their journeys.

The Andean Indians travel 25 kilometers per day over the precipitous and unsurfaced paths of the mountains. Many of their packs are carried by the surefooted llamas. Each llama can carry 50 kilograms, the load cushioned by a dense coat of brown and white wool. The llamas feed on dry *ichu* grass, a tough vegetation found along the barren stretches of Andean trails, but I caught some Indians occasionally treating the animals to handouts of coca leaves. The Indians consider the coca to be a symbolic reward to the animal; the llamas seem unimpressed and their behavior remains unchanged by the token amounts they are given. Unlike the llamas, which must be be coaxed and encouraged lest they sit down and refuse to budge, the human coca chewers moved with a relentless determination worthy of any expeditionary force. What would happen to the slow but steady pace of the llamas if they were allowed to eat such quickening amounts of coca?

I examined the effects of coca and cocaine on a small herd of domesticated llamas on a California ranch. The female llamas, with their large eyes and long feminine lashes, seemed to be perfectly suited to their names: Harriet, Lana, and Louise. Having been leased out as pack animals to some hikers, the males were absent, with the exception of Lloyd who, at six feet, stood several handsome feet above his harem. Llamas are pretty to look at, but difficult to handle if they are mistreated or startled by an interloper. If they feel threatened, they may respond with karate-style jumping kicks. They can also spit a blistering mixture of saliva and gastric juices. I kept a respectful distance during my observations.

I saw that the llamas got along with each other and there was only a little side jostling at feeding time. The animals sometimes used their long, slender necks to gain advantage over each other, pushing or pressing the other's neck down, but I rarely saw this behavior. Then I provided the llamas with pellets made from compressed coca leaves that had been grown commercially in the Huánuco area of Peru. The leaves were of average potency, containing 0.58 percent cocaine, and they were fashioned into 1-gram pellets held together with a little gum arabic paste, the same ingredient used in commercial chewing gum. Each pellet also contained a small quantity of sodium bicarbonate that would help the cocaine come out of the leaves when the pellet was chewed. The llamas accepted these pellets as part of their normal feed. They were allowed to eat as much as they wanted, but individual llamas, which weighed the same as an average adult human, would take no more than the amount consumed by native Andean Indians.

This dosage was insufficient to change behavior in dramatic ways. The animals appeared slightly more aggressive at feeding time, holding their pointed ears back while making various vocal noises. Behavior in the open grassland showed only minor changes. Their chasing and playing was more frisky than normal, and Harriet wouldn't let her owner give her the usual petting, but these minor effects disappeared quickly. And the animals did not want to eat any greater quantities of coca.

One week later I provided the llamas with coca pellets spiked with additional amounts of cocaine hydrochloride, or "street cocaine," a salt of the alkaloid that renders it quickly and efficiently absorbed through the mucous membranes of the mouth. They would now be given, like it or not, a larger dose than could be obtained from the leaves. More important, the cocaine would be delivered quickly without waiting to be extracted by the slow process of chewing. Each llama now got the equivalent of three times the amount it chewed on its own.

Lana snapped at Harriet's front legs. Louise kicked Lana, then spit at Harriet. Lana snapped at Louise. Lloyd drove them all away with a frontal attack, jumping and kicking. Then he spit in Harriet's direction. This circus of fighting llamas was over almost as soon as the animals dispersed from the food area. A few hours later, when they were rounded up for a quick medical checkup, Lana accidentally jostled Lloyd. He brought her to her knees with a neck press. The irritability gradually faded and by the next day there were no long-lasting effects as the herd resumed its normal routine. The llamas had demonstrated what most coca-chewing Indians already knew—coca was not cocaine.

The intake of the cocaine alkaloid was automatically regulated for the Indians in the packaging of the coca leaf. Although they still experienced a boost in energy, they didn't go around kicking each other. If they had fed their llamas more treats of coca, they might have gotten even more work from the animals, yet the animals would have had none of the problems associated with the cocaine-spiked leaves. The animals would have been in no more danger of fighting on the edge of an Andean cliff than the Indians, who neither fought nor fell with coca. It is also unlikely that a llama would have overdosed on coca; despite limitless supplies, no Indian was ever poisoned by coca.

When coca leaves are chewed, the leaves are placed in the mouth and masticated with saliva into a wad, or quid. The quid is held in the cheek and periodically rechewed. The resulting juice is swallowed and some of the leaves may also be swallowed. Through this process, which is much like the chewing of tobacco, some of the cocaine is extracted from the leaves and absorbed into the bloodstream. The process becomes more efficient if an alkaline substance like sodium bicarbonate is added. The native Indians, with their ecological empiricism, acquired the same knowledge and developed the custom of chewing coca with a preparation of either lime, plant ashes, or powdered calcareous shells. These alkaline additives also impart characteristic sweet tastes to the coca, thus effectively overshadowing the natural bitterness.

In as few as five minutes after chewing coca, there are measurable cocaine levels in plasma, which reach peak concentrations over the next two hours. Subjectively, these levels coincide with reports of local anesthesia in the mouth and a stimulating effect. The stimulation is reflected in feelings of more vigor and strength. Fatigue is reduced as are sensations of hunger, thirst, and cold. Coca is just as useful for Indian trekkers in the Andes as cocaine tablets were for Shackleton. It is as useful today for making long journeys on foot through the mountainous Andes or Amazonian forests as it was when running messages back and forth during Incan battles. Coca is also chewed by farmers, herders, fishermen, hunters, miners, and even long-distance Andean truck drivers. Yet the natives know the effects are temporary and they use coca only to postpone the necessity for food, never to replace it.

There are other benefits to coca when it is used as a medicine. Quids of coca leaves or infusion teas have been used as remedies for a number of gastrointestinal disorders ranging from mild indigestion and stomachaches to ulcers and dysentery. Coca is effective in treatment of *soroche*, the high-altitude sickness characterized by nausea, dizziness, cramps, and severe headaches. The Incas discovered that wads of partially chewed coca leaves were useful as local anesthetics in primitive trephining operations designed to open the skull and relieve compression from fractures. This was a common injury when warfare with spiked clubs was a daily occurrence. The anesthetic effects from the juice of chewed leaves is still used in rural Andean villages to treat open wounds, eye and throat irritations, and toothaches. The list of minor ailments treated with coca includes respiratory problems for which patients inhale fumes from burning coca leaves and seeds. This practice evolved from the ritual of burning and smoking coca leaves in homage to the gods.

Coca is offered not only to the gods, but to strangers traveling in the Andes. A bundle of coca—a gift from the government of Peru—welcomed my arrival in a hotel that would serve as temporary quarters before journeying into the Quechua villages. My subsequent interviews with the natives confirmed the findings of previous studies: the chewers were titrating or adjusting their intake to a desired level of intoxication.

The bundle I had been given as a token of friendship was minuscule in comparison to the tons of leaves available to my informants. Yet they seemed to be able to take it or leave it. When social gatherings called for chewing sessions lasting eight or ten hours, they obliged because they were Indians and it was their tradition. Afterward they ate healthy meals, and their diet was adequate to prevent malnutrition or weight loss. When they needed to hike to a market or treat a bout of *soka,* a condition of weakness and malaise, they used no more coca than was necessary for relief. If their mood was sad or depressed they chewed only until they felt "high in spirits." They seemed to be very carefully balancing their physical and mental states with the help of coca, thus avoiding the consequences of overindulgence such as sleep loss and irritability. They were traditionalists who practiced the way of using coca without abusing it, like llamas who knew the mountain paths and never fell.

What governs this control? Can other animals master its use? I took my questions to the mountain city of Cuzco, where I visited a Quechua *yatiri,* "one who knows." My interpreter guided me through the old part of town, where we found a small man with a posture as crooked as the narrow cobblestone streets we had followed to his house. In addition to being a local authority on coca, he claimed to have been struck by lightning and to be endowed with the ability to foresee the outcome of future events. Some fortune-tellers ask you to chew coca with them; others burn the leaves with llama fat and study the smoke; still others spit the juice into their hands and watch the drippings for telltale patterns. A few have been known to stick wads of leaves under your shirt and down into your pants. To my great relief, this *yatiri* simply dropped a handful of leaves onto a white tablecloth and studied their features, reading "inkblots" in green and white.

He started to tell me about my future. I asked highly specific questions that did not require any psychic talent. For example: Why did no one misuse coca? "Mama Coca," he answered. As he started to tell the story of Mama Coca, I wondered if he really was psychic—it was my favorite of all Inca legends. Mama Coca was originally a very beautiful woman, he explained, and she was killed because she had been an adulteress. Her body was cut in half and buried. From her remains grew the coca bush. Whenever you chew coca, you are sharing in the spirit of a beautiful woman, Mama Coca. Once only men could pick the leaves and only rulers were allowed to use them, but now everybody could pick and chew coca. Since Mama Coca was a goddess, no one can ever resist her control. The goddess in the plant prevented abuse. Actually, I knew he was referring to the small amounts of cocaine fixed in the leaf, but it would have been rude for me to suggest that Mama Coca was nothing more than a cheap alkaloid you could pick up on any city street.

Can Mama Coca be used for anything other than work or healing? The *yatiri* gestured by patting the fingers of each hand together. "Good for fucking," he said with a straight face and a twinkle in his eye. "Do other animals use coca?" He told me about the llamas, but said there were no others. "Why not?" I asked. He laughed and answered, "No other animal on earth should chew coca." "But if they did," I wondered, "wouldn't Mama Coca protect them from abuse?" The question stopped the *yatiri*'s chatter for a full minute. He seemed shocked. Had I suggested that other animals might have sex with the beautiful woman? "If any other animals dare to use coca," whispered the *yatiri*, "*they are damned!*"

Either the *yatiri* was wrong or my monkeys were destined for an unfavorable judgment. I could not tell if monkeys *should* chew coca, but I had determined that they *would*. In the laboratory at UCLA I had given rhesus monkeys access to the same coca pellets that the llamas ate. All the monkeys had to do was to press a lever, and a pellet would be dispensed automatically into the food chute in their cages. Two alternating lever-pressing requirements were arranged to assess some of the drug effects. A small white light located near the lever signaled the start of the sequence. The monkey was trained to press the lever twenty times and then a coca pellet would drop into the food chute. The signal light would be turned off for a five-minute "coca break," during which the animal could chew under the scrutiny of closed-circuit television cameras. The cage remained well lit by overhead house lights. Then the signal light would be turned on again, but now the monkey had to wait one minute, then press the lever once. This single lever press earned delivery of another coca pellet and another five-minute break. Monkeys could keep earning pellets in this way all day and all night long. By examining the speed of the initial twenty responses, I could obtain a measurement of coca's stimulating effects. If the animals could refrain from lever pressing for the full minute during the next requirement, I would be able to see how coca affected their ability to hold back and control what they were doing.

When working for regular monkey chow, the animals executed the lever-pressing requirements flawlessly. During the next phase, the monkeys had ample supplies of chow and fresh fruit in their cages, and were given the opportunity to earn supplements of coca pellets. Although the monkeys could earn a coca pellet every five minutes, they limited themselves to an average of twenty-four a day, or one each hour. A few of these would be discarded on the bottom of the cage, but most were chewed. It was clear from the videotapes that the monkeys knew what to do with the pellets. Their cheeks bulged as they chewed and sucked, just like the South American natives who were first described by the explorer Amerigo Vespucci.

During the coca breaks, the monkeys remained relatively silent and spent time inspecting their numbed lips and tongues. After chewing a few pellets, they paced around the cage while staring at everything, behavior known as "checking." When it came time to earn another pellet, they seemed eager to get the pellets and often started pressing the lever even before the five-minute break was over. The twenty lever presses came in rapid-fire bursts. The monkeys were so excited that they could not withhold responding during the one-minute intervals. Nevertheless, the coca chewing remained constant, a little at a time. Vespucci marveled at similar eager yet regulated behavior in the natives and couldn't guess the secret. A clue was provided by the daily urine tests of the monkeys. The tests detected the presence of benzoylecgonine, the major cocaine metabolite. And the levels were nearly the same from day to day.

When tested with decocainized pellets that contained all of the ingredients in coca except cocaine, the monkeys took only two or three pellets each day. Their behavior remained unaffected by these placebos, which still contained nutrients, but this was not what the monkeys were after. They seemed to care little about the carbohydrates or vitamins provided by the placebos. In choice tests between placebos and coca, the monkeys preferred the coca nine times out of ten. They wanted cocaine—the same secret ingredient that puzzled Amerigo Vespucci and was destined to be pursued by future inhabitants of the land named after him.

Although the monkeys were after cocaine, they were still capable of titrating their dosage. On a weight basis, they took the same amount used by the Andean Indians. Either the monkeys had all been Indians in some former life, Mama Coca was protecting all primates with the same rules, or there was a built-in mechanism that controlled coca chewing. Undoubtedly, the small quantities fixed in the leaf prevented overindulgence. After all, there had to be a limit to how many bulk leaves one could stuff into the cheeks or swallow. In addition to the physical limitations of chewing more coca, the slow absorption of cocaine from the juices in the mouth and stomach produced a gradual, almost natural stimulation that may have been appealing but not addicting.

If the quids that were chewed contained more cocaine, would control be lost to addiction? The question could be easily answered by combining cocaine with chewing gum, an equally ancient, if not addicting, habit. Gum can hold cocaine as well as any leaf with the added advantage (perhaps disadvantage) that more can be added and the precise dose can be varied. I prepared several different types of cocaine gum for the monkeys in order to assess the effects of dosage on their desire to chew. The gum was flavored with the same natural flavonoids derived from the coca leaf. The aromatic oil methyl salicylate, also present in coca, gave the gum a distinctive wintergreen taste. Each bite-size piece of "Coca-Lets" contained 5 milligrams of cocaine, the same amount found in one of the coca pellets. "Coca-Peps" contained 10 milligrams of cocaine, and "Coca-Jets" provided a whopping 25 milligrams.

The monkeys pressed eagerly for the Coca-Lets, which also increased their rate of lever pressing. They chewed quietly during the break periods, but expressed some impatience for another piece by banging away at the lever before the break was over. Yet the total amount of cocaine they worked for was no greater than the amount they took in coca pellets. They also earned as many pieces of Coca-Peps but discarded more than half of them without chewing. Coca-Jets would have been a commercial disaster if ever marketed to rhesus monkeys; the animals wouldn't work for these at all. Monkeys treated these high-dose pieces with the same lack of enthusiasm that was shown for "Coca-Less," placebo gum prepared with procaine, a local anesthestic devoid of appealing stimulant effects when chewed.

Several experiments were conducted with the mild Coca-Lets. The monkeys worked for the gum but they didn't like too much of it—or too little. In one study, two monkeys were limited to daily two-hour sessions in which they could earn the gum. Apparently this wasn't quite long enough for Lightning, a large female rhesus who earned her name for the speed with which she could pick the lock on her cage and escape. One day she broke out and headed directly for the container of Coca-Lets on my desk. I grabbed it first and then Lightning struck, canines bearing down on my neck. A technician caught the monkey, pinned her arms, and carried her screaming back to her cage.

Both Lightning and her companion in this experiment, Pearl, were high-spirited in other ways. Most of the time these laboratory-reared monkeys seemed depressed. They spent many hours huddled in their home cages. They were always sleeping or picking through the wood shavings at the bottom of the cage, hoping to find something new. They were pictures of simian despair. Cocaine gum lifted them up. The monkeys returned my glances without the usual threat displays, then playfully groomed my hand through the wire cage. They showed renewed interest in their toys and swings, performing showy acrobatics while stretching the gum between their teeth and tiny hands. Reaching into the wood shavings and tossing them in the air, they would then run through the falling pieces like children playing in winter's first snow.

Cocaine is similar to coca when both are chewed. But playing in the snow is a long way from forced marching through it, and neither monkey nor Indian seems eager to swallow more than he can chew. Coca's exhilarating effects appeal to animals and humans, who like the small amounts of cocaine locked in the plant leaves or stuck in the gum. There is plenty of attraction but no abuse.

2

When cocaine is freed from these packaging restraints, individuals cannot always control their own amounts and attraction turns to addiction.

Even the language and the mythology start to change. The *yatiri* knew that when he chewed coca he was touched by the spirit of a very beautiful woman, but the small amounts of cocaine guarded against a more intimate embrace. He never used cocaine itself, although he was aware of the modern practices of sniffing, injecting, and smoking the drug. That, he claimed, would be a bad marriage.

The slang terms that once described cocaine suggested that a good relationship could easily turn sour when the drug was administered via these new routes. Users went to a "snow bank" where they could purchase their illegal "snowcaine." They could then "hook up the reindeer" and go on a spree of use known as a "sleigh ride." By blowing some snow into their noses, the ride could turn into a joyous "snowball"—anyone could be a Cinderella for a night. But they would not always be able to stop at midnight. Once they were under the influence of cocaine they were "caught in a snowstorm," "loaded with coke," and "snowed under." These "snowbirds" would eventually take too much cocaine and turn into "cocaine monkeys."

Toby was a real macaque who learned to sniff enough cocaine for a one-way sleigh ride to the Saint Anne Asylum in Paris. He belonged to a woman who was also a cocaine user. The woman kept her cocaine in a small snuffbox. Toby watched as she or her friends inhaled the powder into their nostrils. He imitated their behavior and started searching through handbags and pockets for the box. When he found it, he opened it and plunged his nose in with obvious delight. Toby was as mischievous as Lightning and learned to break his chain to get at a drawer where a supply of the drug was kept.

Initially, cocaine made Toby excited, then quarrelsome; finally, he started biting people. He pulled the hair out from his legs and arms. When the owner sought treatment at the asylum for her own habit, she took Toby with her. By this time the monkey was hallucinating, waving his hand in the air and trying to grasp imaginary objects. Toby's continuing demand for cocaine could be seen during his examination at the hospital whenever the doctors tested him with boxes of white powder. He rejected their offers of substitutes like baking soda but always took the cocaine. Both he and his owner were denied further access to the drug and successfully detoxified.

There are many stories of other pets that have turned into demanding cocaine monkeys when provided with supplies of the drug. Archie, a pet cat living in Hollywood, would mew and beg for sniffs or licks from a vial of cocaine. Dexter, a grey Manx, was given a sniff of cocaine every morning and evening for five years. If the owner forgot the handout, the cat's incessant whining would remind him. Floozy, a kitten, would run to her owner whenever cocaine was being used, and wait patiently for puffs of cocaine smoke to be blown in her face. Then she would start purring and running about the house. After about two hours, Floozy would lie down and go to sleep, yet she could be quickly aroused again by the smell of cocaine smoke.

But some animals have been turned into real beasts when they get too much. Robert Louis Stevenson gave us a glimpse of this behavior when he wrote *The Strange Case of Dr. Jekyll and Mr. Hyde* in six days and nights under the influence of cocaine. The fictional Dr. Jekyll takes a drug—modeled after cocaine—that turns him into a demonic murderer called Mr. Hyde. Screen versions of the story often portray Hyde as a mad, hairy ape. Cocaine can change cute monkeys into miniature Mr. Hydes in laboratories where lever pressing delivers an automatic injection of cocaine rather than a piece of gum. The most famous of these laboratories was located at the University of Michigan Medical School. The monkeys self-administered cocaine around the clock. They managed to keep this up for about five days, or until they were exhausted. Then they slept fitfully, ate heartily, and resumed the cycle of injections.

During the course of these cycles the Michigan monkeys made Toby look tame in comparison. Their eyes sprang open and locked. Their hairs stood erect as they shook and trembled. They lost coordination, muscle mass, and the ability to control their movements. It was a haunted and emaciated look. Yet they ignored all this, passed up candy treats, and continued to press the lever for cocaine. A few started biting and scratching their hands, producing extensive wounds, even amputating their own fingers. With bloody and decaying stumps they still pressed for cocaine. I had once seen a young Bolivian boy who had chewed off two fingers on his left hand because of his love for cocaine. Only a very special love could make one do such terrible things. The monkeys clenched their teeth in fear grimaces. The *yatiri* would have called it a bad marriage. The curse of Mama Coca is mistaking addiction for love.

The tenacity with which animals hang on to cocaine, despite alarming changes in their bodies, is all the more remarkable when other physical consequences are considered. Monkeys, as well as rodents and dogs, show increases in respiration, heart rate, blood pressure, body temperature, and electrical activity in the brain. The animals do more than lose sleep over their chemical love. Psychomotor stimulation may progress from mild arousal to tremors, jerking movements, and seizures. Binges of cocaine use may be followed by respiratory depression and cardiovascular collapse. Long-term consequences include weight loss, skin disorders, and liver damage. Surprisingly, these animals are not permanently addicted to cocaine. The cycle of addiction was easily broken for the Michigan monkeys when the injections were discontinued. Most toxic effects could be reversed, although fingers do not regenerate and livers may never be the same.

In other laboratories where monkeys were limited in access to the cocaine they could inject, intake was well regulated and signs of toxicity were seldom seen despite daily use that went on for years. The monkeys injected themselves at regular intervals, almost as if they were titrating the dose by some internal clock. They were stimulated, sometimes agitated, but they never displayed the toxicity seen in monkeys given free access to cocaine. Even when the experimenters increased the dose delivered in each injection, the animals decreased their rate of injections in order to maintain a constant amount. Monkeys simply do not lose control of cocaine use unless they are given unlimited access as happened in the Michigan studies.

The ability of monkeys to self-regulate cocaine seems to hold true for smoking, a route of administration that results in even faster and more intense intoxication. The Bolivian boy who chewed his fingers had been smoking coca paste, a crude extract of coca leaf. The refined cocaine hydrochloride can also be made into a smokable product once the hydrochloride salt is "freed" from the cocaine alkaloid by free basing, a chemical process developed by North American smokers. More than a decade before cocaine free base was given the slang name "crack," our monkeys were quietly smoking it in a basement laboratory at UCLA.

When given a choice between nontobacco lettuce cigarettes or ones laced with human doses of cocaine free base, all the monkeys preferred the cocaine cigarettes. They continued to smoke cocaine, even when no other rewards were offered, yet they limited their use. When given unlimited access to cocaine cigarettes for twenty days, the monkeys spent only four hours a day smoking. They consumed an average of five cigarettes a day, most of them smoked during the early morning hours.

Several monkeys became hyperactive and puffed up a storm of smoke. Phoebe, a fifteen-year-old rhesus, seemed unable to stop puffing and went through twenty-five cigarettes a day. Yet she still managed to control her intake of cocaine by reducing the duration of her drags on each cigarette. Her daily urine levels of cocaine metabolite remained as steady as the other monkeys. Thus the amount of cocaine could be controlled by regulating either the frequency or the duration of puffing. The important point was not how fast the monkeys could smoke or how big a cloud they could produce—as entertaining as it was to watch Phoebe licking some of these clouds—but that they chose to maintain a particular level of intoxication. This is an example of the same natural control exhibited by people, llamas, and monkeys when they chew coca. But why monkeys can limit cocaine smoking and most people cannot is an important question that remains unanswered.

The chosen level of intoxication was sufficient to arouse behavior.

Immediately after the monkeys finished smoking their morning cocaine cigarettes, loud barks and high-pitched calls echoed throughout the steel cages. The monkeys engaged in their characteristic pacing and swinging with a cage-rattling intensity. At this time any attempt to look through the cages at the monkeys was greeted by fear grimaces and threats. Pupi, a petite female rhesus who always greeted my approach with affectionate grooming and lip smacking, now performed the monkey "salute." In this salute, Pupi cupped her hand like a good little scout and brought it up to the side or top of her eyebrow. The salute is used by some monkeys to hide their eyes from onlookers and is particularly useful in avoiding threats. Monkeys reared in isolation or those rendered slightly paranoid by stimulants may do the same. Some monkeys "salute" with their feet by waving a foot in front of the eyes. Pupi was more ladylike. The salute meant that I had to leave the room. If I didn't walk away, Pupi would become so angry and frustrated that she would start biting herself. I learned that by shielding my own eyes from hers, I could suppress the self-biting. Whenever Pupi saluted, I saluted back.

Stopping animals from pursuing cocaine is not so simple as saluting. The allegiance to cocaine outranks most other behavior. Other animals will work hard for injections of cocaine. Rats, dogs, and baboons, in addition to several species of monkeys, will press levers with the same general patterns. They will learn to execute complex programs that require sequential responding on several levers for a reward of cocaine at the end of the program. These programs or rules are successful in controlling the behavior whether the animals are seeking food, water, or many of the drugs abused by humans. Yet cocaine, more than food and most other drugs, can stretch the rules to the breaking point. It can drive the animal or person over the brink to death.

The breaking point can be demonstrated when the program requires an animal to press the lever 100 times for the initial cocaine injection; then the requirement might double to 200, 400, 800, and so on. This program is known as a progressive ratio schedule and the critical measure of behavior is the highest ratio completed in a given period of time. The ratio at which the animal will no longer work for the drug reward is the breaking point, and it provides an index of the reinforcing strength of the drug. Cocaine's breaking point was 2 to 16 times higher than for other drugs, and some monkeys would press up to 12,800 times for each cocaine infusion!

Not all animals will hold out longer for cocaine. Individual baboons will work just as hard for high doses of secobarbital, a sedative that may be appealing to the high-strung baboons used in laboratory studies. Some monkeys find cocaine no more rewarding than cathinone, the principal alkaloid from khat. Rats generally like cocaine as much as monkeys but some find that repeated infusions are mildly aversive and they will try to avoid it. Nonetheless, given a choice between cocaine and most other stimulants, animals prefer cocaine. Dogs like it better than nicotine or amphetamine, and many people feel the same. High doses of cocaine are usually preferred to low doses but low doses are sometimes better than a friend: In a choice test between a low dose of cocaine and the opportunity to have visual contact with other monkeys, the low dose of cocaine wins.

Despite these individual differences, cocaine is a universally powerful reward. In a sense, monkeys can exceed the breaking point in tests where they choose intravenous cocaine over food, even when threatened with starvation. Whereas coca might sustain the animals past these breaks, cocaine provides no nutrition and the experimenters have to intervene in the studies and stop the injections when the animals start losing too much weight. It is dangerous to let the animals get carried away.

A group of Canadian researchers was not afraid to allow rats continuous and unlimited access to intravenous cocaine. Every time the rats pressed a lever, a motor-driven syringe pumped the drug solution through an intravenous catheter for ten seconds. Pressing the lever during the injection interval had no consequences but rats could self-administer another infusion immediately after the ten seconds. They could do this twenty-four hours a day for a maximum of thirty days. Not every rat liked to do this but 83 percent of the Canadian rats became regular heavy users.

The rats engaged in episodes of use just like monkeys or people. They would take large amounts of cocaine during one twenty-four-hour period and much less during the next. These patterns continued throughout the thirty-day experiment. Animals lost almost a third of their body weight, groomed very little, and lost their general health.

Several had full-blown seizures but as soon as the convulsions subsided, they approached the lever and pressed again. By the end of the experiment, 90 percent of the animals were dead.

Starvation and weight loss alone would not have killed as quickly as cocaine. Cocaine was doing much more to the animals through its depression of central nervous system functions and respiratory paralysis. Yet the initial kick of stimulation kept rats self-administering until the end. Despite the seizures and other incipient signs of death, the rats continued, acting more like suicidal lemmings than the streetwise survivalists they had evolved to be.

Can animals be stopped in this mad pursuit? Can they be taught to say "No"? Electric shock is an effective "stop sign" to keep animals from injecting cocaine, but only if it is severe enough. If rhesus monkeys get an injection of cocaine coupled with a brief electric shock delivered through wires implanted at the base of the skull, they will earn decreasing amounts of cocaine as the shock intensity increases. However, they can adapt to a moderate amount of shock and maintain responding at low levels for cocaine. They will completely suppress responding for cocaine *only* when extremely high intensities of shock are used.

The difficulty in punishing monkeys for using cocaine is also demonstrated when they are given a choice between two intravenous solutions of cocaine. When one solution is delivered with shock, most monkeys will choose the nonshocked solution if it is an equal dose. With typical primate individualism, some monkeys will actually prefer the shocked dose. If the dose of the shocked solution is made substantially greater than the nonshocked choice, all monkeys prefer the higher shocked dose despite the pain. The choice is unfortunate for many, because chronic cocaine use may render animals hypersensitive to the shock.

The sensitivity extends to almost everything in the environment. Sounds seem louder. Vision seems more acute. Minor sounds or movements can easily startle the animals. Just the presence of other mice is sufficient stimulation to lower the lethal dose of cocaine and kill a greater proportion of mice. Primates under the influence of cocaine also suffer from an exaggerated sensitivity to each other and are easily irritated by the most innocent social interactions.

This evolves into suspiciousness and hyperactivity. The suspiciousness progresses to paranoia; the hyperactivity becomes agitation, overreactivity, and panic. Hallucinations and delusions flourish in the final psychotic stage. This is not schizophrenia, but cocaine psychosis is very close to it. If Shackleton's men engaged in heavy cocaine use and had been trapped in a camp rather than spread out on the glacier, the effects might have been very different. Their increased sensitivity would not be a direct physical danger, but the group still would have been on thin ice. They might not have stayed together as a team because of this psychotic paranoia.

Little was known about the effects of either cocaine or coca on small groups of primates, so I planned a series of studies on a family of island-dwelling chimpanzees. In the years 1975 to 1977 I carried an assortment of coca leaves and cocaine syringes on a series of field trips to South Island. South Island was small, only 300 square meters, and was located on a small lake in a California game park. A naked oasis of dirt, jagged boulders, and twisted dead trees, the island looked like a miniature model of the Skull Island set used in the movie *King Kong*. A huge wooden box stood incongruously on one end of the island. It was home to a group of four chimpanzees. The group included OJ, a large dominant male; Mickey, an older male who was a retired ice-skating star; Suzie, a fully mature female who had lost her left arm to a park lion; and Xerox, a juvenile male who appeared on the island one day but nobody knew where he came from.

Our teams had been observing the island for many months in the course of several different studies, so the chimps were not alarmed as I rowed my boat to their home. I dumped a large box of coca leaves on the beach and rowed to a safe distance to watch. OJ quickly raked in the leaves and started to inspect them. The others joined him and soon leaves could be seen in hands, mouths, and on top of Mickey's head. Although the animals received two boatloads of food and fresh fruit daily, any edible addition to the barren island was a novelty worthy of experimental eating. Most of the leaves were eventually chewed and swallowed.

The coca had been provided in the same amounts that would be chewed by four humans in one day. But without an alkaline ash, the effects on the chimps were going to be as gradual and mild as the handouts of leaves given to the llamas in Peru. The chimps seemed to move about more quickly than usual. All other behavior looked normal. Mickey and Suzie stayed near each other, and sometimes Mickey would drape his arm around her shoulders. Little Xerox did his usual begging for grapes or bananas gathered by the adults at feeding time. OJ roamed the island's perimeter alone or joined the others in climbing about the trees.

I prepared the chimps for the next phase of the study by tossing them peanuts from the boat. I developed my throwing ability so that I could accurately target individual animals. A few days later I tossed pieces of Coca-Jets to each chimp. There had been a surplus of this high-potency gum in the lab ever since the rhesus monkeys rejected them. Each chimp seemed to know exactly what to do and quickly scooped up its piece and started chewing. I continued to toss pieces every fifteen minutes until each animal had consumed four pieces, the equivalent of an intoxicating dose for an adult human. Vocal communication in the group escalated with a chorus of grunts and a few soft barks, a coughing sound that is a mild form of threat. Mickey and Suzie kept their distance from each other while OJ rapidly circled the island again and again. Xerox hid in the shelter. This first cocaine intoxication had produced mild stimulation without dramatic outbursts, behavior also seen in first-time users at human cocaine parties.

I was not convinced that the chimps had eaten all their gum—I saw two pieces floating on the lake the next day—and they didn't seem eager to take more, probably because of the numbing effect in their mouths. In the final phase, I darted individual animals with cocaine. Each dart was a miniature syringe that was fired from a carbon-dioxide-powered rifle kept on the boat. The dart automatically and instantaneously injected a solution of cocaine hydrochloride when it hit the thick, muscular thighs of the animal. The dose was the same as four pieces of Coca-Jets—delivered all at once. A small barb on the dart's hollow needle prevented it from bouncing off the animal and ensured that each chimp received the full dose, yet it could be easily pulled out by the chimp after impact. An antibiotic coating on the darts protected the chimps from infection.

The cocaine darts turned the normal facial expressions into bold-faced demonstrations of aggression. Each chimp would become the focal point of the group's attention as soon as it was darted. When the darts were placebos, the entire group would gather around to inspect the situation—the dart was sometimes passed around for study. But cocaine rendered the darted animal irritable and the group's approach was met with explosive barks and charging displays. Fortunately, the island provided sufficient room for everybody to disperse, thereby eliminating serious fights. Mickey and Suzie made faces at each other, exchanged a few slaps, then moved to separate boulders. OJ stamped and drummed on the top of the box. Xerox happened to be inside, but he managed to run out and climb to the safety of a tree. OJ then jogged around the island at a record pace.

Over the next two hours I made several attempts to land on the island to retrieve the darts. OJ's bobbing and flailing blocked every approach. At one point, he threw stones at the boat, then waded into the shallows and jumped on board. I screamed and drummed the oars on the boat until he jumped off and returned to the beach. I had seen these same effects in my clinical practice with cocaine users. Mickey and Suzie reminded me of married couples driven to separation by cocaine problems, and more than one of OJ's human cousins attacked me during a cocaine rage.

Across the lake from South Island was North Island, an identical island whose inhabitants were the polar opposites of OJ and company. Alice was a large, scraggly chimpanzee and the highest-ranking female on the island. Cheryl, another mature female, had oversize ears that protruded at almost right angles to her head. She had several bumps just above her eyebrows that twitched with her facial expressions. I named an adolescent female Twiggy because she was always digging for something with a dead twig or small branch. The lone male, a giant of a chimp, was a picture of intimidation, from the unruly tufts of hair that formed epaulets on his broad shoulders to his name—Godzilla. His physical appearance belied his real character. He was extremely gentle and formed a close-knit family with the three females. The group was full of warmth and affection. They huddled together most of the time, groomed each other, and embraced without hesitation. When they put on their "play faces"—a slight retraction of the lip corners—tickling, wrestling, and mock biting was enjoyed by all.

North Island proved to be a suitable dumping ground for the

leftover gum. I limited each chimpanzee to just one piece of Coca-Jets a day until my supply was exhausted two weeks later. The animals became enthusiastic chewers. They allowed me onto the island to dispense the gum and Alice once accepted her ration from my outstretched hand. Godzilla never trusted me and sat at a distance until I tossed the gum to him. He always took it. The behavior of the group showed none of the outbursts that characterized the larger doses given on South Island. The animals seemed to groom themselves more, rock back and forth a little faster, and play harder. But the sparring never got out of hand. During their social play, the chimpanzees made soft panting sounds, vocalizations that have been identified as laughing. The low-dose preparations could be controlled. If South Island was a reminder of people in clinical crises with cocaine, then North Island was a flash-back to the happy coca-chewing families I interviewed in Peru. The behavior seemed so radically different from any that we had observed in other drug studies on North, that I was tempted to rename the gum with a slang term once used for cocaine: "paradise."

The temptation vanished when the first cocaine dart hit Alice. She pushed away from the others and moved quickly to a boulder. Godzilla followed her as she tried to find a secluded refuge. Eventually, she climbed to the top of the island's tallest tree and perched on a small branch. Godzilla, expressing calls of concern, started climbing up to her. Alice clutched the tree. Godzilla continued to advance. Alice screamed. Godzilla came closer. He was almost on top of her when she reached behind her back, grabbed a handful of excrement, and threw it at her best friend and mate. Godzilla turned around and left her alone.

But Alice couldn't relax or sit still for long. She kept changing her position on the tree. When a flock of low-flying ducks from the lake startled her, she lowered her head and covered her face with both arms. Leaving the tree, she continued to roam the island, hiding from visual contact with the others. When she got dangerously close to the water, we had to sting her with a pellet gun to keep her from a final march into the sea.

A few days later I went back to North and South Islands to retrieve the darts. Behavior had already returned to normal. The chimpanzees did not suffer any ill effects. The islands had been big enough to allow the intoxicated chimps to isolate themselves, thereby avoiding more serious consequences from their cocaine-induced aggression. Now they sat and groomed each other as before. Even OJ seemed to forgive me and took several bananas from my hand. But he refused to give up one of the silver darts, which he held onto as a souvenir from the time there had been a cocaine problem on the island.

Years later, while visiting the Fitz Hugh Ludlow Memorial Library in San Francisco, I found a rare book describing one man's problem with cocaine. It was a 1927 German edition of *Kokain,* a novel that told the story of a young man, Tito, who recaptured for a fleeting moment the Paradise of Eden when he sniffed cocaine.

Like Tito, the chimpanzees had their fun with low doses of cocaine in the leaf or gum, laughing and somersaulting around their island. Tito kept using more and more. If the chimps had been darted often enough with cocaine, they would have stopped laughing and lapsed into a schizophrenic psychosis, just as Tito did. The real danger of cocaine was psychological, not physical. Unlike the chimpanzees who could run away from aggressive encounters, animals confined to cages or people locked in close relationships cannot escape from their feelings. "Cocaine literally uncouples and splits your individuality in twain," explained Tito. "It accomplishes the almost electrolytic destruction of one's own conscience."

The result is often increased aggression. Cocaine by itself does not induce aggression, but when aggression is elicited by environmental events, cocaine may render the animals more sensitive and increase the attacks. In one type of freakish experiment, pairs of rats were subjected to unavoidable foot shocks in an escape-proof cage; the animals reflexively stood up and fought. They fought even more with cocaine. In social groups cocaine causes animals to fight and squabble more. Mates are frequent targets of the outbursts. Tito observed that most fights were caused by men and women who either fought over supplies of cocaine or else escalated minor irritations into major arguments. In *Kokain,* a lady under the influence of cocaine rushes up to a male friend, clawing and choking him until she is exhausted. Alice's throwaway gesture aimed at Godzilla seemed oddly more civilized.

Still, Tito, like the many people who have been heroes of romances with cocaine, pursues the drug. He lives a life of almost unlimited access to cocaine, while the author makes us aware that he is on a sleigh ride to death. Blinded by the attachment to the drug, Tito cries out, "Let me kiss you for the last time, Cocaine."

He has no more chance to escape the consequences than do rats trapped in a shock box with cocaine. Worn down by a lifestyle of addiction, Tito eventually welcomed death from typhus and pneumonia as he had welcomed cocaine, as an escape from pain and suffering. Cocaine had turned Tito into a beast and he had consumed himself. When I came to the end of the book, I froze at the sight of the bookplate pasted in the cover. I was told the bookplate was authentic, but whether the plate belonged to this book could be disputed. It was the sign of another beast who had used cocaine:

Ex Libris—Adolf Hitler.

9

A Bevy of Beasts

DRUGS IN THE
SOCIAL GROUP

The beast was marked for an early death. The face had a ghostly pallor; its skin was tight and green, almost moldy.

The beauty, the "divine" Sarah Bernhardt, pushed into the room with eager curiosity. *"C'est magnifique!"* shouted Madame Sarah.

"C'est horrible!" gasped the ladies who accompanied her to this San Francisco opium den in May 1887.

As Bernhardt leaned over the opium smoker and watched his dreamy face, reporters working for William Randolph Hearst, who had engineered this event, prepared to exploit the scene with front-page headlines in the *Examiner*.

Such tactics of creating a startling news story may have been good for circulation, but they were unnecessary dramatizations since Bernhardt's real life, unknown to the reporters, had many similarities to that of the smokers in that Chinatown den. Madame Sarah's likeness adorned advertisements for absinthe as well as a coca wine, to which she credited her health and vitality. "When at times unable to proceed, a few drops give me new life," proclaimed the actress who was a regular user of the cocaine beverage. She was also familiar with the dreams of the opium smoker. Early in her acting career she took opium and once gave a performance under the influence. Describing this incident in her memoirs, she hinted at a nodding acquaintance with other drugs:

"I was in that delicious stupor that one experiences after chloroform, morphine, opium, or hasheesh."

Hearst and other newsmen of the day would not have profited as much from the real story. For them it was worthwhile to enlarge, not shrink, the contrast between beauty and the drug beast. Their mission was to startle and amaze and stupefy readers, thereby increasing sales. In their circulation-hungry eyes they saw drug users not as beautiful, successful women but as animals. Few pictures could show this as well as those that depicted the forbidden fruit of drugs as a beast. In 1922, when Hearst launched an antidrug crusade in his *International* magazine, "dope" was portrayed in an illustration as a giant drooling cheetah, hungrily devouring hordes of helpless human victims. In papers and magazines throughout the country, drugs were pictured as vipers, often encircling people as well as their towns and cities. Other dope predators, fabricated from newspaper and printer's ink, resembled spiders, sharks, vultures, bats, mongooses, wolves, and great apes. Dope was the dragon, the living dead, the grim reaper. It could kill you faster than alcohol. Gin was portrayed as the mythological eagle that slowly tore at Prometheus's liver, but opium was the vampire bat that quickly sucked life from the veins while its wings fanned the victims into a deadly sleep. If a narcotic monster catches you, warned an antidrug film of the time, "It makes beasts of men and women!"

The real message of these crusades was that the consequences of intoxication have little to do with the intentions and dreams that motivate use. Addiction and dependency are unbidden images that change physical, psychological, and social behaviors. The point was not that drugs move you down the phylogenetic ladder, turning people into creatures from the reptilian part of their brains, but that you can change just enough to be strange. When large numbers are intoxicated, behavior may be downright scary to the rest of us. In a sense, the editorial cartoons were correct when they suggested that an exaltation of larks can fly under the influence into an aspect of vulturous behavior.

The antidrug crusades of yesterday and today express a basic and legitimate concern: what will happen to the rest of us when an individual in our midst is under the influence? After all, we are not only individuals but social beings who directly affect others around us. In natural habitats, as we have seen, many species use intoxicants, yet they generally do so alone, apart from the group. Accordingly, the biggest social problems they seem to encounter is when we put them in pairs or groups and *force* the drugs into them. While this is not a natural way for them to use drugs, their reactions tell us why they generally avoid social situations when intoxicated and why such avoidance is the difference between use and abuse of intoxicants.

When intoxicated animals are forced to engage in social behaviors, the results may or may not be dangerous to the individual, but they are often crippling to the group. From the lowly insects to the great apes, social organizations are disrupted in the same ways. Furthermore, the mechanisms that the animal kingdom has evolved for coping with its intoxicated and severely addicted brethren—temporary isolation either forced by the group or chosen by the addict—are ones that best protect everyone.

Despite the normal instincts that govern much behavior in the animal kingdom, drugs are often powerful enough to rub against the genetic grain and change the way animals are programmed to act. Consider what happens to mice who are born with neurological deficits. White mice can inherit a variety of central nervous system disorders that cause them to quake, twirl, or even tumble about the cage. The behavior is almost a neurological rock and roll that is both spontaneous and continual—there is no need for music or drugs. One of the more picturesque of these syndromes is waltzing, in which the mice move in loose circles and figure eights. The circling is so rapid that the eye can hardly follow the dancer's movements. LSD stops the dancing. If a drug is powerful enough to interfere with this basic programming in the brain without disturbing other vital functions, what other behavioral programs can be changed?

Some of the most colorful changes in behavior are demonstrated with hallucinogens in the inherently fixed social behaviors of insects and lower animals. The social behavior of many insects is under rigid genetic control and very little interferes with their determined and stylized activities. The group demands allegiance and service from its members. But a little LSD goes a long way to disrupting behavior in colonies of *Vespa orientalis* hornets. The drugged hornets become hypersensitive and show increased aggressiveness to other members of the colony.

LSD and related hallucinogens, as well as alcohol, cause the same disruption in social colonies of wasps, in gatherings of newts, and in schools of fish. Indeed, LSD in the water supply of tropical fish disturbs social activities to such an extent that the fish appear confused and distressed, the same reactions seen when the temperature suddenly changes or the water becomes fouled. Sex under such conditions, even for perpetual breeders like guppies, is impossible. Caring for the young is equally difficult. African cichlid fish forget to guard their brood and the small fry are quickly devoured by hungry neighbors. And almost all intoxicated fish swim around as if they have lost their way, even those who don't rely on the normal visual senses. Mexican blind cavefish have highly developed senses of touch and smell; they rarely bump into anything. They are known for their close sense of community, but LSD or mescaline bumps the community apart.

Consider the dramatic effects of drugs on the social structure of neon tetra, a tropical fish from the shaded jungle waters of the Brazilian Amazon. The fish swim in tightly controlled schools. The blue-green sheen along their sides is so brilliant that the school appears to be a cloud of fireflies stuck in the "On" position. Schools are highly polarized, with no more than one body-length between individuals. This inter-fish distance, remarkably, never varies and appears to be the minimal distance sufficient for normal swimming behavior. The fish maneuver as a school, forming strings of Christmas tree lights snaking up and down the tank.

The decorum in the school breaks down if only five neons are drugged in a school that numbers fifty. The drugged fish tend to group together and apart from the rest. This division is actually a benefit to the school, which can now swim independently from the drugged subgroup. The subgroup itself stays only loosely aggregated; one or two fish can always be found suspended in a vertical position apart from the others. As long as the drugged fish have room, they stay apart until the drug's effects wear off. But in small tanks where space is limited, the crippling effects are inevitable as sober fish cannot avoid bumping into intoxicated fish, which leads to disorganized swimming for all. In addition, the gentle neons, which rarely fight, start to show some resemblance to a distant relative, the bloodthirsty piranha. The sober neons slyly begin to nip at the fins of their drugged schoolmates.

Similarly, social behavior in birds is disrupted by drugs such as hallucinogens. I conducted experiments with pigeons and found that LSD or THC caused the birds to isolate themselves from nondrugged birds. If there were several intoxicated pigeons, they aggregated into small subgroups, or squads, that refused to participate in the social behavior of the loft. Fighting between the "drug squads" and the rest of the pigeons in the loft was thereby kept to a minimum. Usually there were enough sober birds around so that important mating and nesting chores could still get done.

This isolation strategy works unless everyone is intoxicated. When I treated all the pigeons in the loft to LSD, individuals dispersed, actively avoiding social groupings. Social skills were impaired and the group's ability to maintain functioning was threatened. Drugged pigeons refused to return mating signals, ignored nesting duties, and neglected their own preening and health. They still defended their territories against interlopers, but sometimes fought with their mates out of confusion or irritability. Like the intoxicated fish who were forced to interact in small tanks, the loft pigeons could not escape situations that demanded behavioral responses. They were forced into social situations where they showed dysfunction.

In large social groups where there is room to be alone, rats and mice intoxicated with hallucinogens follow the same isolation strategy seen with fish and birds. Rats given scopolamine, for example, will spread out into the corners of an open field away from sober rats in the same way that grazing animals intoxicated with *Datura* or locoweed move away from the main herds. When a drugged mouse is placed in a spacious colony, it will squeal, squeak, and retreat from investigations by colony members. Such a drugged animal will eventually find refuge in an isolated corner of the colony cage. Put several drugged mice into the colony and they will end up apart from the colony huddles but aggregated with each other, furry snowballs massed in the corners of the cage. This grouping of "druggies" occurs because there is a tendency for drugged mice to huddle together and avoid annoying investigations by the sober animals. The drugged animals don't really pay any attention to each other. Indeed, they may be so inattentive that they sometimes can convince us they no longer see the outside world. In maze tests comparing blind rats with sighted rats, the sighted rats given LSD sometimes did no better than sober blind animals, bumping around like Mexican cavefish out of water. In human terms, the rats are "stoned."

But when all the mice in a colony are stoned, even though they may have little to fear from one another, they are vulnerable to outside threats. When hallucinogens are put in the colony's water supply, for example, the "snowballs" melt as the social huddles break down and members disperse over the cage area. The drugged mice are reluctant to bother each other and there is now no need to huddle in order to avoid investigations. If a mouse from another colony is introduced at this point, it can wander about the literally spaced-out inhabitants with little chance of encountering a fight. Ordinarily, the introduction of a stranger elicits sniffing, nosing, and licking from residents. More often than not the residents will display aggression by assuming offensive upright or sideways postures, rattling their tails, then attacking. But now that the residents are stoned, the stranger can have free access to the colony's territory, including the food supplies. With effects such as these, it is not surprising that hallucinogens were once stockpiled for use in chemical warfare.

The same reactions are seen in social groups of primates when they are given hallucinogens. Monkeys and baboons seek quiet areas and withdraw from group activities. But there is increased fighting between intoxicated cagemates when they cannot avoid each other. Humans are no different. After taking hallucinogenic mushrooms, Komugl men in the New Guinea highlands become so hypersensitive to sounds, they run away from the group's territory until they can find a quiet place to rest. But in their rush to escape the group and avoid confrontation, the Komugl men may run into each other and a struggle will take place.

Sometimes the isolation strategy followed by humans is not a matter of increasing physical distance. For example, at small parties, individuals under the influence of LSD may simply cut off their verbal behavior with others. And while "huddles" of hallucinogenic drug users have been found at times in our culture, as in the hippie communes of the 1960s, individuals can remain in the central population and isolate themselves by embracing attitudes and ideologies of lessened commitment to institutional goals and rules. The expression

"Turn on, tune in, and drop out," coined by social psychologist Timothy Leary, was an apt description of these drug effects.

If the isolation strategy is not followed, mice, rats, cats, and dogs may get into mating difficulties just as we saw with the intoxicated fish and birds. Consider mice who may try to mate while under the influence of hashish. One or two injections of a hashish extract will cause a male mouse to follow an estrous female with more than the usual fervor. Additional injections make them even more interested in the female but they are not particularly adept at mating. They can barely crawl over the females, let alone mount them. Eventually these intoxicated mice start yawning, then turn to more self-directed activities such as grooming and penis licking.

There is also trouble when intoxicated rodents, cats, or dogs have to take care of their young, just as we saw with the inebriated African cichlid fish. For example, mice restricted to ethanol as their only fluid will cannibalize their pups. Rat mothers given alcohol do not eat their young but show less interest in nest-building, nursing, and pup retrieval than do sober mothers. Being stoned on alcohol can also be disruptive to animals who don't have a nest but are trying to start one. Alcohol doesn't diminish sexual motivation in rats, but it does reduce male potency. Furthermore, intoxicated female rats have impaired postural responses that disrupt the performance of even a sober male attempting copulation.

Primates also have difficulties with sex under the influence of alcohol. When small amounts of alcohol are put into the drinking water of a group of monkeys, or injected into them, they become playful and increase their sexual mounting. Even sober monkeys join in the fun. Intoxication may be a barrel of monkeyshines, but drunkenness can be frustrating. Drunk male monkeys become sexually aroused, only to be prevented from copulating by sober dominant males in the colony. The drunk animals resolve the dilemma by masturbating.

Fighting is no easier than sex when drugs get in the way. For example, most mice under the influence of marijuana try to stay by themselves; they usually run away from the first signs of aggression. Even dominant mice are more likely to flee than fight. They simply want to be alone. When a fight breaks out, animals still under the influence are at risk of being abused because they may be too sleepy or immobile to fight well. And even if they are capable of moving but are clumsy and wobbly, the uncoordinated behavior may trigger a pathological attack by a sober animal—the rodent version of "rolling" a drunk. This effect is limited to the small cage. The sober animals show no desire to take advantage of their intoxicated partners if both have enough space.

The effects of intoxicants are not the same for all members of a social group. The temperament of the user is an important factor and the rule that drugs only modify a person's basic personality seems to hold true for most animals. A group of mice may all look the same, but they have recognizable individual personalities. Some are aggressive and will always attack the intruder. Other mice are timid by nature: they "flag"—turning their heads sharply away from the intruder—and evade contact. LSD only strengthens the basic personality of the animal: aggressive mice increase their aggression; timid mice become more defensive.

Similar effects are seen with fish. When it is the nature of fish to be combative, as in the case of Siamese fighting fish, LSD only increases the aggressive displays. Firemouths, red-throated fish from Central America, might act peaceful but they all react in the same aggressive way to LSD because the drug brings out their underlying feisty nature. Convicts, a close relative to the fire-mouths, have a similar reaction to alcohol. The convicts are scrappy tropical fish named for their black and white stripes. They are highly territorial and are always mauling intruding fish. Low doses of alcohol make them even more aggressive. If no intruder is present, the intoxicated convict becomes so mean it may tear apart an aquarium plant or two.

The social hierarchy of animals can also change when specific individuals are under the influence. Consider the case of two rats in a test box with a lever at one end that controls a water-delivery tube at the opposite end of the box. One rat (the "worker" rat) usually ends up doing all the work and pressing the lever, while the other rat stays near the tube and does most of the drinking. If the worker is then treated with THC, the division of labor is altered: the worker rat does far less work but reaps many more rewards because the nonworker now goes to work pressing the lever. Such effects are dependent on how much of the drug goes to which rat; too much marijuana to both rats and no work will get done. Fortunately, these effects subside as the animals recover from the intoxication. When individuals are once again normal, productivity in the rat workplace, as in the human workplace, can also recover.

Sometimes nobody notices the drug user until previously subtle effects become blatant. It may take months or years of chronic drug use before the effects emerge in social behavior and the group takes notice. For example, most studies with *Cannabis* have found that the drug reduces aggression when used in single doses or over a short period. Long-term use may be another story for some animals.

When selected monkeys in a group cage were given daily oral doses of THC for several years, chronic intoxication eventually changed the personality of some animals. During the first two or three months, the sedative effects of the drug predominated and the monkeys appeared relatively relaxed. As tolerance developed, the sedative effects diminished and were replaced with increased hitting, biting, chasing, and attack behavior. The pattern was for drugged animals to become more overtly aggressive as nondrugged animals became more submissive. Finally, low-ranking monkeys that were getting the THC became so aggressive that they began to rise in the dominance hierarchy. The sober monkeys were the ones that really suffered from abuse: they endured serious injuries and elevated levels of stress hormones. Even the young became innocent victims of these effects. In one long-term THC study, several females gave birth. The intoxicated mothers showed irritation and rejection behaviors toward their infants; they even refused to respond to the infants' distress calls.

Most of these beastly effects can be avoided with the proper environment for the intoxication. In the language of human social psychology, this translates to the proper setting. When the environment permits adequate room for the drugged animal to avoid the group, the individual, although still displaying signs of acute intoxication, does not cause such destructive behavior. A consistent finding has been that in large outdoor facilities, groups of primates treated with hallucinogens show fewer social problems than those living in high-density indoor conditions. Finding a place where you can get away from others, isolating yourself or dropping out, can be a real help. In the tight quarters of a laboratory cage, some intoxicated monkeys, desperate to be alone, will throw themselves against the cage door and walls.

Not all drugs antagonize social relationships, split the group, and cause animals to bang their heads against the wall. The type of intoxicant is an important determinant of effects on social behavior. Some drugs cause animals to socialize more than usual. Azaperone, for example, is a synthetic antipsychotic drug that will keep adult pigs from fighting with each other in close quarters, something they do normally when placed together for the first time. The drug also has a therapeutic effect on aggressive sows that refuse to nurse their litters. After treatment, the sows start caring for their piglets and continue to do so even after the acute effects of the drug have vanished.

Other antipsychotics, tranquilizers, and sedatives may reduce the frequency of social interactions among rodents and primates yet allow submissive animals to act more bravely and take a larger share of food. Such calmed animals investigate and explore less, huddling with each other for prolonged periods. Methaqualone, better known by the trade name of Quaalude, increases sexual behavior in male monkeys but also makes their potential female partners more aggressive. Humans interpret this reaction as increased sexual desire on the part of the female, but male monkeys are less chauvinistic and rarely force the issue the way humans do.

Morphine reduces much of the aggression seen in groups of rhesus monkeys. Even if the dominant male is the only animal addicted, less aggression is seen throughout the entire group. At doses that do not impair motor activity, the animals appear more tolerant of each other, sometimes lovable. Juvenile squirrel monkeys treated with morphine will increase the time they spend near their mothers. The young cuddle up to their mothers just as human infants once did after being given soothing opium syrups by their mothers. This cradle of peace and calm is easily rocked during withdrawal: the animals spontaneously fight with each other.

If morphine withdrawal rocks the cradle, then stimulants turn it upside down. Most research on the social effects of these drugs has been done with amphetamine but the few studies on cocaine suggest it has similar but shorter-acting properties. Both drugs can cause animals to withdraw from all social interactions. After receiving the drugs, primate mothers neither engage in normal contact with their infants nor respond to their distress calls. Eye contact between the mother and infant, an important cue for maternal behavior, is almost completely lacking when the mother monkey is under the influence of amphetamine. The mother seems more concerned with grooming herself than with caring for her baby. And if the infant is treated with amphetamine, it will wiggle and squirm continuously while looking around at everything. When the infant is frightened it will cling to the front wall of the cage rather than run to its mother. If it runs to its mother while she is still full of amphetamine, it finds her no different from the cold, hard steel of the cage wall.

Both mother and infant are exhibiting a common reaction of all species under the influence of amphetamines or cocaine: *stereotypy*. This refers to a persistent, mechanical repetition of motor activity that is done at the expense of social interactions. Rats will continually rub their paws and flex their necks. They chase each other around the cage and might just as readily end up sniffing or fighting. Cats engage in compulsive looking movements. Neither loud noises, the cries of kittens, nor catnip can distract them from their preoccupation with the purposeless searching. Monkeys are more active in the day but cocaine or amphetamine turns them into creatures of the night, stalking things that do not exist. They incessantly examine every minute section of their cages and bodies, rubbing and picking themselves until the skin is raw.

Human cocaine and amphetamine abusers exhibit the same aimless and endless behavior. There is enormous energy here but the behavior is directed to tasks that are usually antisocial. The Swedish describe it with the slang term *punding*, which refers to stupid behavior. One person on a binge of amphetamine use stood immobile for forty-eight hours, moving only to get another injection of the drug. Another on cocaine spent several days counting and recounting the number of squares on a stack of graph paper. These abusers might just as well have been counting angels dancing on the head of a pin, for their tasks were destined to continue forever or until the supply of the drug ran dry. The task of *punding* or *freaking*, to use the American slang expression, was the end in itself. In the words of one former freak, cocaine or amphetamine is like any other intoxicant if left uncontrolled: it can negate interest in all else but you and your intoxication.

We have seen that intoxication, for both animals and humans, means a change in many important aspects of social behavior. Whether poisoned, locoed, stuporous, drunk, narcotized, high, coked-up, freaked-out, or addicted, intoxicated animals and people tend to isolate themselves from social behaviors. Of course, some drugs may seem to facilitate social functioning, as with the pigs who received the antipsychotic medication that drew them closer to each other. But even closeness can have its inappropriate aspects. In 1910, six German students had just finished ingesting hashish when one of them decided to drop down on all fours while grunting like a pig. At once his companions imitated him, forming a litter of piglets that circled around the room all evening.

Once again, the point is not that hashish makes you act like a pig, or even that acting like a pig may not be silly and enjoyable for some people, but that when you're down on all fours it is as difficult to greet guests at the door as it is to ward off intruders or answer your baby's cries.

These social consequences of intoxication are potentially dangerous to survival, for both the individual and, potentially, the species. Continually drugged animals will eventually lose the biological advantages of social organization and suffer exposure to reduced breeding potential and increased aggression. They will be less able to adapt to the changes brought about by shifts from the low-stress conditions of isolation to the high stress of social interactions. The pursuit of intoxication is not simply a drinking party or bevy of individuals, but of species.

Our own species is deserving of special focus in Part II because only we can describe what intoxication really feels like and, ultimately, answer the question of why we want to feel this way. But it must be remembered that we are not alone in this pursuit. Certainly, as we have seen, the individual and social behavior of animals under the influence is very familiar to us. We may not be beasts, but we are, like our fellow animals, creatures from the same ark. And the drive to pursue intoxication is within us all.

The Cree Indians believe that all animals are thinking and feeling beings. This is particularly true of the bear, whom they revere as both an intelligent and spiritual creature. The intelligence allows the bear to behave in ways that we recognize as similar to our own. We may never know the spiritual world of our fellow animals like the bear, but if the Cree are right, their visions, both artificial and natural, would also be very familiar to us.

A wild grizzly bear was once darted with the synthetic drug ketamine. The drug literally knocks people down with ecstatic visions, and massive doses are often used to capture wild animals. I have given the drug to many human volunteers, who report being unable to move while mesmerized by feelings of harmony and joy in all that they see. But here the dose was insufficient to knock the bear down and he retreated to a protected ledge high on a mountain. He had escaped the potentially horrific consequences of fighting with his captors or returning to the den, where he would have been unable to interact appropriately. Alone in the privacy of this retreat and safe from abusive effects, he seemed to enjoy the grand view. He sat on his haunches, swinging his head from side to side, silently taking in the landscape. The Cree, speaking for the bear, might echo Sarah Bernhardt's comment and call it magnificent.

PART II

The Drive

10

The Fourth Drive

MOTIVATION
FOR INTOXICATION

1

There is a natural force that motivates the pursuit of intoxication.

This biological force has found expression throughout history. It pushed all the animals from Noah's Ark into patterns of drug-seeking and drug-using behavior. It has been the *basso continuo* in our own behavior since long before we were civilized primates. It has led to the discovery of many intoxicants, natural and artificial, and to demonstrations of its irrepressible drive. It was responsible for Annie Meyers' invention of the "Cocaine Dance."

The time was 1894. Annie C. Meyers, Chicago socialite, patron of the arts, congressional appointee to the World's Columbian Exposition, and recent widow of a distinguished naval officer, had a bad cold. Her lawyer advised her to try Birney's Catarrh Remedy, a popular over-the-counter cold powder containing cocaine. Soon she found herself sniffing cocaine day and night. A month's supply of cocaine cost only 50 cents, but Annie's runaway habit totaled $10 a day, a hefty sum that forced her to forge checks and steal.

Annie was caught shoplifting in the Marshall Field store in Chicago. She had concealed several costly silks and expensive pocketbooks in her clothing and was now confronted by the store detective and manager.

"If we let you go, will you keep out of the store?" asked the manager.

"Gentlemen, excuse me while I take a blow of my cocaine," answered the always polite Mrs. Meyers, who now needed a dose every five minutes. The men were fascinated by this little lady and her white powder. They asked her to show them how it was done. Then they asked to see it again. And again. Eventually they decided to let this "unfortunate" woman go. But a few days later they stopped her in the store just as she was trying to steal a pair of fur gloves.

"Have you any more goods on you?" snapped the detective.

"Search me!" invited Annie as she threw up her hands and stepped toward him.

"Don't come near me," begged the detective. "I am a married man."

He let her go again. Annie still had about $25 worth of goods on her, part of the thousands she would eventually take from that store. She resold the items on the black market.

All the money went for cocaine. After stealing a valuable diamond, she tried to sell it for 10 cents, the amount she was short for another bottle of Birney's. She would pet the bottles and speak to them as "my baby" and "my only friend." The only time she would leave the house was when her cocaine supply was exhausted and she had to go out to the store to buy some more. Detectives were following her everywhere, or so she imagined. Once, in the midst of a drug-induced paranoid episode, she fled to the roof of a house and refused to come down until the police passed her some cocaine via a string she lowered to them. She talked her way out of that arrest, too.

The unstoppable Mrs. Meyers used aliases and disguises, worked in different cities, and learned how to do the "Cocaine Dance"—a dance she would perform at public gatherings, then take up a collection to support her "baby." Late one night, alone with no one to dance for, she took a pair of scissors and pried loose one of her gold teeth. With blood streaming down her face and drenching her clothes, she pawned the tooth for 80 cents. Her baby was very hungry that night.

Throughout it all, Annie was aware of a powerful force that was directing her drive for cocaine. No other experience in her life had made such a pleasing impression on her brain. During the eight years she spent under the influence, she was aware that her pursuit involved many social and psychological problems, but cocaine also stirred something deep inside her that was soothing, enlivening, vitalizing. It seemed to Annie that she was satisfying a natural, biological urge. Like the grizzly bear on the mountain ledge, it was a precarious but magnificent natural feeling.

Calling an event natural is sometimes just reporting that it happens. Over the centuries, people have sought—and drugs have offered—a wide variety of effects, including pleasure, relief from pain, mystical revelations, stimulation, relaxation, joy, ecstasy, self-understanding, escape, altered states of consciousness, or just a different feeling. These statements of motives, of what people say they seek with drugs—and there could be an endless catalogue of such motives—is also what they say they seek without drugs. They are the same internal urges, wishes, wants, and aspirations that give rise to much of our behavior. Plant drugs and other psychoactive substances have been employed as natural tools for satisfying such motives.

The motivation to use drugs to achieve these effects is not innate but acquired. The major primary drives, those associated with survival needs and part of the organism's innate equipment, include the drives of hunger, thirst, and sex. These drives are a function of the organism satisfying certain primary biological needs. We are not born with acquired motivations yet they are not unnatural—they are simply an expression of what we strive to be. The pursuit of intoxication is no more abnormal than the pursuit of love, social attachments, thrills, power, or any number of other acquired motives. Man's primary biological needs may be body-bound, but his acquired addictions soar beyond these needs.

Acquired motives such as intoxication can be as powerful as innate ones. As we have seen, animals will die in pursuit of cocaine with the same absolute determination that drives them in their quest for food or water. Additionally, many of the naturally occurring plant drugs and their derivatives produce effects that directly or indirectly address the needs of hunger, thirst, or sex, thereby increasing their value to the organism. Unlike other acquired motives, intoxication functions with the strength of a primary drive in its ability to steer the behavior of individuals, societies, and species. Like sex, hunger, and thirst, the fourth drive, to pursue intoxication, can never be repressed. It is biologically inevitable.

Annie's dance to the power of this feeling was done in the footsteps and tracks of people and animals who have been inspired by the same driving beat throughout history. It began with Daniel's *Datura* hop through the woods, along a path strewn with accidental encounters. It was where Kaldi's goats pranced with coffee while livestock staggered on range poisons or galloped in addicting circles for locoweed. There were cats who leaped and turned for catnip while creatures everywhere twitched, shook, flipped, and rolled to a symphony of hallucinogens. Almost everyone caroused and reeled with alcohol or glided on opium. Mice jumped to the tune of morphine withdrawal. Grasshoppers did it awkwardly with marijuana resin. Llamas stepped assuredly with coca, and rats couldn't stop with cocaine. And primates, great and small, selected a variety of chemical partners, from tobacco to ergot, so they could dance with their ancestors and gods.

We have seen that intoxication with plant drugs and other psychoactive substances has occurred in almost every species throughout history. There is a pattern of drug-seeking and drug-taking behavior that is consistent across time and species. This behavior is similar for many animals because it has been shaped and guided by the same evolution and environment, the same plants and pressures. In considering an evolutionary explanation of the phenomenon, we might ask if intoxication is in some way beneficial to the species. After all, the pursuit of intoxication with drugs has no apparent survival value and in some situations has certainly contributed to many deaths. The condition is so obviously disadvantageous for some animals, such as insect pollinators, that natural selection acted strongly to eliminate it or helped animals to coevolve adaptive mechanisms. Yet the laws of evolution, even with help from the prohibitive laws of *Homo sapiens,* have not prevented it from surfacing in every age and in every culture.

What then could be the evolutionary value of such a condition? One possibility is that the pursuit of intoxication is a side effect of a beneficial gene or genes. Intoxication with drugs is widespread in animals, especially mammals, and it seems plausible that in order to appear in so extensive a range of genetic contexts it was inextricably associated with something else that was of survival value. The universal pursuit of intoxication implies the existence of direct connections between the molecular chemistry of the drugs and the chemistry of the central nervous system, such as opiate receptors in the mammalian brain, a biological investment that is difficult to think of as arising by accident. We are organisms with chemical brains and drives that pit the chemistry of the individual against that of the environment. We have survived these interactions and learned to thrive on them.

Intoxication, like the syndrome of food poisoning, has adaptive evolutionary value. All species must have been under continual evolutionary pressure to develop protection against chemicals that are true toxins. The intoxication can produce sensory or physiological disturbances that so shake up the individual, they cause ingested food to be rejected by emesis. Recognizing bitter tastes, bad feelings, or other disturbances may also help the individual to learn to avoid future ingestions. These defenses provide an ideal warning system for detecting the early central effects of toxins. The emetic responses or learned taste aversions are highly advantageous for animals accidentally feeding on plant toxins.

Exposure to intoxicants can also produce pleasant experiences, thereby attracting us and forming the familiar "love-hate" fascination described by so many addicts. Annie Meyers described her passion for cocaine as an expression of motherly love and her intoxications were pure enjoyment; yet the cyclical withdrawal was hell. Her nonstop use prevented the agony of withdrawal, except when she was periodically arrested. These occasional unpleasant episodes only strengthened her determination to avoid them by staying "full of cocaine" all the time. The benefits of staying high on cocaine overshadowed the costs of stopping; use continued according to the same economic equation governing other types of intoxications.

This principle of positive effects outweighing negative effects can be illustrated by dizziness, a major drug effect that is triggered by disturbances in sensory input or motor control. When dizziness is accompanied by nausea, as in food poisoning or motion sickness, it is generally unpleasant. Animals as well as people usually reject drugs such as locoweed that produce intense dizziness. But when unaccompanied by nausea or severe physiological disturbances, the dizziness can become a desired state of intoxication, and inebriating amounts of such substances as alcohol will be sought after. Thus dizziness can be a pleasant or an unpleasant experience, and one that we seek almost as often as we avoid it. It is perhaps the most primitive form of intoxication and, aside from sleep and dreams, one of the oldest altered states of consciousness known to our species.

In the initiation rites of the !Kung Bushmen of the Kalahari Desert (the "!" denotes a click sound in their language), the men dance in a circular rut, stamping around and around, hour after hour. The dancing can generate a dizziness so extreme that it induces a trance state marked by visions. In the Umbanda rituals in Brazil, participants create an identical trance by spinning around rapidly as their heads and chests jerk back and forth in opposing directions. The whirling Sufi dervishes dance and spin like tops to achieve a similar altered state of consciousness.

Dizziness is not only an ancient and adult form of intoxication, it is one of the first to be discovered by children. It is common to find three- and four-year-olds whirling and twirling themselves into delirious stupors. Many children have discovered that a good way to induce dizziness is to wind up a swing and let it unwind while they are sitting on it. The "witch's cradle," a U.S. adaptation of the swinging basket once used by witches in the Middle Ages, is a more certain way to swing into a trance. The cradle is actually a metal swing in which a blindfolded rider stands upright. The swing hangs like a pendulum and moves the rider in rotating and horizontal planes in response to the slightest body movements. Typically, a trance is induced in a few minutes, giving the rider visions comparable to those produced by hallucinogens. Many amusement-park rides are designed to induce other thrilling experiences through dizziness. For example, "tilt-a-whirls" move riders in vertical and horizontal planes while spinning them around.

Many intoxicants also whirl people around; at least that is the sensation users report happening in their heads. "I drink to catch me a good little tilt," responded one young patient when I asked him why he drinks so much beer. He reported that other drugs had their own distinctive effects. Barbiturates? "They gummed me up." Quaaludes? "'Ludes make everything feel real rubbery." Amphetamines? "They tweak me out." Hallucinogenic mushrooms? "With 'shrooms I can spin around and see what is on in my brain."

These may be crude descriptions but they illustrate the different feelings of intoxication. Throughout most of his drug experiences, the patient also said he felt dizzy. The term *dizziness* has a pejorative value in medical and psychiatric contexts, but this patient was not using the word to describe unpleasant sensations. Rather, he was using the term to indicate a mental daze that was giddy, light, and totally acceptable to him. As the world tilted about him, he found pleasure in the mismatched perceptions.

Dizziness is a common aspect of drug-induced intoxication and some drugs induce it better than others. More than half of the people who smoke marijuana experience dizziness, and in one study 82 percent of them got dizzy during their very first intoxication. The intoxication with peyote cactus is inevitably marked by dizziness, hallucinations, nausea, and frequent vomiting. Most Indians have learned to minimize the nausea and vomiting by fasting before eating the peyote, then remaining motionless during the intoxication. They maximize the visionary effects by taking peyote during nighttime ceremonies around a flickering fire.

Young children may be introduced to the dizziness experience by dentists who give them laughing gas as an anesthetic. The gas, nitrous oxide, causes a dissociative reaction, a feeling that the mind is free from the body, hence the absence of pain in the dental chair. Sensations of dizziness, floating, and flying are often encountered. The children laugh and giggle. Happily, they are more apt to remember these subjective experiences than the dental procedures themselves.

The young patients frequently describe the world moving around them, and it is this feature which is so often sought after in nonmedical settings where users experiment with tanks of nitrous oxide, which are available over-the-counter. Users are not always careful to have sufficient oxygen available and the resulting hypoxia may cause fainting. For some, even passing out can be a desirable altered state. They take deep inhalations from balloons filled with the gas while standing on a mattress. The mattress is there to cushion their falls when they become unconscious. Young children often experiment with such intoxicating "games" without the aid of a drug. They may deliberately hyperventilate and have other children squeeze them around the chest so that they faint. The panting hyperventilation, central to these effects, produces a lowering of carbon dioxide pressure, cerebral vasoconstriction, and a final dreamy collapse as the world starts to move around them.

As they grow up, these children, who score high on psychological tests measuring their propensity to seek new sensations, sometimes experiment with household drugs that promise similar experiences. Intoxication from sniffing glue, gasoline, paint, or any number of other deliriants have been utilized by children too old to twirl yet too young to have access to other drugs, New Age Tom Sawyers who have found something else to do with the paint besides put it on the fence.

Adults were offered the opportunity to enjoy these "school-boy pleasures" in London theaters of the eighteenth century. The theaters provided "ladies and gentlemen of the first respectability" with the "chemical recreation" of nitrous oxide. People laughed and sang and danced. The gas was celebrated in songs, poems, and plays. And use continued in the nineteenth century. Philosopher William James believed that the intoxication revealed the uniqueness of our species to contemplate the hidden meaning behind language and thought. Writer Oscar Wilde once said that with the gas "I knew everything," although he was surprised to learn that the little pink man he was watching on a distant stage was really his dentist who had just pulled a tooth. Throughout all these recreations and revelations, the people reported an intoxication marked by dizziness, delirium, and delight. A few had to be restrained from hurting themselves or others. Many became sick with symptoms resembling motion sickness.

Experiences with dizziness-provoking drugs like nitrous oxide are illustrative of intoxications in general, which cannot be easily separated into distinctive pleasant and unpleasant feelings. The initial encounters with many drugs are unpleasant and the reported effects for opiates, barbiturates, alcohol, and nicotine include nausea, vomiting, sweating, dysphoria, emotional lability, aggression, drowsiness, and lethargy. There may also be impairments in concentration, thinking, comprehension, memory, and judgment. William James didn't vomit with nitrous oxide but his nonsensical statement that he was experiencing nausea "what's nausea but a kind of -ausea? Sober, drunk, -unk, astonishment" leaves us with a little of our own astonishment at the cognitive dysfunction of this great thinker while under the influence. As a rule, some negative effects are accompanied by some positive effects. Why bother pursuing such a chancy condition?

2

Part of the answer may be found in the study of the self-administration of drugs that continually recycle the user through addiction and withdrawal. As we have seen, animals self-administer the same drugs we use. The behaviors of these animals have told us much about effects such as tolerance and breaking points. Yet with the exception of the pigeons and monkeys that were trained to report their hallucinations, few animal experiments tell us about the internal feelings that motivate use. And so we turn to human subjects for answers about their subjective sensations.

Many addicting drugs such as cocaine or heroin produce a rush of intense pleasure, especially if rapidly delivered through injection or smoking, followed by mild discomfort as the drug loses its euphoric effect through metabolic destruction. The discomfort is both physiological and psychological. Cocaine leaves the user with lethargy and fatigue. Heroin's discomfort can be seen in the user's runny eyes and nose, abdominal pains, clammy skin, and muscular malaise. Psychologically, both drugs create a craving, an aversive state that animals and people will seek to avoid by repeated self-administration of the drug. The aversive state will go away on its own, but the heightened contrast between the previous euphoria and the craving creates a universal impatience.

The important elements of this behavior are the changes in affect. The initial intoxication has a different emotional quality from the subsequent withdrawal. Cocaine's first few doses, for example, produce an initial state of excitement and intense euphoria. The onset of the drug action is the reinforcer. But after the drug effect dissipates, the second state, the unpleasant withdrawal phase, begins. Withdrawal finally disappears with time or another dose. Therefore, both the *onset* of the drug effect and the *removal* of the withdrawal effect acquire the capability of reinforcing or rewarding behavior; both can motivate the continued use of the drug. This can be easily illustrated by cocaine addicts like Mrs. Meyers who continue to use the drug despite the fact that they no longer feel any pleasure or high from the intoxication. They have generated tolerance to the initial euphoric state, yet drug use is maintained because repeated doses act to block or remove the withdrawal effect.

Psychologist Richard Solomon has proposed a model to account for these events. It is known as the *opponent-process theory* and it is helpful in explaining a wide variety of acquired motivations, from addiction to Zen, from rock climbing to free-fall parachuting. According to the model, most organisms behave in the direction of restoring bodily functions to a normal state. Solomon explains that "the brains of all mammals are organized to oppose or suppress many types of emotional arousals or hedonic processes, whether they are pleasurable or aversive, whether they have been generated by positive or negative reinforcers." The opposing processes are automatically set in motion by events that induce disturbances in physiological or psychological systems. These disturbances, in turn, elicit counterreactions that function to correct the imbalances.

For example, the first few doses of heroin produce a rush of euphoria followed by a state of craving. The rush is the positive reinforcer and the craving is the negative one. After many doses the rush is greatly diminished and euphoria is often absent. However, the withdrawal state of craving becomes longer and more intense. While the positive reinforcer (the rush) has lost most of its power, the negative reinforcer (the craving) has gained strength. It has acquired sufficient power to motivate behavior. The user may have become tolerant to the drug, but the intolerance to drug termination or absence drives him on.

The opponent-process model can also account for situations in which the rush is aversive and the withdrawal is positive. For example, a parachutist experiences terror during his first free fall jump. Studies of military parachutists have found that even the bravest men show an initial fear reaction: eyes bulge, lips retract, and the men yell with anxiety. Once they have landed safely, they appear too stunned to talk. Then they experience relief and begin a lively chatter with other jumpers. After many parachute jumps, the fear reaction is undetectable, and affective habituation is said to have occurred. This allows the positive aftereffects of withdrawal—the removal of the anxiety upon landing and the subsequent relief—to reinforce further jumps. Now the parachutists look eager before the jump and report a thrill during the free fall. The landing is followed by a long-lasting feeling of exhilaration.

These concepts help to explain how some drug-induced intoxications can be rewarding despite the occurrence of negative effects. The most unusual and "negative" drug taken by both monkeys and people is phencyclidine (PCP), a compound that produces negative effects in 100 percent of the intoxications and positive effects only 60 percent of the time. It defies convenient classification and has mixed excitatory, sedative, anesthetic, and hallucinatory properties. The intoxications are predictably unpredictable and almost everyone reports bad trips. In a sense, the persistent use and abuse of a drug like PCP seems to be a paradox. Yet the fourth drive is not just motivating people to feel good or bad—it is a desire to feel different, to achieve a rapid change in one's state. The direction of change, up or down, good or bad, is of secondary importance. If we can understand this nature of PCP's attraction, then we can understand how almost any intoxicant can satisfy the fourth drive.

Before PCP reached nonmedical users it was called Sernyl and was used as a surgical anesthetic for humans. The drug did not perform well in clinical tests. Patients were oblivious to the surgery but, in the recovery room, they awoke in the midst of a lingering and confusing delirium resembling schizophrenia. While some patients felt years younger—almost as if they were "born again"—others had a stormy emergence that required constant supervision because they could become violent. Therefore, PCP was restricted to use as an immobilizing agent for animals since veterinarians were generally less concerned about the psychological aftermath in their patients. However, because it was relatively cheap and easy to manufacture and the effects of subanesthetic doses mimicked those of many illegal hallucinogens, PCP began to appear as an adulterant in street drugs. Familiarity bred experimentation. People started to experiment with pure PCP itself and gradually acquired a liking for the drug experience.

PCP is typically smoked, although it can be used in a number of ways, and the symptoms start to appear within a few minutes. Users report peak effects within fifteen to thirty minutes, followed by a prolonged intoxication of several hours. Recovery may take many more hours, even days. The experience is triggered by PCP's direct action on the brain, arousing the user's body and elevating mood. Heart rate and blood pressure increase. The mood turns euphoric. But as the extremities are numbed, motor behavior becomes uncoordinated and the user acts in a drunken manner. Further doses produce bizarre and inappropriate motor movements.

Under PCP's influence Luther R. cut off his own penis and swallowed it. The paramedics found him lying on the kitchen floor in a pool of blood. As they attempted to stop the bleeding, Luther regurgitated his penis. He never felt the pain. At similar points of intoxication users might not be able to feel a surgeon's knife or a blow from a police baton, yet sensory impulses in grossly distorted form do reach the brain.

Seventeen-year-old Martin L. had just finished smoking a PCP cigarette when he started breaking store windows with karate kicks as he walked along the street. When the police arrived, Martin flashed a butcher knife and attacked. The police were unable to subdue him, even after multiple baton blows, and Martin, making no sound whatsoever, was showing no signs of fatigue or pain. Additional officers were called to the scene, six in all, and eventually they restrained and handcuffed the "super-human" Martin. The handcuffs held, although other people under the influence of PCP have mustered the 550 pounds of pressure necessary to snap them. Martin's first words came in the form of a song he sang in the hospital, words that suggested some vague, albeit distorted, awareness of the preceding events: "I'm strong to the finish 'cause I eats my spinach, I'm Popeye the sailorman!"

What is so attractive about the state of PCP intoxication? When users like Martin are examined in the hospital, they do not look as though they should be singing. Flushed, feverish, and dripping with sweat, the users seem consumed by discomfort. There may be excessive salivation and tearing. Speech is slurred and difficult. A blank stare comes over the face. Unable to stand or walk properly, they start shivering, but it's actually preseizure muscle activity. Touch them and their muscles may become tense and rigid. However, the users remain largely detached from these physical discomforts and focus on the subjective experiences. They are so unaware of physical sensations that they often have the sensation of floating clear out of their bodies.

It is precisely this dissociation, not unlike the trance from dizziness or anesthesia from nitrous oxide, that is so attractive to many users. They have dreamlike experiences in which they feel as though they were in a different place, in a different time. A common sensation is the feeling that one is watching oneself from a distance. When we think of the last time we went swimming in the ocean, we might see a mental image of ourselves running along the beach and into the water. This is an entirely fictitious memory. We couldn't possibly have seen ourselves. Yet memory images often contain fleeting glimpses of oneself. PCP users have similar dissociated or out-of-body perspectives but *while* events are taking place. In such an altered state, PCP users report a generalized feeling of well-being and a detachment from worldly tensions and anxieties. In other words, their affect is changed. For many, there is ambivalence or a blanding of affect; users claim even this can be euphoric in light of preexisting depression or unhappiness. Others experience a negativism and hostility, sometimes coupled with feelings of "sheer nothingness" and thoughts about death. This, too, can be rewarding for individuals who can find escape from the stimulus overload of their normal lives and feel stronger after surviving a powerful psychological experience.

The names given to PCP by users tell of these varying stimulus properties: Angel Dust, Devil's Dust, Embalming Fluid, Goon, Peace, Rocket Fuel, Whack, Wobble Weed, and Zombie. Other street names suggest that PCP intoxication can also recapitulate phylogeny, at least experientially: Amoeba, Worm, Busy Bee, Dog, Hog, Pig Killer, Horse Tranquilizer, Elephant Tranquilizer, Monkey Dust, and Gorilla Tab.

According to the Los Angeles Police Department, Lenny B. turned into one of these animals after smoking a tobacco cigarette that had been dipped in liquid PCP. In his mind, Lenny was flying over a duck farm. But in his house he walked like a duck, quacked like a duck, and announced to the startled guests that he was Donald Duck. Then he savagely stabbed a man to death. He was found waddling in a puddle on the sidewalk. Lenny was unaware of these events, and later told me he enjoyed the high and would take PCP again.

Elsewhere, Linda, one of my research subjects who had taken PCP in a controlled environment, had a quiet introspective experience. She reported seeing images of God and heaven: "I was flying with the angels. When I started coming down, I felt sad that I was leaving such a lovely place. I think I even cried. I hadn't done that in years. But most of all I remember the peace and tranquility. Everything was good. I want to be there always."

PCP will not automatically deliver a devilish or angelic experience.

Many of the horror stories retold in the media are true, but the unsung tales of beatific paradises experienced by users like Linda are much more common. As with most mind-altering drugs, the intoxication from PCP is shaped and guided by both pharmacological and behavioral variables. Individual health and personality, the size of the dose, route of administration, and frequency of dosing are a few of the more obvious factors. And so are the set (expectations) of the user and the setting (environment) for the intoxication. Less apparent, but more important, are the patterns of use in which the pursuit of intoxication finds expression. These patterns are the most critical determinants of abuse. In other words, whether or not a drug will get an individual into trouble is often a question of whether an individual gets into a troublesome pattern of use with the drug.

3

The patterns of drug use are individual expressions of the fourth drive. They are structured by psychosocial needs and fall into five basic types that are seen worldwide: experimental, social-recreational, circumstantial-situational, intensified, and compulsive. These patterns describe a continuum from irregular use to highly structured, continual use. Shifts from one part of the continuum to another can occur with changing needs of the individual.

All drug users begin with an experimental pattern that is primarily motivated by curiosity about the drug and a desire to experience the anticipated effects of intoxication. The first reactions are often influenced by the initial set or expectation of what the experience is going to be like. For example, people experimenting with the hallucinogen MDMA are usually searching for what is promised by its street name, Ecstasy; at least half of them experience muscle tension, sweating, and blurred vision so severe that they express no desire to repeat the experience. For the others who anticipate these effects as a prelude to a subsequent euphoria, Ecstasy delivers on its promise, thus encouraging future trials.

The initial setting or environment can also influence these experimental trials. Most people experiment with drugs in the company of someone else, generally a close friend. This may help the individual overcome initial reluctance or anxiety, yet, as we have seen in other animals, social groups may not be the best settings for intoxication. Individuals experimenting with PCP are often looking for a tranquil or mellow experience; a subsequent confused or excitatory reaction to others around them may thwart their future experimentation. Conversely, if they are seeking stimulation in an otherwise boring home environment, as Lenny B. told me, then the hallucinations from high doses of PCP may be rewarding.

When friends or acquaintances get together on a regular basis to share a drug experience perceived by them as both acceptable and pleasurable, it is called *social* or *recreational use*. These are the patterns typically found in alcohol and marijuana parties, at afternoon teas, or at coffee and cigarette breaks. At this stage of drug use, intoxication is still voluntary and, regardless of the duration of use, tends not to escalate to uncontrollable amounts. For example, studies of long-term cocaine users have found that recreational patterns can be maintained for a decade or more without loss of control. Such use tends to occur in weekly or biweekly episodes and users perceive that the effects facilitate social functioning. In a sense, users in these situations monitor and control their own doses, much like monkeys titrating intake.

If use is motivated by a desire to achieve a specific drug effect that is helpful in coping with a particular condition, the pattern of use is called *circumstantial* or *situational*. This category includes long-distance truck drivers who have relied on stimulants to provide extended alertness and endurance, as did the Apollo astronauts who used amphetamine before reentry into the Earth's atmosphere. Both the truck drivers and the astronauts were medicating themselves in order to obtain a certain self-prescribed effect, like the baboons who treated despair with tobacco and alcohol. The same pattern is seen in the case of a student who takes caffeine pills to stay awake, an overweight woman who takes cocaine to lose a few pounds, or a worker who relaxes with an afterwork drink. The pattern is the same although the choices of drugs may not always be prudent or legal. One of the greatest dangers of this pattern is that the user will become accustomed to having the drug in similar circumstances and will be unable to exercise the control that usually accompanies medically prescribed and supervised use. Mrs. Meyers may have felt that cocaine, in addition to helping her cold, also tempered the loneliness of her recent widowhood. It was undoubtedly tempting to use the drug well after her cold was over. She quickly moved into the next pattern: *intensified use.*

When a person perceives a need to achieve persistent effects or maintain such effects, a daily or intensified pattern of drug use may occur. In the case of many drugs, this recurrent drug taking will escalate to states of psychological or physical addiction. Intensified users include the American housewife who regularly consumes tranquilizers, the coca-chewing Bolivian miner, the daily marijuana-smoking laborer in Jamaica, and the opium-munching water buffalo in Vietnam. In these instances the pattern of drug use has become a normal and customary activity of everyday life. Daily PCP users, who are often innercity youths suffering from a high rate of unemployment, frequently cite a need to achieve constant relief from persistent unpleasant internal and external environments. A young secretary who reported that she was using cocaine a few times each day "to white-out" the depression of her recent divorce was also an intensified user who ran the risk of escalating to still greater amounts.

Escalation is common for daily cocaine or heroin users. They use at high-frequency and high-intensity levels, the mark of the *compulsive* pattern of drug taking. They cannot discontinue use without experiencing some physiological discomfort or psychological disruption. Mrs. Meyers was so afraid of withdrawal that she would tear her hair out and throw a temper tantrum whenever she was arrested. The strategy worked; her jailers would take pity on her and sneak her some cocaine. A characteristic of these compulsive users is that they become preoccupied with drug seeking and drug taking, often to the exclusion of other behaviors. Compulsive users are not only the prototypical street junkies, they also include alcohol-dependent white-collar workers and white rats, opiate-dependent physicians and research monkeys, and chain-smokers everywhere. The eight-year cocaine career of socialite Annie Meyers was no different from that of the skid-row alcoholic she was often mistaken for.

Some drugs offer greater risks of developing compulsive patterns than others. Because hallucinogens like LSD stop working when taken daily due to tolerance, intensified and compulsive patterns of use do not develop with these drugs. The tolerance can be so complete that even superdoses have no effect if the person has been taking the drug too often. Therefore, most LSD users will adopt experimental patterns and take the drug no more than ten times over the course of their entire lives. Conversely, cocaine has an extremely short duration of action. It doesn't last long and, coupled with tolerance, can cause even social users to escalate short runs or binges into long-term compulsive patterns. Compulsive cocaine smokers may take hits as frequently as ten times per hour.

In a sense, the escalating patterns of drug use, from experimental to compulsive, can be viewed as points on a continuum. The different patterns cannot be separated easily, and individuals move along this continuum at speeds governed largely by the amount of the drug that is fueling the drive. For example, large and frequent experimental dosages of morphine delivered during a binge may catapult the user directly into compulsive patterns. Conversely, small measured doses can maintain intensified patterns for years without difficulty.

4

These dynamics of the fourth drive are best illustrated by the history of cocaine. The experiences of Annie Meyers came at a turning point in that history, at a time when the dosages of cocaine preparations had recently changed. Before her time, people were prevented from developing runaway compulsive habits because only coca preparations were available.

A widely held belief in Western medicine was that most physical and mental diseases were caused by brain exhaustion and the best way to cure these conditions was to wake up the brain with a stimulating coca tonic. Physicians, pharmacists, and chemists recommended daily doses of coca extracts or wines that delivered an amount of cocaine equivalent to that obtained from chewing the leaves. While intensified dosage patterns were normally prescribed, abuse was held in check by the highly diluted preparations. Most coca wines contained only 10 milligrams of cocaine per fluid ounce, equivalent to one piece of the Coca-Peps gum used in the monkey studies.

Other patterns of use were encouraged by the commercial marketing of coca products. Coca was promoted as a wonder drug not only for medicine but also for social and recreational purposes. To make it more attractive, an assortment of coca preparations were sold, including tonics, gum, cigarettes, and soft drinks. Coca-Cola, originally promoted as a brain tonic for the elderly, was made with a coca extract. It reportedly contained slightly less than 60 milligrams of cocaine per eight-ounce serving, the amount found in a modern intranasal dose.

The tonics of Mrs. Meyers's day were much more potent; cocaine had been recently isolated from the leaf, and the manufacturers substituted it for the coca extracts. Large amounts of cocaine alkaloids or salts could now be readily dissolved in almost any tonic or packed into any powder. Whereas coca products were treated as roughly equivalent to the chewing of the leaves, cocaine was advertised as two hundred times stronger. And it was. Just as the chimps on North and South Island had discovered, coca was not cocaine, and the golden age of coca medicine was in for some lackluster years.

Physicians started increasing the daily dosages to as much as 1,200 milligrams—a lethal dose for most people if taken into the body all at once. The effects of increased doses of cocaine were further complicated by the popularity of the highly efficient intranasal and injection routes of administration. By the time Mrs. Meyers bought her first bottle of Birney's, many snuffs were pure cocaine and patients were instructed to take them as needed. Mrs. Meyers's perceived needs went beyond the bounds of treating her cold and her pattern of use became compulsive.

When Annie Meyers was arrested for the last time, while trying to blow open a safe, she looked awful and she knew it: "My hair was mostly out. A part of my upper jawbone had rotted away. My teeth were entirely gone. My face and my entire body were a mass of putrefying cocaine ulcers. I weighed only about eighty pounds and it would be hard to conceive of a more repulsive sight." Not hard at all. One need only examine more recent cases where users, faced with plentiful supplies of cheap cocaine, danced faster and harder than Mrs. Meyers ever could with her Birney's.

During the early 1970s when cocaine once again became a social-recreational drug of choice for North Americans, the case of Annie Meyers seemed like a historical oddity. Studies of intranasal users during this period revealed that the daily intake averaged only 150 milligrams. But by the end of the decade, many social users had climbed the ladder to more concentrated patterns of use. Sniffing as much as

1,000 milligrams (1 gram) in a single dose, Kenny D. suffered severe nasal erosion. Once when he blew his nose, out came a large glob, thick as a cigar, that stretched across his palm. He displayed it to his amazed wife, who named it "Stillborn." The glob was cartilage tissue. Kenny's nose had collapsed. Cocaine seemed to dull the constant pain and Kenny continued his daily use even after another discharge, "Baby Sparrow," was born.

Many cocaine users became concerned about the risks of such nasal damage and switched to smoking cocaine free base. Some users smoked as much as 85,000 milligrams a day! They were unaware that although their noses might be saved, their bodies and lives would be ruled by compulsive patterns of use.

Mitch R. couldn't afford all the cocaine he wanted to smoke. When his supply was exhausted, he often searched the floors and carpet fibers for specks of cocaine to smoke. Like many cocaine smokers, Mitch had a hacking cough with a black, bloody expectorate. One day he "free-based" his black sputum and smoked it. He decided it was "a good hit" and continued the practice whenever supplies were low. Terry B. had a special glass waterpipe he named "Old Faithful." He had been a super-stitious cocaine smoker for several years and never changed the water in the pipe. The pipe itself was wrapped in aluminum foil to prevent anyone from seeing what was growing in the stagnant, cocaine-saturated water. When Terry was out of cocaine, a swig from "Old Faithful" kept him going until he could replenish his supply.

These users had the same pale, cadaverous features that caused Annie Meyers to describe herself as repulsive. To prove her point, Mrs. Meyers included pictures of herself in her autobiographical book, *Eight Years in Cocaine Hell,* the first drug confession written by a woman and the first confession from a cocaine abuser. Those pictures showed the sunken eyes and emaciated look that was characteristic of Terry B. and so many other compulsive users, including the Michigan monkeys who injected themselves with cocaine. Annie's ulcers were not shown, but a photograph of Terry's leg, full of open sores that he picked while look-ing for "cocaine bugs," was featured in a *Time* magazine cover story. *Time* decided not to use photographs of another patient who tried to remove the hallucinatory bugs from his body with a scalpel and forceps. When that effort failed, the patient attempted to burn them out with a propane torch: the pictures showed second-and third-degree burns covering his thighs and testicles.

Until the advent of the modern cocaine abuser, the odd horror tales associated with other drugs were exactly that: rare examples of highly idiosyncratic reactions to intoxications. There were cases of PCP abusers who had gouged out their own eyes; others had sat quietly while engulfed in flames; some had pulled out their teeth with pliers, and one woman had put her own baby in a caldron of steaming water. But cocaine users provided the quintessential examples of the fourth drive's relentless power. Hit in the eye by a piece of cocaine-encrusted glass from an exploding waterpipe, one user described it as the best hit she ever had. She didn't stop. After clumsily burning his hands with a lighter, a cocaine smoker took to wearing fireproof gloves. He solved the problem of constantly grinding his teeth by wearing a plastic mouth guard. He didn't stop. Faced with increasing expenses for cocaine, a mother adjusted her budget by selling her baby on the black market. She didn't stop.

Arrest finally stopped Annie Meyers from doing her Cocaine Dance. Her treatment consisted of a long stay in a sanitarium coupled with the religious and moral lectures that were popular in her day. Traditionally, society still tries to hold the drive in check through legal and moral controls that employ penalties for use, treatment for users, and preventive education for nonusers. Although these methods haven't worked, our response in the face of such unstoppable examples of the drive as the modern cocaine abuser has been to intensify the controls. Accordingly, punishments escalate, involuntary testing programs for the detection of drug use become more widespread, treatment becomes mandatory, and educational campaigns tend to deliver more hyperbole than honest information, resulting in the recurrent message that "drugs will destroy your brain."

Recently, there have been attempts to quiet the underlying drive itself. Psychiatrists try to block it with isolation, physical and chemical restraints, even electric shock. When all else fails, neurosurgeons in South America have severed the neural pathways in the brains of young cocaine users who refuse to stop. It seems as though the healing profession is stepping in to fulfill the promise that drugs will destroy your brain. In Annie

Meyers's time those in the healing arts also panicked. Dr. Albrecht Erlenmeyer, a famous nineteenth-century drug expert, saw so many unstoppable addicts like Mrs. Meyers that he proclaimed cocaine to be "the third scourge of mankind," after opium and alcohol. It was really only the fourth drive, a drive our species had always danced to and always would.

11

Fire in the Brain

MENTAL MARVELS, MURDER, AND MECHANISMS OF CONTROL

1

The drive to intoxication takes the pursuer deep into the brain, through the doors of perception, and across mental landscapes of heavens and hells. The major drugs we use for the journey act to excite, to quiet, or to distort the chemical and electrical activity within the brain and nervous system. Surprisingly, given the countless varieties of mind-altering drugs and the even greater assortment of individual personalities, the human brain responds in a fixed number of ways. The resulting experience is as universal and fundamental as the drive itself.

The basic experience involves predictable elements and themes that arise from common structures in the human brain and nervous system, common biological experiences, and common reactions of the central nervous system to intoxicants. Differences are only skin deep. Even the hallucinations have fixed patterns that cause the Bushman in Africa and the stockbroker in New York to have similar perceptions, thoughts, and feelings.

A simple analogy can illustrate this process. Picture a man in his living room. He is standing at a closed window opposite the fireplace and looking out at the dark night. As the fire starts to burn, the images of the objects in the room behind him can be seen reflected dimly in the window. As more logs burn and the fire in the fireplace illuminates the room, the man now sees a vivid reflection of himself and the contents of the room, which appears to be outside the window. As the analogy is applied to intoxication, the window is the window of our senses to the world, the fire is the electrical excitation in the brain, and the logs are the drugs that dampen (sedatives) or stoke up (stimulants and hallucinogens) the fire. When the fire is stifled, the man will see very little. But when the fire burns brightly, the glass will reflect the furniture in the rooms of his mind—his images, memories, dreams, and fantasies. The brighter the fire—the more cocaine or LSD or PCP in the brain—the more vivid the reflections become until some users step through the window, like Alice going through the looking glass, and behave as if the images were real.

The outer room to my laboratory at UCLA's Neuropsychiatric Institute was furnished to resemble a living room. There were comfortable chairs, warm Oriental rugs, bookcases, flowers, and soft lighting. The walls, however, were bare. I was counting on the psychonauts to supply their own drawings. The term *psychonaut* was coined by a journalist who covered the experiments; I preferred to think of the young men and women who volunteered for my experiments as "the fireplaces."

Each subject was in top physical and mental condition and was experienced with such drugs as LSD. All had logged many hours learning a new verbal code with which to describe their mental imagery—those inner rooms of the mind that I planned to illuminate with a variety of drugs. Typically, when you close your eyes you do not see a solid black curtain. If you look very carefully, there are things to see. Some images come from certain structures within the eye itself. The structures, or entoptic events, can be visualized when incident light strikes the eye in an appropriate way. One may see black lacework against a background of red, caused by blood vessels that cast shadows on photosensitive cells within the retina. There may be small dancing spots of light, caused by the shadows of red "floater" cells passing through retinal capillaries, or any number of other images.

Most of these images vanish in a totally dark room. But if you relax and pay careful attention, neurons discharging in the retina and in the visual cortex can make the scene appear gray rather than pitch-black. These same neurons may induce phosphenes—spots, disks, streaks of lightning, glowing blue arcs, and even checkerboard patterns. Blinking the eyes will not erase the phosphenes but only flick them into rapid, right-angle turns. Applying pressure by gently rubbing your closed eyes can create even more of these patterns. Yet such momentary phenomena, like the entoptic events, have a vague, washed-out quality.

When LSD enters the picture, so to speak, these lights and images brighten and turn into a cascade of vivid colors and patterns. Like roadside beacons, they warn the traveler that up ahead lies not only the imagery of *2001*'s stargate corridor but also the twilight zone of hallucinations. It is a landscape where images change so quickly, so intensely, that users are left with only short, breathless descriptions: "Wow," "Trippy," and "Far-out" are typical. Previous literary and philosophical explorations aside, most people have difficulty describing both the simple and the complex scenes revealed by such drugs. The psychonauts were trained observers, specialists fully equipped to deal with the cartography of inner space, just as the astronauts have been trained to describe the novel terrain of their voyages. Apollo 14 pilot Edgar Mitchell once reported a flash that appeared "blue with a white cast, like a blue diamond," and *Skylab 4* pilot William Pogue reported "tadpoles about three eighths of an inch long, at arm's length." No one accused these well-trained observers of being mad or victims of some new space hysteria. The reports were studied, analyzed, and subsequently confirmed. Both men were describing phosphenelike images caused by cosmic nuclei interacting with the human optical system. When molecules of drugs impacted on the central nervous systems of the psychonauts, their reports would be accepted with equal credibility.

The psychonauts were trained to describe the images in precise language, defining a color, for instance, to within a few millimicrons of its spectral wavelength. Because some hallucinogens can generate a bewildering assortment of geometric forms, the psychonauts were trained to scan them quickly, abstracting over individual differences while looking for common features with which to classify the images into preset categories. For example, in training related to a tunnel category, I showed them hundreds of different slides of tunnels so that the subjects would have a broad concept of the tunnel form. In this way, new instances of the form, which might not have been seen before, could be appropriately classified. Thus, a twisted alley, perhaps with Day-Glo girders stretching to infinity, could still be appropriately classified as the basic tunnel form it represents. And because drug-induced images are kinetic and do not remain in the mind's eye for very long, the psychonauts were trained to recognize images even if they lasted for only eight milliseconds.

Once the training was mastered, each psychonaut was given a dose of a drug that was calculated to generate a typical intoxication without interfering with the accuracy of his reporting skills. Each was then led from the outer living room to a bed in an inner experimental chamber that was both lightproof and soundproof. Their verbal reports would be recorded automatically while sophisticated communications equipment would keep them in constant touch with medical personnel. All each psychonaut had to do was lie on the bed, keep their eyes open, and watch the fire.

The psychonauts were eager to put their skills to work, and I found that the training paid off. Unlike untrained subjects who I had used in earlier experiments, the psychonauts were able to pay attention and keep up a running commentary on the flow of imagery. They could conveniently classify most images with the code categories. What did they see?

During sessions in which no drugs were administered, the psychonauts reported the normal imagery seen in the dark: phosphenes and amorphous black-and-white forms moving randomly in the visual field. Treatment with depressants such as phenobarbital tended to darken the images and slow them down. A sufficient dose would stop them altogether. Amphetamines certainly stimulated the amount of verbal reporting and chatter but there were no unusual changes in the imagery to talk about.

If these colorless spots and streaks resembled the flickering dust seen on a movie screen as blank film leader is run through a projector, then the movie really started when hallucinogenic drugs were given. The consensus was that the imagery resembled what one would see in a motion picture or a slide show located about one-half meter in front of the eyes. The imagery was characterized by a central bright light that obscured details in the center but allowed images on the periphery to be observed. The location of this point of light created a tunnel-like perspective for the visions.

The forms became less random and more geometric as the experience progressed. Initial black-and-white images began to take on colors. They started to pulsate, moving toward the center of the tunnel or away from the bright light. Some images rotated like pinwheels while others darted across the visual field. The accelerated movements brought many new geometric forms, including various tunnel and lattice arrangements. The lattices included gratings, fretworks, honeycombs, and chessboard designs. There were also multicolored kaleidoscopic forms bursting from the tunnel, like so many flowers from a magician's hat. These geometric forms frequently cloned themselves or combined into ever-changing structures.

Suddenly, complex images started appearing. These complex images were of real scenes and included childhood memories, scenes associated with emotional events, and recent memories. They formed an involuntary reminiscence, a scrapbook that had both depth and detail. The images were more than pictorial replicas; many of them were elaborated and embellished into fantastic scenes. Here one would expect an astonishing array of individual images. Yet because complex images were projected against a background of the simple geometric forms, they tended to appear in lattice-tunnel arrangements and to move in explosive or rotational configurations. These geometric forms are so ubiquitous that they are called "hallucinatory constants." If the fourth drive is the *basso continuo* of our behavior, the constants are the staffs upon which the music of our intoxications is written. There are many individual variations, but the theme is distinctly human.

Since the psychonauts were in an otherwise empty isolation chamber, the images had to be from sources within the subjects themselves; they arose either from memories or from phosphenes and other structures in their bodies. Nonetheless, these images could be so strong that they became part of the visual environment outside the dark chamber. Occasionally I escorted the subjects down the long corridors of the institute, then outside to a botanical garden. As we walked down the halls, the subjects reported that the geometric imagery formed a veil over the real objects in their visual field, almost as if a projector were flashing slides on everything they looked at. When exceptionally strong doses were used, complex memory imagery could be projected onto the blank walls of the corridors. The screen for the projection of the imagery had changed from the darkness of the chamber to the real world. What subjects now saw was a mixture of real and hallucinatory images. People might appear speckled with geometric forms and the air itself full of shimmering clouds and pyrotechnic displays.

Outside in the garden, the subjects lay on the grass, put on blindfold goggles, and reported what they "saw" with their eyes open. At these times the complex imagery was invaded by images of birds, flowers, trees, and other objects suggested by the sounds and smells of the garden. In other experiments, I found it was possible to shape and guide drug-induced imagery by giving the subjects suggestive words or music. Nevertheless, even these primed complex images carried the imprint of the lattice-tunnel arrangement. I concluded that although specific images might be influenced by environmental stimuli, the basic structures were fixed.

After the outdoor tests were completed, I allowed the subjects to remove their blindfold goggles for a short recess in the garden before returning to the institute. Removing the goggles created an effect similar to the scene in the film *The Wizard of Oz* in which Dorothy steps from the black-and-white of her Kansas home into the Technicolor world of Oz. Now at the peak of their intoxication, the psychonauts could experience the awesome nature of a full psychedelic trip. Not only were there visions to behold, but every sensory system was bombarded with enhanced inputs, as the brain's mechanism for filtering information was temporarily suppressed by the drugs. Senses fused as the subjects heard colors, saw sounds, and felt their visions. Altered perceptions of real and imaginary events were woven together as they experienced the full glory of what was going on inside and outside their brain—"that enchanted loom," as the neurophysiologist Charles Sherrington called it.

I guided the subjects around the grounds to a babbling brook, a small waterfall, and exotic plants. They were like children discovering the world anew, carefully inspecting and taking in all that they found. One psychonaut imagined he was walking through a living Impressionist painting, then "saw" characters from a Monet painting stroll by. Another heard a bird sing, thought about similar notes in a symphony, then "saw" a hallucinatory orchestra.

The psychonauts had found a unique feature of the hallucinatory world: the transformation of thoughts into vivid pictures. In his experiments with hashish, Moreau had described hallucinations as being similar to dreams in which imagined stimuli seem to be real. The psychonauts discovered that the key to the hallucinatory process was the gradual change from thoughts or mental images to visual imagery. As the electrical excitation increased in their brains, abrupt and spontaneous thoughts would take on a concreteness and vividness that put them "out there" in the visual field. These visualized thoughts sometimes took on a life of their own and irrelevant cognitive associations could not always be voluntarily controlled.

Given sufficient doses, all the hallucinogens produced the same typography of imagery for the psychonauts. The remarkable form constants lead to a consideration of their universal nature. Do people in other cultures see the same things? Could these forms be the same primordial forms or archetypes that psychoanalyst Carl Jung described as part of the human collective unconscious?

In an effort to verify these findings cross-culturally, I studied a group of peyote-using Huichols who had remained relatively isolated since Aztec times in the high Sierra Madre range of Mexico. I persuaded several Huichols to put on blindfold goggles during peyote intoxications and to describe their imagery. One vision was described as "a big spiral and I saw the fire god in the center and rushing out toward me." When he removed the goggles, the Indian saw geometric lattices "against the sky and everywhere I looked into the night." The Indians also saw familiar images, including deer, eagles, relatives, and village huts, all projected onto a waving and pulsating screen of the basic geometric motifs.

The most plausible explanation is that this universality of experience occurs because we *Homo sapiens* are wired the same way. That is, the structure and functioning of our central nervous systems are similar. The geometries are not only related to the structure of our optical system but also to the electrical excitation of organized groups of cells in the visual cortex of the brain. When these cortical areas are stimulated by electrodes placed in surgical patients, the patients report seeing moving colored lights, geometric forms, and complex memory images projected out in front of their eyes. Some patients have described multiplying images as when a memory image of a toy soldier turned into a line of marching toy soldiers, not unlike the report by a psychonaut on mescaline who saw a single valentine heart multiplying into hundreds of valentines filling the squares of a giant chessboard. It is almost as if entire columns of organizing cells within the brain are being fired at once, either by the electrodes or by the drugs. The resulting images can generate strong feelings in both patients and psychonauts, like viewing an emotional movie in a theater rather than in their heads. In this sense, we seem to be operating as living, feeling projectors.

In the experimental chamber, the film for the projector must come from the psychonauts. The valentine heart was not inside the capsule of mescaline but encapsulated in the memory of the subject. These quasi perceptions are forms of mental imagery that lie on a continuum of vividness, thought images being the least vivid and images of hallucinations being the most vivid. The transition from one form of imagery to another along this continuum depends on the arousal state; when arousal is low, there are minimal firings by cortical cells, and they are represented by the imagery of colorless, amorphous forms. The imagery is projected in the mind's eye and reflects elements of physical structures (entoptic events) and experiences (memories). At first such projections appear as weak thought images. When arousal is increased, however, retrieval of memories by this system is obtained more successfully. The imagery may now appear to be projected more vividly and may contain increasing amounts of complex imagination and fantasy material. When arousal is increased further, imagery may appear to be projected on a sensory field outside the body, especially if other sensory inputs are reduced—as when subjects put on the blindfold goggles.

Hallucinations occur when imagery is projected outside the observer and is viewed as separate from the projector. In the case of a young anesthesiologist who tried the hallucinogen ketamine in our experiments, the screen was the ceiling above his bed and the hallucinations were all from a previous film. He had no previous experiences with hallucinogens and his only expectation was that the trip would be something like the movie *2001: A Space Odyssey*. During the session, as he lay strapped to a gurney while an intravenous tube delivered the ketamine, he saw a hallucinatory replay of the entire movie on the ceiling of his hospital room. For several hours I endured his off-key humming of "The Blue Danube" waltz while he reported floating through space with the movie spaceship.

In the controlled set and setting of the experiments, neither the anesthesiologist nor the experienced psychonauts became lost in this mental space. During the peak hallucinatory periods, the psychonauts held on to the experimental demands and kept up their detached reporting. The untrained subjects, however, frequently described themselves as having become part of the imagery. At such times they stopped using similes in their reports and asserted that the images *were real*. This point marked the transition from pseudohallucination to true hallucination, a distinction first noted by William James in his experiments with nitrous oxide.

James defined a pseudohallucination as a false perception but one which you know is not real—it doesn't fool you. A subject having a true hallucination would have the concomitant delusion that it was real. An untrained subject under the influence of marijuana became frightened and his voice filled with terror when he saw puppets being attacked by killer bats while clowns looked on and laughed. He forgot that he was in the experimental chamber and screamed: "Omigod! I see these things!" He knew they were not real but I sensed from the tone of his voice that he was having difficulty distinguishing these mental images from real ones. A little later in the same session, when one of the bats appeared to swoop down toward his face, he insisted that a real bat was in the chamber with him. He had made the jump from pseudo- to true hallucination and was now acting in accordance with the belief that the bat was real. The trained psychonauts, however, remained firmly grounded in objective reality and always knew the images they experienced were unreal projections. The psychonauts had learned how to tame the bats from inner space.

2

The difference between a good trip and a bad one is often a slight shift in the delicate balance between dosage, set, and setting. Alone, in the privacy of the psychonaut's body and the experimental chamber, a glowing fire in the brain from small doses can be amusing and entertaining. We can easily understand why the monkeys smoked DMT cigarettes in the isolation chamber. But when a fire roaring in the brain sends people running out of their rooms into the streets, the result is often madness. Here we see parallels with intoxicated animals who are forced to interact with others, bringing dysfunction to the social group and a bad trip for all.

Consider the case of Steven, who was looking for a good job in electronics, not a bad trip from an electrical seizure in his brain, when he moved to Marin County, California. Known to residents as "Coke County," the area provided Steven with access to abundant, inexpensive cocaine. It had been a month since he had used any cocaine. During that last exposure, he was on a binge of cocaine smoking and experienced intense central nervous system excitation. The first signs were flashes of light in the corners of his visual field. He ignored these "snow lights," early warning sparks from the building fire in his brain, and kept smoking. Then he heard a noise in his head, like the sound of rushing water. Suddenly his limbs started shaking and jerking. Then he blacked out.

One month later, the seizure was all but forgotten. Steven was more excited about his new, high-salaried job in the computer industry. He decided to celebrate and bought two grams of cocaine to smoke. "The first hit felt real good," explained Steven, and the earlier seizure was the furthest thing from his mind. But his brain still remembered, because once a seizure occurs, the fire in the brain acts as if it were already kindled and the next seizure or roaring fire will occur with a much lower dose of cocaine. This is especially true after a period of abstinence when there is no longer any tolerance or resistance to these electrical storms.

In a few short minutes, Steven became extremely uncomfortable. He couldn't sit still. His ears were ringing. Everything seemed extra loud and extra irritating. He was rushing around now and in his confusion he couldn't find his keys or wallet. He thought he might have left them at his friend Betty's house when he visited her earlier in the day. Although it was now three in the morning, Steven bicycled several miles up a hill to where she lived. He knocked on the door.

Steven asked to come inside to look for his keys and wallet. Betty helped him look but they couldn't find anything. Next Steven called his girlfriend to see if he had left them with her. He mentioned he was at Betty's place. His girlfriend became enraged, told Steven that their relationship was over, and hung up. Steven put down the telephone and turned around. He started trembling and his wide eyes rolled up into the sockets.

Steven watched Steven. He struggled with Betty. She had two butcher knives. One had just stabbed her in the head; she pulled the other out of her stomach. She was on the attack. Steven ran outside to the garden. He threw an empty five-gallon water bottle at her, then tried to scale a fence. Betty was screaming something. Steven wanted to scream, too, but he couldn't make a sound. He found a couple of tomato stakes in the garden and tried to fend off Betty by brandishing them like swords. He retreated into the house, ran to the bedroom, and locked the door. He *knew* she was still coming and would kill him if she got the chance. He kicked the window, then dove through the broken glass headfirst.

Steven hovered in the air while he watched the other Steven land, run to his bike, then ride off a ten-meter cliff, crashing the bike and hitting his head. He staggered down the road. Lights from a car were coming at him. He flagged it down. *Thank God!* he thought. It was a police car. The two Stevens passed out together.

At the hospital, Steven was back in his body, which was shaking with a pulse of 108 and threatening to explode with a hypertensive blood pressure. At first he thought he had been robbed of his keys and wallet, and attacked by a crazed woman. It couldn't have been a hallucination—everything seemed so vivid and intense.

Events were clear because the fire in the brain had literally catapulted Steven onto the other side of the window. Already kindled by a previous history of seizures, and fanned by the anger and irritation of the evening, the two-gram cocaine fire suddenly ignited with napalmesque consequences. It produced a minor seizure, followed by a dissociative reaction and panic. Steven did not understand that he had been guilty of the initial attack on Betty, who recovered, until he heard the evidence in court.

The court held that Steven must assume responsibility for his criminal conduct. In the wonderland of cocaine intoxication, in between doses that stimulate all users and those that cause seizures in all, there are acts controlled by individual variables. The drug did not cause the attack but it did release a paranoid idea within Steven's brain. Events had been dictated largely by his personality and his previous reactions to mental stress. Steven admitted to being bothered by murderous ideas for a long period of time; he tried to suppress them by getting high with cocaine. But the thoughts only got stronger and he feared that something evil was about to happen. Under the influence of cocaine, he spent many nights sitting alone, cradling an ax. His plan of action was already formed when the paranoia seized him again in Betty's house and he panicked. One could blame Steven, but not cocaine. The drug did not force him into the specific acts of aggression, it only kindled a preexisting propensity to act in those directions.

Many bad trips are a function of personality; not everybody is a good subject for a mind-altering drug experience. And even experienced users can have a bad day. Steven would have been a poor subject for my experiments. Harold, a veteran of one thousand LSD trips, wanted to volunteer to be a psychonaut but he had a history of violence, both on and off the drug. "Ever since I was small," confessed Harold, "I go ape when I'm bothered."

Whenever Harold took LSD, he would also go wild: screaming, fighting, and scaring his friends, just as OJ the chimp had done on South Island. Then there was the incident at Red Rock in March 1984. Red Rock is a wilderness camping area not far from President Reagan's ranch in Santa Barbara County. Harold had gone there to relax. He had been bothered by financial problems. He was passing bad checks and had failed to make child-support payments to his ex-wife. As he drove his truck into the area, he drank some beer, smoked a little marijuana, and swallowed a few amphetamine tablets along with a full dose of LSD. He stopped near a stream, turned up the volume on the tape deck in the truck, put the speakers outside the cab, and "partied."

Harold's party spirit changed when a friend came by and told him there was a warrant out for his arrest. Harold vowed they wouldn't take him alive. He decided to go back to town and force "them" to kill him. He put on his camouflage army gear, Vietnam boots, and loaded the shotgun. He started down the trail.

"I remember walking down a trail, watching myself walking, checking everything out, tripping. The ground was moving up and down, the wind going about a thousand miles a hour. . . . I felt detached from myself, like a camera. I walked to the swimming pond, tripping out on the water. I felt someone behind me. I turned around and two people were right in front of me. The guy grabbed the shotgun and tried to take it away."

No one takes Harold's gun. "You're fucking crazy!" screamed Harold, then hit the man with the butt of the gun. The man and his wife dove into the pond and tried to swim away. Harold stalked them like ducks.

"I'm going to kill you, kill someone, kill someone," chanted Harold as he fired buckshot at the targets. He had to reload several times. The couple tried to stay underwater as long as possible. But they had to come up for air. "So now whats ya gonna do? Now whats ya gonna do?" screamed Harold as the man surfaced.

Then the woman came up for air into the arms of her husband. They were face to face in the deep water; the husband was holding her around the back with one arm while protecting her head with the other. Another blast and he could feel her body go limp. The water turned red. Harold had just killed the female duck.

Cases like Harold's tend to confuse the issue of intoxication and violence. Violent people are often intoxicated but the violence is usually rooted in the personality, not the drug. People may panic under the influence of LSD or any other drug that makes them feel different, just as Steven panicked with cocaine. What seems difficult for us to understand is that despite overt behaviors, the subjective experience can still be fun. In other words, one's inner feelings and sensations can be under the influence but such influence may not extend to outside acts in the real world that remain chillingly sober. This is most difficult to accept if users are obviously intoxicated when they commit criminal acts. The subjective intoxication can remain an enjoyable experience, despite our desire to blame the fires inside for the destruction outside.

Even when someone is actively hallucinating, as twenty-year-old Jeffrey told me he was when he stabbed a neighbor and her daughter to death, the fire in the brain may have little or no influence over behavior. Unlike Steven and Harold, who flew through the windows of their hallucinations and ended up in places where previously buried thoughts and impulses came alive, Jeffrey was a user who remained firmly grounded in reality despite the fires. We might be fooled by Jeffrey's hallucinations, but he never was.

Jeffrey had a dealer who assured him that the "acid" (LSD) he was selling was "fun acid." The smiling dolphin on the little squares of blotter paper seemed to be saying the same thing. Jeffrey bought five doses, or "hits." The first trip was pure joy. So the next time Jeffrey ate four dolphins—four times the fun. He put on a pair of stereo headphones, turned on a strobe light, and watched the geometric and complex patterns dance around his bedroom. He had a good time. Then he had a dream; his report to me, months later, was fragmented as I recorded it verbatim:

> In a woman's bedroom.
> "What do you want?"
> "I want to make love to you."
> In another room.
> "I want to make love."
> "I'm on my period."
> "Take off your negligee."
> "Please don't hurt me."
> Her breasts are swollen. The carpet is moving. The
>   air is thick with dots and patterns.
> Downstairs.
> "Do you have any valuables?" In the kitchen.
> There is a little girl on the telephone. I am stabbing
>   her. Her mouth is wobbling. She looks like an
>   ugly pumpkin.
> I get hit on the head.
> Running after the woman in slow motion.
> Stabbing her.
> "Die. Die. Die. Die. Die. Die. Die."
> "Stop! I'm already dead."
> "Die."
> Running through quicksand.
> Sirens.
> Waking up in bed.

Since Jeffrey had actually killed two people during this acid "dream," it is easy to take the view that LSD was the real culprit. The dreamlike recall was a strong indication that Jeffrey was hallucinating. And there were multiple stab wounds to the mother's body, eight major ones corresponding to the eight "Dies" Jeffrey heard in his dream. One might also suspect contributory influences from the satanic music he was listening to earlier—it was the same music that has been blamed for a number of youthful suicides and homicides. The fact that he had also been watching *Helter Skelter,* a television movie depicting the Manson LSD-linked murders, would seem to provide further evidence that Jeffrey was a victim of these combined influences. The press would have had a field day with this information if I had turned it over to them, but it would have been misleading. Despite all appearances, LSD did not cause Jeffrey to kill.

Many details had been lost from his memory over the months between the incident and my examination. The intoxication had prevented these details from becoming embedded in long-term memory storage. When the fire burns brightly in the brain, information from short-term memory buffers cannot be consolidated, or stored, in long-term memory areas due to electrical and chemical interference. Therefore, one tends to remember only the more dramatic subjective and objective events such as the feeling of running through quicksand or the flash of a knife. The psychonauts had to be debriefed immediately after the experiment; a delay of even a day or two would have wiped out much valuable data. Fortunately, Jeffrey was "debriefed" by the police within a few hours after the incident.

Wringing his hands and weeping, Jeffrey told the police that he left his bedroom and entered the neighbor's house looking for money. As he went through the house, the mother came up behind him and hit him over the head with a candlestick holder. He grabbed her and forced her to have sex with him. He noticed the little girl holding the kitchen telephone, grabbed the phone away from her, then stabbed her with a kitchen knife. He turned to finish off the mother. He was still slashing and yelling "Die" when neighbors started banging on the front door. He fled to his own house where he faked a burglary to make it look as if someone had robbed both houses. He threw away the knife and changed his clothes. Then he went to bed.

Jeffrey was not under the influence to the extent that he did not know what he was doing. He knew he was committing a crime; he knew right from wrong; and he had the capacity to conform his conduct to the requirements of the law. He was still experiencing some enjoyable perceptions: the patterns in the air, the moving carpet, and the slow-motion effects. But he was clearly aware of carving up people, not pumpkins, and he knew enough to try to mask his involvement with another burglary. If Jeffrey had been more severely intoxicated he might have followed in the footsteps of the intruder mice who are often attacked by the residents. Such was the fate of a ski-masked rapist, a bear of a man, who broke into a Vermont home and terrorized the two men and three women inside. When they realized how stoned the rapist was, the residents turned on him, took his gun away, and subdued him.

Under special circumstances, behavior *can* be directly controlled by the drug. This happened to a teenage boy who drank wine, sniffed glue, then had sex with his girlfriend on a California beach. According to witnesses, as the two were making love, a seizure locked the boy's hands around his girlfriend's neck and she strangled to death. Sometimes the effects of the drug are unexpected and catch the user in the wrong situation. A Los Angeles biochemist, for instance, was trying to synthesize a "peace pill" by twisting a ring of cyclohexane molecules when he discovered PHP, an analog of PCP. After swallowing the pill, he stripped, climbed a pole, and was shot six times, fatally, by a policeman who felt threatened by the bizarre behavior. And sometimes the intoxication is involuntary. An elderly woman took some medicine that her son, a doctor, had given her to relieve depression. The medicine turned out to be cocaine that—unknown to the son—had been adulterated with PCP. The woman started cleaning the house, then remembered she had to go cash a check at a bank across the street. She entered the bank unaware that she was still carrying a broom. When the teller asked about the broom, the woman, feeling a little mischievous, held it like a shotgun and joked that it was a robbery. Alarms were sounded and the woman was taken into custody. She was released after her son convinced the authorities that his mother was being medicated for mental problems.

But reactions to intoxicants can be controlled. In our experiments at UCLA, there was never a bad trip or adverse reaction to any drug. A major reason for the successful control of intoxications was the preparation and guidance given to each subject. Each person was thoroughly briefed about the drugs and given information regarding expected and unexpected effects. In addition, they were surrounded by the best emergency medical equipment available. They were fully protected and they knew it. When someone seemed preoccupied with a particularly stressful experience, I simply distracted him with another thought. A key to the success of this guidance lies in the fact that the users' perceptions can be as easily shaped by verbal suggestions as by their own internal memories. Once, while I was escorting an LSD subject down the hospital hallway, we passed a uniformed police officer. The subject thought the officer was a Nazi and wanted to confront him. I suggested that the officer was only a wax dummy that would melt away. The subject then saw the figure melt. An experienced guide can navigate trippers out of such difficult mental waters. Unfortunately, most street users do not have good information or guides. No one was there to help a student in Israel who took LSD, thought an Israeli soldier was a Nazi, then stabbed him to death.

Set and setting, personality, and guides are not the sole programmers of intoxication. Sometimes previous trips themselves can shape the experience. In the classic film *City Lights,* Charlie Chaplin saves a drunken millionaire from attempted suicide and so becomes his good friend. When the millionaire is sober he does not remember Charlie. But when he is drunk again, he recognizes Charlie and treats him like a long-lost friend. He takes Charlie home with him. In the sobriety of the morning after, he forgets that Charlie is his invited guest and has the butler throw him out. These scenes illustrate the process of state-dependent learning: events experienced or learned in one drug state are highly dependent on that same or similar physiological state for recall. This is illustrated by the following case of a man I will call Donald Ike.

In the dark movie theater, Donald Ike chuckled as he watched the 1976 movie, *J. D.'s Revenge,* because the hero of the film was also named Ike. The fictional Ike stops at a nightclub where a hypnotist selects him from the audience and puts him in a trance. While under hypnosis, Ike has the distinct feeling that he is a hoodlum called J. D. who is murdered in a slaughterhouse. In the days that follow the nightclub visit, Ike is taken over more and more by J. D.'s violent personality. He sees J. D.'s image in the mirror, starts to comb his hair like J. D., and walks and talks like J. D. He even beats his wife the way J. D. might have done. Ike's transformation to J. D. is so complete it finally draws out the original killer, who is shot to death at the end of the movie.

Watching this while under the influence of PCP, Donald Ike saw many recognizable scenes. The bloodstained walls and rusting meathooks of the slaughterhouse were familiar to Donald because he had worked with his father, who was a butcher. J. D. had lost a sister in the movie; Donald had lost two sisters in real life. Donald identified so much with J. D. that he saw the movie four more times, each time while under the influence of PCP.

A few days later, Donald smoked another PCP cigarette. He looked into the mirror and saw J. D. looking back! As he studied his body, he saw parts of J. D.'s physique replacing his own. The vision passed quickly, but Donald couldn't sleep all that night. The following day he smoked another PCP cigarette and started feeling uneasy again. He stared at his bedroom ceiling, where images from the movie kept him awake for another night.

The next day Donald visited a hairdresser and had his hair styled like J. D.'s. As he drove along the street with a girlfriend, he checked his rearview mirror; J. D. winked at him! But J. D. was looking more and more like the devil. Each time Donald looked in the rearview mirror, a figure that increasingly resembled the devil glared back at him. Donald rolled down his window and threw out his false teeth, but that didn't stop the transformation from completing itself. He stopped the car on the side of a major boulevard.

"I'm the devil! I'm the devil! King of the throne!" yelled Donald with J. D.'s accent. "Where do you want to go, bitch? Heaven or hell? Because I'm going to kill you." The girl became hysterical and leaped out of the car. Donald grabbed a .45-caliber blue steel automatic and jumped out after her. "I'm the devil now," repeated Donald. He fired the gun in the air. He danced around the car, laughing and yelling just as J. D. did in the movie.

This is the last gun in the world, thought the devil. *Armageddon is at hand. Nixon and Watergate were the first signs. I'm in charge here now. I'll start by getting Nixon. Nixon? You messed it all up! Nixon? Where are you?*

Donald stopped another car on the road. He went to the passenger window. "Do you know where I can find Nixon?" asked the devil.

"Bring that bitch back!" demanded Donald. He didn't wait for a response and killed the passenger. *Everything I do is okay 'cause I'm the devil. I'm the king of the throne.* He chased the driver around the car and fired several more rounds. Then Donald left in his own car.

A yellow Cadillac! This is the perfect car for me, thought the devil. *What's that? Police cars? Police want me because this is the only gun in the world. If they want me they have to come and get me.*

They did. After a shoot-out with the police, Donald was arrested and taken to a police station. There, in the privacy of his cell, the "voices" assured him that *It's okay 'cause you the devil, you the king of the throne. In order for you to be free you must read the message.* Donald looked around the cell and saw some cryptic writing on the walls. It looked Egyptian. Maybe this would explain how to get out. But it was taking him forever to decipher the writing.

The voices became impatient. *Think! Think!* they wailed. *You must think back to the key to the message. Otherwise we gonna dig through the ceiling and get you.*

Donald asked the deputies for help. He walked around his cell, pointing out where the voices were coming from. He even asked for medication. The deputies refused. After all, they had the devil under lock and key, safely tucked away for the night. They were wise to his tricks.

That night stretched into several weeks before Donald recovered from his PCP psychosis. Blood tests and psychopharmacological evaluations confirmed the diagnosis. "I really thought I was the devil," Donald told me in the infirmary of the Los Angeles County Jail. "The devil came inside me. He used my body and possessed me."

The devil, of course, was nothing more than a bunch of cortical cells programmed with images from a movie and activated by a powerful dissociative anesthetic agent. Donald played the part exactly the way the script had been written for him. He had learned the lines by sitting through the movie five times while under the influence of PCP. Another stiff dose of PCP, some hairstyling for the part, a few prompts from the car mirror, and Donald was ready to act. But it was Donald who was onstage, not the drug. It was Donald who chose how to interpret the role when it was thrown at him by the process of state-dependent recall. PCP and the movie were functioning as the producer and writer. In all fairness to the actor, Donald's background must also be acknowledged. Those credits included brief work in his father's slaughterhouse, where he developed a fascination for the scenery; a stint in a local street gang where he earned the nickname "Mr. Dog" for always coming out on top in fights; a well-ingrained streak of paranoia, honed to a fine edge by a long criminal career; and years spent studying movies involving devil themes.

When Donald was charged with murder stemming from his realistic portrayal of the devil, he tried to tell the detectives all about the devil. They were seasoned investigators of drug-related homicides and knew the difference between a devil choking a victim in a seizure and a devil who can drive a car, shoot a gun, then attempt to escape. They *told* Donald he knew exactly what he did and asked him how he felt about having killed the victim. Donald answered for himself and for all those logs still burning in his brain: "Guilty." Silently, he wondered where he could find Nixon.

Donald continued to have flashbacks to the incident for months, and they probably would last for many years. He found it hard to look in a mirror for a long period of time and not see a flash of J. D. or the devil: a slanted eyebrow here, a hollow cheek there. And he would remember. The memory would come as a vicarious retrieval of events, and Donald would sometimes be overwhelmed by a feeling of panic or a sensation of dissociation. The duration of these flashbacks was brief—most lasted only one or two seconds—and I assured him that they would decrease in duration and frequency, eventually disappearing altogether. Most will occur within the immediate recovery period from the intoxication, although flashbacks are unrelated to residual metabolites floating around in the body. They are, in the words of French novelist Marcel Proust, vitalized "remembrances of things past."

When we listen to a song that we originally heard when we first fell in love, we sometimes spontaneously recall the loved one. We form mental images of the person; we might even find ourselves momentarily overcome by nostalgia. Some will respond to the flashback by telephoning or writing to the person. Others will simply enjoy the memory. There are melodies that can do the same for people who share the same cultural images. Many cannot listen to the strains of "As Time Goes By" without flashing on images from *Casablanca*, the classic wartime love film with Humphrey Bogart and Ingrid Bergman. Few today will fail to associate the song "Somewhere Over the Rainbow" with images from *The Wizard of Oz*.

Flashbacks from drug experiences work in a similar way. The state-bound memories can be evoked not only by melodies, imagery, and other symbols from the content of an experience, but also by simply inducing the particular level of arousal that prevailed during the initial experience. Donald's recall of scenes from *J. D.'s Revenge* was triggered by the same PCP-induced arousal that prevailed during his initial viewing of the movie. While authorities familiar with Donald's crimes may be thankful that the movie was not as popular as *Casablanca* or *The Wizard of Oz*, they have little to fear from those who saw it or those countless others who continue to view violence-laden films and television programs while under the influence. The bug-eyed killer in *Reefer Madness*, for example, has been seen by millions of marijuana smokers, and theaters are often filled with the fragrance of marijuana smoke, a telltale sign that many in the audience are also high at the time. Yet it is the comedy rather than the killing that people flash back to when they get intoxicated again. Still, shouldn't we be worried that we might be programming an underground army of "Manchurian Candidates" who will someday surface in the Armageddon that Donald felt was at hand?

The answer is clearly no, as long as the drug produces low levels of arousal, as does marijuana, and the violent images are also of weak or unrealistic intensity. Yet even if stronger drugs and stronger images are used, the susceptibility of the individual user is generally the deciding factor. Few, if any, street users screen themselves as thoroughly as I screened the research subjects. Still, surprisingly few react violently to combinations of strong drugs and movies. My study of drug-related homicide cases has revealed only a handful of defendants like Donald who were strongly influenced by violent films or television programs. The personalities of the defendants appeared so volatile that their dangerousness might have been predicted independent of intoxicant use. When they happened to take a drug like PCP, many defendants spoke of being "whacked out" or of "snapping." In those graphic, almost visible terms they were describing PCP's unique property of causing a sudden, drastic alteration of the underlying personality. Experienced users know this and try to avoid violent settings. But when the violence is already in the personality, even watching TV on a lazy afternoon can be dangerous when mixed with PCP. It was for Sergio.

Sergio never liked violent movies. He was frightened enough by the stories about Satan that he and his wife heard every Sunday in church. Pictures of Jesus and religious scenes hung on every wall of their home. None showed Satan, but Sergio pictured him as a tall man with beef-jerky skin and hair all over his body. He prayed that he would never meet Satan but if he did, Sergio prayed that he would be strong enough to cast him out.

Sergio and his wife had just returned home from church when they decided to relax and smoke some PCP. They turned on the television and started watching a cooking program. The chef was explaining how to clean fish: descaling, removing the head and fins, then the bones. Sergio thought he drifted to sleep.

He awoke to a funny odor, then heard a sound like a washing machine. His watch had stopped. He turned to his wife. The creature standing there had beef jerky for skin. There was a black hole where the face should have been. Steam was coming out of the body. The voice of the Lord told him this was Satan. He cleaned Satan like the slimy fish he was. Then he went to a priest and reported what he had done.

Sergio had killed and mutilated his wife during this vision. Presumably, many Satan-fearing, God-loving people watch cooking programs, and some may also be under the influence of intoxicants like PCP at the time. Should we ban cooking programs along with violent films and PCP? Sergio's bizarre mutilation murder of his wife was a result of many other forces coming together. He had had a violent marriage and expressed considerable suspicion and jealousy over his wife's attention to other men. Furthermore, he had never been able to control his temper, lashing out at the least provocation. The morning of the murder, Sergio had found a strange "love bite" on his wife's neck. He had planned to confront her about this after he relaxed with a little PCP. But he was angry enough to kill her without waiting for the PCP to take effect.

Subsequent interviews with Sergio confirmed that he did most of his

PCP smoking—and hallucinating—after he killed his wife. He tried to follow the chef's instructions. He washed the body in the bathtub and drained the blood. The process gave the body the wrinkled look of beef jerky. It was hard work cutting off the legs and Sergio took frequent PCP breaks. He hid the body parts in various locations, cleaned the floors, put his clothes in the washing machine, then took a steaming shower. Images from these scenes were found throughout his reported vision.

He told the officers that he used a hatchet, which he hid at his grandmother's house. Despite his intoxication, Sergio was trying to cover up for the murder that he—not PCP—had committed. Much later, Sergio told me that if he ever got out of prison he would hang a picture of Satan in the house—it would be his own police mug shot. Roughly one hundred years earlier, Dostoevsky told us the same thing when he wrote, "If the devil doesn't exist, but man has created him, he has created him in his own image and likeness."

No one, not even the perceptive Dostoevsky, expected the devil to wear white and sparkle like snow. Yet the real violence in the drug world comes not from the flames in the brain, or the dark memories and stored images they tickle so vicariously. Rather, the majority of the violence comes from the fueling of the fire itself, the gathering of tinder and logs for the cerebral celebrations. The fuel—the quest for which creates the most blistering effects, rivaling the sun-god itself in disturbing the entire planet—is cocaine.

"I'll do anything to get me some cocaine," admitted accused bank robber Eddie Love.

"Anything?" I asked. I was grateful that the federal marshals had chained Eddie to the oak chair in my office.

Eddie replied with a homeboy expression from his Los Angeles neighborhood, "Sure you right."

"Tell me."

"If you had my release papers on the desk here, and over there you had an o.z. [ounce of cocaine], I'd take the o.z. even if I had to spend the rest of my life in jail."

Eddie had been in prison for only a few weeks, not long enough to get over the craving. He told me he'd make a deal with the devil himself to get cocaine. "But Ed. You're facing serious bank robbery charges and looking at years of time. Would you really make that kind of deal?"

"Sure you right. I *love* cocaine," squealed Eddie.

I studied Eddie carefully as he told me about his cocaine habit. Life really didn't start for Eddie until he discovered cocaine at age twenty-eight. He had sniffed it a few times before that but never experienced any noticeable effects. This time he injected it, a half gram all at once. Immediately after pulling out the needle he could taste it, a slightly bitter sensation. He heard a hissing roar in his ears. His heart started to pound in unison with the roaring. He started to sweat. Then he ejaculated through a flaccid penis. Eddie was in love.

"If God wanted to make the *perfect* drug," explained Eddie, "he would have made cocaine. Since cocaine is perfect, it must be God's gift. When I take cocaine into my body, I am partaking of God himself."

Eddie told me he had smoked opium, dropped acid, and even took amphetamines when he was only eight years old. "I've had every drug conceivable. Cocaine is *God.*"

He went on a religious crusade to get his sacrament. He robbed banks, then bought cocaine. Sometimes he went through an ounce a day. Literally. "I'd take a shower, then throw a whole o.z. into the air and run through it. I'd rub it in my nose, in my hair, in my ears. God, how I *loved* cocaine." The chains were straining against the wooden armrests of the chair. "I'd like some right now."

"If you were free, say you were on the street right now, how would you get it?"

"The only way I know. I'd rob me a bank."

That is exactly what Eddie had done. He first made sure he wouldn't hurt anyone by taking the bullets out of the gun. Then, dressed in a natty suit and running shoes, he would walk into a bank and take the money. Once he even left a note on a teller's counter reading, "I robbed this lady." At home, much to his wife's chagrin, Eddie lived in the bathroom with cocaine. He refused to walk into the living room for fear of helicopters. He strip-searched his wife for hidden recorders and weapons. Three weeks and three seizures later he got caught. Crazy! At least that's what nine out of the twelve jurors thought at his trial.

The real craziness lies in the vast numbers of cases that are typified by Eddie. Judging from the backlogged calendar in criminal courts throughout the United States, people *will* do anything for cocaine. Five thousand years ago the Indians picked the coca leaves and other psychoactive flora from the trees and bushes. Today users must hunt and gather in a different type of jungle for the fuel to kindle the same fires in the brain. The fires that roar in the violent brain may produce violence, but the greater damage is done from the ceaseless struggles to ignite or extinguish the fourth drive in the body politic.

The interior landscapes that are illuminated are the same for people throughout the world. There is a harmony that unites us all, from cultural choices in drugs to the geometric arrangements of the intoxicated worlds they create. There are neither angels nor devils here. For drugs are not magical elixirs that automatically transform law-abiding citizens into self-realized gods or crazed criminals. With proper attention to set and setting, personality and dosage, the fires in the brain can be controlled. However, since the use of most intoxicating drugs is still viewed as inherently deviant and immoral, if not evil and beastly as well, it is not unexpected that the drugs, like the people who use them, should be the targets of war.

Nowhere was this response more succinctly stated than on the walls of my laboratory. There, hanging with the psychedelic pictures I had encouraged the psychonauts to draw of images they saw while under the influence, was the title page from Eddie's indictment: *"The United States of America* versus *Love."*

The title page was a study in contradiction. As we shall see in the next two chapters, America has always had a love-hate relationship with drugs. As we accept some intoxicants, we reject others. As we condemn excessive use of all drugs as unhealthy, we continue promoting those intoxicants that help the economic health of the nation. The study of this contradiction is a lesson in the power of the fourth drive to rule the behavior of a nation.

12

Star-Spangled Powders

DRUGS AND
THE AMERICAN WAY

1

I find it helpful to picture America in a tug-of-war between the laws of the land and the drives of the people. On one side are people seeking and taking intoxicants; on the other, government policies of regulation and prohibition. These forces have pulled the nation into a series of all-out wars; the recent war on drugs is an old story. As America grew from a colonial society of virgin forests and roaming game into a modern one of skyscrapers and supermarkets, these wars illuminated our basic struggle with the pursuit of artificial paradise.

Standing in the middle of that tug-of-war have been the presidents. Their behavior is shaped by the laws they uphold and, as representatives of the people, by the same drives that influence the rest of us. Their personal drug use, even when at odds with public morality or laws, is a reflection of our own continuing struggles with the fourth drive. To look at the history of drug use in America, and by its presidents, is to see why the primal urge to use intoxicants remains an integral part of the present and future history of our society.

The fourth drive did not come to America with the first hard-drinking explorers. It was already here, expressing itself in the use of tobacco. The ancient Mayan and Aztec custom of smoking cigars and pipes had already spread to American tribes when the first Old World visitors arrived. Early settlers discovered that tobacco smoking offered a novel and stimulating source of gratification. As sailors returned to the Old World, they introduced this New World habit. Before the end of the sixteenth century, Spanish and Dutch merchantmen were crossing the Atlantic on a regular basis to load cargoes of tobacco for sale in Europe. Many European rulers, such as King James I, detested smoking, but New World settlers, who valued the psychological and economic effects, protested against any interference with their drugs or their trade. The spirit of America was to fight for its habits. When the director-general of New Amsterdam issued an arbitrary ban on smoking in 1639, the city's smokers—virtually the entire male population—camped outside his office in a massive silent protest. In other settlements, regulations on smoking in public or use by teenagers failed to change any habits. Although some magistrates and courts were on record as against tobacco, they recognized its importance as a home industry and carried out little enforcement.

As America's exports of tobacco grew, the foreign demand for tobacco also grew. In England the prices soared and for a while tobacco became worth its weight in silver. The demand was not curbed by this inflationary cost. When use spread to the very poor, the cigarette evolved in order to provide a cheap smoke that delivered more actual smoke per ounce than the pipe or cigar. In every country where tobacco was introduced there appeared unquenchable demands. By the middle of the seventeenth century the addicting nature of tobacco was clearly visible throughout Europe. Official edicts banning smoking were issued by several popes and by Bavaria, Saxony, Zurich, and many other states. Draconian punishments were introduced—the slitting of the nostrils in Russia and the death penalty in Turkey—yet tobacco use continued to spread around the world.

This demand for tobacco formed the economic basis for the establishment of the first colonies in Virginia and Maryland. The colonists continued to resist controls on tobacco. The tobacco industry became as American as Yankee Doodle and the Spirit of Independence. People protested and evaded controls on other drugs as well. When British teas were taxed, colonists boycotted them, smuggled them, or searched for native herbs to use as substitutes. In 1776 the American tobacco industry was strong enough to help finance the Revolution. So England tried to eradicate the crop. British armies, trampling across the South, went out of their way to destroy large inventories of cured tobacco leaf, including those stored on Thomas Jefferson's plantation. But tobacco survived to pay for the war and sustain morale. General George Washington, one of the wealthiest tobacco planters of his day, told his countrymen how to help the Revolution: "If you can't send money, send tobacco." In addition to generating revenue from tobacco sales, Washington would dispense tobacco to the troops, who used it to relieve the stress of battle, a pattern of use employed in all wars since that time.

Marijuana, or Indian hemp, as it was called, was initially ignored as a drug because its intoxicating effects were generally unknown in the colonies. Instead Washington encouraged farmers to grow the fibrous plant for clothing, paper, and cordage for ships. Washington grew his own for the seeds and called on his fellow countrymen to sow them throughout the land. One who answered the call was Robert "King" Carter, an early ancestor of President Jimmy Carter. He raised hemp on his vast acreage in Virginia and supplied much of the fiber needed to clothe General Washington's troops. Ironically, when Americans finally discovered a drug use for these native plants, drug agents during President Carter's administration were charged with the responsibility of destroying the wild plants that had their origins in these early colonial seeds.

In addition to growing tobacco and hemp, Washington distilled whiskey, brewed his own beer and ale, and learned how to mix drinking with the art of politics. Treating the public to alcohol at elections was a colonial custom borrowed from England. When Washington sought a seat in the Virginia House of Burgesses in 1758, he was determined to provide sufficient liquor to ensure election. He had lost a previous election by refusing to treat and wrote to his campaign manager that he must not spare the expenses for victory. To win, Washington gave away 144 gallons of rum, punch, wine, hard cider, and beer; he received 307 votes, better than 2 votes per gallon. The important aspect of treating was not the dispensing of strong beverages, which was expected, but the style and manner of the candidate. Congeniality in giving away drinks demonstrated an affinity with the common man. If the candidate also became inebriated, it would show voters that he was an independent man of strong character. Washington was the perfect politician: he showed generosity in offering liquor, and a desire to indulge. Yet with a political double-talk that would become all too common for future presidents, Washington called distilled spirits "the ruin of half the workingmen in this country."

The tobacco and alcohol habits exemplified by Washington were seen in citizens and presidents alike. John Adams, Washington's immediate successor, railed against distilled spirits for half a century, yet he drank a tankard of hard cider every morning. Adams was always trying to quit tobacco and even tried, unsuccessfully, to stifle his craving with large quantities of Madeira wine. In those days, Madeira was frequently prescribed for increasing the strength of patients because it was so fattening. Thomas Jefferson boasted that he had cured friends and family members of fevers with daily pints of Madeira. But he found better uses for other imported wines.

The aristocratic Jefferson had a taste for fine French wines and sherry. Inside his mansion at Monticello, he designed a dumbwaiter to bring bottles from the wine cellar to the dining room in order to service another of his inventions: the presidential cocktail party. At these parties he usually drank double or triple the number of glasses consumed by his guests. The president apparently tolerated these indulgences with few adverse effects despite political criticism that he was habitually drunk. Soon fine wine cellars and cocktail parties became the mark of successful politicians thoughout the country.

Despite the widespread political importance of alcohol, Jefferson recognized the same potential problems foreseen by Washington and Adams. Jefferson was worried about the cheap whiskey that was "spreading through the mass of our citizens." But he was more worried about tobacco and abstained from using it, declaring that "tobacco is productive of infinite wretchedness." After the Revolution he had hoped that wheat would replace tobacco in the fields of Virginia; but tobacco was no more likely to vanish than whiskey or the amber waves of grain it came from. Indeed, before he became president, James Madison, who used snuff with his wife, protested when Congress considered a levy on all tobacco commodities. Madison argued that the pleasures of life consisted in a series of "innocent gratifications," among which was the social use of tobacco.

These innocent gratifications were destined to continue, as tobacco and alcohol were widely consumed by everyone. James Monroe was the first heavy drinker to occupy the White House. His successor, John Quincy Adams, was the first to have been a heavy smoker, although he had quit many years earlier. He was against tobacco thereafter and wanted to see everyone who was "afflicted with this artificial passion" freed from its power and every acre of tobacco land turned into a wheat field. Such Jeffersonian dreams could hardly happen in a young America where the tobacco industry was enriching the country and alcohol was still buying the votes.

The next presidents upheld these American traditions. Andrew Jackson kept the alcohol flowing and the tobacco burning throughout his administration. Even his wife smoked a pipe, a habit adopted by many frontier women. And treating with alcohol became bigger than ever. William Henry Harrison, who ran against Martin Van Buren, used the images of a log cabin and a jug of hard cider on his campaign banner, although he probably drank very little himself. It was during this period that the word *booze* became part of the language. In the election campaign, E. C. Booz, a Philadelphia distiller, started putting whiskey into bottles shaped like log cabins and calling it "Old Cabin Whiskey." Soon the word *booze* was synonymous with distilled liquor.

It was only a matter of time before the first alcoholic president came to power. Franklin Pierce came into the executive office in 1853, during a time when the temperance forces in American society were finding political power. The anti-alcohol campaign had been launched around 1810 by a small number of reformist clergymen. Several churches had already adopted rules strictly limiting use of distilled spirits, but the temperance movement worked for total prohibition. In the 1840s it brought about local licensing, and, in the 1850s, state prohibitions. Total national prohibition remained a continuing goal.

Publicly, Franklin Pierce led a temperate administration that brought approval from these crusaders. The Pierces served no alcoholic beverages at their receptions and no wine was served at state dinners. Privately, the president was not so puritanical. The son of a tavern keeper and an alcoholic mother, Pierce had had a drinking problem since his college days. He had an uncomfortable marriage and his only son was tragically killed in front of his eyes just prior to the inauguration. The president turned more and more to the solace of the whiskey bottle. Political crises also triggered binges wherein he isolated himself from official duties. His frequent administrative blunders may have been more than coincidentally related to his constant drinking. Pierce eventually died from cirrhosis of the liver and hepatic coma.

The Civil War was looming and, just before his death, Pierce asked, "What can the next president do but drink?" His successor, James Buchanan, seemed to agree, but only in the context of official parties. When Buchanan moved into the White House, he chided his liquor merchants for delivering small bottles of champagne: "Pints are very inconvenient in this house," he explained, "as the article is not used in such small quantities." Buchanan was a serious drinker and was praised for his ability to keep drinking while his guests were falling down in alcoholic stupors.

Abraham Lincoln used to say he was getting drunk and ready to fall down after a sip of wine, but he was only joking. Lincoln tried his best to refrain from overindulgence. It wasn't just the temperance movement that shaped his habits, but the experience of his mother. When Lincoln was nine years old, his mother, Nancy Hanks, died because a local cow had grazed *Datura*. The toxins passed into the cow's milk, Nancy drank it, and caught the "milk sickness"—a slow but fatal disease.

"I promised my precious mother only a few days before she died, that I would never use anything intoxicating as a beverage, and I consider that promise as binding today as it was the day I gave it," explained Lincoln when he refused to taste a rare wine that was offered to him after his election to Congress. As a young man he hadn't kept his word and drank whiskey and smoked tobacco, although he didn't like the taste or the effects, so it was easy to avoid excessive use. Lincoln understood the difference between use, as in medicines, and abuse, which rendered one dysfunctional. He kept an account at the Corneau & Diller drugstore in Springfield, Illinois, where from 1855 to 1861 he purchased such items as brandy and liniment containing hemlock and laudanum, among many other preparations. When he purchased three sticks of cough candy for 25 cents, he was probably unaware that there was opium in every piece. But the sticks worked and coughs were suppressed.

According to historian Henry Pratt, on October 12, 1860, Abraham Lincoln walked into the drugstore and purchased a bottle of cocaine for 50 cents. If true, this would have made Lincoln the first American to buy this newly available product. Previously, only coca products were sold. However, I examined the original daybooks of Corneau & Diller and found the purchase recorded as "Cocoaine." This spelling was sometimes used for coca extract products, coca wine, and cocaine-based local anesthetic preparations. But it was also the trade name for a coconut-oil hair product sold in 50-cent bottles and manufactured by the Joseph Burnett Company in Boston. Burnett was famous for its flavoring extracts used for cooking purposes, and such extracts were stocked by Corneau & Diller. The Lincoln family used them, and it seems likely that Lincoln's purchase of Cocoaine was for his hair, not for his stomach or nose. Indeed, the following week he started growing a beard and the next month he was elected the sixteenth president of the United States.

Although Lincoln came to office in the midst of a growing temperance movement, his administration quickly became enmeshed in the Civil War. While focusing his energy on preserving the Union, Lincoln allowed the alcohol and tobacco industries to flourish. He taxed tobacco when funds were needed for the Union Army and allowed his officers to drink as long as they could stand and fight. When a temperance committee asked him to fire General Grant because he drank too much, Lincoln inquired as to Grant's brand of whiskey so that he could send a barrel of it to his other generals. But Lincoln was honest enough to acknowledge that excessive alcohol use wasn't good for the body or mind. In a speech before a gathering of reformed drunkards, Lincoln attributed the "demon of intemperance" to a universal appetite for intoxication:

> Nobody knows when the use of intoxicating liquors commenced; nor is it important to know. It is sufficient that to all of us who now inhabit the world, the practice of drinking them is just as old as the world itself. . . . When all such of us . . . first opened our eyes upon the stage of existence, we found intoxicating liquor recognized by everybody, used by everybody, and repudiated by nobody. It commonly entered into the first draught of the infant and the last draught of the dying man. . . . In my judgment such of us as have never fallen victims have been spared more by the absence of appetite than from any mental or moral superiority over those who have.

The battlefields of the Civil War produced a new drug phenomenon: morphine addiction. The widespread use of morphine, injected with the newly introduced hypodermic syringe, created a large postwar population of addicts. Other technological developments changed patterns of tobacco and alcohol use. In the post-Civil War era, cigarettes became more widely available, along with the safety match, which was invented in 1855. These matches allowed smokers to leave their indoor lamps and candles and thus indulge freely in a portable habit. Within a few years the Diamond Match Company introduced a "drunkard's match" that was self-extinguishing at midpoint and enabled Americans to combine their two favorite intoxications.

The Civil War and its aftermath marked an important turning point in the patterns of intoxication within America as illustrated by the habits of its chief executives. Before that time, Lincoln's predecessors used the same intoxicants: tobacco and alcohol. Over the early days of the Republic they had become familiar with growing hemp for fiber and using opium for medicines, but neither were popular intoxicants. Now the widespread availability of drugs such as morphine and cocaine would shape a gradual change in habits. Familiarity was breeding nonmedical experimentation. For example, after the war William Hammond, Lincoln's surgeon general of the army, recommended coca wines as a general tonic and stimulant. When pure cocaine became available, Dr. Hammond personally took some of the largest doses on record and became convinced that the drug was a cure for depression. As for the "so-called cocaine habit," the enthusiastic Hammond was certain that it did not exist.

Lincoln kept himself informed about the latest developments in pharmacology. He certainly knew what to take and when. In 1862 the president had a toothache and visited Dr. G. S. Wolf, who had offices near the White House. As Dr. Wolf prepared to extract the tooth with forceps, Lincoln waved his hand. "Just a minute, please," said the president, taking a small bottle of chloroform from his vest pocket. The drug was a popular recreational intoxicant in America, but it had not yet been used for dental anesthesia in Washington. It is unknown why Lincoln had his own bottle. Lincoln inhaled deeply a few times, then drowsily gave a signal for the dentist to proceed.

The changing medical and nonmedical habits of the presidents and those around them illustrate how the country embraced these new drugs. The major point is not that these men used drugs that were once legal and are now prohibited or even that we once had drunks and addicts as leaders of our country. As the men who occupied the White House changed places, the country changed and so did the types of drugs available. What never changed was the fourth drive, the universal appetite that Lincoln so aptly described. Because of that appetite all early wars waged with legislative controls and prohibitions were destined to fail.

2

Alcohol intoxication remained a national recreation. President Andrew Johnson was said to be rarely sober; he delivered a rambling, incoherent speech when inaugurated as vice president to Lincoln. Ironically, he warned the country against sinful complicity with the liquor traffic and advocated prohibition: "If King George III oppressed the colonies with the iron heel of tyranny, King Alcohol is more severely oppressing the nation today." Johnson called for a new leader to free the nation from alcohol dependency. He went to sleep that night, as he always did, by sedating himself with whiskey.

Ulysses S. Grant was our next leader, but not the one to answer Johnson's call. Grant was an alcoholic. As a soldier, Grant acquired a taste for alcohol that escalated from social use to compulsive, solitary drinking. After his marriage, he pledged to stop and joined the Sons of Temperance, but he failed to maintain his abstinence. As he advanced through military promotions, he drank more and adhered less to military discipline, sometimes appearing dead drunk before his soldiers. During the Civil War, General Grant's chief of staff, John Rawlins, banished liquor from his headquarters and gave secret orders to keep alcohol away from the general. But Grant always seemed to find a bottle.

As president, Grant managed to avoid falling deeper into the morass of his own alcoholism. Instead he smoked an average of 750 cigars a month! During his retirement, Grant complained of mouth pain and was examined by Dr. John Douglas, a throat specialist. Douglas found evidence of cancer and dabbed cocaine on the diseased areas, which brought immediate relief to Grant. The treatments were continued twice daily. The newspapers accused Douglas and his colleagues of experimenting on the president with a new and potentially dangerous medicine. Grant wanted to defend the medicine himself and replied:

> It is not true that they are experimenting on me with a single medicine about which they know little or nothing . . . . The medicine alluded to as the one being experimented with is, I presume, Cocaine. That has never been given me as a medicine. It has only been administered as an application to stop pain. It is well known that it accomplishes that result without leaving injurious effects behind. It is only applied when much needed.

The president was receiving cocaine as a local anesthetic, yet the pleasurable psychoactive effects did not escape his notice. As the cancer progressed, Douglas increased the dosage and Grant started to experience tolerance: "My mouth hurts me and cocaine ceases to give me the relief it once did. If its use can be curtailed I hope it will soon have its effect again."

Grant's poor health weakened him but he continued to write his memoirs. Indeed, it was this sole activity, sustained by cocaine, that seemed to motivate him to stay alive. He took the opportunity to prepare a brief essay extolling the virtues of cocaine:

> I have tried to study the question of the use of cocaine as impartially as possible considering that I am the person affected by its use. The conclusion that I have come to in my case is: taken properly it gives a *wonderful* amount of relief from pain. . . . When the medicine is being applied the tendency is to take *more* than there is any necessity and *oftener.* On the whole, my conclusion is to take it when it seems to be so much needed as it was at times yesterday. I will try to limit its use. This latter you know how hard it is to do. [emphasis added]

Toward the end of his life, Grant, who owned a well-thumbed copy of De Quincey's opium confessions, received frequent injections of morphine followed by combinations of morphine and brandy, in addition to the cocaine. The doctors had accidentally stumbled upon the same euphoric mixture of drugs used in Brompton's Cocktail, a traditional British prescription for terminal cancer patients. After Grant's death, his three chief physicians confessed that for the last five months of Grant's life they had also given him a coca extract known as Thé Mariani. Grant was receiving oral doses equal to 160 milligrams of cocaine, three to six times a day, more than enough to cause intoxication as well as dependency. It was this extract, not the local anesthetic cocaine swabs, that was the "experimental" medicine referred to by the newspaper stories. According to Angelo Mariani, the chemist who formulated the extract, "it was owing to this medicament that the general was enabled each day to spend several hours working at his book, and he could not have completed the same without the strengthening effect of *Thé Mariani.*"

No one appreciated the virtues of this treatment more than Mark Twain, who had a vast financial interest in keeping Grant alive to finish the book. Twain had engineered a publishing contract and a $10,000 advance for Grant's memoirs. He visited his author regularly, sometimes daily, and was present on occasions when Grant was given a cup of milk mixed with the Thé Mariani. It was not surprising that Grant always seemed to pick up strength and write more whenever his publisher was around.

The sustaining power of coca was well known to Twain. As a young man of nineteen, he had read an account of exploration in the Amazon Valley and was fired with a desire to open up a global trade in coca. He financed his adventure with a fifty-dollar bill and went to New Orleans to catch a ship for Brazil. He found no ships, ran out of money, and was forced to become a pilot on a riverboat. Twain called the incident a "turning-point of my life" and described it in a 1910 essay. But he remained impressed with the virtues of coca, and may have even suggested it for the dying president. If Twain was not the dealer, he was still capable of profiting from Grant's cocaine-inspired writing. Grant's *Personal Memoirs* was a best-seller for Twain's publishing company and earned Grant's estate nearly half a million dollars. The general himself now adorns the fifty-dollar bill.

If temperance forces were dismayed by Grant's excesses, they felt renewed hope with the administration of Rutherford B. Hayes. The new president had one cup of coffee for breakfast, one cup of tea for lunch, and never used tobacco or alcohol. His wife, Lucy, the first college graduate to become First Lady, became the patron saint of the Women's Christian Temperance Union.

Wine was served at their first official White House dinner, but never again. President Hayes had decided "that the example of excluding liquors from the White House would be wise and useful, and would be approved by good people generally." He also knew it would be particularly gratifying to his wife and members of temperance organizations whom he wanted to bring into the Republican party. Seasoned party members thought it was too high a price to pay for votes. After all, the temperance philosophy went against the whole notion of treating, which now took the form of official dinners at the White House. Politicians joked that "the water flowed like champagne" at the dinners and blamed "Lemonade Lucy" for their sober times.

Toward the end of his life, Hayes wondered if he had been too puritanical and pondered the Madisonian doctrine of innocent gratifications: "In avoiding the apearance of evil, I am not sure but I have sometimes unnecessarily deprived myself and others of innocent enjoyments."

Those innocent enjoyments and gratifications finally reappeared when President Chester Arthur restored alcohol to official White House dinners. Arthur criticized the executive mansion as a "badly kept barracks" and called in Louis Comfort Tiffany to remodel. Twenty-four wagons full of old furnishings were sold at auction. One of those items, a sideboard presented to Lucy Hayes by the Women's Christian Temperance Union, ended up in a saloon on Pennsylvania Avenue, where it was kept loaded with liquors. Tiffany replaced everything with flags, golden eagles, and other ornate decorations. In keeping with this new style, the presidential dinners became famous for their fine wines, rich foods, and after-dinner liqueurs. Arthur grew obese, suffered painful attacks of indigestion, developed gallbladder problems and nephritis. The constant misery prevented him from sleeping and he eventually resorted to narcotics in the months prior to his death.

The president's drug use was not unusual. Many Americans tried narcotics during this period, an era referred to as the golden age of "patent" medicines. Narcotics and other mood-altering drugs were becoming readily available and people were being encouraged to use them. The demand was so great that coca and opium became major import items and domestic hemp was finally cultivated as a drug plant. Almost every corner pharmacist mixed alcohol, *Cannabis,* cocaine, morphine, and opium into a cornucopia of over-the-counter nostrums.

The preparations were neither patented nor labeled with ingredients, but that didn't stop manufacturers from promoting them. Drug advertisements became as American as treating with alcohol or smoking cigars. Testimonials from celebrities were a major feature of the ads. When Sigmund Freud said he liked the taste and price of American cocaine better than German cocaine, the manufacturer, Parke, Davis & Company, rushed to include his remarks in a promotional booklet. After Dr. George Miller Sternberg, the deputy surgeon general under President Grover Cleveland, supplied Mariani's coca wine to hospitals, Sternberg's endorsements became regular features in Mariani ads. Even Cleveland's young and attractive wife, Frances, appeared in patent medicine advertisements for a New Jersey pharmaceutical company.

Grover Cleveland preferred alcohol. During his last term there was gossip that he drank heavily and physically abused his wife. The White House issued a strong denial. They also tried to quash a sensationalistic press report that the president had used cocaine while on a friend's luxury yacht.

The latter rumor turned out to be true, but the full story of what took place onboard the yacht was kept secret for another twenty-four years. President Cleveland had a cancerous growth on the roof of his mouth and part of his jaw was removed in a daring operation employing nitrous oxide, ether, and cocaine. The anesthesia was particularly risky due to the president's use of alcohol, which rendered him somewhat resistant to the ether. However, the use of cocaine solved the problem and helped to eliminate the pain.

Whereas Grover Cleveland may have escaped a personal link with intoxication or drug endorsements, his successor William McKinley wasted no time in becoming associated, albeit unintentionally, with advertisements for coca products. After his election as twenty-fifth president, McKinley received a case of Vin Mariani coca wine direct from the publicity-wise Angelo Mariani, the chemist who supplied Grant with the more concentrated and potent Thé Mariani. The

Mariani line of coca and cocaine preparations was now the favorite of leaders around the globe who used the products for work and pleasure. Vin Mariani was endorsed by six presidents of France, a president of Argentina, royalty throughout Europe and Asia, and three popes. Six years before he pressed McKinley for a testimonial, Mariani received what some consider his greatest compliment. Frédéric Bartholdi, the celebrated sculptor of the Statue of Liberty, wrote "*Vin Mariani* seems to brighten and increase all our faculties; it is very probable that had I taken it twenty years ago, the Statue of Liberty would have attained the height of several hundred metres."

Mariani, a pusher par excellence, undoubtedly wanted to add President McKinley to his list of such enthusiastic customers. He had missed with Grant and Cleveland, getting testimonials only from their physicians. He was still after a direct endorsement from *the* president, something that might survive as well as Baby Ruth—the candy bar named after Grover Cleveland's daughter who died at the age of twelve.

Mariani must have been disappointed when he received a reply not from President McKinley but from his secretary, John Addison Porter:

> Please accept thanks in the President's behalf and my own for your courtesy in sending a case of the celebrated *Vin Mariani*, with whose tonic virtues I am already acquainted and will be happy to avail myself of in the future, as occasions may require.

Mariani salvaged what he could from the reply. He juxtaposed the letter, which was typed on Executive Mansion letterhead, with a signed picture of President McKinley and published it in advertisements circulated around the world. He also secured an endorsement from Dr. William Van Reypen, McKinley's surgeon general of the navy, who issued Vin Mariani on the U.S. hospital ships *Solace* and *Relief*.

If McKinley did not directly endorse the drinking of coca wine, he did support tobacco smoking. Tobacco use in America was greater than ever. So when funds were needed for the Spanish-American War, McKinley simply tripled the excise tax on tobacco, a tax that lowered domestic sales but not the president's personal use. He loved cigars and smoked from ten to twenty each day, much to the dismay of the anti-tobacco lobby, which claimed the president was physically weakened by his habit. After he was fatally shot by anarchist Leon Czolgosz on September 6, 1901, he still craved tobacco on his deathbed. McKinley's physician withheld the cigars and gave him several whiskeys and small injections of morphine. The physician stated that the president would have survived the shooting if he had not had "a tobacco heart."

After McKinley's assassination, Vice President Theodore Roosevelt became the nation's youngest president. He was described as a non-smoker, a character trait cited by the anti-tobacco movement as the reason he survived an assassin's bullet in 1912 and McKinley had not. Actually, the bullet that struck Roosevelt had been slowed down by a metal spectacle case and a folded manuscript in his breast pocket so that it did not penetrate the vital organs of his body.

Theodore Roosevelt had a coffee habit that escalated from the small amounts he used in his youth to arrest asthma attacks to compulsive drinking by the time he was president. The president's coffee mug was said to resemble a bathtub. Just as Mariani sought presidential testimonials, coffee merchant Joel Clark attempted to get President Roosevelt to endorse his new blend of coffee, which was named after a celebrated hotel, the Maxwell House. In 1907 Clark set up a concession booth on the grounds of the Hermitage, Andrew Jackson's home in Tennessee, for the anniversary celebration of the former president's birth. President Roosevelt arrived and Clark poured him a cup. Before Clark could ask for the endorsement, the president gulped the entire cup, turned to the crowd, and announced that it was "Good to the last drop!" A new advertising slogan was born. Mariani couldn't have done better himself.

Mariani was doing a brisk business in Europe, but he was having a hard time keeping his U.S. markets open. There were over seventy competing brands of coca or cocaine beverages, including Coca-Cola. And problems were brewing. Some southerners were consuming fifty bottles a day of Coca-Cola in order to get more of the cocaine. Pure cocaine was also sold over-the-counter, and people like Annie Meyers were showing signs of abuse and addiction. Opiates were just as plentiful and pure. The American Medical Association was starting to expose the "evil" contents of these nostrums. By this time congressional sentiment was calling for some regulation of the patent medicine industry.

3

Ever since the Civil War ended, the government had been unable to control the new drugs. Measures to control opium, for example, included import taxes, penalties against opium smoking, and closure of public opium dens. But these efforts only drove users and distribution underground where no regulatory measures were able to root them out. And now with the opium and cocaine patent medicines openly available, legislators were getting nervous. Anticipating this legislative mood, and attempting to separate themselves from the word *dope,* which had become synonymous with their popular soda fountain drink, the makers of Coca-Cola removed the cocaine in 1903.

Three years later, the Pure Food and Drug Act required contents to be listed on labels, a regulation that ended up only advertising cocaine and opium by identifying them on the package labels. Further control was needed. But when the importation and possession of opium was finally banned by legislation in 1909, smuggling increased, as did the price of opium. Then users shifted to cheaper, more widely available morphine and heroin products. As for the cocaine beverages, most manufacturers elected to remove the cocaine and substitute caffeine.

The great Mariani, who was considered to be the Merlin of the advertising world, refused to change. He flooded the marketplace with elegant announcements claiming that "*Vin Mariani* has never produced cocainism" because coca was not as dangerous as cocaine. Mariani conjured up sophisticated propaganda methods—sponsoring plays and using billboards—to keep his wine in the minds of as many people as possible. But prohibitive laws seemed just around the corner, and Mariani eventually retreated from the U.S. market. In his later years, Mariani sequestered himself in his Paris office, described by some as a shrine to Mama Coca. The rugs, furniture, paintings, and other objects all depicted coca in some artistic way. Amid the splendor of these furnishings Mariani passed away in 1914, the year in which the Harrison "Narcotics" Act was passed in the United States and signed by President Wilson.

The Harrison Act was widely interpreted as national prohibition of "narcotics" (opium, morphine, heroin, coca, and cocaine), but it was merely a law for the orderly marketing of these drugs in small quantities over-the-counter and in larger quantities on a physician's prescription. Marijuana was not included because of strong lobbying by the pharmaceutical industry. Tobacco was not included because it was so entrenched it could always be found in snuffboxes on the desks of the senators who voted on the legislation. The Harrison Act effectively stopped sales of most over-the-counter narcotics. But new black markets emerged immediately in brothels and red-light districts where police enforcement was minimal. Within a few years after the Harrison Act, the underground traffic in narcotics had linked up with newly established international smuggling operations. Americans were as good at finding supplies of narcotics as they were at finding teas during colonial days of British restraints.

Woodrow Wilson, like most subsequent presidents who were elected to enforce these new laws, seemed determined to keep American bodies as pure as the Pure Food and Drug Act. Wilson was always concerned about "poisons and toxins" in his own body. He started each day by swallowing a stomach tube and pumping out his stomach with soothing liquids, a practice later replaced by a special White House diet. It was once reported that President Wilson advocated tobacco but it was his vice president, Thomas Marshall, who made the classic remark, "What this country needs is a really good five-cent cigar!"

What the country didn't need, at least in the opinion of most lawmakers, was overindulgence in any habit; public drunkenness was particularly distasteful. It was during the Wilson administration that the anti-alcohol movement, exemplified by the zeal of Carry Nation, was winning legislative victories. Despite state prohibitions, a brisk and legal interstate traffic in alcohol flowed from wet to dry states during the early 1900s. The Webb-Kenyon Act in 1913 prohibited such shipments. With alcohol laws on the books, the liquor traffic started to move underground just as the narcotic traffic had done in 1914. Congress passed the Eighteenth Amendment (Prohibition) in 1917. By the time Prohibition was implemented in 1920, the organization for the manufacture, distribution, and sales of alcohol was well in place to meet the demand. The demand did not disappear with legislation. Many of the speakeasies in the nation's skid rows now provided both alcohol and narcotics.

Despite Prohibition, President Warren Harding drank whiskey and beer behind the closed doors of his White House bedroom. In public, Harding chewed tobacco and smoked cigars and cigarettes. The pictures of the president smoking delighted the tobacco industry but irritated Miss Lucy Gaston, who championed the cause to outlaw tobacco.

The cause was joined by many prominent Americans who saw cigarettes as the new form of slavery. Henry Ford published a hard-hitting book, *The Case Against the Little White Slaver,* with a foreword by Thomas Edison and a special section on how the cigarette habit was destroying the American workplace, a theme later repeated for marijuana and cocaine in the workplace of the 1980s. Politicians agreed with the case against the "white slavers," and several cities and states banned the sale or use of cigarettes just as colonial governments had attempted to do. New York City passed the Sullivan Ordinance, which banned women from smoking in public. More than one hundred regulatory measures were eventually introduced in twenty-eight state legislatures. Although these controls reduced cigarette sales, the smoking public only switched to cigars or chewing tobacco. In areas where the tobacco bans were enforced, cigarettes were manufactured illegally and many new smokers were drawn to this forbidden fruit.

By 1921, states began to repeal their anti-tobacco laws. Lucy Gaston fought back with fiery propaganda: America must be saved from tobacco or fall to Bolshevism. Her evidence: many cigarettes sold in the United States were imported from Russia. But her cries of white slavery or liberty had no effect on the ever-increasing consumption of tobacco. When she started the movement in 1899, 4.4 billion cigarettes were consumed. In the year of her death, 1924, more than 73 billion cigarettes were sold. Ironically, the nonsmoking Gaston died of throat cancer.

Tobacco consumption continued to soar outside and inside the White House. President Calvin Coolidge, who abstained from alcohol, smoked cigars heavily and the aroma of Virginia cigars perfumed every room in the White House. Outside, cigar smoking enjoyed a new following among Americans, especially young politicians who followed the presidential lead. The power of the president to influence behavior was comically illustrated at a White House breakfast. Coolidge poured his coffee and cream into a saucer. Several guests politely did the same. Then, as the politicians waited for the president to take a sip, he smiled, leaned over, and placed the saucer on the floor for the nation's First Cat.

When it came to alcohol, however, the country did not follow the public displays of presidential abstinence. Instead people and presidents did what they felt like doing. Alcohol use continued even when Herbert Hoover became President. Hoover was strongly sympathetic to Prohibition and called it "a great social and economic experiment, noble in motive and far-reaching in purpose." Outwardly dedicated to the law, the president remained inwardly loyal to gin fizzes throughout this noble period. In homes and speakeasies across America the experiment was failing. If Lincoln could drink and even operate a tavern in Illinois despite a pledge to his mother, so could others despite the law or their sworn duty to uphold it. McSorley's tavern in New York, like hundreds of other establishments, continued to serve alcohol throughout Prohibition. Their patrons included the very policemen charged with its enforcement.

Despite increased law-enforcement budgets and escalating penalties, Prohibition didn't work and probably never did, at least in terms of stopping supply and demand. The thirteen years of Prohibition were unlucky in that all the efforts to change patterns of alcohol use in America failed. Alcohol was abundantly available. People still got drunk, became alcoholics, menaced the highways, and filled up courts, jails, and hospitals. Some things were worse than before. Adulterated and contaminated "rot-gut," produced without safeguards or standards, caused blindness, paralysis, and death. There was a shift from the large bottles of wine and beer to hard liquors that were less bulky and easier to transport on the black market. Organized crime syndicates took control of alcohol distribution. And consumption of other intoxicants such as marijuana and ether soared. People saw the law as an outrageous and senseless invasion of personal liberty. The nation rebelled. The Twenty-first Amendment, the repeal of Prohibition, was finally ratified in 1933, the year that Franklin Delano Roosevelt took office. His four administrations would now be confronted with other drug problems.

Prohibition of alcohol had stimulated the rise of marijuana smoking and black marketing in the drug. Marijuana "tea pads"—reminiscent of the opium dens of the previous century—started to appear in New Orleans and other southern cities that were the ports of entry for marijuana smuggled from Cuba and Mexico. Increasing numbers of Mexican immigrants, who brought with them a tendency to use marijuana for relaxation and entertainment, traveled from Louisiana to all parts of the United States. By 1930 there were five hundred tea pads in New York City alone and many others could be found in cities along the Mississippi.

Marijuana use had spread up the Mississippi with migrant workers, jazz, and sensational newspaper accounts of this new drug habit. The affected states started passing laws to stop the traffic. By 1937, 46 of the 48 states and the District of Columbia had laws against marijuana with penalties and definitions equating it to a narcotic. The federal Marihuana Tax Act was enacted in 1937. Like the Harrison Act, the Marihuana Tax Act was a revenue measure requiring any person dealing with marijuana to register and pay a special tax. At the same time, the law attempted to regulate use by making it extremely difficult for people to acquire marijuana for nonmedical purposes.

The response by marijuana users was almost a replay of the behavior that followed Prohibition. Tea pads moved into the former speakeasies and a sizable subculture started domestic cultivation of marijuana. Enforcement directed at eradication had only minimal effects because marijuana was officially replanted in many states during World War II when foreign hemp sources were cut off. In an effort to inflate the budget for their enforcement activities, the Federal Bureau of Narcotics consistently exaggerated the extent of marijuana use and publicized the drug as a violent menace.

The propaganda did not affect the patterns of marijuana use. Users then, as now, seemed to be listening only to the "message" the drug produced in their own bodies. That message told them that the marijuana intoxication felt good and that it was not hurting them. They retained an appetite for such innocent gratifications and enjoyments. Consequently, users developed attitudes of distrust for the exaggerated official information. When World War II obstructed the international heroin trade, smugglers began importing marijuana on a large scale. When the heroin trade resumed after the war, both heroin and marijuana became available from the same sources. As a result, their users were linked together. The view of marijuana as a violence-producing menace was now joined to the stepping-stone theory, which incorrectly argued that marijuana use led to heroin addiction, although any intoxicant can always be a gateway to experimentation with others. Despite increased penalties that officially equated marijuana to heroin, use continued to spread from lower-class groups to the middle class. Organized illicit traffic flourished. By 1945 the border seizures of marijuana exceeded domestic seizures.

FDR was president during this period, a period of pharmacological advances that went far beyond the accomplishments of the patent-medicine era. Medical science provided such new drugs as phenobarbital, which the president received for high blood pressure. FDR's nonmedical choices were the politician's staples of alcohol and tobacco. He was an expert in the American way of treating. He also smoked up to four packs of cigarettes a day. In the tradition of George Washington, FDR recognized that tobacco and cigarettes were valuable morale boosters to the American fighting man and he seldom failed to display a cigarette in his press photographs. Tobacco was also financing much of World War II, as it had the Revolution. Nonetheless, as tobacco consumption set new records, the antismoking movement vehemently complained about the image of the president in his seer-sucker suit, grinning around his uptilted ivory cigarette holder.

Subsequent presidents managed to keep their patterns of alcohol or tobacco use—as well as their use of less accepted drugs—more private, confining use to official toasts, private affairs in the White House living quarters, or on board the *Air Force One* jetliner. John F. Kennedy usually had a cigar in his mouth on board *Air Force One*. But prior to landing he would hide it in his coat pocket, a habit that burned many pockets. It was during the Kennedy years that recreational drug use started to peak in America. So it was not unexpected when there were published whispers about JFK's use of marijuana and LSD in the White House, and speculation that the frequent "vitamin" injections he received, which left him flushed and excited, were really amphetamines or cocaine. Since there was no hard evidence for these claims, only hearsay from such pro-drug figures as Timothy Leary, they can only be viewed as the projected fantasies of a growing population of recreational drug users.

The electorate's use of drugs continued to escalate and Congress increased restrictions and penalties. By 1970, fifty-five federal drug laws (excluding alcohol laws) had been passed to tighten the Harrison Act and state legislatures voted for hundreds of others. Taken together, these laws failed to stop drug use. Although they may have slowed the rate of addiction in the population, they certainly created the black market and transformed patterns of distribution and use. The fourth drive remained alive and well in America's hidden pockets of drug use: inner-city ghettos and shooting galleries, middle-class suburban homes, and bathrooms everywhere.

In the tradition of Abraham Lincoln, the modern presidents continued to support the tobacco and alcohol industries and to joke about intoxication. Nixon was once speaking about his travels in South America, where stones were thrown at him, and stated: "I got stoned in Caracas. I'll tell you one thing; it's a lot different from getting stoned at a Jaycee convention." But Nixon was not joking when he signed the Comprehensive Drug Abuse Prevention and Control Act of 1970, which superseded all other federal narcotic laws. It was designed to establish control over the manufacture, importation, and distribution of drugs. Among the act's most significant provisions was the classification of drugs into schedules with distinctive regulations, controls, and penalties. This part of the legislation was known as the Controlled Substances Act. Drugs were placed into one of five schedules depending on the potential for abuse, accepted medical use and safety, and potential for physical or psychological dependence. Heroin, marijuana, and most hallucinogens were judged to be unsafe and to have a high potential for abuse with no current medical use. They were placed in Schedule I, the most restrictive classification. Cocaine, along with opium, was placed in Schedule II. Provisions were made to add new drugs as they became a problem but the more established drugs of tobacco and alcohol remained unscheduled.

President Ronald Reagan continued to support the tobacco industry, to permit alcohol use, and to accept medical use of powerful narcotics. After his colon surgery in 1985, painkilling morphine was injected into the president's spinal column, bypassing the circulation to the brain and thereby minimizing the mental grogginess. Still, the euphoric effects may have contributed to the president's unexpected postoperative cheer and his jaunty remark: "I feel fit as a fiddle."

Little had changed from the early days of the country when the presidents and the people they represented used tobacco, alcohol, coca, and opium. We have seen a consistent pattern of drug-seeking and drug-taking behavior. Equally commonplace have been policies of regulation and prohibition, always greeted with protest and evasion. From the earliest settlements on the continent, with their use of homegrown tobacco plants and imported teas, to today's preference for homegrown marijuana and imported cocaine, the drive continues. It was the pursuit of cocaine, however, that really sent users into overdrive in order to fulfill their demands for this "ideal recreational drug." By the 1980s, users of cocaine, representing 10 percent of the population and feeling as fit as 24 million fiddles, called it the all-American drug. The commander in chief called it *war*.

13

War on Drugs

ENDURING SUPPLIES
AND DEMANDS

1

The catapult rolled silently into position. At least it looked like a scale-model of a catapult. I watched carefully as the Professor loaded the deadly charge into the two tiny wooden spoons that served as throwing arms. A single latch held both arms down against tightly coiled springs. When the latch was released, the arms would spring up and throw their loads in unison. A miniature gargoyle carved out of Black Forest wood bedizened each arm and gazed upward to where the target would lie. The effect was ominous.

The Professor adjusted the aim by sighting through an intricate system of mirrors. He spoke in a rapid-fire babble of angles, vectors of force, and German craftsmanship. He was close enough to the machine to kiss it. I tensed as his bony fingers reached for the latch. He whispered words of encouragement to the catapult, exhaled, and released the loads. The arms snapped and the Professor's head jerked backward as the twin charges of cocaine powder rammed deep into his nostrils. Two perfect hits!

The title "Professor" was an honorary one I had bestowed on him for the inventiveness he displayed in engineering new drug accessories.

The devices he developed and tested were turned over to manufacturers in exchange for a small consultant fee. The inventions eventually appeared in stores and mail-order catalogues, part of the one-billion-dollar-a-year market in drug accessories. He passed the catapult tome.

I was fascinated by this latest in cocaine dispensers, which he had copied from a European design. It was crafted to resemble a war machine, an appropriate embodiment of the word *paraphernalia,* which originally referred to mechanical devices used by the military in ancient Greece. Most modern instruments used to administer cocaine connote some type of militaristic assault on the body: needles shoot it, straws and "tooters" rocket it, and liquid sprays blast it. Other devices available in the paraphernalia market help camouflage drug use. There are aerosols to mask and disperse marijuana, cocaine, or PCP smoke. "Chamber" pipes offer the users a self-contained odorless and smokeless way to use their favorite combustible drug. Underwater pipes can make marijuana smokers as difficult to spot as frogmen. "Camelflage" papers turn marijuana joints into innocent-looking Camel cigarettes. Cocaine dispensers disguised as jewelry, lipsticks, belt buckles, and coins can make any user feel like a secret agent. If this wasn't war, it was a most unusual peacetime activity.

2

A new war on drugs was formally declared by President Nixon in a message to Congress in 1971, again by President Ford in 1976, and once again by President Reagan in 1982. This war, like past wars, was based on a supply-and-demand analysis. The major strategy was aimed at cutting off the drugs available to users and prospective users while reducing demand.

In its simplest terms, the specific drugs chosen by users are viewed as a function of availability and need. Availability is measured by supply, which has been traditionally attacked by international agreements, eradication, interdiction, and other efforts aimed at preventing the drugs from entering the country or getting to the users. Reduce the available supplies, so goes the reasoning, and drug abuse declines. Needs, reflected by patterns of use, are equated to the demand side of the economic equation and have been addressed by programs of treatment, rehabilitation, and preventive education. Reduce the needs, then supplies will disappear.

A war based on such an analysis was doomed to failure because it neglected to factor into the equation the basic operating principle of the fourth drive: the unstoppable pursuit of intoxication that creates the needs in the first place. As enforcement dramatically affects the supplies of or demands for specific drugs, users manifest protest or evasion or they merely shift to other supplies or other drugs that allow them to continue their pursuit of intoxication. Reducing supplies or demands has never stopped the pursuit of intoxicants and never will. Presidential declarations could not make the outcome of this war any different from those of past wars.

And so it became a real war. Throughout the 1970s and 1980s, the war against supply continually escalated. On the international front the U.S. intelligence community came to play a more important role in the nation's antidrug efforts. So did the U.S. Customs Service, the U.S. Coast Guard, the Border Patrol, the Department of Defense, the Federal Aviation Administration, the National Oceanic and Atmospheric Administration, the Federal Communications Commission, even NASA. National Security Agency satellites tracked shipments of ether to processing labs in Colombia. American military teams went into the front lines in foreign countries. They helped eradicate coca crops, destroy laboratories, and interdict shipments. In Bolivia, a physician working with a U.S. helicopter team was decapitated by the helicopter rotor when he jumped from the craft while it was attempting an emergency landing. Yet there was no legal inquiry or trial because this was the twilight zone of a real war, not a make believe movie.

Drug Enforcement Administration (DEA) agents went to work in over forty foreign countries. Many were assassinated, or put on hit lists. Colombian traffickers offered a $350,000 bounty for the murder of any top DEA official in the United States or Colombia, and threatened to kill five Americans for every Colombian drug trafficker extradited to America. State Department-backed teams tried to eradicate coca plants in fourteen countries: nineteen members of one team in Peru were hacked to death. Four had been tortured first. In the Upper Huallaga Valley of Peru, another seventeen eradicators were murdered by a band of fifty traffickers armed with automatic weapons. Less direct methods were tried: teams taught Peruvian peasants who depended on coca for their livelihood to substitute tobacco and potatoes. At the same time, however, little was done to persuade American marijuana farmers, who were raising the nation's largest cash crop, to give up their livelihood.

Foreign governments were praised for these and other international antidrug efforts. The kudos were undeserved. Despite the putative successes, the impact on reducing drug use in the United States has been negligible. Why?

Because drug use, the unstoppable fourth drive, has proved to be extremely adaptable to changing supplies and pressures from abroad. The mechanisms were clear in 1969 following the very first significant international campaign: Operation Intercept, the first major assault on marijuana use. This operation captured 493 drug runners at the Mexican border. But very few drugs were confiscated and no change in marijuana use inside the United States was recorded.

Twenty days later, the name of the program was changed to Operation Cooperation and it enlisted the support of Mexican police to destroy the marijuana plants themselves. Marijuana fields in northern Mexico were burned. But the operation back-fired. Smugglers were forced to trade farther south into Mexico, where they found more potent varieties of marijuana. They also found supplies of strong marijuana in other countries such as Thailand and superior hashish from North Africa and the Near East. Subsequently, the percentage of THC in street samples of marijuana in the United States increased sevenfold. This created a connoisseur demand for regular supplies of higher-potency preparations. And so, the final ironic result of Operation Cooperation was to promote north of the border cultivation of *sinsemilla*, a high-potency seedless marijuana.

The homegrown industry became as effective as bootlegging in satisfying the demands of users. In 1978 the United States conducted paraquat-spraying programs on Mexican marijuana, providing yet another incentive for more domestic cultivation. Ironically, when the United States started growing marijuana for medical research, government scientists sought the advice of growers from northern California. American homegrown marijuana and its farmers had become the best in the world.

The war had ignored the ability of American users to circumvent shortages produced by operations waged on foreign soil. Even if the coca and marijuana fields were destroyed with defoliants and nuclear fire, as one Peruvian general suggested at a 1979 conference; even if the Amazon itself were salted with Agent Orange, as two Colombian officials recommended; even if interdiction were 100 percent successful, as three former White House advisers claimed it could be; we would always have Miami, Los Angeles, or hundreds of other cities and towns as centers of trafficking, distribution, and use. The war would have to come home to America.

Domestic enforcement began by attacking supplies utilizing such diverse agencies as the FBI, the DEA, and the Marshals Service. The Treasury Department contributed the services of the U.S. Customs Service, the IRS, and the Bureau of Alcohol, Tobacco, and Firearms. Intelligence was supplied by the CIA, the National Institute on Drug Abuse, and the Immigration and Naturalization Service. A total of 11 cabinet departments, 13 independent agencies, 9 executive offices, 31 executive branch agencies, and 95 subagencies joined the fight. The National Guard was called out in 19 states to assist in spotting and destroying marijuana plants. Reconnaissance was supported by Air Force U-2s, RF-4C jet aircraft, even AWACS.

The domestic efforts were backed by new legislation. Laws were passed to enhance penalties, control new drugs, require forfeiture of cash and drug-related assets, tighten bail requirements, increase reporting for currency and foreign exchange transactions, and provide massive amounts of more financial aid, hardware, and rhetoric for the battles. In the tradition of colonial protests against regulations on tea and tobacco, contemporary users created organized political movements dedicated to changing the drug laws. The most visible protest group has been the National Organization for the Reform of Marijuana Laws (NORML). This group organized public protests and "smoke-ins," constitutional challenges to state and federal marijuana laws, and challenges to aerial surveillance and eradication efforts.

Those who grew marijuana were some of the most defiant resistance fighters in the domestic war on drugs. California marijuana growers formed an organization that supported legal action to protect domestic cultivation. Growers in other states organized guilds to promote local varieties of marijuana and soon bales of American "grass" carried such designer labels as "Sunny Mountain Brand" and "Sierra Sinsemilla." A trade journal was started in 1980 to provide farmers with technical tips. Handbooks on the cultivation of marijuana covered such subjects as pest control and methods for camouflaging fields. Growing tips from George Washington were sprinkled throughout these publications and readers were encouraged to follow his advice to sow hemp seeds throughout the land.

A new breed of Johnny Appleseeds started planting marijuana on private and public lands. The Emerald Triangle, a ten-thousand-square-mile stretch of national forest in northern California, became the heartland of domestic cultivation. As efforts to restrict domestic supplies escalated and helicopters spied on America's backyards and national parks, growers started planting marijuana among existing crops such as corn and sunflowers, or concealed in patches of ditchweed. However, it became apparent that a shift to indoor cultivation would be the best way to avoid detection. The cultivation books turned to an emphasis on indoor gardening techniques. Mail-order catalogs advertised halide growing lights and other advanced technical equipment. One company offered a closet to anyone who needed a place to grow marijuana. The closet was a handsome oak cabinet outfitted with a complete system of lights, hydroponic tanks, and nutrients, all for the "closet farmer." The farmers even developed shorter marijuana plants more suited to the new indoor environment. "Skunk #1," originally developed in California, and just under a half meter in height, was described as "little more than a popsicle stick coated with resinous marijuana flowers." George Washington would have been amused to find that marijuana had become America's largest cash crop, outranking corn, wheat, and all the other grains combined! America was now supplying at least 27 percent of the needs of over 64 million marijuana users.

The same pattern of domestic cultivation started to develop for coca, which, contrary to widespread beliefs, grows in North American climates. By 1977 the seeds were available to users in the United States. They started growing coca for personal use in greenhouses and window boxes, a level of cultivation similar to the novelty gardening of marijuana during the 1960s. The technology for large-scale commercial coca farming, for the extraction of coca paste, and for the refinement of cocaine hydrochloride became available to users a few years later.

Outdoor coca fields were found in Florida, Hawaii, and Puerto Rico. Indoor commercial coca farms and cocaine production facilities were discovered in Colorado and California. If supply reduction and interdiction efforts against foreign cocaine becomes more successful, more domestic coca farms and labs will prosper.

Opium cultivation in the United States is following a similar pattern. After Turkey effectively banned poppies in 1972, thereby drastically cutting off heroin supplies to North America, demands were filled by Mexico. The Mexican poppy eradication program started in 1976 and by 1979 had reduced the availability of heroin in the western United States, forcing traffickers to turn to other sources. By 1985 small opium poppy fields were detected on private and public lands from California to New England. But the Mexican eradication program failed, Mexican heroin became more plentiful and cheaper than ever, and opium cultivation in the United States never had to become a large-scale commercial operation. Yet the technology and seeds exist to handle any future shortage.

Marijuana, coca, and poppies can be grown indoors, thus escaping most methods of visual detection. Law enforcement agents have had to resort to new tactics such as monitoring the electricity utilized by suspected growers, who need enormous amounts of power to run the lights and temperature-control systems. None of these monitoring tactics, however, is effective when the drugs need only a dark cellar in which to grow. Accordingly, hallucinogenic mushrooms have become the second most popular and widespread homegrown drug in America.

Chemical manufacture can also circumvent supply problems. Books including *The Construction and Operation of Clandestine Drug Laboratories* by "Jack B. Nimble" or *The Whole Drug Manufacturers Catalog* make the chemical synthesis of drugs seem as simple as whipping up a batch of hashish brownies. The handbooks simplified the laboratory procedures and provided information on where to purchase all the necessary raw materials and equipment. By the mid-1970s, information on the synthesis of drugs for "fun and profit" was available for amphetamines, cocaine, and PCP, among others. The DEA raided illicit laboratories and found that even the smallest ones were capable of enormous outputs. Theoretically, almost any kitchen or bathroom could be converted into a lab capable of turning out the world's supply of a synthetic drug.

The Controlled Substances Act had anticipated the possibility of such clandestine manufacturing by listing the immediate precursors of controlled substances in the schedules. The essential ingredients for making drugs such as LSD, amphetamine, methamphetamine, and PCP were specifically listed. Other precursors were placed on a "watched list" and their sales were monitored by the DEA. In response, underground chemists started to manufacture the precursors, sometimes even making the chemicals needed to make the precursors, thereby avoiding the use of monitored ingredients.

Perhaps the most dramatic and prophetic example of how users evaded supply problems through chemistry has been the "designer drugs" of the 1980s. By slightly altering molecular structures, chemists have been able to design legal substitutes for illegal drugs. Many designer drugs were simple to make and they became more and more popular. New synthetics appeared on the market almost weekly with such names as "Eve" and "U4EUH." State and federal authorities raced against the chemical reactions to identify and prohibit the new drugs; the Controlled Substance Analogue Act was passed in 1986. Consequently, many users turned to existing sources of substitute drugs. Heroin substitutes were often found in combinations of other less restricted drugs that produced similar effects. For example, a mixture of codeine and glutethimide (Doriden) produces a heroinlike euphoria. The combination is popular among young users because it can be obtained for approximately one-fifth the cost of heroin.

When cocaine is in short supply, users do not need the magic of designer chemistry or innovative mixtures of prescription drugs; they can use mixtures of legal powders. These substitutes contain over-the-counter stimulants such as caffeine, ephedrine, and phenylpropanolamine. They may also contain readily available local anesthetics, such as lidocaine, which produce cocainelike effects when smoked. Disguised as incenses or vitamins, the substitutes are widely distributed via the paraphernalia industry.

The same mixtures are also packaged in capsules and tablets resembling legitimate pharmaceutical preparations of amphetamines. They form a new class of drugs known as "look-alikes." Imitation pills of almost every variety have been marketed. Look-alike depressants and tranquilizers, for example, may contain over-the-counter sleeping aids mixed with aspirin. Since look-alikes only contain noncontrolled substances, no federal agency has been able to stop them.

The true master of disguise in the war on drugs is not the fake speed pill or the hollow lipstick full of cocaine, but the new American outlaw. The outlaws dealing drugs were as hard to find as the drugs themselves. By the 1980s, drugs had become big business and as indistinguishable from American society as the Protestant ethic and the spirit of capitalism. One police narcotics manual advised officers that cocaine couriers may be dressed as priests or wearing gold Rolex watches.

From the rebellious cocaine-dealing youth of the 1969 movie *Easy Rider* to the senior citizen dealing cocaine in the 1981 film *Atlantic City*, the cocaine outlaw, like the marijuana outlaw, became part of the American life-style. "Your Neighbor's Business Could Be Drugs" announced the front page headline in the December 1, 1985, issue of the *Miami Herald*. The article included a detailed map with street locations for major drug dealers, houses where drugs have been sold, and cocaine labs. If you didn't have money but just wanted some fast cash or free dope, you could buy Rex Feral's *How to Rip Off a Drug Dealer* and get step-by-step instructions in the art of terrorizing and robbing dealers.

The enormous profits generated by this drug economy have attracted terrorist and insurgent groups in many areas of the world. These groups often ally themselves with trafficking organizations: traffickers supply American dollars and weapons in return for protection and assistance in smuggling. There is so much money that even one or two sizable drug shipments can finance a limited revolutionary cause. Militant organizations linked with the drug trade have included the leftist M-19 movement in Colombia, which took over the Colombian Palace of Justice, murdered eleven supreme court justices, and destroyed records on cocaine traffickers; the Maoist Shining Path, which incited rural peasants in Peru to rebel against coca eradication projects; the Burmese Communist Party, which levied a protection tax on southeast Asian opium growers; and Armenian, Druze, and Shiite groups that have been partially financed by hashish and heroin production in Lebanon's Bekaa Valley. The Nicaraguan Contras have been linked to cocaine trafficking, as has CORU, a Cuban terrorist group that operates in Costa Rica. In Bolivia, a ruthless paramilitary army known as the Black Eagles extorted protection payments from major cocaine traffickers. The Black Eagles were trained by neo-Nazis recruited by former Gestapo chief Klaus Barbie, the "Butcher of Lyon."

Terrorist tactics, some borrowed and some invented by the new American outlaws, have filtered down into organizations operating within the United States. For example, Florida cocaine dealer Carlos H. promised his little band of juvenile couriers that if they were caught and cooperated with the police in any way, they would win a free tie! To explain the nature of this gift, Carlos displayed a photograph of the famous "Colombian necktie." The photo showed one of Carlos's former employees spread-eagled on a vertical board. His neck had been slit vertically, from the chin to the collarbone, which severed the larynx and prevented any screaming. The tongue had been pulled through the slit, thus strangling him on what now resembled a blue necktie. In Kansas, a cocaine importer used all-American methods: polygraph examinations to uncover disloyal employees, then cattle prods or simulated lynchings to ensure future obedience.

The new narcoterrorism caused many observers to echo the fear that America, in its zeal to win this runaway war on drugs, would have to become a police state. Yet even in the Soviet Union and Eastern Europe, where borders are highly controlled and internal police seem to be everywhere, drug abuse was out of control. In many Soviet cities the police called drugs their number-one problem. Opium and hashish were widely available from drug crops grown illicitly in central Asia. The Soviet Union launched operation Poppy 86 and arrested four thousand drug dealers and destroyed 250,000 acres of marijuana. Drug use did not stop. Soldiers returning from the war in Afghanistan continued to smuggle all types of drugs, including heroin, and drug use continued to escalate. The users proved to be as resourceful as their American counterparts. In Czechoslovakia, where opium and marijuana were more difficult to find, users learned to mix over-the-counter drugs to produce an intoxicating cocktail called *pernik*. In Poland, an epidemic number of youth became addicted to *kompot,* a form of heroin prepared by combining household chemicals with poppy stalks.

Demands for drugs remained equally undiminished in countries where military and police joined forces to attack opium supplies. A major opium production area, the Golden Triangle, is formed by the mountainous confluence of Burma, Laos, and Thailand. Thailand is at the center of the Triangle and of the trafficking. When Thailand started attacking its opium problem, farmers switched to marijuana, which they discovered grew even better than poppies. They increased their export of the fire-cracker-potent "Thai stick," a clump of resinous marijuana leaves wrapped around a splinter of bamboo. This added considerable spice to the Thai marijuana trade, which soon provided record amounts to the world markets. Even in the war-torn Golden Crescent—the opium-producing area made up of Iran, Afghanistan, and Pakistan—trafficking managed to penetrate borders that were lined with armies. Throughout the Iran-Iraq war, Iranian smugglers, who risked facing the firing squad if caught, continually shipped opium into Syria via Iraq. Despite Soviet occupying forces, Afghanistan continued to smuggle its opium into Pakistan. As the general in charge of the Thai war on drugs noted: "Fighting narcotics is like squeezing a big balloon. When you grab one end, the other bulges."

A police state seems no more likely to suppress drug use than are individual police. Law enforcement officers who fought the drug war became corrupted by the climate of easy money and high times. In some areas of America it was hard to tell the good guys from the bad. DEA agents, Coast Guard officers, customs agents, soldiers, lawyers, prosecutors, judges, elected government officials, and entire police departments have been charged with involvement in the drug trade. The frequent opportunities to run off with narcodollars or drugs, the bribery of public officials, the destabilization of financial institutions, the corruption of police, the growing disrespect for the law—all of these activities, in the words of a former U.S. attorney general, threatened the very foundation of law and order.

3

President Reagan's Commission on Organized Crime reviewed the progress of the war on drugs in 1986 and concluded what was obvious: "Despite continuing expressions of determination, America's war on drugs seems nowhere close to success." The commission's report noted that the past seventy-five years of federal efforts to reduce drug supplies had failed to reduce social, economic, or crime problems related to drugs. The reason for this was equally apparent: the continuing and overwhelming demand for drugs. They suggested a war against demand. In the parlance of the antiwar movement, this meant a war against "U.S.ers."

The justification for attacking users was an old one: individual actions have tremendous fallout on the group. In colonial America, five hundred chests of tea were dumped into Boston harbor in December 1773. The actions were carried out by a small band of spirited protesters. Afterward, the harbor water was so contaminated with caffeine that the fish started to taste bad. Some speculated that the fish had contracted nervous disorders and it was feared that people might catch the same from eating them. The logic of the war on drugs called to mind such examples when it stated that even if individual users are not poisoned, the rest of us are at risk of catching some of the bad effects. A high-ranking military adviser to the war on drugs stated the logic with his own brand of "Newspeak": "Cocaine produces paranoia! The police say we could all catch it!" He advocated locking users up for their own good as well as to preserve the sanity of society.

The strategy was to target users and prospective users within the borders of the United States. Anything that tended to depress demand was expected to reduce trafficking-related crime, supplies, and, ultimately, drug abuse. One major tactic was to employ street-corner sting operations to inspire fear and paranoia among individual customers. The commission endorsed several other methods including drug education programs that would utilize anti-drug advertising. They reasoned that drug dealers cannot openly advertise their products but we can advertise the fact that drugs are no longer fashionable and that "all illicit drug use is unacceptable in light of the effects of drugs on individuals, families, communities, and governments."

Several antidrug campaigns embraced those exact words and, despite warnings from the commission that information must be honest and continually updated, they repeated the hyperbolic errors of past campaigns. One ad displayed a picture of an egg (identified as "your brain"), a simmering frying pan ("This is drugs"), and a fried egg ("This is your brain on drugs"). If this ad referred to alcohol it might be excused as Madison Avenue shorthand for explaining the dementia following prolonged, heavy ingestion of alcohol. But if the ad were referring to cocaine, marijuana, LSD, or any number of other intoxicants, which are not so destructive, it could expect to have as much lasting impact on users as the film *Reefer Madness* did several wars ago.

While few advisers to the nation's war efforts felt that such propaganda would stop current users, at the very least they hoped to deter prospective users. Accordingly, they targeted very young children who had not yet been exposed to the teachings of the drug experience. The war went into the classrooms, into health-education texts and comic strips, even into animated television commercials. The commission had acknowledged that changing attitudes and reducing demand for drugs would take a long time. They might teach young children to turn down drugs by saying "No." But it would take several generations for these children to grow up and replace the Yes-sayers. Yet the present baby-boomers had once been exposed to antidrug messages in the fifties and they were the ones doing most of the drugs today! Success with this approach seemed unlikely.

The growing frustration in stemming the flow of drugs was now compounded with the frustration of not being able to stop users, especially the children. Despite all efforts, cocaine was more abundant and cheaper than ever. U.S. production of home-grown marijuana, methamphetamine, and designer drugs was breaking records every year. The 1987 U.S. marijuana crop was worth $33.1 billion—a 150 percent increase from 1981—and the government was able to seize only 16 percent. Supplies were up and demands were ceaseless. Only the patterns of use changed. For example, when cocaine seemed no longer fashionable in upper-class circles, it became a street-corner drug. Ready-to-smoke forms such as crack became available in pieces shaped like french fries, wrapped like dime-store candy, or in aspirin-size tablets with the brand name "Easy Access." They could be purchased from "rock houses" that were better hidden and fortified than any opium den, tea pad, or speakeasy. Crack was being consumed by younger and younger children.

The scare tactics were not working. When Nancy Reagan spoke on the subject in Los Angeles in 1987, she observed that only 12 percent of the teenagers in California said they were afraid of cocaine. That remark caused at least one journalist to escalate the verbal war in the *Los Angeles Times*. "It [cocaine] may be doing to this country what

Hitler, the Kaiser, the Spanish fleet, the Confederacy or the British Crown could never do—bring it to its knees. It's destroying our children." What was interesting about the journalist's remark was that surveys had suggested that fewer than 12 percent of those same kids knew who Hitler was or when the Civil War took place. Some probably didn't even know that Reagan was president, yet all of them knew about cocaine and many were using it despite the prophecy of destruction.

According to government statistics, the drugs were also destroying the workplace, and with it the economic foundations of America. Shortly before his reelection, President Reagan announced that drug abuse cost society $60 billion a year. The figure included estimates of lost and reduced productivity, hospital and medical treatment, and criminal justice costs. Yet, according to the economist who worked out the figures, the yearly societal costs of tobacco were over $95 billion and alcohol-related costs were running more than $116 billion. Tobacco and alcohol, however, were not officially declared part of the drug abuse problem. Since more than half of the total cost of drug abuse was estimated to be impaired or lost productivity, the next target in the war would be the American worker.

"Help an Addict. Threaten to Fire Him," advised one anti-drug poster. The cries against witches in the Dark Ages, who were usually detected by hidden marks on their skin, could not have been very different. Now the war started testing for drug abuse with urine and blood tests. But urine and blood did not speak any more scientifically than witches' marks did. Assuming that the tests and laboratories were accurate—several studies found that false results were common—the results only showed past exposure to a particular drug.

The tests failed to answer the important questions of when the exposure took place, how and why it happened, and what were the effects. The tests failed to identify the source of the drug, which might have been an over-the-counter or a prescribed preparation. Because they were so ultrasensitive, the new tests could not differentiate between the morphine injected by an addict and the morphine absorbed from poppyseed rolls eaten at lunch. Eating poppyseed cakes, such as strudels, can keep your urine looking like a junkie's for several days. The tests read the same positive results for someone who had just snorted cocaine and for someone who recently drank an unlabeled over-the-counter herbal tea containing fragments of coca leaf. The tests also failed to reveal the history of drug use that is so essential to a diagnosis of abuse and so important in formulating plans for treatment. Most tests routinely ignored tobacco, a major health problem, and alcohol, a drug capable of seriously impairing job performance.

Despite these pharmacological quirks and shortcomings, the presence of an illegal drug in the urine marked many workers for immediate diagnosis as drug abusers or addicts. Many were compelled to undergo mandatory treatment or face termination of employment. In an age of technological sophistication in medical diagnosis, when no one would dare let a surgeon perform an operation based on a single blood or urine test, America allowed her workers to be severed from their jobs, their livelihoods, and sometimes their freedom on the basis of this new epidemic: test abuse.

Test abuse was the misinterpretation and misapplication of highly sophisticated chemical procedures. Urine tests were becoming so sensitive that they could detect traces of drugs that either had been used weeks earlier or had stayed in the body for long periods, yet no longer influenced behavior. The tests could also detect traces in the urine of nonusers. Bystanders at parties or in closed vehicles may passively inhale the smoke from marijuana, cocaine, or other smokable drugs that can produce detectable urinary metabolites, even intoxication. Emergency rooms in Los Angeles have seen many infants under the influence of PCP because they were too close to the cigarettes being smoked by their parents. Still, it was commonly assumed that urine testing would function as a good deterrent to drug use, thus reducing demand.

Methods of evading these tests, however, were widely known and practiced. The most common technique was to drink voluminous quantities of water before a urine test so that the concentration of drugs or metabolites was below the detectable limits of the tests. Yankee ingenuity developed other techniques, including chemicals to render your samples unanalyzable. When labs started to report such manipulated samples as "positive," some users switched to mechanical devices that would secretly squirt clean urine, obtained from a friend or even a pet dog, into the collection container. If the testing facility employed observers to visually monitor individuals while they gave the urine sample, other methods could be adopted. A group of female probationers in Los Angeles started marketing a tamponlike container that could be filled with clean urine, sealed with a thin plastic film, then inserted into the vagina. A simple poke with a sharp fingernail would rupture the film and allow the urine to flow into a collection jar.

Several labs started analyzing hair samples for drug metabolites. Because head hair is constantly absorbing chemicals from the blood as it grows at the rate of approximately a centimeter each month, hair analysis offered the advantage of providing a longer history of drug exposures than other tests. Slower-growing body hair, such as pubic hair, provides a drug history that may extend back into time as long as three or four years. Hair can be snipped directly from patients, and contamination from smoke adhering to the outside cuticle of the hair strand can be removed by washing the hair before analysis, leaving only drugs in the cortex of the hair shaft that were absorbed from the blood. While hair analysis was circumventing many of the problems encountered by urine tests, users quickly learned how to bleach and dye their hair so as to remove all drug metabolites. They, too, were fooling this newest high-tech test.

One of the incidental results of using these high-tech tests as a weapon in the war on users has been the revelation that drugs have contaminated the entire environment. In fact, by 1987, chemical studies showed that 94 percent of American paper currency was contaminated with traces of cocaine. The findings were not surprising. The fibers in currency act like a sponge, absorbing tiny particles of powders that are placed in contact with it. Since one out of every three bills in U.S. circulation is involved in cocaine transactions, and the money is often placed in suitcases or other locations shared with the drug, this contact and absorption is to be expected. Other money may be contaminated by users who sniff through rolled-up bills or count money while using cocaine. Although transfer of these traces from currency to urine or blood through normal handling of the money is unlikely, a sufficient bundle of bills—$1,000 to $1,500 in small denominations—could trigger the attention of a narcotic-sniffing dog. Therefore, when dogs were brought into banks to sniff deposits of suspected money launderers or into factories to sniff employee lockers, they were no more likely to detect illicit activities than the new smell of American capitalism.

Hair analysis was also revealing widespread contamination. Marijuana residue was regularly detected on the hair of elementary school children, even preschoolers, who used no drugs themselves but either socialized with pot-using peers or had parents who used the drug. PCP, heroin, and cocaine were regularly detected *in* the hair of inmates in jails and prisons throughout the United States. The exposures were occurring while the inmates were in custody, supposedly cut off from supplies of drugs. Most shocking of all, a large number of recovering drug users in both inpatient and outpatient treatment programs had drugs both on and in their hair—they were still associating with drug users and using drugs themselves.

Many people remained hopeful that America could wash the drug problems out of her hair, scrub the money, cleanse the air, purify her vital fluids, and, if necessary, wash old attitudes out of the brain itself. A White House Conference for a Drug Free America declared that the U.S. national policy must be "zero tolerance" for illegal drugs. But there was frustration at curbing drug supplies and demands. First came the collective paranoia, then the panicked responses.

Everyone was on guard: police, teachers, doctors, parents, kids, even pets. Correctional authorities in Canada employed gerbils to work undercover near the entrance to the Warkworth medium-security prison in Ontario. The gerbils were trained to sniff out drugs, then push a lever activating a red light if they smelled them on prisoners or visitors.

Good cops, like good gerbils, can also make reliable detections of drug users. A study of the best drug detectors in the Los Angeles Police Department found that the officers could detect intoxication 98 percent of the time and even identify the type of drug used in over 91 percent of the cases. Well-trained doctors and substance-abuse workers can also make reliable evaluations but they employ numerous diagnostic aids. According to guidelines of the American Psychiatric Association, they should look for a variety of psychological and physical symptoms in addition to the chemical tests before making a diagnosis of intoxication or dependence. Unfortunately, the war on drugs was largely in the hands of untrained, albeit well-intentioned, warriors excited to fever pitch by the paranoid call to arms. Many, including some of the well trained, panicked. At this stage, had they tried to enter Warkworth, the gerbils, also sensitive to the high flow of adrenaline from overly fearful people, would have sounded the alarm.

Hot lines used for years by police for anonymous tips on drug dealers now became numbers for workers to call and report on the activities of fellow workers. Drug-education classes began to evoke images of Nazi youth who reported on their parents when, following intensive drug-education lectures, at least two schoolgirls in California turned in their drug-using parents to police. Lawmakers called for legislation requiring users to relinquish their driver's licenses and government benefits. The director of the White House Office of Drug Abuse Policy finally declared: "I think we're ready now to start arresting users." But perhaps this wouldn't be enough.

Malaysia already had the death penalty, or at least life imprisonment plus whipping, for trafficking in dangerous drugs including marijuana; what was America waiting for? The commander in chief was asked that very question in 1986. Acknowledging that drug users should be helped rather than punished, President Reagan declared that, while no final decisions had yet been reached, *drug dealers deserved the death penalty.* Some could not wait for final decisions. Police in Los Angeles brought in a motorized battering ram to break into the heavily fortified houses where drug dealing was suspected. Network TV crews accompanied police on mass roundups of crack dealers, and millions watched it live. One group advised parents to get tough and handcuff their children to keep them away from drug-using schoolmates. A few overly zealous parents actually applauded when an angry group of mothers chased down and stabbed to death a cocaine peddler in Carini, Sicily.

Finally, it did happen here. On September 14, 1986, President Reagan pleaded that "for the sake of our children, I implore you to be unyielding and inflexible in your opposition to drugs." Two days later, a local police officer in Sauk City, Wisconsin, approached the driver of a Ford pickup truck that was stopped along the road. The truck had Texas plates. The driver was wearing a cowboy hat. The green plants in the back *looked like* marijuana. The officer wrestled the driver out of the truck, slammed him down on the cement, and handcuffed his hands behind his back. Next the policeman pulled out his snub-nosed .357 Magnum and fired two execution-style shots into the back of the driver's head. After his trial, the officer was committed to a mental-health center for treatment. In similar incidents, a motel manager in Pompano Beach, Florida, angered over neighborhood cocaine dealers using his parking lot, shot one of them. On June 3, 1987, a mother in Los Angeles "just snapped." She picked up a butcher knife and stabbed her teenage daughter to death because the daughter was using cocaine. The mother was found cradling her daughter's body, the knife still sticking in the chest. "I'm sorry. I'm sorry. I love you. Don't die. Don't die," sobbed the mother as she rocked the dead child back and forth.

The fanaticism of narcoterrorism had turned into the craziness of the final narcosolution. All efforts to control drugs such as marijuana and cocaine have been no more successful than those directed at tobacco and alcohol. Despite the war effort, use of intoxicants continues to spread. We cannot eliminate the fourth drive, although we can certainly destroy ourselves trying.

4

I went back to visit the Professor to see what new weapons the resistance had waiting in the wings. It had been eight years since I last saw the catapult, which was now gathering dust on the shelf in his den. The Professor was wearing a white shirt and regimental tie. He seemed to have put on some weight and his sinus condition had improved.

"What's new, Professor?" I asked, feeling very much like the little boy who visited Mr. Wizard on the weekly television show in the fifties.

The Professor cocked his head up into the air. "Ack Ack!" he barked.

"Ack Ack? What's that? Sounds like a gun."

"Exactly! You dip the lighted end of a cigarette into this here powder, tilt your head back to prevent it from falling off the end of the cigarette, then smoke."

He demonstrated the technique. The lighted end of the cigarette pointed upward like an antiaircraft gun in action, hence the appellation. The Professor explained that Ack Ack was a method used by Hong Kong addicts who smoked heroin. It was never as popular as inhaling the fumes from heating heroin on aluminum foil. The fumes would appear to take the shape of the undulating tail of a dragon, hence the popular term "dragon chasing." Chasing the dragon volatilized heroin at an ideal low temperature, yielding a whopping dose, whereas Ack Ack cigarettes burned so hot that most of the heroin was destroyed. Ack Ack was more convenient than fussing with foil but it simply couldn't deliver the hypereuphoric doses that users got from the dragon.

Through the miracle of designer chemistry, the Professor had mixed a synthetic opiate with several cool-burning additives to yield a smokable Ack Ack powder that had all the power of mainlining heroin itself. Furthermore, the Professor maintained that the metabolites of this compound were undetectable by normal urine tests. He was now experimenting with several ways of volatilizing the Ack Ack powder without the use of tobacco. The Professor did not approve of tobacco.

"Like my lamp?" the Professor asked with a mischievous glint in his eye as he directed my attention to a device that looked more like an expensive piece of modern art than a desk lamp. The lamp was shaped like a sleek, black faucet with a place for the light to stream out from where the water would flow. "It uses a special quartz bulb, perfect temperature for heroin, cocaine free base, or Ack Ack," he explained. "I exposed the bulb, fashioned a special cup to hold it, and added a dead man's trigger switch. Behold!"

The Professor swiveled the faucet so it was now pointed directly at his face. He sprinkled a few flecks of Ack Ack powder into the faucet, opened his mouth, then briefly pressed the trigger switch. A stream of light and smoke bathed his face with the brilliance of a flashbulb. The flash blinded him for a moment and I was certain he could not see that, despite the designer molecules and high-tech paraphernalia and test-resistant urine, he was still chasing the tail of a very old dragon, one that we could never slay.

14

Waking Dreams

DRUGS IN
THE FUTURE

1

What is the answer? Can there ever be a peaceful resolution to the war that began in Eden and still is waged today? Finding the shard, and all the animal and human stories it represented, had revealed our almost inherent drive to use plant chemicals to change our mood or state. The pursuit of intoxication is inevitable and unstoppable. Supplies of intoxicants will never disappear. Can *Homo sapiens*, the king of intoxication and master of invention, figure a way out of the dilemma?

Is legalization of drugs the answer? That solution has been proposed since the heyday of recreational drug use in the 1960s. Many eminent social scientists, economists, and policy advisers who have studied the question say that legalization of illicit drugs such as marijuana and heroin would be economically and medically healthier than their continued prohibition. It would certainly lower the social costs, most of which are absorbed by the criminality of the drugs. In addition, legalization would eliminate a source of funds for organized crime while permitting government health programs to profit from tax revenues on the legal sales. Furthermore, if drugs like marijuana replaced the more toxic ones such as tobacco, there would be a net gain in lives since far fewer die from all the illegal drugs put together than from either tobacco or alcohol alone.

But these drugs are not totally safe. For example, the list of adverse health consequences associated with marijuana, which was once considered the prototype of a safe recreational drug, is growing with each new medical study. Licensing and dispensing of marijuana, even by physicians, would undoubtedly lead to increased use and such use is not entirely harmless, even if greater societal harm is generated by prohibition. We must worry about the safety of these drugs and the certainty that some abuse would still remain while health costs for treating more abusers would increase.

Opponents to these legalization proposals have reminded us that we already have our hands full with alcohol and tobacco abuse; we do not need to start condoning marijuana and heroin abusers, however small that number might be. How can we put the government seal of approval on such appealing yet imperfect substances? We can't. Legalization isn't the answer.

2

Is the answer to persuade drug users to use the relatively safer plant intoxicants instead of their extracted and purified chemicals? There are some plant drugs that by nature of their form and substance have their own built-in safety mechanisms. Coca leaf, for example, is safe to chew. But extraction of the cocaine for administration by sniffing or injection is as potentially hazardous as using purified nicotine from tobacco leaf: both alkaloids can be dangerous poisons when used in such concentrated amounts. Why not, then, put the alkaloids back into their naturally occurring packages?

In each major category of intoxicant used by our species, there appear to be one or two drug plants that researchers have noted are more controllable, hence safer, than all the other plants or synthetics in that category. Coca leaf stands out among all the stimulants, licit and illicit, as the easiest to control and the one least likely to produce toxicity or dependency. Khat is a close second. Among the narcotics, which include opium and its derivatives, there is lactucarium, the smokable extract derived from *Lactuca virosa*. In the category of sedative hypnotics, which includes alcohol, it is kava, the drink prepared from a pepper plant that grows on islands in the South Seas. And for hallucinogens, which include marijuana, the smokable leaves and flowers of a Mexican marigold *(Tagetes lucida)* seem to qualify as the premier controllable psychedelics.

Controllable does not necessarily mean it will be preferred by all users. Coca is acceptable to natives in South America where it is viewed as a "divine plant," superior to caffeinated beverages or other available stimulants. Khat is the great Scrabble word that can be spelled khat, chat, kat, or qat. To natives in northeast Africa and the Arabian peninsula it is the "flower of Paradise" that spells relief from the hardships of life. Both coca and khat stimulate the mind of the chewer and enable him to climb mountains, breathe easier, and ward off hunger and fatigue. They do so with almost no toxicity or abuse; the bitterness limits use to just so many leaves. But in countries where cultural recipes do not encourage leaf chewing, few would volunteer to take a step backward to the original plant, however safe that retreat would be.

It is possible, however, that such cultural phobias apply only to chewing the leaf. Millions of Americans found coca tea acceptable during a three-year national experiment that started in 1983. The experiment was the brainchild of the Peruvian government's National Enterprise of Coca. This agency controls Peru's coca industry by licensing producers and providing coca leaves to native consumers as well as to international pharmaceutical companies. They were seeking new markets in order to channel the country's enormous coca production into legal products and away from the illegal drug market. It was decided to export the native *mate de coca,* or coca tea, to the United States. The Peruvians were clever enough to add lemongrass and other flavors to make the taste acceptable to North American palates.

Importers in New York and other U.S. cities were told that the tea had been decocainized. Millions of tea bags with such labels as Health Inca Tea were sold through mail-order ads and in grocery and health-food stores. In San Francisco the National Addiction Research Foundation provided patients with as much of the tea as they desired while detoxifying from cocaine. They reported that the tea was helpful in satisfying the patient's craving for cocaine itself. That result was hardly surprising. I, together with a number of colleagues, found that the tea had not been decocainized! Each tea bag contained approximately five milligrams of cocaine, the same dose normally found in a single, small coke spoon of street cocaine. Rather than detoxifying, the patients were simply adjusting to a lower and slower-acting dose.

I rounded up representative coca-tea drinkers who were each drinking an average of two cups per day. The examinations confirmed the effects expected from the small amounts of cocaine: mild stimulation, mood elevation, and increased pulse rate. Most important, the coca-tea drinkers did not satisfy the diagnostic criteria for cocaine abuse, and their claims of controlled use seemed to be correct. The drinkers were getting high, but the intoxication was totally harmless. In 1986, when our team published these findings in the *Journal of the American Medical Association,* the tea was declared illegal and the experiment with this over-the-counter cocaine package was over.

Did this experiment convert cocaine sniffers, shooters, and smokers to the tea? No. Many cocaine users, addicted to the exhilarating euphoria of concentrated cocaine rushing through their veins, did not accept the subtle high from drinking the tea. Despite controllability or palatability, plants like coca or khat are not appealing to the addict's taste for a quick intoxication. Users want drugs that deliver their effects speedily and conveniently. Once alkaloids are freed from the plants, it is difficult to put them back. The users may be willing to accept safety controls but they are unwilling to compromise on the reinforcing properties—their drug of choice must still satisfy demands for a quick, pleasurable high.

The high must also be intense. Although *Tagetes lucida* has been used as a hallucinogen since Aztec times, few modern users would consider such a weak drug a worthwhile choice. The smoke of this plant has a pleasant licorice taste and gentle intoxication: through the mental window users gaze upon heaven with rarely a glimpse of hell. That's good enough for the Mexican Indians who smoke it, but American users seem to want the more intense visions of LSD and other synthetics, despite the possibility of bad trips. When it comes to choices in psychedelics, users prefer drugs that do not appear risk-free, even if they really are.

Drugs of choice must taste good to the body and the mind. Most important, the intoxication must be consistently effective—no placebos are allowed in the discriminating consumer marketplace. Consider the case of lactucarium, which never caught on as a modern opium substitute because it was either so mild or so inconsistent in quality that people thought it was a fake.

Lactucarium smells like opium and tastes just as bitter. When smoked or swallowed, it is so mildly intoxicating it remains legal. There are no visions like the ones De Quincey had from eating opium, but the euphoria and dreamy intoxication last slightly longer. Although lactucarium is structurally unrelated to the opiates, it will still soothe irritating coughs, ease minor pains, and help induce sleep, hence its more common name of "lettuce opium." The history of lettuce opium in America paralleled that of coca tea. Both drugs enjoyed widespread medical use in the nineteenth century and brief periods of experimental nonmedical use in more recent years.

In the mid-1970s, smokable extracts of lettuce opium were marketed throughout the United States under such brand names as L'Opium and Lettucene. "Buy your lettuce before they make it illegal!" announced the national ads. Hundreds of thousands did exactly that when the craze peaked in the late 1970s. There was not a single case of toxicity or dependency. But there was a lot of competition as different manufacturers rushed to get a share of the new market. Most of these newer brands were made from ordinary garden lettuce, which lacked the intoxicating lactucarium. Subsequently, sales fell, some suppliers of real lactucarium went out of business, and the fad all but disappeared. While lactucarium is still available, heroin users are not rushing to buy it and probably never will: it's simply too weak.

If the intoxication, however safe and tasty, is unfamiliar to a culture, it has a hard time being accepted. Alcohol is firmly implanted in our culture and kava will never replace it despite its many advantages. Tea made from kava roots is drunk cold but it still retains an attractive lilac aroma. A pungent and numbing aftertaste keeps users from drinking too much. The intoxication is similar to that of alcohol in that it produces a short euphoric state, relaxation, and some loss of social inhibitions. There is no hangover, even for seasoned kava drinkers. But it is strangely disappointing to many who find that while they are happy and content, their mental alertness remains unaffected. This would seem to be a benefit for problem drinkers but they balk at such unfamiliar sobriety and return to the dizziness of alcohol. To achieve stronger effects it is necessary to chew the kava root, a fibrous and unappetizing course that even native kava drinkers dislike. Furthermore, such high doses can be as addicting and as debilitating as alcohol.

While our culture accepts drugs, we are suspicious of new ones. We insist they be studied and tested. They may be superior to alcohol and all the rest, but to be accepted into our culture any imported intoxicant will require much scientific scrutiny, followed by a long period of assimilation.

Substituting the more controllable plant intoxicants for risky chemicals is not the answer. Thus far, these plant drugs have not been popular enough to persuade users of cocaine, heroin, and other drugs to leave their habits for greener pastures.

3

If users cannot be persuaded to switch to more controllable drugs, can we get them to control themselves better with the ones they are already using?

One approach has been to teach people, especially the very young, to control absolutely their urges to use intoxicants, to abstain from all illegal drugs, to say "No." Supporters of this approach acknowledge that little can be done to alter the behavior of the current drug-using population, but they believe we can raise future generations of abstainers. This effort to eliminate the demand for drugs by educating the young may eventually change attitudes toward some drugs, but, as we have seen, there will always remain an abundance of intoxicants. Unless we also outlaw pharmacies, gardening, and kitchen cooking, there will always be sources of store-bought, homegrown, and homemade intoxicants.

There are other advocates of control who suggest we teach people how to use drugs and not abuse them. The illegal drugs would remain illegal and we would continue efforts at preventive education. At the same time, however, we would try to reduce the number of drug abusers by changing them into controlled *users*. This notion is not as unthinkable as it sounds.

In recent years it has become apparent that some individuals can control the street use of cocaine and other illegal intoxicants with no greater health problems than those seen with over-the-counter products or an assortment of medically prescribed stimulants, tranquilizers, and sedatives. These controlled intoxicant users have been the subject of a new field of research. The central focus of these studies has been to identify the ways in which some people manage to control marijuana, cocaine, heroin, LSD, or any other illegal intoxicant and thereby avoid abuse. Studies of the controlled user, who is far more common than the abuser, have not been popular among those committed to the view that illegal drug use *is* abuse. However, the research exposes the mechanisms by which a variety of potentially hazardous substances—alcohol, caffeine, sugar, and hundreds of thousands of other natural plant products—can be used, if not with health benefits, then at least without creating health costs.

Consider the case of heroin. Heroin is probably the most feared drug because it has the reputation as the hardest. There are cases of hardened users who come to the attention of the medical and legal systems. Society has hardfisted attitudes toward the users. People serve hard time for dealing or endure hard times when using. The social costs are hard to bear. It's hard for nonusers to understand why people use it and users are equally hardheaded when it comes to kicking the habit.

It took a war in Vietnam to soften these perceptions about heroin. Southeast Asian heroin was cheap and plentiful for the enlisted men. The heroin was so inexpensive and so potent that smoking it, a more desirable method for the soldiers than injecting, was effective. Approximately one out of every three soldiers tried heroin while in Vietnam and half of them became addicted. The point is not whether they were good or bad soldiers, but that heroin use did not necessarily result in dysfunction and lifelong enslavement to the habit. When the men returned to the United States, and were removed from the social setting of the war, their craving was minimal. Although heroin was less accessible and more expensive in the States, half the returnees who had been addicted in Vietnam used heroin again at home. Surprisingly, only 12 percent became readdicted—a remarkably low recidivism rate. Many soldiers found they could use heroin, even at the rate of more than once a week, without readdiction.

How? Users of heroin can engage in such occasional use, known as "chipping," and thereby avoid dependency. This pattern of use lies between experimental and social patterns and allows users to maintain long-term use without dysfunction or abuse. As early as 1947 the "joy popper" was recognized as a heroin user who used intermittently and never got hooked. Some 1947 joy poppers may still be around since such controlled use can be maintained for an indefinite period of time, even for life.

The occasional user of narcotics and other drugs is more common than most people realize. These users are difficult to study because they do not appear regularly in hospitals, clinics, coroner's offices, courts, or other places where *abusers* surface. Most studies concentrate on the abusers: the physically and psychologically dysfunctional addicts who are also the more obvious and noticeable drug takers. What about the individuals who do not have problems? Even if most heroin addicts had once been chippers, why didn't all chippers become addicts? Is there a secret to controlled intoxicant use?

Some of the answers come from epidemiological studies that have managed to tap into populations of controlled users of heroin, cocaine, marijuana, and even hallucinogens like PCP. The dose and form of the drug are major factors in control, as they were in the use of coca tea. But there is more to control than simply packaging the drug in an abuse-proof form such as a tea bag. Social controls are important. These controls include informal rules of conduct, as in the maxim associated with alcohol use, "Don't drink and drive." They also incorporate social rituals surrounding the use of drugs. For example, drinking wine at a family meal or sharing a marijuana cigarette at a party usually controls excessive behavior just as rats drink less alcohol when they are with other rats.

For many occasional illicit drug users, the social controls operate to structure intoxication just as the coffee break at work or an afternoon beer at the baseball field regulate licit drug use. These social factors are not always effective, as in cases where the individual may be the target of peer pressure to take more of a drug than is either desired or appropriate for the social situation. After all, social intoxication is expected to be moderate. However, even when control breaks down, as at wedding celebrations or an adolescent's first drunk, excessive behavior may still be accepted.

Of course, society has always attempted to provide guidelines for drug use by creating and enforcing rules. Laws tell us what substances will be legally available, in what forms, how they will be taxed, where they will be manufactured and sold, and what the penalties will be for violations. Laws of the land are not suspended when citizens enter the church, school, or workplace. But in the home and at play, formal rules are often less important than the informal social rules. The informal rules have no clearcut mechanisms for enforcement; they are handed down by the family, peers, and other social groups as traditions. These informal controls develop cultural recipes, menus describing what substances can be used, in what amounts, how, when, and with whom in order to achieve desired effects. For example, many recreational drug users have informal sanctions that limit use of their intoxicants to weekends so as to avoid conflict with the formal rules of the weekday workplace. LSD users generally adopt the ritual of using the drug only in settings where they can avoid having to drive a car, answer a telephone, or apply other skills that may be impaired by the intoxication. Marijuana users will frequently adjust their dosage to avoid becoming overly intoxicated and dysfunctional. And almost all drug users seeking *intense* intoxications seem instinctively to obey, as do animals, the rule of isolation from the social group.

Some policy advisers searching for a reduction in drug abuse have suggested that these formal and informal rules can be improved so that controlled intoxicant use might be possible for more people. Accordingly, they have advocated that accurate information on the best ways to achieve desirable substance effects while avoiding the most harmful effects would be more advantageous to users than hysterical and hyperbolic antidrug information. They suggest, furthermore, that efforts to teach people to control their drug use and to avoid excessive amounts or dangerous practices would be more in tune with the reality of a complex modern society in which citizens must learn to control a variety of potentially addicting behaviors including eating, gambling, and television-viewing.

The theory behind this proposal boils down to teaching people how to control their intoxications—not unlike teaching people how to eat a healthy diet or have safe sex. It won't work because of one simple fact: our most popular drugs cannot be endorsed as really safe.

Some drugs are inherently unsafe even in moderate patterns of use. While smoking and no-smoking zones may regulate social use of tobacco, and commercial cigarette filters may partially remove noxious substances from the smoke, and laws may govern age of use, and high taxes limit availability to some users, tobacco remains unhealthful. And the essential ingredient, nicotine, remains addictive. The notion of controlling such an unhealthy intoxicant is not only unwise, it's unrealistic. Educational messages and package warnings undoubtedly discourage excessive use, but use and abuse would continue even if colonial prohibitions were resurrected.

Another glaring example of why controlled use of current drugs won't work is provided by the problem of prescription drug abuse. Even when strong guidelines are employed, as with prescription drugs, abuse and other unwanted side effects still occur. Consider the fact that Americans take more than $17 billion worth of prescription medicines each year, and half of these medicines are taken incorrectly. As a result, 10 percent of all hospital admissions are related to prescription abuse. The total social costs of prescription drug problems are estimated at $10 to $15 billion per year. These costs do not include the 125,000 Americans who die each year as a consequence of prescription drug problems.

Controlled intoxicant use sounds good. It has a lot of attractive features, but it is not the answer. Regardless of how adept we become at controlling them, the major intoxicants still have dangers and risks attached to them. Of course, we tolerate the problems associated with another type of controlled drug use: prescription drugs. But it is medical drug use. It is morally acceptable. The use of intoxicating drugs is seen by our culture as nonmedical use. It is morally unacceptable. And therein lies the major obstacle in solving the drug dilemma.

4

The use of intoxicants, whether controlled or uncontrolled, safe or risky, will never be accepted as long as we view intoxication as nonmedical.

Most of us will resist the notion that the use of intoxicants serves a medical purpose. We have strong moral resistance to such a view. Society has taught us that getting intoxicated with drugs is unhealthy, if not immoral as well. I began to question my own resistance to this view when I met a crippled woman by the name of Peggy Sue. She, along with hundreds of other people I studied, showed me that even the most dangerous of these intoxicants was really functioning as a medicine.

Peggy Sue went square dancing. I saw the pictures and I still couldn't believe it. She was sitting in my office, passing photographs to me from the family album, and explaining what had happened. Peggy Sue was seventy-three and she looked very tired; the pictures told the story of better days. In her youth she had been a champion square dancer; Bill, her husband and partner, had posed with the trophies to prove it. He still moved with grace as he guided her through the examination procedures. They now lived in a retirement village where Bill took care of Peggy. He helped her out of bed in the morning and tucked her in at night with all the tenderness of a lovesick boy. Peggy could only smile back. Sex was too difficult.

As I examined her, I realized she needed Bill's help. Her hands were gnarled; her limbs were stiff; and her joints were red and swollen. She could move only short distances with a slow shuffle. While she was able to hold a glass of water with two hands, turning a doorknob was impossible. She needed help in the bath and with grooming. None of these signs of advanced rheumatoid arthritis caused me to disbelieve her story of square dancing. It's just that she got out of her wheelchair to do it.

The medical records told of Peggy Sue's battle with arthritis for almost twenty years. She had received all the conventional treatments, including gold shots, anti-inflammatory drugs, even surgery on her hands. She sought unconventional steroid treatments in Mexico and was desperate enough to try every new diet, exercise, or massage that promised to ease the progressive stiffness and pain. Then she moved to a desert clinic in California where she received Esterene. Several weeks later, Peggy Sue danced.

The charts in her file showed an increased range of motion as muscle and joint functions became less restrained. Her strength improved, the inflammation and swelling of her joints subsided, and all the examining physicians agreed that Esterene had greatly improved Peggy's condition. Although she never looked forward to taking the Esterene— she thought sniffing was a most peculiar way to take medicine—Peggy Sue had to agree she felt better, suffered less pain, could move her neck and body more freely, and could do without the dozen aspirins she normally took each day. Even when she was told that Esterene was a stimulant, she still didn't get a rush from the drug. Bill was the one who seemed excited, though, especially now that his lover could once again get into bed on her own.

I remained skeptical. Peggy Sue's rising out of the wheelchair seemed like an act straight from a faith healer's tent show, not the result of medical treatment by a national arthritis center, and Esterene was, after all, a slick trade name for crack! If used intranasally, crack, which is cocaine free base, would be ever so slowly absorbed by the mucous membranes of the nostrils. This would eliminate the rush that Peggy Sue denied experiencing, but would it also prevent abuse? There were over two hundred other people in the Esterene treatment program that I had been asked to evaluate. I was hopeful that detailed study of these patients would provide the answer.

Esterene had been used for more than two years on hundreds of patients, yet I was unable to find a single case of abuse. Some patients had been taking as much as 750 milligrams per day with no ill effects. The program had not proven that Esterene was a cure for arthritis—at best it was only acting as an analgesic and psychomotor stimulant—but it did show that *use* of a drug, even one with the addicting power of crack, did not have to lead to *abuse*. It was important to understand how such use could be achieved. If crack could be used without abuse, then maybe any drug could be used safely.

The key to this safety was the ultra-slow absorption of cocaine free base from the nasal membranes. Unlike the smoking of the drug, which results in almost instantaneous intoxication, the effects from topical application were like a time-release capsule. The nose functioned as the capsule and the cocaine free base slowly leached out into the blood. Users experienced mild intoxication but one that seemed to last for hours and didn't need frequent boosts. It was the same effect achieved by chewing coca. Another aspect of safety seemed to be the medical set and setting for the Esterene use. Users were *good patients* who were under the direct supervision of physicians; they followed their doctor's orders and the instructions on their Esterene labels. What would happen to users in nonmedical settings? Would the Esterene preparation fulfill the needs of users who wanted to "medicate" themselves for social or recreational purposes?

I didn't have long to wait for a group of such users to surface for study. Sensational press stories about the Esterene program had prompted many people to experiment with intranasal cocaine free base. Some were cocaine users attracted to the report that snorting the free base was safer than snorting cocaine hydrochloride. Others were elderly people just like Peggy Sue who were seeking treatment for arthritis or depression. The state of California had halted the Esterene program and disciplined the physicians, and as a result people started whipping up home brews of the drug. The authorities were understandably worried. Cocaine free base was not a miracle cure for rheumatoid arthritis, but if people started believing it and feeling better we might have a new population of illegal drug users to worry about: senior citizens! They could just as readily be sold on the idea of cocaine as on Coca-Cola, which was originally intended as a cocaine tonic for elderly people who became easily tired. We would no more be able to raid retirement homes looking for little old ladies sniffing cocaine than to bust into cancer clinics where patients sometimes received other unconventional drugs.

I found a total of 175 users in the greater Los Angeles area. Surprisingly, most were not experiencing problems. They reported antifatigue effects, as well as suppression of chronic pain and discomfort, but they failed to experience the rapid and reinforcing euphoria that gives cocaine its addictive potential. Unlike daily cocaine hydrochloride users who repeatedly dose themselves throughout the day, people sniffing cocaine free base administered the drug infrequently and did not show signs of dependency. Some had financial or legal problems associated with their use; several also experienced loss of appetite or sleep. Yet their ability to maintain daily doses as high as 1,000 milligrams without severe dysfunction suggested that safe use was possible, even in nonmedical settings.

The major conclusion of the Peggy Sue story is not that Esterene should be made available by prescription. Rather, we see that people can *use* certain forms of intoxicants. They can do so as safely on the streets as in the clinics. How? In the prescriptions of Esterene the doses of cocaine were as carefully fixed as they had been in the coca tea bags. Even street users, without the constraints of a medical set or setting, were handling these preparations. Conversely, the uncontrolled doses of street cocaine or smokable crack can easily lead to *abuse* if not to toxicity itself. The apparent safety of the Esterene emphasized the dictum that a major difference between drug use and abuse is one of dose.

But our culture also views the difference in terms of medical approval. Peggy Sue was engaged in a medical pattern of use. Her crack was a medicine, therefore acceptable. When used by street users for purposes that are not approved by medicine, the pattern of use is called nonmedical, therefore unacceptable and immoral. Their crack is a poison. Yet the street users were medicating their needs for psychological or physical stimulation, improving their mood or state, and therefore medicating their health, with the same relative safety that Peggy Sue and other clinical patients enjoyed while medicating the symptoms of arthritis. The resulting intoxication in both cases was *medical,* not nonmedical.

The medical purpose of intoxication is easier to understand if we think of intoxicating drugs as *adaptogens.* Technically, an adaptogen is a substance that helps people adjust to changes in their physical or psychological environments. Adverse fluctuations in physiological, chemical, biological, or neurological systems may be corrected by some adaptogens. Thus, if the body or mind is tired, an adaptogen perks up functioning. Conversely, if one is overly excited, another adaptogen may temper the arousal. Some adaptogens not only correct imbalances but also perform a normalizing function by helping even healthy humans increase their resistance to potential changes.

Many adaptogenic substances are of plant origin and the most famous is ginseng, a plant that can rival cocaine in costs for some exotic preparations. Ginseng has been used worldwide to help the body perform under stress, correct fluctuations in blood pressure, even repair damage from radiation. Many people find it has a mild stimulating effect and also use it for fatigue, depression, and sexual indifference. But this is really no different than the reasons chosen for using other drugs, such as coca. Proportionally, there is no greater incidence of abuse among the millions who use ginseng than among the comparative number who consume coca.

These findings do not mean that we should outlaw ginseng any more than we should legalize coca. What they show is that coca, cocaine, heroin, marijuana, alcohol, tobacco, and the hallucinogens are just as much medicines as ginseng when used to help us adapt to changes in our psychological or physical environment. Intoxicating drugs medicate the needs of the fourth drive for a change in state or mood. Whether we use coca tea to help us cope with high altitude sickness or cocaine to fight a fatiguing day at sea level, whether we use Esterene to alleviate the pain and depression of arthritis or heroin to fight the gloom and despair of consciousness, we are still medicating our needs. The pursuit of intoxication serves a legitimate medical purpose.

The solution to the drug problems of our species begins when we acknowledge the legitimate place of intoxication in our behavior. We must ensure that the pursuit of intoxication with drugs will not be dangerous. How can we do that?

5

The answer is to make drugs perfectly safe.

The best way to proceed in improving intoxicants is to utilize the technology that is our human distinction. The search for improved drugs, botanical and synthetic, is a time-honored quest for the pharmaceutical industry, which spends billions of dollars each year for research and development of magic bullets and wonder drugs. The goal is to maximize desired effects and benefits and to minimize risks and dangers. A tacit but guiding notion has been that one shouldn't feel too good. The Food and Drug Administration approved synthetic THC for clinical use in treating the nausea and vomiting encountered by many cancer patients undergoing chemotherapy. But the approved form, Marinol, was a soft gelatin capsule containing sesame seed oil to retard the high.

This Calvinistic pharmacology has prevented us from seeing pleasurable changes in the body or mind as fulfilling health needs. It is time to rid ourselves of such notions and recognize intoxicants as medicines, and intoxications as treatments for the human condition. We must expand the definition of self-medication to include drug use for purposes of intoxication. Yet even if some of us can admit that intoxication serves medical or adaptogenic purposes, almost everyone, however, is afraid it will lead to loss of control and abuse. The research and development of intoxicants that are as unabusable and safe as the foods we eat are as worthy of pursuit as are those leading to any magic bullet or wonder drug.

In the meantime, supplies of drugs cannot be eliminated. The drive to pursue intoxication cannot be suppressed. We must work patiently to solve the daily problems resulting from the use and abuse of imperfect drugs. We have to take care of the abusers and do what we can to prevent new ones from joining the ranks. We must continue our preventive education programs and step up our treatment and rehabilitation efforts. There are no short-term solutions. The ongoing destructive nature of the war on drugs is something we will have to endure until, ultimately, the demands of those seeking artificial paradise are addressed.

Intoxicants have been a natural part of the diet of life ever since it began on this planet. Intoxication, by definition the entry into a state of toxicity, will never be totally risk free, but it will always be. Man has experimented with many intoxicating drugs but found none that was perfect. In Homer's *Odyssey*, Helen of Troy filled wine cups with nepenthe, an opium-based potion that banished pain and sorrow. The mythical nepenthe represented an ideal drug, perfectly safe and enjoyable. Seeking to remedy their ills and misfortunes, the ancient Greeks replaced human sacrifice, in which the victims were called *pharmakoi*, with better living through pharmacology. Many of their herbs and drugs are found in today's medicines, but the ideal nepenthe for both therapeutic and social use has remained the holy grail of psychopharmacology.

From Homer to Huxley, dreams of a brave new world of intoxicants have haunted our literature and inspired our research. Huxley's fictional mind-lulling "soma" is now the trade name of a modern muscle relaxant; a few puffs of PHP, a synthetic analogue of PCP, can magically transform Dr. Jekyll into Mr. Hyde faster than cocaine did for the author, Robert Louis Stevenson; and in the 1970s Moksha Laboratories, named after the psychedelic in Huxley's utopian novel *Island*, searched worldwide for botanical nepenthes. Just as the discovery of the rubber tree was one of the elements that made possible the Industrial Revolution, new investigations in the plant kingdom—90 percent of which remains unstudied—may spawn equally dramatic changes in our development.

The quest has been guided by the dreams and nightmares of science fiction elixirs. Author Robert Silverberg reviewed these elixirs for the National Institute on Drug Abuse and noted that future drugs, like his own fictional potions—"tingle" and "mind-blot"—will be used as euphorics, panaceas, mind expanders, and controllers. Science fiction writers imagine that some drugs will be products of technology whereas others will be discovered when we explore the flora of other worlds.

Why wait to stumble over these drugs on some alien planet? Why can't we find safer ones here? Why can't we make them perfectly safe now? Scientists and futurists from academia, the Rand Corporation, and the Hudson Institute predict that we could do it in the twenty-first century. We could do it with molecular chemistry, twisting and bending already known psychoactive molecules. It seems equally likely that we could find new and more suitable molecules in nature's own botanical laboratory. Advances in chromatographic and spectroscopic techniques now permit the isolation and analysis of biologically active plant constituents that could not have been found in earlier times. New techniques for the manipulation of plant cells, genes, and enzymes could provide a host of new agents.

In the future, fashions in drugs will change, just as they have in the past. Heroin was once viewed as chic; today it has a reputation for being ugly and dangerous. Cocaine's image is undergoing a similar transformation. Although such changing images may mark a decline in a drug's popularity, it is certain that new drug fads will appear. We have a chance, now, to design those future choices.

The ideal intoxicants would balance optimal positive effects, such as stimulation or pleasure, with minimal or nonexistent toxic consequences. The drugs would be ingested as fast-acting pills or liquids or breathed in the form of gases. They would have fixed durations of action and built-in antagonists to prevent excessive use or overdoses. The drugs could even be engineered to provide brief but safe surges of intense effects, thus appearing more dangerous and thrilling than they really are.

Ideal drugs would deliver desired effects without unwanted side effects. If the drug is used to enhance mood, for example, it should not keep someone from eating or sleeping. The ideal tranquilizer would reduce anxiety without being so comforting that the user became passive and nonproductive. Similarly, if the drug was designed to entertain our senses, it would not distract us from performing normal activities.

Molecular chemists have already designed some interesting possibilities, including drugs for enhancing sensation, reliving childhood fantasies, unblocking creativity, or taking a weekend trip. One promising drug, 2C-B, appears to enhance all the senses without distortion, turning the everyday world into a museum of interesting perceptions. Another new intoxicant, DIPT, seems to alter auditory, input signals and not visual ones, giving sounds an electronic-like embellishment while keeping the dyes firmly focused on reality. Chemists keep changing the rules of molecular architecture, making hundreds of new psychoactive compounds each year, and no one can guess how close to the ideal the next new molecule will be. Thus far, however, the trips are not always pleasant or controllable and, to the relief of those still unwilling to accept the solution of perfectly safe drugs, much more research and development is needed.

Future molecular architects may be able to mix and match desirable properties of drugs, creating the perfectly safe nepenthes. For example, they may combine buprenophine, a semisynthetic opioid that is similar to morphine but seems to block its own overdose, with pentozine, a synthethic as nice as heroin but with considerably less abuse potential. They may be able to combine the effects of Ro15-4513, a drug that makes drunk animals sober, with the inebriating aspects of alcohol itself. They may be able to couple Esterene preparations with nitrenidipene, a chemical that reverses cocaine overdoses, thereby creating a nonlethal and controllable form of cocaine. They may eventually create a synthetic coca leaf that is so far removed from the original plant in appearance, name, and emotional history that it will be accepted on its own merits. Like the New Age alchemists they will be, they will turn a wartime pharmacology that constantly pits the needs of the individual against those of a mistaught society into a pharmacology of harmony.

Winning the war on drugs by eradicating nonmedical drug use is neither possible nor desirable. We need intoxicants—not in the sense that an addict needs a fix, but because the need is as much a part of the human condition as sex, hunger, and thirst. The need—the fourth drive—is natural, yes, even healthy. Our use of intoxicating drugs is just as natural and can be, if we apply our ingenuity, just as healthy as the medicating drugs that we use should be. This is not moral surrender to the war on drugs. The development of safe, man-made intoxicants is an affirmation of one of our most human drives and a challenge for our finest talents.

If the road to safe intoxicants leads to a society free of drug abuse, and is not merely a science fiction fantasy, travel to such a future will probably have to await changes in societal thinking, not to mention the research and development that may be necessary to produce the compounds. In the meantime, just as animals protect against abusive effects by isolation, and experienced human users do it with the appropriate set and setting, our society must find a place in its thinking for intoxication. We must recognize the drive to get there, then pursue safe paths.

Perhaps there will be new utopian drugs that control themselves, but we will have to perfect them. For now, the utopiates, like children's dreams of a mountain paradise in Robert Browning's "Pied Piper of Hamelin," remain elusive yet fetching possibilities. While we still cannot move mountains to know for certain what lies in that future paradise, we need not fear the *Datura* witches, tobacco gods, pink elephants, hashish assassins, opium dragons, and cocaine bugs we meet along the path; they are only reflections of ourselves, the dreams and nightmares born of our fourth drive. We need not fear the street sorcerers who can change spices like nutmeg into enchanting but imperfect elixirs like Ecstasy; we can master their art of designer chemistry and do better. Though our every step is challenged by plants with thorns and bittersweet chemicals, though voices cry out for us to come back, we can no more turn back than climb down the evolutionary ladder. We must learn from these encounters and move on. To "just say No" is to deny all that we are and all that we could be.

Epilogue

César had disappeared. There was a rumor that he had gone into the cocaine business and was killed in a jungle shoot-out. A *yatiri* told me he was spirited away by a UFO while hiking in the mountains. Wherever he was, he had taken the shard with him. I was angry.

I wanted a laboratory to date the shard more precisely. When I showed my sketch of it to other experts, they told me the style resembled that of the Moche people, who had a relatively recent culture. If it was Moche art, it could only be hundreds of years old, not thousands as César thought. Did César deliberately overestimate its age to please me? He knew how much I dreamed of finding such proof for my theory and he told me where I should look. Did he also tell me what I wanted to hear? The questions made me uneasy.

But I couldn't remain angry for long. Even if the shard was a piece of a dream, it had been enough to start me on the hunt for real pieces to the puzzle of intoxication, a puzzle born of the collective dreams of an entire planet. The picture they formed was real, all right, but, like the rough edges of the shard, imperfect. And so we are forced to dream again, a dream of making intoxication picture perfect.

Thank you César, wherever you are.

Acknowledgments

My thanks are first due to the late Ada E. Hirschman, my chief research assistant, who helped organize the dozens of file cabinets that filled with data over the twenty years of this research. She retrieved many rare references, provided expert translations, and managed the office during my many field trips.

I was extremely fortunate in having several remarkable students who assisted with observations in the laboratory and field. For contributing their energy and talent to the research I thank Mark Brodie, D.D.S.; Kirk J. Brower, M.D.; Laura A. Freberg, M.A.;Jean Poole, B.A.; Pauline B. Popek, M.A.; and Susan E. Valadez, M.A.

For their expert assistance in the field, and for helping with everything from animal observations to translations with native tribes, I am grateful to the following: James Amundson (Mexico); William Bergin, D.V.M. (Hawaii); Lawrence Blair, Ph.D. (Malaysia and Indonesia); Gary L. Bogue (California); Enrico C. Chavez, M.D. (Mexico); Peter R. Collings (Mexico); Steve Craig (California); José Luis Diaz, Ph.D. (Mexico); Donald Dooley, D.V.M. (California); David Dorrance, M.D. (Mexico); Robert Ellsworth, Ph.D. (Yemen); Howard Johnson (California); Philip Lowenthal (Hawaii); Bruce Moffitt (Australia and New Guinea); and the late Ivan Tors (Africa and Asia). Thanks are also due to the following individuals for providing helpful information on animal-plant interactions: T. F. Corfield (Kenya); E. C. Goss (Kenya); W. Harding (Africa); P. Moulet (France); and D. S. Sade (Cayo Santiago).

I wish to thank the following for logistical support and assistance with the field research: Alexander Lindsay Junior Museum, Walnut

Creek, California; Centro Coordinator para el Desarrollo de la Región Huichot, Tepic, Nayarit, Mexico; U.S. Department of State, U.S. Drug Enforcement Administration; Instituto Ecuatoriano de Adiccionología y Psicoterapía, Guayaquil, Ecuador; Ginseng Research Institute, Seoul, South Korea; Lion Country Safari, Laguna Hills, California; Max Planck Institut für Psychiatrie, Munich, West Germany; Ministerio de Salud, División Salud Mental, Bogota, Colombia; Pan American Health Organization; Peruvian Ministry of the Interior; San Diego Zoo; San Jose Police Department; U.S. Forest Service; Stanford Outdoor Primate Facility; and the World Health Organization.

For assistance in library research and for access to rare documents in their possession I am grateful to Michael Aldrich, Ph.D., Michael Horowitz, and William Dailey of the Fitz Hugh Ludlow Memorial Library, San Francisco. I thank the staff at the following libraries and museums for generous help in finding references: American Institute of the History of Pharmacy; Harvard Botanical Museum; Historic New Orleans Collection; Illinois State Historical Library; Library of Congress; Lloyd Library; Mutter Museum of the College of Physicians of Philadelphia; National Library of Medicine; La Pharmacie Française; Historical Pharmacy Museum, New Orleans; Pharmacy Museum, University of Minnesota; and the UCLA Biomedical Library. I am particularly grateful to John V. Dennis and Leonard A. Eiserer, Ph.D., for sharing references on alcohol intoxication in birds; to James T. Hickey, curator of the Lincoln Collection at the Illinois State Historical Library, for helpful services; to John Mann for providing a collection of contemporary folklore; and to my late mother, Frieda Siegel, for her care and diligence in providing newspaper clippings. A number of office assistants joined the task of collecting research materials, and I am grateful to Stella Gardner, Debra Hartley, Lori Hack, Beverly Lowe, and Erin McCormick.

Over the years I have worked with several colleagues in laboratory studies that are referenced in this book. I am indebted to the following for the opportunity to work and learn with them: Werner A. Baumgartner, Ph.D.; Joan M. Brewster, Ph.D.; Ellen R. Gritz, Ph.D.; Barbara E. Gusewelle, M.D., Ph.D.; Werner K. Honig, Ph.D.; Murray E. Jarvik, M.D., Ph.D.; Cheryll A. Johnson; Gerald D. Robinson, Ph.D.; and Ian P. Stolerman, Ph.D. I also wish to thank the following for technical assistance with the research: Tom Hesterberg, Virginia Hill, Monroe A. Lee, and Charles Scott.

For helpful discussions along the way, I thank: Robert Byck, M.D.; the late Sidney Cohen, M.D.; James A. Duke, Ph.D.; William Emboden, Ph.D.; Lynn Fairbanks, Ph.D.; Dino Fulgoni, J.D.; John Garcia, Ph.D.; William L. Hearn, Ph.D.; Jack Herer; Oscar Janiger, M.D.; Reese Jones, M.D.; Weston La Barre, Ph.D.; the late William H. McGlothlin, Ph.D.; the late Alan Nodell; G. Reichel-Dolmatoff, Ph.D.; Marlene Dobkin de Rios, Ph.D.; Shepard Siegel, Ph.D.; Neil B. Todd, Ph.D.; J. Thomas Ungerleider, M.D.; Andrew Weil, M.D.; Louis Jolyon West, M.D.; Johannes Wilbert, Ph.D.; and Roy A. Wise, Ph.D.

I also want to thank Reid Boates, my literary agent, and Joyce Engelson, my editor, for their encouragement and advice throughout the writing. I am equally grateful to Stephen Peters for his friendship and help. I want to give special thanks to Erica Blomquist, my project editor at Inner Traditions, for her careful attention to editing details that have greatly improved the quality of this edition.

Finally, I thank the many local people who joined our teams in the field and helped cook, carry equipment, and care for the animals and team members. Their support was greatly appreciated. I also extend my appreciation to the nurses, residents, and staff members at the UCLA Center for Health Sciences who provided support services for the clinical studies. And my thanks to the many informants, respondents, and subjects, human and nonhuman, who helped in this pursuit.

I am particularly grateful to Claude, Alex, Lucy, Pupi, and all the other nonhuman primates in my studies. They sensitized me to the plight and rights of laboratory animals, propelling me to shift my research out of the laboratory and into the field, where intoxication is not only natural but right.

Bibliography

INTRODUCTION

Baudelaire, C. 1860. *Les paradis artificiels: Opium et hashchish.* Paris: Poulet-Malassis et de Broise.

Buck, D. P. February 1964. "Come Where My Love Lies Dreaming." *Fantasy and Science Fiction,* no. 153: 113–26.

1. WAR IN EDEN

Alvarez, W., Kauffman, E. G., Surlyk, F., Alvarez, L. W., Asaro, F., and Michel, H. V. 1984. "Impact Theory of Mass Extinctions and the Invertebrate Fossil Record." *Science* 223:1135–41.

Ames, O. 1939. *Economic Annuals and Human Cultures.* Cambridge: Botanical Museum of Harvard University.

Atsatt, P. R., and O'Dowd, D. J. 1976. "Plant Defense Guilds." *Science* 193:24–29.

Beck, C. E., ed. 1976. *Origin and Early Evolution of Angiosperms.* New York: Columbia University Press.

Bever, O. 1970. "Why Do Plants Produce Drugs? Which Is Their Function in the Plants?" *Quarterly Journal of Crude Drug Research* 10:1541–49.

Brallier, Floyd. 1922. *Knowing Birds Through Stories.* New York: Funk & Wagnalls Company.

Brantjes, N. B. M. 1981. "Ant, Bee and Fly Pollination in Epipactis palustris (L.) Crantz (Orchidaceae)." *Acta Botanica Neerlandica* 301:59–68.

Bristol, M. L. 1969. "Tree Datura Drugs of the Colombian Sibundoy." *Botanical Museum Leaflets,* Harvard University 22:165–227.

Carroll, C. R., and Hoffman, C. A. 1980. "Chemical Feeding Deterrent Mobilized in Response to Insect Herbivory and Counteradaptation by Epilachna tredecimnotata." *Science* 209:414–16.

Carroll, M. E., and Meisch, R. A. 1984. "Increased Drug-Reinforced Behavior Due to Food Deprivation." *Advances in Behavioral Pharmacology* 4:47–88.

Dobkin de Rios, M. 1984. *Hallucinogens: Cross-Cultural Perspectives.* Albuquerque: University of New Mexico Press.

Edmunds, G. F., and Alstad, D. N. 1978. "Coevolution in Insect Herbivores and Conifers." *Science* 199:941–45.

Eisner, T., and Halpern, B. P. 1971. "Taste Distortion and Plant Palatability." *Science* 172:1362.

Emboden, W. A. 1974. *Bizarre Plants*. New York: The Macmillan Company.
————. 1979. *Narcotic Plants*. New York: The Macmillan Company.
Farb, P., and Armelagos, G. 1980. *Consuming Passions: The Anthropology of Eating*. Boston: Houghton Mifflin Company.
Folkard, R. 1884. *Plant Lore, Legends, and Lyrics*. London: Sampson Low, Marston, Searle, & Rivington.
Freeland, W. J., and Janzen, D. H. 1974. "Strategies in Herbivory by Mammals: The Role of Plant Secondary Compounds." *The American Naturalist* 108:269–89.
Furst, P. T. 1976. *Hallucinogens and Culture*. San Francisco: Chandler & Sharp.
Geleperin, A. 1975. "Rapid Food-Aversion Learning by a Terrestrial Mollusk." *Science* 189:567–70.
Gilbert, L. E., and Raven, P. H., eds. 1975. *Coevolution of Animals and Plants*. Austin: University of Texas Press.
Gowdy, J. M. 1972. "Stramonium Intoxication." *Journal of the American Medical Association* 221:585–87.
Grant, V., and Grant, K. A. 1983. "Behavior of Hawkmoths on Flowers of Datura meteloides." *Botanical Gazette* 144:280–84.
Hamblin, D. J. May 1987. "Has the Garden of Eden Been Located at Last?" *Smithsonian* 18:127–35.
Hansen, H. A. 1978. *The Witch's Garden*. Santa Cruz, Calif.: Unity Press.
Harner, M. April 1977. "The Enigma of Aztec Sacrifice." *Natural History* 86:47–51.
Harner, M. J. 1973. "The Role of Hallucinogenic Plants in European Witchcraft." In *Hallucinogens and Shamanism,* ed. M. J. Harner, 125–50. New York: Oxford University Press.
Huxley, A. 1978. *Plant and Planet*. Middlesex, Eng.: Penguin Books.
Jacob, F. 1977. "Evolution and Tinkering." *Science* 196:1161–66.
Jacobs, K. W. 1974. "Asthmador: A Legal Hallucinogen." *The International Journal of the Addictions* 9:503–12.
Jones, S. B. 1977. "Vernonicae—Systematic Review." In *The Biology and Chemistry of the Compositae,* ed. V. H. Heywood, J. B. Harborne, and B. L. Turner, 503–21. New York: Academic Press.
Keeler, R. F. 1979. "Toxins and Teratogens of the Solanaceae and Liliaceae." In *Toxic Plants,* ed. A. D. Kinghorn, 59–82. New York: Columbia University Press.
Ketchum, J. E., Sidell, F. B., Crowell, E. B., Aghajanian, G. K., and Hayes, A. H. 1973. *Atropine, Scopolamine, and Ditran: Comparative Pharmacology and Antagonists in Man*. Edgewood Arsenal Technical Report EB-TR-73028, EATR 4761. NTIS no. AD-767257. Aberdeen Proving Ground, Md.: Department of the Army.
Kingsbury, J. 1964. *Poisonous Plants of the United States and Canada*. Englewood Cliffs, NJ.: Prentice-Hall.
Lehane, B. 1977. *The Power of Plants*. Maidenhead, Eng.: McGraw-Hill.
Levinson, H. Z. 1976. "The Defensive Role of Alkaloids in Insects and Plants." *Experientia* 32:408–11.
Lloyd, J. U. 1921. *Origin and History of All the Pharmacopeial Vegetable Drugs, Chemicals and Preparations with Bibliography*. Cincinnati: The Caxton Press.
Midgley, M. 1978. *Beast and Man, The Roots of Human Nature*. Ithaca, N.Y.: Cornell University Press.
Ott, J. 1976. *Hallucinogenic Plants of North America*. Berkeley: Wingbow Press.
Pammell, L. 1911. *A Manual of Poisonous Plants*. Cedar Rapids, Iowa: Torch Press.
Regal, P. J. 1977. "Ecology and Evolution of Flowering Plant Dominance." *Science* 196:622–29.

Ridley, H. N. 1930. *The Dispersal of Plants Throughout the World*. Ashford, Eng.: L. Reeve & Co.

Rosenthal, G. A., and Janzen, D. H., eds. 1979. *Herbivores: Their Interaction with Secondary Plant Metabolites*. New York: Academic Press.

Russell, D. A. 1982. "The Mass Extinctions of the Late Mesozoic." *Scientific American* 246 (1):58–65.

Schleiffer, H., ed. 1973. *Sacred Narcotic Plants of the New World Indians*. New York: Haffner Press.

Schultes, R. E., and Hofmann, A. 1979. *Plants of the Gods*. Maidenhead, Eng.: McGraw-Hill.

———. 1980. *The Botany and Chemistry of Hallucinogens*. Springfield, Ill.: Charles C. Thomas.

Schuster, C. R., and Balster, R. L. 1977. "The Discriminative Properties of Drugs." *Advances in Behavioral Pharmacology* 1:85–138.

Siegel, R. K. 1976. "Herbal Intoxication: Psychoactive Effects from Herbal Cigarettes, Tea, and Capsules." *Journal of the American Medical Association* 236:473–76.

Siegel, R. K., and Jarvik, M. E. 1974. "Learning in the Land Snail (*Helix aspersa* Muller)." *Bulletin of the Psychonomic Society* 4:476–78.

Spruce, R. 1908. *Notes of a Botanist on the Amazon and Andes*. London: The Macmillan Company.

Steinberg, P. D. 1984. "Algal Chemical Defense Against Herbivores: Allocation of Phenolic Compounds in the Kelp Alaria marginata." *Science* 223:405–407.

Swain, T. 1974. "Cold-blooded Murder in the Cretaceous." *Spectrum* 120:10–12.

Taylor, A. S. 1875. *On Poisons in Relation to Medical Jurisprudence and Medicine*. Philadelphia: Henry C. Lea.

Taylor, J. E. 1884. *The Sagacity and Morality of Plants*. London: Chatto & Windus.

Thorpe, W. H., and Davenport, D., eds. 1964. *Learning and Associated Phenomena in Invertebrates*. Animal Behaviour Supplement 1. London: Bailliere, Tindall & Cassell.

Trease, G. E., and Evans, W. C. 1983. *Pharmacognosy*. 12th ed. Eastbourne, Eng.: Bailliere, Tindall.

Tyrrell, E. Q. 1985. *Hummingbirds: Their Life and Behavior*. New York: Crown Publishers.

Van Emden, H. F., ed. 1973. *Insect/Plant Relationships*. Symposia of the Royal Entomological Society of London, no. 6. Oxford: Blackwell Scientific Publications.

Watt, J. M., and Breyer-Brandwijk, M. G. 1962. *The Medicinal and Poisonous Plants of Southern and Eastern Africa*. London: E. & S. Livingstone.

Weintraub, S. 1960. "Stramonium Poisoning." *Postgraduate Medicine* 28:364–67.

Zechmeister. 1845. "Vergiftung durch Datura stramonium." *Medizinische Wochenschrift* 29:57.

2. A TRIP OF GOATS

Abdo Abbasy, M. 1957. "The Habitual Use of 'Qat.'" *Internationales Journal für Prophylaktische Medizin und Sozialhygiene* 1:20–22.

Allegro, J, M. 1970. *The Sacred Mushroom and the Cross*. London: Hodder and Stoughton.

Arnold, H. L. 1944. *Poisonous Plants of Hawaii*. Rutland, Vt.: Charles E. Tuttle.

Austin, G. A. 1978. *Perspectives on the History of Psychoactive Substance Use*. National Institute on Drug Abuse Research Issues 24. DHHS Publication no.

(ADM) 79–810. Washington, D.C.: Superintendent of Documents, U.S. Government Printing Office.

Balls, E. K. 1962. *Early Uses of California Plants*. Berkeley: University of California Press.

Biocca, E. 1970. *Yanoáma*. Trans. D. Rhodes. New York: E. P. Dutton.

Blyth, A, W. 1895. *Poisons: Their Effects and Detection*. London: Charles Griffin & Company.

Bourke, J. G. 1894. "Popular Medicine, Customs, and Superstitions of the Rio Grande." *The Journal of American Folk Lore* 7:119–46.

Brodie, E. D. 1977. "Hedgehogs Use Toad Venoms in Their Own Defense." *Nature* 268:627–28.

Ciba Pharmaceutical Products. 1954. *The Rauwolfia Story*. Summit, N.J.: Ciba.

Cooke, M. C. c.1860. *The Seven Sisters of Sleep: Popular History of the Seven Prevailing Narcotics of the World*. London: James Blackwood.

Cowan, J. 1870. *The Use of Tobacco vs. Purity, Chastity and Sound Health*. New York: Cowan & Company.

Dayton, W. A. 1960. *Notes on Western Range Forbs: Equisetacea Through Fumariacea*. Washington, D.C.: U.S. Government Printing Office.

Dobkin de Rios, M. 1984. *Hallucinogens: Cross-Cultural Perspectives*. Albuquerque: University of New Mexico Press.

Duran-Reynals, M. L. 1946. *The Fever Bark Tree*. Garden City, N.Y.: Doubleday & Company.

Fenton, W. N. 1941. "Iroquois Suicide." *Bureau of American Ethnology* 128:79–137.

Fernald, M. L., and Kinsey, A. C. 1943. *Edible Wild Plants of Eastern North America*. Cornwall-on-Hudson, N.Y.: Idlewild Press.

Fisher, M. F. K. 1961. *A Cordiall Water*. Boston: Little, Brown & Company.

Folkard, R. 1884. *Plant Lore, Legends, and Lyrics*. London: Sampson Low, Marston, Searle, & Rivington.

Forsyth, A. A. 1968. *British Poisonous Plants*. London: Her Majesty's Stationery Office.

Fulder, S. 1980. *The Root of Being: Ginseng and the Pharmacology of Harmony*. London: Hutchinson.

Garcia, J., Hankins, W. G., and Coil, J. D. 1977. "Koalas, Men, and Other Conditioned Gastronomes." In *Food Aversion Learning*, ed. N. W. Milgram, L. Kramer, and T. M. Alloway, 195–218. New York: Plenum Press.

Getahun, A., and Krikorian, A. D. 1973. "Chat: Coffee's Rival from Harar, Ethiopia. I: Botany, Cultivation and Use." *Economic Botany* 27:378–89.

Gilges, W. 1955. *Some African Poison Plants and Medicines of Northern Rhodesia*. Paper no. 11. Livingston, Zambia: Rhodes-Livingston Museum.

Gimlette, J. D. 1929. *Malay Poisons and Charm Cures*. London: J. & A. Churchill.

Grossinger, R. 1980. *Plant Medicine*. Garden City, N.Y.: Anchor Books/Doubleday.

Guizot, E-J. A. 1864. *Essai sur les cantharides*. Paris: A. Parent, Imprimeur de la Faculté de Médecine.

Gunther, E. 1974. *Ethnobotany of Western Washington: The Knowledge and Use of Indigenous Plants by Native Americans*. Seattle: University of Washington Press.

Hamel, F. 1969. *Human Animals: Werewolves and Other Transformations*. New Hyde Park, N.Y.: University Books.

Hinton, H. E., and Dunn, A. M. S. 1967. *Mongooses*. London: Oliver & Boyd.

Hoehne, F. C. 1939. *Plantas e Substancias Vegetais Toxicas e Medicinais*. São Paulo: Graphicars.

Jacob, D. A. 1965. *A Witch's Guide to Gardening*. New York: Taplinger.

Jacob, H. E. 1935. *The Saga of Coffee: The Biography of an Economic Product*. Trans. E. and C. Paul. London: George Allen & Unwin.

Keast, A. 1958. "The Influence of Ecology on Variation in the Mistletoebird *(Dicaeum hirundinaceum)*." *Emu* 58:195–206.

Kingsbury, J. M. 1964. *Poisonous Plants of the United States and Canada*. Englewood Cliffs, N.J.: Prentice-Hall.

Krikorian, A. D. 1984. "Kat and Its Use: An Historical Perspective." *Journal of Ethnopharmacology* 12:115–78.

Laing, R. M., and Blackwell, E. W. 1957. *Plants of New Zealand*. Christchurch: Whitcombe & Tombs.

Lehner, E., and Lehner, J. 1973. *Folklore and Odysseys of Food and Medicinal Plants*. New York: Farrar, Straus & Giroux.

Lewin, L. [1924] 1931. *Phantastica: Narcotic and Stimulating Drugs*. Trans. P. H. A. Wirth. London: Kegan Paul, Trench, Trubner and Co.

MacCulloch, J. A. 1911. *The Religion of the Ancient Celts*. Edinburgh: T. & T. Clark.

Marsh, C. D. 1909. *The Loco-Weed Disease of the Plains*. U.S. Department of Agriculture, Bureau of Animal Industry, Bulletin 112. Washington, D.C.: U.S. Government Printing Office.

———. 1924. *Stock-Poisoning Plants of the Range*, U.S. Department of Agriculture, Bulletin 1245.

Mességué, M. 1973. *Of Men and Plants*. New York: The Macmillan Company.

Molyneux, R. J., and James, L. F. 1982. "Loco Intoxication: Indolizidine Alkaloids of Spotted Locoweed *(Astragalus lentiginosus)*. *Science* 216:190–91.

Murphy, J. M. 1964. "Psychotherapeutic Aspects of Shamanism on St. Lawrence Islands, Alaska." In *Magic, Faith, and Healing*, ed. A. Kieve, 53–83. New York: Free Press.

Norman, J. R. 1931. *A History of Fishes*. New York: Frederick A. Stokes Company.

Northcote, R. 1971. *The Book of Herb Lore*. New York: Dover Publications.

Olson, S. L., and Rasmussen, D. T. 1986. "Paleoenvironment of the Earliest Hominoids: New Evidence from the Oligocene Avifauna of Egypt." *Science* 233:1202–04.

Penfold, A. R., and Willis, J. L. 1961. *The Eucalypts*. London: Leonard Hill.

Quinn, V. 1937. *Leaves: Their Place in Life and Legend*. New York: Frederick A. Stokes Company.

Riddle, J. M. 1985. *Dioscorides on Pharmacy and Medicine*. Austin: University of Texas Press.

Ridley, H. N. 1930. *The Dispersal of Plants Throughout the World*. Ashford, Eng.: L. Reeve & Co.

Robin, P. A. 1936. *Animal Lore in English Literature*. London: John Murray.

Russell, A. 1973. *Horns in the High Country*. New York: Alfred A. Knopf.

Safford, W. E. 1916. "Narcotic Plants and Stimulants of the Ancient Americans." *Annual Report of The Smithsonian Institution* 1916: 387–424.

Sanyal, P. K. 1964. *A Story of Medicine and Pharmacy in India*. Calcutta: Shri Amitava Sanyal.

Selander, R. B. 1960. *Bionomics, Systematics, and Phylogeny of Lytta, a Genus of Blister Beetles (Coleoptera, Meloidae)*. Illinois Biological Monographs no. 28. Urbana: University of Illinois Press.

Selden, C. 1979. *Aphrodisia*. New York: E. P. Dutton.

Speck, F. G. 1944. "Catawba Herbals and Curative Practices." *Journal of American Folklore* 57:37–50.

Srivastava, G. P. 1954. *History of Indian Pharmacy*. Calcutta: Pindars.

Survival, Evasion, and Escape. 1969. Department of Army Field Manual no. 21–76. Washington, D.C.: Superintendent of Documents, U.S. Government Printing Office.

Taylor, A. S. 1875. *On Poisons*. Philadelphia: Henry C. Lea.

Taylor, N. 1945. *Cinchona in Java*. New York: Greenberg.

Vogel, V. J. 1970. *American Indian Medicine*. Norman: University of Oklahoma Press.

Watt, J. M., and Breyer-Brandwijk, M. G. 1962. *The Medicinal and Poisonous Plants of Southern and Eastern Africa*. London: E. & S. Livingstone.

Wootton, A. C. 1910. *Chronicles of Pharmacy*. Vols. 1 and 2. London: Macmillan and Co.

3. FALLING BIRDS AND FLYING CATS

Abramson, H. A., and Evans, L. T. 1954. "Lysergic Acid Diethylamide (LSD 25): II: Psychobiological Effects on the Siamese Fighting Fish." *Science* 120:990–91.

———— and Jarvik, M. E. 1955. "Lysergic Acid Diethylamide (LSD-25): IX: Effect on Snails." *Journal of Psychology* 40:337.

Arbit, J. 1974. "Learning in Annelids and Attempts at the Chemical Modification of This Behaviour." In *Learning and Associated Phenomena in Invertebrates*, ed. W. H. Thorpe and D. Davenport, 83–88. Animal Behaviour Supplement. London: Bailliere, Tindall & Cassell.

Balls, E. K. 1962. *Early Uses of California Plants*. Berkeley: University of California Press.

Bates, R. B., and Sigel, C. W. 1963. "Terpenoids: *Cis-trans-* and *transcis*-Nepetalactones." *Experientia* 19:564–65.

Bejerot, N. 1972. "A Theory of Addiction as an Artificially Induced Drive." *American Journal of Psychiatry* 128:76–80.

Bell, C. R. 1971. "Breeding Systems and Floral Biology of the Umbelliferae of Evidence for Specialization in Unspecialized Flowers." In *The Biology and Chemistry of the Umbelliferae*, ed. V. H. Heywood, 93–107. London: Academic Press.

Bergtold, W. H. 1930. "Intoxicated Robins." *Auk* 47(4):571.

Berry, F. 1955. "Intoxicated Robins." *Audubon Magazine* 57:198.

Bralliar, F. 1922. *Knowing Birds Through Stories*. New York: Funk & Wagnalls Company.

Butler, R. A. 1953. "Discrimination Learning by Rhesus Monkeys to Visual-Exploration Motivation." *Journal of Comparative and Physiological Psychology* 46:95–98.

————. 1957. "The Effect of Deprivation of Visual Incentives on Visual Exploration Motivation in Monkeys." *Journal of Comparative and Physiological Psychology* 50:177–79.

Chapelle, M. 1981. *Pour que vive la truffe noire*. Evreux: Compagnie Jean-Jacques Pauvert.

Chavin, R. 1970. *The World of Ants*. Trans. G. Ordish. London: Victor Gollancz.

Chessick, R. D., Knonholm, J., Beck, M., and Maier, G. 1964. "Effect of Pretreatment with Tryptamine, Tryptophan and DOPA on LSD Reaction in Tropical Fish." *Psychopharmacologia* 5:390–92.

Christiansen, A., Baum, R., and Witt, P. N. 1962. "Changes in Spider Webs Brought About by Mescaline, Psilocybin and an Increase in Body Weight." *Journal of Pharmacology and Experimental Therapeutics* 136:31–37.

Claus, R., Hoppen, H. O., and Karg, H. 1981. "The Secret of Truffles: A Steroidal Pheromone?" *Experientia* 37:1178–79.

Cornell, R. D. 1938. *Conspicuous California Plants*. Pasadena: San Pasqual Press.

Doty, R. W. 1970. "On Butterflies in the Brain." In *Electrophysiology of the Central Nervous System*, ed. V. S. Rusinov, 97–106. New York: Plenum Press.

Efron, D. H., ed. 1967. *Ethnopharmacologic Search for Psychoactive Drugs*. U.S. Public Health Service Publication no. 1645. Washington, D.C.: U.S. Government Printing Office.

Elliot, O. 1971. "Adverse Reactions to Lysergic Acid Diethylamide in Animals: Nest-building and General Maternal Care in Rats." *The Philippine Journal of Science* 100:267–88.

Evans, L. T., Geronimus, L. H., Kornetsky, C., and Abramson, H. A. 1956. "Effect of Ergot Drugs on *Betta splendens.*" *Science* 123:26.

Fabing, H. D. 1956. "On Going Berserk: A Neurochemical Theory." *The American Journal of Psychiatry* 113:409–15.

Fall, M. W., Medina, A. D., and Jackson, W. B. 1971. "Feeding Patterns of *Rattus rattus* and *Rattus exulans* on Eniwetok Atoll, Marshall Islands." *Journal of Mammalogy* 52:69–76.

Gjerstad, G. 1971. "Naturally Occurring Hallucinogens: II." *Quarterly Journal of Crude Drug Research* 11: 1797–1805.

Granier-Doyeux, M. 1956. "Una Toxicomania Indígena: El Uso de la *Piptadenia peregrina.*" *Revista Técnica* 2:49–55.

Grinnell, J. 1926. "Doped Robins." *Condor* 28(2):97.

Harney, J. W., Leary, J. D., and Barofsky, I. V. 1974. "Behavioral Activity of Catnip and Its Constituents: Nepetalic Acid and Nepetalactone." *Federation Proceedings* 33:481.

Hatch, R. C. 1972. "Effect of Drugs on Catnip *(Nepeta cataria)* -Induced Pleasure Behavior in Cats." *American Journal of Veterinary Research* 33: 143–55.

Jackson, B., and Reed, A. 1969. "Catnip and the Alteration of Consciousness." *Journal of the American Medical Association* 207:1349–50.

Jacobs, B. L., ed. 1984. *Hallucinogens: Neurochemical, Behavioral, and Clinical Perspectives.* New York: Raven Press.

Jarvik, M. E. 1957. "Effect of LSD-25 on Snails." In *Neuropharmacology: Transactions of the 3rd Conference*, ed. H. A. Abramson, 29–38. New York: Josiah Macy, Jr. Foundation.

Johnston, J. F. W. 1855. *The Chemistry of Common Life*. New York: D. Appleton & Co.

Keller, D., and Umbreit, W. 1956. "Chemically Altered 'Permanent' Behavior Patterns in Fish and Their Cure by Reserpine." *Science* 124:407.

Kieve, A., ed. 1964. *Magic, Faith, and Healing*. New York: Free Press.

Kingsbury, J. M. 1964. *Poisonous Plants of the United States and Canada*. Englewood Cliffs, N.J.: Prentice-Hall.

Kirk-Smith, M., Booth, D. A., Carroll, D., and Davies, P. 1978. "Human Social Attitudes Affected by Androstenol." *Research Communications in Psychology, Psychiatry and Behavior* 3:379–84.

Lambert, M., and Heckel, F. 1901. "Sur la racine d'iboga et l'ibogine." *Comptes Rendus Hebdomadaires des Séances de l'Académie des Sciences* 133:1236–38.

Leyhausen, P. 1973. "Addictive Behavior in Free Ranging Animals. In *Psychic Dependence*, ed. L. Goldberg and F. Hoffmeister, 58–65. New York: Springer-Verlag.

Lyons, P. C., Plattner, R. D., and Bacon, C. W. 1986. "Occurrence of Peptide and Clavine Ergot Alkaloids in Tall Fescue Grass." *Science* 232:487–89.

Michell, J., and Bickard, R. J. M. 1982. *Living Wonders*. London: Thames & Hudson.

Mirocha, C. J., and Christensen, C. M. 1974. "Fungus Metabolites Toxic to Animals." *Annual Review of Phytopathology* 12:303–30.

Morris, R., and Morris, D. 1965. *Men and Snakes*. London: Hutchinson.

Myerhoff, B. G. 1974. *Peyote Hunt: The Sacred Journey of the Huichol Indians*. Ithaca, N.Y.: Cornell University Press.

Orians, G. 1971. "Ecological Aspects of Behavior." In *Avian Biology*, ed. D. S. Farner and J. R. King, vol. 1, 513–46. New York: Academic Press.

Palen, G. F., and Goddard, G. V. 1966. "Catnip and Oestrous Behaviour in the Cat." *Animal Behaviour* 14:372–77.

Park, O. 1964. "Observations upon the Behavior of Myrmecophilous Pselaphid Beetles." *Pedobiologia* 4:129–37.

Piercy, P. L., Hargis, G., and Brown, C. A. 1944. "Mushroom Poisoning in Cattle." *Journal of the American Veterinary Medical Association* 105:206–208.

Pierqujn, P. 1839. *Traité de la folie des animaux, de ses rapports avec celle de l'homme et les législations actuelles*. vol. 1. Paris: Libraire de la Faculté de Médecine de Paris.

Pope, H. G. 1969. "*Tabernanthe iboga*: An African Narcotic Plant of Social Importance." *Economic Botany* 23:174–84.

Rand, A. L. 1954. "Social Feeding Behavior of Birds." *Field Museum of Natural History, Chicago, Zoology* 36:1–71.

Reichel-Dolmatoff, G. 1975. *The Shaman and the Jaguar*. Philadelphia: Temple University Press.

Robière, J. 1967. *La truffe du Perigord*. Périgueux: Pierre Fanlac.

Sai-Halasz, A., and Endroczy, E. 1959. "The Effect of Tryptamine Derivatives on the Behaviour of Dogs During Brain-Stem Stimulation." In *Neuropsychopharmacology*, ed. P. B. Bradley, P. Deniker, and C. Radouco-Thomas, 405–407. Amsterdam: Elsevier.

Schneider, J. A., and Sigg, E. B. 1957. "Neuropharmacological Studies on Ibogaine, an Indole Alkaloid with Central-Stimulant Properties." *Annals of the New York Academy of Sciences* 66:765–76.

Siegel, R. K. 1978. "Hallucinogens and Attentional Dysfunction: A Model of Hallucinations, Illusions and Reality-Testing." In *Psychopharmacology of Hallucinogens*, ed. R. Willette and R. Stillman, 268–96. New York: Pergamon Press.

——— and Jarvik, M. E. 1980. "DMT Self-Administration in Monkeys in Isolation." *Bulletin of the Psychonomic Society* 16:117–20.

——— and West, L. J., eds. 1975. *Hallucinations: Behavior, Experience, and Theory*. New York: John Wiley.

Stillman, R. C., and Willette, R. E., eds. 1978. *The Psychopharmacology of Hallucinogens*. New York: Pergamon Press.

Sturtevant, F. M., and Drill, V. A. 1956. "Effects of Mescaline in Laboratory Animals and Influence of Ataraxics on Mescaline-Response." *Proceedings of the Society of Experimental Biology and Medicine* 92:383–87.

Syroechkovskii, E. E., ed. [1975] 1984. *Wild Reindeer of the Soviet Union*. Trans. S. H. Paranjpye. New Delhi: Oxonian Press.

Todd, N. B. 1963. "The Catnip Response." Ph.D. diss., Harvard University.

Turner, W. J. 1956. "The Effect of Lysergic Acid Diethylamide on *Betta splendens* I." *Diseases of the Nervous System* 17:193–97.

Uyeno, E. T. 1967. "Lysergic Acid Diethylamide and Dominance Behavior of the Squirrel Monkey." *Archives Internationales de Pharmacodynamie et de Thérapie* 169:66–69.

———. September 1968. "Hallucinogens and the Underwater Lashley III Maze." Paper presented at the 76th Annual Convention of the American Psychological Association, San Francisco, Calif.

Van Lawick-Goodall, H., and Van Lawick-Goodall, J. 1971. *Innocent Killers.* Boston: Houghton Mifflin Company.

Waller, G. R., Price, G. H., and Mitchell, E. D. 1969. "Feline Attractant, Cis, Trans-Nepetalactone: Metabolism in the Domestic Cat." *Science* 164:1281–82.

Wasson, R. G. 1968. *Soma: Divine Mushroom of Immortality.* New York: Harcourt Brace Jovanovich.

———, Ruck, C. A. P., and Hofmann, A. 1978. *The Road to Eleusis.* New York: Harcourt Brace Jovanovich.

Wasson, V. P., and Wasson, R. G. 1957. *Mushrooms, Russia and History.* vols. 1 and 2. New York: Pantheon.

Watt, J. M., and Breyer-Brandwijk, M. G. 1962. *The Medicinal and Poisonous Plants of Southern and Eastern Africa.* London: E. & S. Livingstone.

Weckowicz, T. 1967. "Animal Studies of Hallucinogenic Drugs." In A. Hoffer and H. Osmond, *The Hallucinogens,* 555–94. New York: Academic Press.

Weslager, C. A. 1973. Magic Medicines of the Indians. Somerset, N.J.: Middle Atlantic Press.

Wilson, E. O. 1971. *The Insect Societies.* Cambridge: Harvard University Press.

Witt, P. N. 1951. "D-Lysergsäure-Diäthylamid (LSD-25) im Spinnentest." *Experientia* 7:310.

———. 1956. *The Effect of Substances on the Construction of Webs by Spiders as a Biological Test.* Berlin: Springer-Verlag.

———. 1975. "Effects [of LSD] on Insects and Lower Organisms." In D. V. S. Sankar, *LSD—A Total Study,* 603–25. Westbury, N.Y.: PJD Publications.

4. A SHREWDNESS OF APES

Albert, R. E., Alessandro, D., Lippmann, M., and Berger, J. 1971. "Long-term Smoking in the Donkey." *Archives of Environmental Health* 22:12–19.

Ando, K., and Yanagita, T. 1981. "Cigarette Smoking in Rhesus Monkeys." *Psychopharmacology* 72:117–27.

Ardrey, R. 1961. *African Genesis.* New York: Atheneum.

Ashton, H., and Stepney, R. 1982. *Smoking: Psychology and Pharmacology.* London: Tavistock,

Ator, N. A., and Griffiths, R. R. 1981. "Intravenous Self-Administration of Nicotine in the Baboon." *Federation Proceedings, Federation of the American Societies for Experimental Biology* 40:298.

Barker, L. M., Best, M. R., and Domjan, M., eds. 1977. *Learning Mechanisms in Food Selection.* Waco, Tex.: Baylor University Press.

Berger, B. D., Cwengel, P., Peshkin, N., and Schuster, R. 1979. "Social Factors in Taste Aversion." *Neuropharmacology* 18:1003–06.

Bond, N. W. 1984. "The Poisoned Partner Effect in Rats: Some Parametric Considerations." *Animal Learning & Behavior* 12:89–96.

————, ed. 1984. *Animal Models in Psychopathology*. Orlando, Fla.: Academic Press.

Brooks, J. E. 1952. *The Mighty Leaf: Tobacco Through the Centuries*. Boston: Little, Brown & Company.

————, ed. 1937–1952. *Tobacco: Its History Illustrated by the Books, Manuscripts and Engravings in the Library of George Arents, Jr.* vols. 1–5, parts 1–10 (1958–1969). New York: Rosenbach Company.

Brown, W. H. 1925. *Tobacco Under the Searchlight*. Cincinnati: Standard Publishing Company.

Cahan, W. G., and Kirman, D. 1968. "An Effective System and Procedure for Cigarette Smoking by Dogs."*Journal of Surgical Research* 8:567–75.

Cassell's Popular Natural History. 1861. London: Cassell, Petter, & Galpin.

"Chimp Capers." Summer 1985. *Fortean Times*, 23.

Cooke, M. C. c.1860. *The Seven Sisters of Sleep: Popular History of the Seven Prevailing Narcotics of the World*. London: James Blackwood.

Coombes, S., Revusky, S. H., and Lett, B. T. 1980. "Long-Delay Taste-Aversion Learning in an Unpoisoned Rat: Exposure to a Poisoned Rat as the Unconditioned Stimulus." *Learning and Motivation* 11:256–66.

Cowan, J. 1870. *The Use of Tobacco vs. Purity, Chastity and Sound Health*. New York: Cowan & Company.

Darwin, C. 1871. *The Descent of Man and Selection in Relation to Sex*. London: John Murray.

Deneau, G. A., and Inoki, R. 1967. "Nicotine Self-Administration in Monkeys." *Annals of the New York Academy of Sciences* 142:277–79.

Domino, E. F. 1986. "Nicotine: A Unique Psychoactive Drug-Arousal with Skeletal Muscle Relaxation." *Psychopharmacology Bulletin* 22:870–74.

Durrell, G. 1956. *The Drunken Forest*. New York: The Viking Press.

Ellenberger, H. F. 1960. "Zoological Garden and Mental Hospital." *Canadian Psychiatric Association Journal* 5.136–49.

Emily, G. S., and Hutchinson, R. R. 1984. "Behavioral Effects of Nicotine." In *Advances in Behavioral Pharmacology*, ed. T. Thompson, P. B. Dews, and J. E. Barrett, vol. 4, 105–129. Orlando, Fla.: Academic Press.

Fairbanks, L. 1975. "Communication of Food Quality in Captive *Macaca nemestrina* and Free-Ranging *Ateles geoffroyi*." *Primates* 16:181–90.

Furst, P. T. 1972. "To Find Our Life: Peyote Among the Huichol Indians of Mexico." In *Flesh of the Gods: The Ritual Use of Hallucinogens*, ed. P. T. Furst, 126–84. New York: Praeger.

Galef, B. G., and Beck, M. 1985. "Aversive and Attractive Marking of Toxic and Safe Foods by Norway Rats." *Behavioral and Neural Biology* 43:298–310.

Garner, W. W. 1946. *The Production of Tobacco*. Philadelphia: Blakiston Company.

Glick, D. S., Canfield, J. L., and Jarvik, M. E. 1970. "A Technique for Assessing Strength of Smoking Preference in Monkeys." *Psychological Reports* 26:707–10.

Goldberg, S. R., Spealman, R. D., and Goldberg, D. M. 1981. "Persistent Behavior at High Rates Maintained by Intravenous Self-Administration of Nicotine." *Science* 214:573–75.

Grabowski, J., and Sunkin, J. 1976. "The 'Pill Popper': A Device for Drug Capsule Self-Administration by Primates." *Behavior Research Methods and Instrumentation* 8:495–97.

Griffiths, R. R., Bigelow, G. E., and Henningfield, J. E. 1980. "Similarities in Animal and Human Drug-Taking Behavior." In *Advances in Substance Abuse: Behavioral and Biological Research*, ed. N. K. Mello, vol. 1, 1–90. Greenwich, Conn.: JAI Press.

————, Brady, J. V., and Bradford, L. D. 1979. "Predicting the Abuse Liability of Drugs with Animal Drug Self-Administration Procedures: Psychomotor Stimulants and Hallucinogens." In Advances in Behavioral Pharmacology, ed. T. Thompson and P. B. Dews, vol. 2, 163–208. New York: Academic Press.

Gritz, E. R., and Siegel, R. K. 1979. "Tobacco and Smoking in Animal and Human Behavior." In Modification of Pathological Behavior, ed. R. S. Davidson, 419–76. New York: Gardner Press.

Grunberg, N. E. 1986. "Nicotine as a Psychoactive Drug: Appetite Regulation." Psychopharmacology Bulletin 22:875–81.

Heimann, R. K. 1960. Tobacco and Americans. New York: McGraw-Hill.

Huxley, A. 1962. Island. New York: Harper & Brothers.

Janiger, O., and Dobkin de Rios, M. August 1973. "Suggestive Hallucinogenic Properties of Tobacco." Medical Anthropology Newsletter 4:6–11.

Jarvik, M. E. 1967. "Tobacco Smoking in Monkeys." Annals of the New York Academy of Sciences 142:280–94.

Jenkins, J. H., Hayes, F. A., Feurt, S. D., and Crockford, J. A. 1961. "A New Method for the Live Capture of Canines with Applications to Rabies Control." American Journal of Public Health 51:902–08.

Jensen, L. B. 1970. Poisoning Misadventures. Springfield, Ill.: Charles C. Thomas.

Johanson, C. E., and Schuster, C. R. 1981. "Animal Models of Drug Self-Administration." In Advances in Substance Abuse: Behavioral and Biological Research, ed. N. K. Mello, vol. 2, 219–97. Greenwich, Conn.: JAI Press.

Kamen-Kaye, D. 1971. "Chimo: An Unusual Form of Tobacco in Venezuela." Botanical Museum Leaflets, Harvard University 23:1–58.

Keehn, J. D., ed. 1979. Psychopathology in Animals. New York: Academic Press.

Kellogg, J. H. 1923. Tobaccoism or How Tobacco Kills. Battle Creek, Mich.: Modern Medicine Publishing Company.

Kimmens, A. C. 1975. Tales of the Ginseng. New York: William Morrow.

Koganezawa, M. 1974. "Food Habits of the Japanese Monkey (Macaca fuscata) in the Boso Mountains." Contemporary Primatology, 380–83.

Ksir, C. 1983. "Taste and Nicotine as Determinants of Voluntary Tobacco Use by Hamsters." Pharmacology Biochemistry and Behavior 19:605–08.

Lane, B. I. 1845. The Mysteries of Tobacco. New York: Wiley & Putnam.

Lavin, M. J., Freise, B., and Coombes, S. 1980. "Transferred Flavor Aversions in Adult Rats." Behavioral and Neural Biology 28:15–33.

Mangin, G. L., and Golding, J. F. 1984. Psychopharmacology of Smoking. New York: Cambridge University Press.

Marais, E. 1940. My Friends the Baboons. New York: McBride Co.

————. 1969. The Soul of the Ape. New York: Atheneum.

Mason, J. A. 1924. "Use of Tobacco in Mexico and South America." Field Museum of Natural History Anthropology Leaflet 16. Chicago: Field Museum of Natural History.

McCann, J. 1977. "Baboons Smoke a Lot Like People." The Journal 6(3):5.

McKey, D. 1974. "Ant-Plants: Selective Eating of an Unoccupied Barteria by a Colobus Monkey." Biotropica 6:269–70.

McKinney, W. T., and Bunney, W. E. 1969. "Animal Model of Depression: I: Review of Evidence: Implications for Research." Archives of General Psychiatry 21:240–48.

Meller, H. J. 1832. Nicotiana; or the Smoker's and Snuff-Taker's Companion. London: Effingham Wilson.

Pickens, R., Thompson, T., and Muchow, D. C. 1973. "Cannabis and Phencyclidine Self-Administration in Animals." In *Psychic Dependence,* ed. L. Goldberg and F. Hoffmeister, 78–87. New York: Springer-Verlag.

Piper, W. A., and Cole, J. M. 1973. "Operant Control of Smoking in Great Apes." *Behavior Research Methods and Instrumentation* 5:4–6.

Pomerleau, O. F. 1986. "Nicotine as a Psychoactive Drug: Anxiety and Pain Reduction." *Psychopharmacology Bulletin* 22:865–69.

Ratner, S. C., Katz, L., and Denny, M. R. 1974. "Training a Surrogate for Evaluation of Tobacco Smoking of Humans: Rationale and Outcome." *The Psychological Record* 24:365–72.

Revusky, S., Coombes, S., and Pohl, R. W. 1981. "Failure of Albino Guinea Pigs to Exhibit Lavin's Poisoned Partner Effect." *Behavioral and Neural Biology* 32:111–13.

Ridley, H. N. 1930. *The Dispersal of Plants Throughout the World.* Ashford, Eng.: L. Reeve & Co.

Robicsek, F. 1978. *The Smoking Gods: Tobacco in Maya Art, History, and Religion.* Norman: University of Oklahoma Press.

Rodriguez, E., Aregullin, M., Nishida, T., Uehara, S., Wrangham, R., Abramowski, Z., Finlayson, A., and Towers, G. H. N. 1985. "Thiarubrine A, a Bioactive Constituent of *Aspilia* (Asteraceae) Consumed by Wild Chimpanzees." *Experientia* 41:419–20.

Rucker, W. L. 1971. "An Analysis of the Cigarette Puffing Response in Woolly Monkeys." Ph.D. diss. University of Rochester. Available from University Microfilms, Ann Arbor, Michigan.

Schaller, G. B. 1963. *The Mountain Gorilla: Ecology and Behavior.* Chicago: University of Chicago Press.

Schenk, G. 1955. *The Book of Poisons.* Trans. M. Bullock. New York: Rinehart & Company.

Shaw, J. 1849. *Tobacco: Its History, Nature, and Effects on the Body and Mind.* New York: Fowlers & Wells.

Siegel, R. K., Collings, P. R., and Diaz, J. L. 1977. "On the Use of *Tagetes lucida* and *Nicotiana rustica* as a Huichol Smoking Mixture: The Aztec 'Yahutli' with Suggestive Hallucinogenic Effects." *Economic Botany* 31:16–23.

Slifer, B. L., and Balster, R. L. 1985. "Intravenous Self-Administration of Nicotine: With and Without Schedule-Induction." *Pharmacology Biochemistry & Behavior* 22:61–69.

Stainton, H. 1941. "Addiction in Animals." *British Journal of Inebriety* 41:24–31.

Thomason, G. 1938. *Science Speaks to Young Men: On Liquor, Tobacco, Narcotics, and Marijuana.* Mountain View, Calif.: Pacific Press.

Tugrul, L. 1985. "Abuse of Henbane by Children in Turkey." *Bulletin on Narcotics* 37:75–78.

Watt, J. M., and Breyer-Brandwijk, M. G. 1962. *The Medicinal and Poisonous Plants of Southern and Eastern Africa.* London: E. & S. Livingstone.

Weber, S. A., and Seaman, P. D., eds. 1985. *Havasupai Habitat: A. F. Whiting's Ethnography of a Traditional Indian Culture.* Tucson: University of Arizona Press.

Wilbert, J. 1972. "Tobacco and Shamanistic Ecstasy Among the Warao Indians of Venezuela." In *Flesh of the Gods: The Ritual Use of Hallucinogens,* ed. P. T. Furst, 55–83. New York: Praeger.

———. 1975. "Magico-Religious Use of Tobacco Among South American Indians." In *Cannabis and Culture,* ed. V. Rubin, 439–61. The Hague: Mouton.

———. 1987. *Tobacco and Shamanism in South America*. New Haven: Yale University Press.

Wilkie, D. M., MacLennan, A. J., and Pinel, J. P. J. 1979. "Rat Defensive Behavior: Burying Noxious Food." *Journal of the Experimental Analysis of Behavior* 31:299–306.

Wolf, F. A. 1962. *Aromatic or Oriental Tobaccos*. Durham, N.C.: Duke University Press.

Woods, J. H. 1983. "Some Thoughts on the Relations Between Animal and Human Drug-Taking." *Progress in Neuro-Psychopharmacology & Biological Psychiatry* 7:577–84.

5. ARK ON THE ROCKS

"Absinthe." 17 April 1869. *The British Medical Journal*, 353.

Allegro, J. M. 1970. *The Sacred Mushroom and the Cross*. London: Hodder & Stoughton.

Amory, R. 1868. "Experiments and Observations on Absinth and Absinthism." *Boston Medical and Surgical Journal* 78:70–71.

Arvola, A., and Forsander, O. A. 1963. "Hamsters in Experiments of Free Choice Between Alcohol and Water." *Quarterly Journal of Studies on Alcohol* 24:591–97.

Beard, G. M. 1871. *Stimulants and Narcotics; Medically, Philosophically, and Morally Considered*. New York: G. P. Putnam's Sons.

Benedict, F. G. 1936. *The Physiology of the Elephant*. Washington, D.C.: Carnegie Institution of Washington.

———. 1938. *Vital Energetics: A Study in Comparative Basal Metabolism*. Washington, D.C.: Carnegie Institution of Washington.

Blair, L. 1988. *Ring of Fire*. New York: Bantam.

Carrighar, S. 1965. *Wild Heritage*. Boston: Houghton Mifflin Company.

Carrington, R. 1959. *Elephants*. New York: Basic Books.

Conrad, B. 1988. *Absinthe: History in a Bottle*. San Francisco: Chronicle Books.

Corner, E. J. H. 1964. *The Life of Plants*. Cleveland: World Publishing Company.

Crane, J. T. 1871. *Arts of Intoxication*. New York: Canton & Lanahan.

Critchlow, B. 1986. "The Powers of John Barleycorn." *American Psychologist* 41:751–64.

Darwin, C. 1871. *The Descent of Man and Selection in Relation to Sex*. London: John Murray.

Dennis, J. V. June 1979. "Are They Birds or Do We See W. C. Fields in Triple Vision?" *Smithsonian* 10:144.

Dixon, R., and Eddy, B. 1924. *The Personality of Insects*. New York: Charles W. Clark.

"Dog Can Be Sot on Beer Saucer." 18 August 1977. *Commercial Appeal* [Memphis]:14.

Drummond, W. H. 1875. *The Large Game and Natural History of South and Southeast Africa*. Edinburgh: Edmonston & Douglas.

"Drunken Animals." October 1979. *Omni* 2:58.

"Drunken Animals." Spring 1985. *Fortean Times*, no. 43, 44–45.

Ehrlich, P., and Ehrlich, A. 1981. *Extinction*. New York: Random House.

"Elephants Rampage, Trample 5 in India." 1 January 1985. *Los Angeles Times*, part I:19.

"Elephant with a Snoot Full." 3 September 1975. *San Francisco Chronicle*: 17.

Ellison, G. D. 1977. "Animal Models of Psychopathology." *American Psychologist* 32:1036–45.

——— and Potthoff, A. D. 1983. "Social Models of Drinking Behavior in Animals: The Importance of Individual Differences." In *Recent Developments in Alcoholism*, ed. M. Glanater, vol. 2, 17–36. New York: Plenum Press.

Eltringham, S. K. 1982. *Elephants*. Poole, Dorset: Blandford Press.

Evans, E. P. 1906. *The Criminal Prosecution and Capital Punishment of Animals*. London: William Heinemann.

Farb, P., and Armelagos, G. 1980. *Consuming Passions: The Anthropology of Eating*. Boston: Houghton Mifflin Company.

Fisher, M. F. K. 1961. *A Cordiall Water*. Boston: Little, Brown & Company.

Fitz-Gerald, F. L. 1972. "Voluntary Alcohol Consumption in Apes." In *The Biology of Alcoholism*, ed. B. Kissin and H. Begleiter, vol. 2: *Physiology and Behavior*, 169–92. New York: Plenum Press.

Gaster, M. 1915. *Rumanian Bird and Beast Stories*. London: Sidgwick & Jackson.

Hadaway, P. F., Alexander, B. K., Coambs, H. B., and Beyerstein, B. 1979. "The Effect of Housing and Gender on Preference for Morphine-Sucrose Solutions in Rats." *Psychopharmacology* 66:87–91.

Hirschman, A. E., and Siegel, R. K. 1987. "Absinthe and the Socialization of Abuse: A Historical Note and Translation." *Social Pharmacology* 1:1–12.

Holland, W. J. 1968. *The Moth Book*. New York: Dover Publications.

"Inebriated Birds." August 1979. *Smithsonian* 10:14.

Janson, H. W. 1952. *Apes and Ape Lore in the Middle Ages and the Renaissance*. Vienna: Brüder Rosenbaum.

Kellner, E. 1971. *Moonshine: Its History and Folklore*. New York: Barre Publishing.

Lalou, S.-D. 1903. *Contribution à l'étude de l'essence d'absinthe et de quelques autres essences*. Paris: C. Naud.

Lane, F. W. 1951. *Animal Wonder World*. New York: Sheridan House.

Lehner, E., and Lehner, J. 1973. *Folklore and Odysseys of Food and Medicinal Plants*. New York: Farrar, Straus & Giroux.

Leslie-Melville, B., and Leslie-Melville, J. 1973. *Elephants Have Right of Way*. Garden City, N.Y.: Doubleday & Company.

Lewin, L. [1924] 1931. *Phantastica: Narcotic and Stimulating Drugs*. Trans. P. H. A. Wirth. London: Kegan Paul, Trench, Trubner & Co.

Lindsay, W. L. 1879. *Mind in the Lower Animals*. Vol. 2, *Mind in Disease*. London: C. Kegan Paul & Co.

Loeb, E. M. 1943. "Primitive Intoxicants." *Quarterly Journal of Studies on Alcohol* 4:387–98.

Magnan, V. 1873. "Recherches de physiologie pathologique avec l'alcool et l'essence d'absinthe—épilepsie." *Archives de Physiologie*: 117–42.

———. 1874. *De l'alcoolisme*. Paris: Adrien Delahaye.

Majchrowicz, E. 1975. "Induction of Physical Dependence upon Ethanol and the Associated Behavioral Changes in Rats." *Psychopharmacologia* 43:245–54.

Masserman, J. H. 1957. "Stress Situations in Animals and the Nature of Conflict." In *Neuropharmacology: Transactions of the Third Conference*, ed. H. A. Abramson, 147–67. New York: Josiah Macy, Jr. Foundation.

Medawar, P. B., and Medawar, J. S. 1983. "A Natural Glossary." *The Sciences* 23:54–59.

Meisch, R. A. 1977. "Ethanol Self-Administration: Infrahuman Studies." In *Advances in Behavioral Pharmacology*, ed. T. Thompson and P. B. Dews. vol. 1, 35–84. New York: Academic Press.

———. 1984. "Alcohol Self-Administration by Experimental Animals." In *Research Advances in Alcohol and Drug Problems*, ed. R. G. Smart, H. D. Cappell, F. B. Glaser, Y. Israel, H. Kalant, R. E. Popham, W. Schmidt, and E. M. Sellers, vol. 8, 23–45. New York: Plenum Press.

Mello, N. K. 1973. "A Review of Methods to Induce Alcohol Addiction in Animals." *Pharmacology, Biochemistry and Behavior* 1:89–101.

Mello, N. K., Bree, M. P., Mendelson, J. H., and Ellingboe, J. 1983. "Alcohol Self-Administration Disrupts Reproductive Function in Female Macaque Monkeys." *Science* 221:677–79.

Menninger, E. A. 1967. *Trees*. New York: The Viking Press.

Nashe, T. Quoted in Muir, F. 1976. *An Irreverent and Thoroughly Incomplete Social History of Almost Everything*, 304–05. New York: Stein & Day.

Nilsson, L. A. 1978. "Pollination Ecology of Epipactis palustris (Orchidaceae)." *Botaniska Notiser* 131:355–68.

Novick, A. May 1973. "Bats Aren't All Bad." *National Geographic* 143: 615–37.

Park, E. October 1979. "Around the Mall and Beyond." *Smithsonian* 10:34–42.

Pasteur, L. 1876. *Études sur la bière, ses maladies, causes qui les provoquent, procédé pour la rendre inaltérable, avec une théorie nouvelle de la fermentation*. Paris: Gauthier-Villars.

Pieper, W. A. 1975. "Alcoholic Monkeys." *Yerkes Newsletter* 12(2):15–17.

———, Skeen, M. J., McClure, H. M., and Bourne, P. G. 1972. "The Chimpanzee as an Animal Model for Investigating Alcoholism." *Science* 176:71–73.

"Pink Elephants." 1 November 1975. *The Journal* 4:10.

"Plastered Parrots Stopped at Border." December 1976. *National Screw* 1:56.

Porter, T. 14 December 1976. "Beer Puts Losing Racehorse on the Right Track—Five Wins in a Row." *National Enquirer:* 41.

Richter, C. P. 1957. "Production and Control of Alcoholic Cravings in Rats." In *Neuropharmacology: Transactions of the Third Conference*, ed. H. A. Abramson, 39–146. New York: Josiah Macy, Jr. Foundation.

Ridley, H. N. 1930. *The Dispersal of Plants Throughout the World*. Ashford, Eng.: L. Reeve & Co.

"Runaway Chimp a Chump for Wine." 19 August 1975. *Los Angeles Herald Examiner*.

Rybot, D. 1972. *It Began Before Noah*. London: Michael Joseph.

"Screwdrivers a Threat in the Pig Pen." March 1977. *U.S. Journal of Drug and Alcohol Dependence* 1:4.

"Sheep Wolfs Down Vodka by Quart." 29 June 1976. *Star-News*. A1.

Siegel, R. K., and Brodie, M. 1984. "Alcohol Self-Administration by Elephants." *Bulletin of the Psychonomic Society* 22:49–52.

Sieveking, P., ed. 1980. *Man Bites Dog: The Scrapbook of an Edwardian Eccentric, George Ives*. London: Jay Landesman.

Sikes, S. 1971. *The Natural History of the African Elephant*. London: Weidenfeld & Nicolson.

"Six-Pack Kid." 6 September 1982. *Time*. 25.

Stainton, H. 1941. "Addiction in Animals." *British Journal of Inebriety* 41:24–31.

Suzdak, P. D., Glowa, J. R., Crawley, J. N., Schwartz, R. D., Skolnick, P., and Paul, S. 1986. "A Selective Imidazobenzodiazepine Antagonist of Ethanol in the Rat." *Science* 234:1243–47.

Thompson, Z. 20 August 1980. "Peacock Drowns His Sorrow in Stout." *Los Angeles Times,* part 2, 1.

Tolstoy, L. [1890] 1975. *Why Do Men Stupefy Themselves? and Other Writings.* Trans. A. Maude. Hankins, N.Y.: Strength Books/East Ridge Press.

Wilkinson, A. 1985. *Moonshine.* New York: Alfred A. Knopf.

Wolin, M. J. 1981. "Fermentation in the Rumen and Human Large Intestine." *Science* 213:1463–68.

Woods, J. H., and Winger, G. D. 1974. "Alcoholism and Animals." *Preventive Medicine* 3:49–60.

Younger, W. 1966. *Gods, Men, and Wine.* Cleveland: Wine and Food Society/World Publishing Company.

6. MILK OF PARADISE

Baumgartner, A. M., Jones, P. F., Baumgartner, W. A., and Black, C. T. 1979. "Radioimmunoassay of Hair for Determining Opiate-Abuse Histories." *The Journal of Nuclear Medicine* 20:748–52.

Berridge, V., and Edwards, G. 1981. *Opium and the People: Opiate Use in Nineteenth-century England.* London: Allen Lane.

Boissière, J. 1896. *Propos d'un intoxiqué.* Paris: Louis-Michaud.

Charvet, A. P. 1826. *De l'action comparée de l'opium, et de ses principes constituans sur l'économie animale.* Paris: F. C. Levrault.

Cocteau, J. |1930| 1957. *Opium: The Diary of a Cure.* Trans. M. Crosland and S. Road. London: Icon Books: 61.

Cooke, M. C. c.1860. *The Seven Sisters of Sleep: Popular History of the Seven Prevailing Narcotics of the World.* London: James Blackwood.

Courtwright, D. T. 1982. *Dark Paradise. Opiate Addiction in America Before 1940.* Cambridge: Harvard University Press.

Crothers, T. D. 1902. *Morphinism and Narcomanias from Other Drugs.* Philadelphia: W. B. Saunders & Company.

Danby, F. 1916. *Twilight.* New York: Dodd, Mead & Company.

Dayton, W. A. 1960. *Notes on Western Range Forbs: Equisetacea Through Fumariacea.* Washington, D.C.: U.S. Government Printing Office.

Dekobra, M. 1931. *Perfumed Tigers.* Trans. M. Wood. London: Cassell & Company.

[De Quincey, T.] 1822. *Confessions of an English Opium-Eater.* London: Taylor & Hessey.

DeVèze, E. R. 1895. *Traité theorique et pratique du haschich et autres substances psy-chiques.* Paris: Chamuel.

Dickens, C. 1870. *The Mystery of Edwin Drood.* London: Chapman & Hall.

Duke, J. A. 1973. "Utilization of Papaver." *Economic Botany* 27:390–400.

————, Gunn, C. R., Leppik, E. E., Reed, C. F., Solt, M. L., and Terrrell, E. E. 1973. *Annotated Bibliography on Opium and Oriental Poppies and Related Species.* Agricultural Research Service Publication ARS-NE-28. Washington, D.C.: U.S. Department of Agriculture.

Frumkin, K., and Zych, K. November 1973. *Insect Chemical Detection.* Technical Report no. LWL-CR-08B73. Aberdeen Proving Ground, Md.: U.S. Army Land Warfare Laboratory.

Guimbail, H. 1892. *Les morphinomanes.* Paris: Librairie J.-B. Baillière et Fils.

Harrison, J. B. 1854. "The Psychology of Opium-Eating." *The Journal of Psychological Medicine* 7:240–52.

Harthoorn, A. M. 1965. "The Use of a New Oripavine Derivative with Potent Morphine-like Activity for the Restraint of Hoofed Wild Animals." *Research in Veterinary Science* 6:290–99.

Hayter, A. 1968. *Opium and the Romantic Imagination.* Berkeley and Los Angeles: University of California Press.

Jones, J. 1700. *The Mysteries of Opium Revealed.* London: Richard Smith.

Kane, H. H. 1882. *Opium-Smoking in America and China.* New York: G. P. Putnam's Sons.

Kramer, J. C. 1980. "The Opiates: Two Centuries of Scientific Study." *Journal of Psychedelic Drugs* 12:89–103.

Kumar, B. 1972. "Morphine Dependence in Rats: Secondary Reinforcement from Environmental Stimuli." *Psychopharmacologia* 25:332–38.

Lagneau, F., and Gallard, P. 1946. "Intoxication des bovins par l'oeillette." *Recueil de Médecine Vétérinaire* 122:310–13.

Lefebure, M. 1974. *Samuel Taylor Coleridge: A. Bondage of Opium.* London: Victor Gollancz.

Lenz, G. R., Evans, S. M., Walters, D. E., and Hopfinger, A. J. 1986. *Opiates.* Orlando, Fla.: Academic Press.

Lewin, L. [1924] 1931. *Phantastica: Narcotic and Stimulating Drugs.* Trans. P. H. A. Wirth, London: Kegan Paul, Trench, Trubner & Co.

Lewis, G., and Fish, B. 1978. *I Loved Rogues.* Seattle. Superior Publishing.

Lezy, Dr. 1946. "Intoxication des bovins par des capsules d'oeillette." *Recueil de Médecine Vétérinaire* 122:23–24.

Marsh, J. 1987. *Pre-Raphaelite Women: Images of Femininity.* New York: Harmony Books.

McNaughton, I. H., and Harper, J. L. 1964. "Papaver L." *The Journal of Ecology,* no. 3:767–93.

Merlin, M. D. 1984. *On the Trail of the Ancient Opium Poppy.* Rutherford, N.J.: Fairleigh Dickinson University Press.

Mitchell, S. W. 1869. "On the Insusceptibility of Pigeons to the Toxic Action of Opium." *American Journal of the Medical Sciences* 57:37–38.

———. 1870. "On the Effect of Opium and Its Derivative Alkaloids." *American Journal of the Medical Sciences* 59:2–33.

O'Carroll, P. 1981. "Trademarks of the Traffic." *Drug Enforcement* 8:27–32.

Palmer, C., and Horowitz, M. 1982. *Shaman Woman, Mainline Lady.* New York: William Morrow.

Parssinen, T. M. 1983. *Secret Passions, Secret Remedies: Narcotic Drugs in British Society 1820–1930.* Philadelphia: Institute for the Study of Human Issues.

Pichon, G. 1889. *Le Morphinisme.* Paris: Octave Doin.

"Poppy Goes the Weevils." November/December 1976. *Head:* 16.

Ridley, H. N. 1930. *The Dispersal of Plants Throughout the World.* Ashford, Eng.: L. Reeve & Co.

Roudil, H., ed. 1960. *La Drogue.* Paris: Tour Saint Jacques.

Schmidt, J. E. 1959. *Narcotics: Lingo and Lore.* Springfield, Ill.: Charles C. Thomas.

Scully, V. 1970. *A Treasury of American Indian Herbs.* New York: Crown Publishers.

Siegel, R. K. 1984. "LSD-Induced Effects in Elephants: Comparisons with Musth Behavior." *Bulletin of the Psychonomic Society* 22:53–6.

———, Gusewelle, B. E., and Jarvik, M. E. 1975. "Naloxone-Induced Jumping in Morphine Dependent Mice: Stimulus Control and Motivation." *International Pharmacopsychiatry* 10:17–23.

———— and Hirschman, A. E. 1983. "Charvet and the First Psychopharmacological Studies on Opium: A Historical Note and Translation." *Journal of Psychoactive Drugs* 15:323–29.

Siegel, S. 1983. "Classical Conditioning, Drug Tolerance, and Drug Dependence." In *Research Advances in Alcohol and Drug Problems,* ed. R. G. Smart, F. B. Glaser, Y. Israel, H. Kalant, R. E. Popham, and W. Schmidt, vol. 7, 207–46. New York: Plenum Press.

Spears, R. A. 1986. *The Slang and Jargon of Drugs and Drink.* Metuchen, N.J.: Scarecrow Press.

Spragg, S. D. S. April 1940. "Morphine Addiction in Chimpanzees." *Comparative Psychology Monographs* 15, no. 79.

Stuart, D. M. 1957. *A Book of Birds and Beasts: Legendary, Literary and Historical.* London: Methuen & Co.

Terry, C. E., and Pellens, M. 1928. *The Opium Problem.* New York: Bureau of Social Hygiene.

De Waal, M. 1980. *Medicinal Herbs in the Bible.* York Beach, Me.: Samuel Weiser,

Williams, J. H. 1950. *Elephant Bill.* London: Rupert Hart-Davis.

Zimmerman, D. 1 September 1974. "To Kill a Poppy." *The Journal:* 5.

7. EMERALD LAUGHTER

Abel, E. L. 1980. *Marihuana: The First Twelve Thousand Years.* New York: Plenum Press.

Allen, J. L. 1900. *The Reign of Law: A Tale of the Kentucky Hemp Fields.* New York: The Macmillan Company.

Ames, F. R., Brownell, B., and Zuurmond, T. J. 1979. "Effects of the Oral Administration of Cannabis sativa (Dagga) on Chacma Baboons (Papio ursinus)." *South African Medical Journal* 55:1127–32.

"Apes on Drugs." January 1985. *High Times:* 8.

Baldwin, P. H., Schwartz, C. W., and Schwartz, E. R. 1952. "Life History and Economic Status of the Mongoose in Hawaii." *Journal of Mammalogy* 33:335–56.

Baudelaire, C. 1860. *Les paradis artificiels: Opium et hashchisch.* Paris: Poulet-Malassis et de Broise.

Black, D. W. 1984. "Laughter." *Journal of the American Medical Association* 252:2995–98.

Burton, R. F. 1901. *Supplemental Nights to the Book of the Thousand Nights and a Night,* vol. 4. Denver: Burton Society.

Cardassis, J. 1951. "Intoxication des équidés par *Cannabis indica." Recueil de Médecine Vétérinaire* 127:971–73.

Cherniak, L. 1979. *The Great Books of Hashish,* Vol. 1, book 1. Berkeley: And/Or Press.

Clarke, E. G. C., Greatorex, J. C., and Potter, R. 1971. "Cannabis Poisoning in the Dog." *Veterinary Record* 88:694.

"Contented Cows." May 1981. *Playboy:* 63.

Corcoran, M. E. 1973. "Role of Drug Novelty and Metabolism in the Aversive Effects of Hashish Injections in Rats." *Life Sciences* 12, part 1:63–72.

Corcoran, M. E., and Amit, Z. 1974. "Reluctance of Rats to Drink Hashish Suspensions: Free-Choice and Forced Consumption, and the Effects of Hypothalamic Stimulation." *Psychopharmacologia* 35:129–47.

Cooke, M. C. c. 1860. *The Seven Sisters of Sleep: Popular History of the Seven Prevailing Narcotics of the World.* London: James Blackwood.

Cutler, M. G., MacKintosh, J. H., and Chance, M. R. A. 1975. "Behavioural Changes in Laboratory Mice During Cannabis Feeding and Withdrawal." *Psychopharmacologia* 44:173–77.

Davenport, J. 1966. *Aphrodisiacs and Love Stimulants*. New York: Lyle Stuart.

Elsmore, T. F., and Fletcher, G. V. 1972. "Δ⁹-Tetrahydrocannabinol: Aversive Effects in Rat at High Doses." *Science* 175:911–12.

Everett, B. 31 March 1975. "Postscript: The Continuing Saga of Marty M. Mouse; A Pier Held Dear; Lion Country Revisited." *Los Angeles Times,* part 2, 1.

———. 12 January 1976. "Postscript: Where Do Yugo from Here: Longrun Bankruptcy; Marty Mouse Awards." *Los Angeles Times,* part 2, 1.

Ferster, C. B., and Skinner, B. F. 1957. *Schedules of Reinforcement*. New York: Appleton-Century-Crofts.

Frank, M., and Rosenthal, E. 1978. *Marijuana Grower's Guide*. Berkeley: And/Or Press.

Gautier, T. 1846. "Le Club des Haschichins." *Revue des Deux Mondes* 13:520–35.

Girl, M. 1977. *The Primo Plant: Growing Sinsemilla Marijuana*. Berkeley: Leaves of Grass/Wingbow Press.

Gottheil, E., Druley, K. A., Skoloda, T. E., and Waxman, H. M., eds. 1983. *Alcohol, Drug Abuse and Aggression*. Springfield, Ill.: Charles C. Thomas.

"The Great Smokeout." March 1980. *High Times:* 44–46.

Grunfeld, Y., and Edery, H. 1969. "Psychopharmacological Activity of the Active Constituents of Hashish and Some Related Cannabinoids." *Psychopharmacologia* 14:200–10.

Harris, R. T., Waters, W., and McLendon, D. 1974. "Evaluation of Reinforcing Capability of Delta-9-Tetrahydrocannabinol in Rhesus Monkeys." *Psychopharmacologia* 37:23–29.

"High Living." 25 September 1978. *Time:* 27.

Hinton, H. E., and Dunn, A. M. S. 1967. *Mongooses: Their Natural History and Behaviour*. Edinburgh and London: Oliver & Boyd.

"Insect Munchies." 1975. *Marijuana Monthly,* no. 5, 12.

"Intensive Hunt Ends with Mouse Going to Seed." 24 December 1974. *Los Angeles Times:* 1, 3.

Kimmens, A. C. 1977. *Tales of Hashish*. New York: William Morrow.

Latif, A., and El Daly, M. A. 1973. "Search for New Fixed Oils," part 2, "Edible Oil from the Seeds of Hemp." *Agricultural Research Review* 51:123–29.

Levi, W. M. 1957. *The Pigeon*. Sumter, S. C.: Levi Publishing Company.

Lewis, B. 1968. *The Assassins*. New York: Basic Books.

Maeder, J. 4 January 1976. "Pot-Eating Marty Mouse Is Eulogized." *Miami Herald:* 2A.

"Marty Eludes Police but It's Close Squeak." 19 December 1974. *Los Angeles Times,* part 1, 34.

"Marty Mouse." 3 January 1975. *Daily Bruin* [UCLA]: 5.

"The Marty Mouse Fan Club." 5 January 1976. *Los Angeles Times,* part 1, 2.

"Marty Mouse Fans Rally." 3 January 1975. *Daily Bruin* [UCLA]: 2.

McMillan, D. E. 1977. "Behavioral Pharmacology of the Tetrahydrocannabinols." In *Advances in Behavioral Pharmacology,* ed. T. Thompson and P. B. Dews, vol. 1, 1–34. New York: Academic Press.

Meriwether, W. F. 1969. "Acute Marijuana Toxicity in a Dog." *Veterinary Medicine* 64:577–78.

Miczek, K. A. 1976. "Mouse-Killing and Motor Activity: Effects of Chronic Δ^9-Tetrahydrocannabinol and Pilocarpine." *Psychopharmacology* 47:59–64.

Mikuriya, T. H., ed. 1973. *Marijuana: Medical Papers. 1839–1972*. Oakland, Calif.: Medi-Comp Press.

Morrison, F. B. 1957. *Feeds and Feeding*. Ithaca, N.Y.: Morrison Publishing Company.

Myerscough, R., and Taylor, S. 1985. "The Effects of Marijuana on Human Physical Aggression." *Journal of Personality and Social Psychology* 49:1541–46.

"National Weed." February 1979. *High Times*: 36.

"Newsmakers." 6 January 1975. *Newsweek*: 32.

Oldham, A. August 1978. "Rat Exposed in Big Top Pot Heist." *High Times*: 35.

Paris, M., Boucher, F., and Cosson, L. 1975. "The Constituents of *Cannabis sativa* Pollen." *Economic Botany* 29:245–53.

Payne, J., ed. 1901. *The Book of the Thousand Nights and One Night*, vol. 2. London: Khorassan Edition.

Peck, W. 24 December 1974. "Marty Named House Mouse." *San Jose Mercury*: 1.

Pickens, R., Thompson, T., and Muchow, D. C. 1973. "Cannabis and Phencyclidine Self-Administration by Animals." In *Psychic Dependence*, ed. L. Goldberg and F. Hoffmeister, 78–86. New York: Springer-Verlag.

Pierquin, D. 1839. *Traité de la folie des animaux, de ses rapports avec celle de l'homme et les législations actuelles,* vol. 1. Paris: Libraire de la Faculté de Médecine de Paris.

"Police Marijuana Evidence Gone—Suspects Squeal." 15 April 1974. *Los Angeles Times,* part 1, 3.

"Rats Get High as a Flag on 'Pot' in Courthouse." 30 September 1978. *Los Angeles Times,* part 1, 7.

"Readers' Harvest Report." January 1987. *High Times*: 25–27.

Robinson, V. 1912. *An Essay on Hasheesh*. New York: Medical Review of Reviews.

Rodman, E. J. 13 January 1975. "Marijuana Mouse Nibbles His Way to UCLA." *Daily Bruin* [UCLA]: 1, 17.

———. 13 January 1975. "Doper Mouse Seeks Freedom." *Daily Bruin* [UCLA]: 17.

Romano, B. 17 December 1974. "Marijuana Mouse May Go to College." *San Jose Mercury*: 1, 20.

Rosenthal, F. 1971. *The Herb. Hashish versus Medieval Muslim Society.* Leiden: E. J. Brill.

Rubin, V., ed. 1975. *Cannabis and Culture*. The Hague: Mouton.

Santos, M., Sampaio, M. R. P., Fernandes, N. S., and Carlini, E. A. 1966. "Effects of *Cannabis sativa* (Marihuana) on the Fighting Behavior of Mice." *Psychopharmacologia* 8:437–44.

Siegel, R. K. 1969. "Effects of *Cannabis sativa* and Lysergic Acid Diethylamide on a Visual Discrimination Task in Pigeons." *Psychopharmacologia* 15:1–8.

———. 1973. "An Ethologic Search for Self-Administration of Hallucinogens." *International Journal of the Addictions* 8:373–93.

———. 1978. "Hallucinogens and Attentional Dysfunction: A Model of Hallucinations, Illusions and Reality-testing." In *Psychopharmacology of Hallucinogens*, ed. R. Willette and R. Stillman, 268–96. New York: Pergamon Press.

———. 1979. "Natural Animal Addictions: An Ethological Perspective. In *Psychopathology in Animals: Research and Clinical Implications,* ed. J. D. Keehn, 29–60. New York: Academic Press.

———— and Hirschman, A. E. 1984. "Hashish Near-Death Experiences." *Anabiosis* 4:69–86.

————. 1985. "Hashish and Laughter: Historical Notes and Translations of Early French Investigations." *Journal of Psychoactive Drugs* 17:87–91.

Solomon, D., ed. 1966. *The Marihuana Papers.* Indianapolis: Bobbs-Merrill Company.

Strachan, D. February 1976. "Death of a Mouse: An Obituary for Marty." *Marijuana Monthly* 2:35–37.

Takahashi, R. N., and Singer, G. 1979. "Self-Administration of Δ⁹-Tetrahydrocannabinol by Rats." *Pharmacology Biochemistry and Behavior* 11:737–40.

Ueki, S., Fujiwara, M., and Ogawa, N. 1972. "Mouse-Killing Behavior (Muricide) Induced by Δ⁹-Tetrahydrocannabinol in the Rat." *Physiology and Behavior* 9:887–98.

Vaughan, J. G. 1970. *The Structure and Utilization of Oil Seeds.* London: Chapman & Hall.

Walton, R. P. 1938. *Marihuana: America's New Drug Problem.* Philadelphia: J. B. Lippincott.

Wolff, P. O. 1949. *Marihuana in Latin America: The Threat It Constitutes.* Washington, D.C.: Linacre Press.

Yoshimura, H., and Ueki, S. 1981. "Regional Changes in Brain Norepinephrine Content in Relation to Mouse-Killing Behavior by Rats." *Brain Research Bulletin* 7:151–55.

8. FORCED MARCH

Aigner, T. C., and Balster, R. L. 1978. "Choice Behavior in Rhesus Monkeys: Cocaine versus Food." *Science* 201:534–35.

Antonil. 1978. *Mama Coca.* London: Hassle Free Press.

Baber, A. March 1983. "Behind Hollywood's Mirrors." *Playboy:* 120–22, 192–203.

Beals, C. 1934. *Fire on the Andes.* Philadelphia: J. B. Lippincott.

Bedford, J. A., Wilson, M. C., Elsohly, H. N., Elliott, C., Cottam, C., and Turner, C. E. 1981. "The Effects of Cocaine Free Extracts of the Coca Leaf on Food Consumption and Locomotor Activity." *Pharmacology Biochemistry and Behavior* 14:725–28.

Bergman, J., and Johanson, C. E. 1981. "The Effects of Electric Shock on Responding Maintained by Cocaine in Rhesus Monkeys." *Pharmacology Biochemistry and Behavior* 14:423–26.

Bozarth, M. A., and Wise, R. A. 1985. "Toxicity Associated with Long-Term Intravenous Heroin and Cocaine Self-Administration in the Rat." *Journal of the American Medical Association* 254:81–83.

Briand, M. 1913. "Un singe cocainomane." *Société Clinique de Médecine Mentale* 6:380–83.

Burchard, R. E. 1975. "Coca Chewing: A New Perspective." In *Cannabis and Culture,* ed. V. Rubin, 463–84. The Hague: Mouton.

Burczynski, F. J., Boni, R. L., Erickson, J., and Vitti, T. G. 1986. "Effect of *Erythroxylum coca,* Cocaine and Ecgonine Methyl Ester as Dietary Supplements on Energy Metabolism in the Rat." *Journal of Ethnopharmacology* 16:153–66.

Coquero, M. 1977. *The Coca Cultivator's Handbook.* Ukiah, Calif.: L'eaf Press.

Deneau, G., Yanagita, T., and Seevers, M. H. 1969. "Self-Administration of Psychoactive Substances by the Monkey." *Psychopharmacologia* 16:30–48.

Ellinwood, E. H., and Kilbey, M. M., eds. 1977. *Cocaine and Other Stimulants.* New York: Plenum Press.

Foltin, R. W., Preston, K. L., Wagner, G. C., and Schuster, C. R. 1981. "The Aversive Stimulus Properties of Repeated Infusions of Cocaine." *Pharmacology Biochemistry and Behavior* 15:71–74.

Freeman R. W., and Harbison, R. D. 1981. "Hepatic Periportal Necrosis Induced by Chronic Administration of Cocaine." *Biochemical Pharmacology* 30:777–83.

Griffiths, R. R., Brady, J. V., and Snell, J. D. 1978. "Progressive Ratio Performance Maintained by Drug Infusions: Comparison of Cocaine, Diethylproprion, Chlorphentermine and Fenfluramine." *Psychopharmacology* 56:5–13.

Griffiths, R. R., Findley, J. D., Brady, J. V., Dolan-Gutcher, K., and Robinson, W. W. 1975. "Comparison of Progressive-Ratio Performance Maintained by Cocaine, Methylphenidate and Secobarbital." *Psychopharmacologia* 43:81–83.

Grove, R. N., and Schuster, C. R. 1974. "Suppression of Cocaine Self-Administration by Extinction and Punishment." *Pharmacology Biochemistry and Behavior* 2:199–208.

Hendrikson, R. 1976. *The Great American Chewing Gum Book*. New York: Stein & Day.

Heston, L. L., and Heston, R. 1979. *The Medical Casebook of Adolf Hitler*. New York: Stein & Day.

Huntford, R. 1986. *Shackleton*. New York: Atheneum.

Johanson, C. E. 1977. "The Effects of Electric Shock on Responding Maintained by Cocaine Injections in a Choice Procedure in the Rhesus Monkey." *Psychopharmacology* 53:277–82.

———. 1984. "Assessment of the Dependence Potential of Cocaine in Animals." In *Cocaine: Pharmacology, Effects, and Treatment of Abuse*, ed. J. Grabowski. NIDA Research Monograph 50, 54–71. Washington, D.C.: U.S. Government Printing Office.

———, Balster, R. L., and Bonese, K. 1976. "Self-Administration of Psychomotor Stimulant Drugs: The Effects of Unlimited Access." *Pharmacology Biochemistry and Behavior* 4:45–51.

Johnson, C. A., Brewster, J. M., and Jarvik, M. E. 1976. "Cocaine Self-Administration in Monkeys by Chewing and Smoking." *Pharmacology Biochemistry and Behavior* 4:461–67.

Kelleher, R. T., and Goldberg, S. R. 1977. "Fixed-Interval Responding Under Second-Order Schedules of Food Presentation or Cocaine Injection." *Journal of the Experimental Analysis of Behavior* 28:221–31.

Kennedy, J. 1985. *Coca Exotica: The Illustrated Story of Cocaine*. Cranbury, N.J.: Associated University Presses.

Lucchitta, B. K., and Ferguson, H. M. 1986. "Antarctica: Measuring Glacier Velocity from Satellite Images." *Science* 234:1105–08.

Markham, C. R. 1862. *Travels in Peru and India*. London: John Murray.

Mitchell, G. 1972. "Looking Behavior in the Rhesus Monkeys." *Journal of Phenomenological Psychology* 3:53–67.

Mortimer, W. G. 1901. *Peru: History of Coca: "The Divine Plant" of the Incas*. New York: J. H. Vail & Company.

"Names in the News." 30 July 1983. *Los Angeles Times*, part 3, 4.

Pacini, D., and Franquemont, C., eds. 1986. *Coca and Cocaine: Effects on People and Policy in Latin America*. Cambridge, Mass.: Cultural Survival.

Pitigrilli [Dino Segre]. [1921] 1974. *Cocaine*. San Francisco: And/Or Press.

Plowman, T. 1984. "The Ethnobotany of Coca (Erythroxylum spp., Erythroxylaceae)." *Advances in Economic Botany* 1:62–111.

——— and Weil, A. T. 1979. "Coca Pests and Pesticides." *Journal of Ethnopharmacology* 1:263–78.

Poma, H. [1567–1615] 1978. *Letter to a King.* Trans. C. Dilke. New York: E. P. Dutton.

Post, R. M., Lockfeld, A., Squillace, K. M., and Contel, N. R. 1981. "Drug-Environment Interaction: Context Dependency of Cocaine-Induced Behavioral Sensitization." *Life Sciences* 28:755–60.

Schmidt, J. E. 1959. *Narcotics: Lingo and Lore.* Springfield, Ill.: Charles C Thomas.

Shuster, L., Quimby, F., Bates, A., and Thompson, M. L. 1977. "Liver Damage from Cocaine in Mice." *Life Sciences* 20:1035–42.

Siegel, R. K. 1982. "Cocaine and Sexual Dysfunction: The Curse of Mama Coca." *Journal of Psychoactive Drugs* 14:71–74.

———. 1982. "Cocaine Smoking." *Journal of Psychoactive Drugs* 14(4).

——— and Jarvik, M. E. 1980. "Self-Regulation of Coca-Chewing and Cocaine-Smoking by Monkeys." In *Cocaine 1980,* ed. F. R. Jeri, 1–10. Lima, Peru: Pacific Press.

Tatum, A. L., and Seevers, M. H. 1929. "Experimental Cocaine Addiction." *Journal of Pharmacology and Experimental Therapeutics* 36:401–10.

Thomsen, C. E. 1974. "Eye Contact by Non-Human Primates Toward a Human Observer." *Animal Behaviour* 22:144–49.

Wilson, M. C., Hitomi, M., and Schuster, C. R. 1971. "Self-Administration of Psychomotor Stimulants as a Function of Unit Dosage." *Psychopharmacologia* 22:271–81.

Woods, J. 1977. "Behavioral Effects of Cocaine in Animals." In *Cocaine: 1977,* ed. R. C. Petersen and R. C. Stillman. NIDA Research Monograph 13, 63–95. DHEW Publication no. (ADM) 77–741. Washington, D.C.: U.S. Government Printing Office.

Woolverton, W. L., and Johanson, C. E. 1984. "Preference in Rhesus Monkeys Given a Choice Between Cocaine and *d,l*-Cathinone." *Journal of the Experimental Analysis of Behavior* 41:35–43.

Yanagita, T. 1973. "An Experimental Framework for Evaluation of Dependence Liability in Various Types of Drugs in Monkeys." *Bulletin on Narcotics* 25:57–64.

9. A BEVY OF BEASTS

Bernston, G. C., Beattie, M.S., and Walker, J. M. 1976. "Effects of Nicotine and Muscarinic Compounds on Biting Attack in the Cat." *Pharmacology Biochemistry and Behavior* 3:235–39.

Borgesová, M., Kadlecová, O., and Kršiak, M. 14 January 1971. "Behaviour of Untreated Mice Towards Alcohol- or Chlordiazepoxide-Treated Partners." Paper presented at 13th Annual Psychopharmacological Conference, Jesenik, Czechoslovakia.

Brower, K. J., and Siegel, R. K. 1977. "Hallucinogen-Induced Behaviors of Free-Moving Chimpanzees." *Bulletin of the Psychonomic Society* 9:287–90.

Burgess, J. W., Witt, P. N., Phoebus, E., and Weisbard, C. 1980. "The Spacing of Rhesus Monkey Troops Changes When a Few Group Members Receive Δ9THC or D-amphetamine." *Pharmacology Biochemistry and Behavior* 13:121–24.

Calkins, A. 1871. Opium and the Opium Appetite. Philadelphia: J. B. Lippincott.

Callear, J. F. F., and Van Gestel, J. F. E. 1971. "An Analysis of the Results of Field Experiments in Pigs in the UK and Ireland with the Sedative Neuroleptic Azaperone." *Veterinary Record* 89:453–58.

Chapman, L. F., Sassenrath, E. N., and Goo, G. P. 1979. "Social Behavior of Rhesus Monkeys Chronically Exposed to Moderate Amounts of Delta-9-Tetrahydrocannabinol." In *Marihuana Biological Effects*, ed. G. G. Nahas and W. D. M. Paton, 693–712. Oxford: Pergamon Press.

Chessick, R. D., Knonholm, J., Beck, M., and Maier, G. 1964. "Effect of Pretreatment with Tryptamine, Tryptophan and DOPA on LSD Reaction in Tropical Fish." *Psychopharmacologia* 5:390–92.

Cohen, H. 1972. *The Amphetamine Manifesto*. New York: Olympia Press.

Cutler, M. G., and Mackintosh, J. H. 1984. "Cannabis and Delta-9-Tetrahydrocannabinol: Effects on Elements of Social Behaviour in Mice." *Neuropharmacology* 23:1091–97.

————, Mackintosh, J. H., and Chance, M. R. A. 1975. "Behavioural Changes in Laboratory Mice During Cannabis Feeding and Withdrawal." *Psychopharmacologia* 44:173–77.

Ellinwood, E. H., and Duarte-Escalante, O. 1972. "Chronic Methamphetamine Intoxication in Three Species of Experimental Animals." In *Current Concepts on Amphetamine Abuse*, ed. E. H. Ellinwood and S. Cohen, 59–68. DHEW Publication no. (HSM) 72–9085. Washington, D.C.: Superintendent of Documents, U.S. Government Printing Office.

———— and Kilbey, M. M. 1975. "Amphetamine Stereotypy: The Influence of Environmental Factors and Prepotent Behavioral Patterns on Its Topography and Development." *Biological Psychiatry* 10:3–16.

Elliot, M. L., and Sbordone, R. J. 1982. "Drug-Induced Ataxia in Opponents Elicits 'Pathological' Fighting in Undrugged Rats Exposed to Footshock." *Pharmacology Biochemistry and Behavior* 16:63–66.

Elliot, O. 1971. "Adverse Reactions to Lysergic Acid Diethylamide in Animals: Nest-Building and General Maternal Care in Rats." *The Philippine Journal of Science* 100:267–88.

Ellison, G. D., and Potthoff, A. D. 1983. "Social Models of Drinking Behavior in Animals: The Importance of Individual Differences." In *Recent Developments in Alcoholism*, ed. M. Galanter, vol. 2, 17–36. New York: Plenum Press.

Figler, M. H., and Peeke, H. V. S. 1978. "Alcohol and the Prior Residence Effect in Male Convict Cichlids (Cichlasoma nigrofasciatum)." *Aggressive Behavior* 4:125-32.

Floru, L., Ishay, J., and Gitter, S. 1969. "The Influence of Psychotropic Substances on Hornet Behaviour in Colonies of *Vespa orientalis* F (Hymenoptera)." *Psychopharmacologia* 14:323–41.

Giono-Barber, P., Paris, M., Bertuletti, G., and Giono-Barber, H. 1974. "L'action du cannabis sur le comportement de domination du singe Cynocéphale [Cannabis effects on dominance behavior in the Cynocéphale monkey]." *Journal of Pharmacology* 5:591–602.

Gritz, E. R., and Jarvik, M. E. 1975. "Psychoactive Drugs and Social Behavior." In *Psychoactive Drugs and Social Judgment: Theory and Research*, ed. K. R. Hammond and C. R. B. Joyce, 7–45. New York: John Wiley.

Haber, S., Barchas, P. R., and Barchas, J. D. 1977. "Effects of Amphetamine on Social Behaviors of Rhesus Macaques: An Animal Model of Paranoia." In *Animal Models in Psychiatry and Neurology*, ed. I. Hanin and E. Usdin, 107–14. New York: Pergamon Press.

Heinze, W. J., Schlemmer, R. F., Tyler, C. B., and Davis, J. M. 1983. "The Comparative Behavioral Effects of N,N-dimethyltryptamine and N,N-diethyltryptamine in Primate Dyads." *Biological Psychiatry* 18:829–36.

Kršiak, M., Borgesová, M., and Kadlecová, O. 10 January 1971. "LSD-accentuated Individual Type of Social Behaviour in Mice." Paper presented at 6th Annual Seminar on Therapeutic Use of Psychodysleptics, Jesenik, Czechoslovakia.

———, Sulcová, A., Tomašíková, Z., Dlohožková, N., Kosař, E., and Mašek, K. 1981. "Drug Effects on Attack, Defense and Escape in Mice." *Pharmacology Biochemistry and Behavior* 14 (Supplement 1):47–52.

———, Sulcová, A., Donat, P., Tomašíková, Z., Dlohožková, N., Kosař, E., and Mašek, K. 1984. "Can Social and Agonistic Interactions Be Used to Detect Anxiolytic Activity of Drugs?" *Progress in Clinical and Biological Research* 167:93–114.

Martin, C. 1978. *Keepers of the Game.* Berkeley: University of California Press.

Masur, J., Martz, R. M. W., and Carlini, E. A. 1972. "The Behavior of Worker and Non-Worker Rats Under the Influence of (—) Δ^9-trans-Tetrahydrocannabinol, Chlorpromazine and Amylobarbitone." *Psychopharmacologia* 25:57–68.

Miczek, K. A., 1983. *Ethopharmacology: Primate Models of Neuropsychiatric Disorders.* New York: Alan R. Liss.

———, and Yoshimura, H. 1982. "Disruption of Primate Social Behavior by d-Amphetamine and Cocaine: Differential Antagonism by Antipsychotics." *Psychopharmacology* 76:163–71.

Mitsuda, H., and Fukuda, T., eds. 1974. *Biological Mechanisms of Schizophrenia and Schizophrenia-like Psychoses.* Tokyo: Igaku Shoin.

Reay, M. 1965. "Mushrooms and Collective Hysteria." *Australian Territories* 5:18–28.

Sassenrath, E. N., and Chapman, L. F. 1975. "Tetrahydrocannabinol-Induced Manifestations of the 'Marihuana Syndrome' in Group-Living Macaques." *Federation Proceedings* 34:1666–70.

Schenk, S., LaCelle, G., Gorman, K., and Amit, Z. 1987. "Cocaine Self-Administration in Rats Influenced by Environmental Conditions: Implications for the Etiology of Drug Abuse." *Neuroscience Letters* 81:227–31.

Schiørring, E. 1977. "Changes in Individual and Social Behavior Induced by Amphetamine and Related Compounds in Monkeys and Man." In *Cocaine and Other Stimulants,* ed. E. H. Ellinwood and M. M. Kilbey, 481–522. New York: Plenum Press.

Sidman, R. L., Green, M. C., and Appel, S. H. 1965. *Catalog of the Neurological Mutants of the Mouse.* Cambridge: Harvard University Press.

Sieber, B. 1982. "Influence of Hashish Extract on the Social Behaviour of Encountering Male Baboons, *(Papio c. anubis)." Pharmacology Biochemistry and Behavior* 17:209–16.

———, Frischknecht, H.-R., and Waser, P. G. 1980. "Behavioral Effects of Hashish in Mice: I: Social Interactions and Nest-Building Behavior of Males." *Psychopharmacology* 70:149–54.

———. 1980. "Behavioral Effects of Hashish in Mice: III: Social Interactions Between Two Residents and an Intruder Male." *Psychopharmacology* 70:273–78.

———. 1981. "Behavioral Effects of Hashish in Mice: IV: Social Dominance, Food Dominance, and Sexual Behavior Within a Group of Males." *Psychopharmacology* 73:142–46.

———. 1982. "Behavioural Effects of Hashish in Mice in Comparison with Other Psychoactive Drugs." *General Pharmacology* 13:315–20.

Siegel, R. K. 1971. "Studies of Hallucinogens in Fish, Birds, Mice and Men: The Behavior of 'Psychedelic' Populations." In *Advances in Neuro-Psychopharmacology*, ed. O. Vinař, Z. Votava, and P. B. Bradley, 311–18. Amsterdam: North-Holland Publishing Company.

———. 1978. "Hallucinogens and Attentional Dysfunction: A Model of Hallucinations, Illusions and Reality-testing." In *Psychopharmacology of Hallucinogens*, ed. R. Willette and R. Stillman, 268–96. New York: Pergamon Press.

———, Brewster, J. M., and Jarvik, M. E. 1974. "An Observational Study of Hallucinogen-Induced Behavior in Unrestrained *Macaca mulatta*." *Psychopharmacologia* 40:211–23.

——— and Poole, J. 1969. "Psychedelic-Induced Social Behavior in Mice: A Preliminary Report." *Psychological Reports* 25:704–06.

Silver, G., ed. 1979. *The Dope Chronicles: 1850–1950*. San Francisco: Harper & Row.

Stewart, W. J. 1976. "Effects of Undrugged Partners on Scopolamine-Induced Changes in Activity and Sociability." *Psychopharmacology Communications* 2:131–39.

Swanberg, W. A. 1961. *Citizen Hearst*. New York: Charles Scribner's Sons.

Van Der Poel, A. M., and Remmelts, M. 1971. "The Effect of Anticholinergics on the Behavior of the Rat in a Solitary and in a Social Situation." *Archives Internationales de Pharmacodynamie et de Thérapie* 189:394–96.

Van Ree, J. M., Niesink, R. J., and Nir, I. 1984. "Delta 1-Tetrahydrocannabinol but not Cannabidiol Reduces Contact and Aggressive Behavior of Rats Tested in Dyadic Encounters." *Psychopharmacology* 84:561–65.

Varlet, T. 1930. *Aux paradis du hachich*. Paris: Société Française d'Éditions Littéraires et Techniques.

Weckowicz, T. 1967. "Animal Studies of Hallucinogenic Drugs." In A. Hoffer and H. Osmond, *The Hallucinogens*, 555–94. New York: Academic Press.

Yoshimura, H., and Ogawa, N. 1984. [Pharmaco-ethological analysis of agonistic behavior between resident and intruder mice: Effects of psychotropic drugs.] *Folia Pharmacologica Japonica* 84:221–28.

10. THE FOURTH DRIVE

Allen, T. E., and Agus, B. 1968. "Hyperventilation Leading to Hallucinations." *American Journal of Psychiatry* 125:632–37

Andersen, K. 11 April 1983. "Crashing on Cocaine." *Time*: 22–31.

Bejerot, N. 1972. *Addiction: An Artificially Induced Drive*. Springfield, Ill.: Charles C. Thomas.

Blum, R. H., and Associates. 1969. *Society and Drugs*. San Francisco: Jossey-Bass.

Clouet, D. H., ed. 1986. *Phencyclidine: An Update*. National Institute on Drug Abuse Research Monograph 64. DHHS Publication no. (ADM) 86–1443. Washington, D.C.: Superintendent of Documents, U.S. Government Printing Office.

Domino, E. F., ed. 1981. *PCP (Phencyclidine): Historical and Current Perspectives*. Ann Arbor, Mich.: NPP Books.

Erickson, P. G., Adlaf, E. M., Murray, G. F., and Smart, R. G. 1987. *The Steel Drug: Cocaine in Perspective*. Lexington, Mass.: D.C. Heath.

Galanter, M. 1976. "The 'Intoxication State of Consciousness': A Model for Alcohol and Drug Abuse." *American Journal of Psychiatry* 133:635–40.

Griffen, J. 1825. *Chemical Recreations*. Glasgow: Richard Griffin.

James, W. [1896] 1915. *The Will to Believe and Other Essays in Popular Philosophy.* New York: Longmans, Green & Co.

Jones, E. 1961. *The Life and Work of Sigmund Freud.* vol. 1. New York: Basic Books.

Llosa, T., and Hinojosa, H. 6 May 1982. "Cingulectomia en la farmaco-dependencia a la pasta básica de cocaina." Paper presented to the Peruvian Psychiatric Association, Lima.

Malcolm, A. I. 1971. *The Pursuit of Intoxication.* Toronto: Addiction Research Foundation Books.

McKim, W. A. 1977. "Childhood Consciousness Altering Behavior and Adult Drug Taking." *Journal of Psychedelic Drugs* 9:159–61.

Mello, N. K. 1978. "Control of Drug Self-Administration: The Role of Aversive Consequences." In *Phencyclidine,* ed. H. C. Petersen and R. C. Stillman, 289–308. National Institute on Drug Abuse Research Monograph 21. DHEW Publication no. (ADM) 78–728. Washington, D.C.: Superintendent of Documents, U.S. Government Printing Office.

Meyers, A. C. 1902. *Eight Years in Cocaine Hell.* Chicago: Press of the St. Luke Society.

Midgley, M. 1978. *Beast and Man: The Roots of Human Nature.* Ithaca, N.Y.: Cornell University Press.

Money, K. E. 1970. "Motion Sickness." *Physiological Reviews* 50:1–39.

Morgan, J. P., and Kagan, D. 1980. "The Dusting of America: The Image of Phencyclidine (PCP) in the Popular Media." *Journal of Psychedelic Drugs* 12:195–204.

Oglesby, E. W., Faber, Samuel J., and Faber, Stuart J. 1982. *Angel Dust: What Everyone Should Know About PCP.* Los Angeles: Lega-Books.

Prince, R., ed. 1968. *Trance and Possession States.* Montreal: R. M. Bucke Memorial Society.

Ram Dass [Alpert, Richard]. 1974. *The Only Dance There Is.* Garden City, N.Y.: Anchor Press/Doubleday.

Sharpe, M. H. 1969. *Living in Space: The Astronaut and His Environment.* Garden City, N.Y.: Doubleday & Company.

Sheldin, M., and Wallechinsky, D. 1973. *Laughing Gas.* San Francisco: And/Or Press.

Siegel, R. K. 1977. "Cocaine: Recreational Use and Intoxication." In *Cocaine 1977,* ed. R. C. Petersen and R. C. Stillman, 119–36. National Institute on Drug Abuse Research Monograph 13. DHEW Publication no. (ADM) 77–741. Washington, D.C.: Superintendent of Documents, U.S. Government Printing Office.

————. 1978. "Phencyclidine and Ketamine Intoxication: A Study of Four Populations of Recreational Users." In *Phencyclidine,* ed. R. C. Petersen and R. C. Stiliman, 272–88. National Institute on Drug Abuse Research Monograph 21. DHEW Publication no. (ADM) 78–728. Washington, D.C.: Superintendent of Documents, U.S. Government Printing Office.

————. 1979–80. "Dizziness as an Altered State of Consciousness." *Journal of Altered States of Consciousness* 5:87–107.

————. 1985. "New Patterns of Cocaine Use: Changing Doses and Routes." In *Cocaine Use in America: Epidemiological and Clinical Perspectives,* ed. N. J. Kozel and E. H. Adams, 204–20. National Institute on Drug Abuse Research Monograph 61. DHHS Publication no. (ADM) 85–1414. Washington, D.C.: Superintendent of Documents, U.S. Government Printing Office.

————. 1985. "Treatment of Cocaine Abuse: Historical and Contemporary Perspectives." *Journal of Psychoactive Drugs* 17:1–9.

————. 1986. "MDMA: Nonmedical Use and Intoxication." *Journal of Psychoactive Drugs* 18:349–54.

Siegel, S. 1983. "Classical Conditioning, Drug Tolerance, and Drug Dependence." In *Research Advances in Alcohol and Drug Problems,* ed. R. G. Smart, F. B. Glaser, Y. Israel, H. Kalant, R. E. Popham, and W. Schmidt, vol. 7, 207–46. New York: Plenum Press.

Singer, J. L. 1973. *The Child's World of Make-Believe.* New York: Academic Press.

Smith, P. B. 1972. Chemical Glimpses of Paradise. Springfield, Ill.: Charles C. Thomas.

Smith, W. D. A. 1982. *Under the Influence: A History of Nitrous Oxide and Oxygen Anaesthesia.* Park Ridge, Ill.: The Wood Library-Museum of Anesthesiology.

Solomon, R. L. 1980. "The Opponent-Process Theory of Acquired Motivation." American Psychologist 35:691–712.

Spector, M., ed. 1967. *Dizziness and Vertigo: Diagnosis and Treatment.* New York: Grune & Stratton.

Szasz, T. 1974. *Ceremonial Chemistry.* Garden City, N.Y.: Anchor Press/ Doubleday & Company.

Tart, C. T. 1971. *On Being Stoned.* Palo Alto, Calif.: Science and Behavior Books.

Treisman, M. 1977. "Motion Sickness: An Evolutionary Hypothesis." *Science* 197:493–95.

Weil, A. 1972. *The Natural Mind.* Boston: Houghton Mifflin Company.

11. FIRE IN THE BRAIN

Adamson, S., ed. 1985. *Through the Gateway of the Heart.* San Francisco: Four Trees Publications.

Barter, J. T., and Reite, M. 1969. "Crime and LSD: The Insanity Plea." *American Journal of Psychiatry* 126:113–19.

Fauman, M. A., and Fauman, B. J. 1979. "Violence Associated with Phencyclidine Abuse." *American Journal of Psychiatry* 136:1584–86.

Hanson, B., Beschner, G., Walters, J. M., and Bovelle, E., eds. 1985. *Life with Heroin: Voices from the Inner City.* Lexington, Mass.: D.C. Heath.

Oglesby, E. W., Faber, Samuel J., and Faber, Stuart J. 1982. *Angel Dust: What Everyone Should Know About PCP.* Los Angeles: Lega-Books.

Pernanen, K. 1976. "Alcohol and Crimes of Violence." In *Social Aspects of Alcoholism,* ed. B. Kissin and H. Begleiter, 351–444. New York: Plenum Press.

Pinsky, L. S., Osborne, W. Z., Bailey, J V, Benson, R. E., and Thompson, L. F. 1974. "Light Flashes Observed by Astronauts on Apollo 11 Through Apollo 17." *Science* 183:957–59.

Pinsky, L. S., Osborne, W. Z., Hoffman, R. A., and Bailey, J. V. 1975. "Light Flashes Observed by Astronauts on Skylab 4." *Science* 188:928–30.

Reich, B., and Hepps, R. B. 1972. "Homicide During a Psychosis Induced by LSD." *Journal of the American Medical Association* 219:869–71.

Siegel, R. K. 1978. "Cocaine Hallucinations." *American Journal of Psychiatry* 135:309–14.

————. 1979. "The Experimental Analysis and Modification of Hallucinations." In *Modification of Pathological Behavior,* ed. R. S. Davidson, 69–108. New York: Gardner Press.

————. 1980. "PCP and Violent Crime: The People vs. Peace." *Journal of Psychedelic Drugs* 12:317–30.

——— and Jarvik, M. E. 1975. "Drug-Induced Hallucinations in Animals and Man." In *Hallucinations: Behavior, Experience and Theory,* ed. R. K. Siegel and L. J. West, 81–161. New York: John Wiley.

12. STAR-SPANGLED POWDERS

Abel, E. L. 1980. *Marihuana: The First Twelve Thousand Years.* New York: Plenum Press.

American Medical Association. 1911. *Nostrums and Quackery.* Chicago: American Medical Association.

Anderson, P. 1981. *High in America.* New York: The Viking Press.

Avorn, J. L. 1980. "The Role of Cocaine in Treating Intractable Pain in Terminal Disease." In *Cocaine 1980,* ed. F. R. Jeri, 227–35. Lima, Peru: Pacific Press.

Back, J. B. 1971. *The Pleasures of Cigar Smoking.* New York: Rutledge Books.

Bain, J. 1903. *Tobacco Leaves.* Boston: H. M. Caldwell Co.

Baron, S. 1962. *Brewed in America: A History of Beer and Ale in the United States.* Boston: Little, Brown & Company.

Boller, P. F. 1981. *Presidential Anecdotes.* New York: Oxford University Press.

———. 1984. *Presidential Campaigns.* New York: Oxford University Press.

Boyce, S. S. 1912. *Hemp.* New York: Orange Judd Company.

Brecker, E. M. 1972. *Licit and Illicit Drugs.* Boston: Little, Brown & Company.

Breen, T. H. 1985. *Tobacco Culture: The Mentality of the Great Tidewater Planters on the Eve of Revolution.* Princeton, N.J.: Princeton University Press.

Brown, W. H. 1925. *Tobacco Under the Searchlight.* Cincinnati: Standard Publishing Co.

Burnett's Floral Handbook. 1878. Boston: Joseph Burnett & Co.

Byck, R., ed. 1974. *Cocaine Papers by Sigmund Freud.* New York: Stonehill.

Cannon, P., and Brooks, P. 1968. *The Presidents' Cookbook.* New York: Funk & Wagnalls Company.

Church, G. J., and Thomas, E. 22 July 1985. "Anxiety over an Ailing President." *Time:* 16–20, 23.

Clark, L. P. 1933. *Lincoln: A Psycho-Biography.* New York: Charles Scribner's Sons.

Courtwright, D. T. 1982. *Dark Paradise: Opiate Addiction in America Before 1940.* Cambridge: Harvard University Press.

Curtis, T., and Cantor, R. 1968. "The Maxillofacial Rehabilitation of President Grover Cleveland and Dr. Sigmund Freud," *Journal of the American Dental Association* 76:359–61.

Daniel, P. 1985. *Breaking the Land: The Transformation of Cotton, Tobacco, and Rice Cultures Since 1880.* Urbana and Chicago: University of Illinois Press.

Davidoff, Z. 1967. *The Connoisseur's Book of the Cigar.* New York: McGraw-Hill.

Dean, A. 1850. *Principles of Medical Jurisprudence: Designed for the Professions of Law and Medicine.* New York: Banks, Gould & Co.

Donaldson, N., and Donaldson, B. 1980. *How Did They Die?* New York: St. Martin's Press.

Everett, M. 1901. *The Life of William McKinley and Complete Story of His Assassination.* Published by author.

Ford, H. 1916. *The Case Against the Little White Slaver.* vols. 1–4. Detroit: Henry Ford.

Frazier, J. 1974. *The Marijuana Farmers: Hemp Cults and Cultures.* New Orleans: Solar Age Press.

Gehman, J. M. 1943. *Smoke over America*. East Aurora, N.Y.: Roycrofters.

Gilbert, R. M. 1976. "Tea Toxicity." *Journal of the American Medical Association* 236:1452.

Goldhurst, R. 1975. *Many Are the Hearts: The Agony and the Triumph of Ulysses S. Grant*. New York: Reader's Digest Press.

Gray, L. C. 1958. *History of Agriculture in the Southern United States to 1860*. vol. 1. Gloucester, Mass.: Peter Smith.

Greden, J. F. 1976. "The Tea Controversy in Colonial America." *Journal of the American Medical Association* 236:63–66.

Hammond, W. A. November 1887. "Coca: Its Preparations and Their Therapeutic Qualities, with Some Remarks on the So-called 'Cocaine Habit.'" *Transactions of the Medical Society of Virginia:* 212–26.

Heimann, R. K. 1960. *Tobacco and Americans*. New York: McGraw-Hill.

Halfand, W. H. 1980. "Vin Mariani." *Pharmacy in History* 22:11–19.

Kurzeja, W. S. 1984. *The Presidential Quotient*. Chicago: Chicago Review Press.

Lasagna, L. January 1982. "Grant's Last Stand." *The Sciences:* 6.

Leary, T. 1983. *Flashbacks*. Los Angeles: J. P. Tarcher.

Lee, M. A., and Shlain, B. 1985. *Acid Dreams: The CIA, LSD and the Sixties Rebellion*. New York: Grove Press.

Lyons, A. B. 1899. *Hand Book of Practical Assaying of Drugs and Galenicals*. Detroit: Nelson, Baker & Co.

[Mariani, A.]. 1886. *Coca Erythroxylon: Its Uses in the Treatment of Disease*. 4th ed. New York: Mariani & Co.

Marx, R. 1960. *The Health of the Presidents*. New York: G. P. Putnam's Sons.

Mayor's Committee on Marihuana. 1944. *The Marihuana Problem in the City of New York*. Lancaster, Pa.: Jaques Cattell Press.

"McKinley: Président des Etats-Unis." 1899. A. LaLauze, L. Dautrey, W. Barbotin, and E. Van Muyden, *Figures Contemporaines: Tirées de l'album Mariani*, vol. 4. Paris: Librairie Henri Floury.

Miller, H. R. 1973. *Scandals in the Highest Office*. New York: Random House.

Morgan, H. W. 1974. *Yesterday's Addicts: American Society and Drug Abuse, 1865–1920*. Norman: University of Oklahoma Press.

Moses, J. B., and Cross, W. 1980. *Presidential Courage*. New York: W. W. Norton.

Musto, D. F. 1973. *The American Disease: Origins of Narcotic Control*. New Haven and London: Yale University Press.

Neider, C., ed. 1982. *The Selected Letters of Mark Twain*. New York: Harper & Row.

Nelson, H. 15 July 1985. "Rare Morphine Technique Speeds Reagan's Progress." *Los Angeles Times:* 1, 5.

Pratt, H. E. 1943. *The Personal Finances of Abraham Lincoln*. Springfield, Ill.: Abraham Lincoln Association.

Rienow, R., and Rienow, L. T. 1965. *Of Snuff, Sin and the Senate*. Chicago: Follett Publishing Company.

Rorabaugh, W. J. 1979. *The Alcoholic Republic: An American Tradition*. New York: Oxford University Press.

Roueché, B. 1963. *Curiosities of Medicine: An Assembly of Medical Diversion 1552–1962*. Boston: Little, Brown & Company.

Sandburg, C. 1954. *Abraham Lincoln: The Prairie Years and the War Years*. New York: Harcourt, Brace.

Shaw, E. R., ed. 1910. *The Curse of Drink or, Stories of Hell's Commerce*. Published by author.

Shepherd, J. 1975. *The Adams Chronicles*. Boston: Little, Brown & Company.

Shutes, M. H. 1933. *Lincoln and the Doctors: A Medical Narrative of the Life of Abraham Lincoln*. New York: Pioneer Press.

Sobel, R. 1978. *They Satisfy: The Cigarette in American Life*. Garden City, N.Y.: Anchor Books/Doubleday.

Swanberg, W. A. 1961. *Citizen Hearst*. New York: Charles Scribner's Sons.

Taylor, A. H. 1969. *American Diplomacy and the Narcotics Traffic, 1900–1939*. Durham, N.C.: Duke University Press.

Townsend, W. H. 1934. *Lincoln and Liquor*. New York: Press of the Pioneers.

Twain, M. [1910] 1973. "The Turning Point of My Life." In *The Works of Mark Twain: What Is Man? and Other Philosophical Writings*, ed. P. Baender, 455–64. Berkeley: University of California Press.

Wagner, S. 1971. *Cigarette Country: Tobacco in American History and Politics*. New York: Praeger Publishers.

Younger, W. 1966. *Gods, Men, and Wine*. Cleveland: Wine and Food Society/World Publishing Company.

Zall, P. M., ed. 1982. *Abe Lincoln Laughing*. Berkeley: University of California Press.

13. WAR ON DRUGS

Abel, E. L. 1980. *Marihuana: The First Twelve Thousand Years*. New York: Plenum Press.

"Angry Moms Kill Cocaine Peddler." 23 September 1986. *Weekly World News*: 1.

Bigelow, G. E., Bickel, W. E., Roache, J. D., Liebson, I. A., and Nowowieski, P. May 1985. "Identifying Types of Drug Intoxication: Laboratory Evaluation of a Subject-Examination Procedure." National Highway Traffic Safety Administration Report no. DOT-HS 806–753. Springfield, Va.: National Technical Information Service.

Brown, R. E., and Associates. 1968. *The Psychedelic Guide to Preparation of the Eucharist*. Austin, Tex.: Linga Sharira Incense Co.

Bruun, K., Pan, L., and Rexed, I. 1975. *The Gentlemen's Club: International Control of Drugs and Alcohol*. Chicago: University of Chicago Press.

Bureau of International Narcotics Matters, Department of State. 1 February 1985. *International Narcotics Control Strategy Report*. vol. 1.

Cervantes, J. 1983. *Indoor Marijuana Horticulture*. Portland, Ore.: Interport U.S.A.

Chapple, S. 1984. *Outlaws in Babylon*. New York: Pocket Books.

Cone, E. J., and Johnson, R. E. 1986. "Contact Highs and Urinary Cannabinoid Excretion After Passive Exposure to Marijuana Smoke." *Clinical Pharmacology & Therapeutics* 40:247–56.

Conot, R. 12 April 1987. "L.A. Gangs: Rock and a Hard Place." *Los Angeles Times*, part 5, 3, 6.

Cousteau, J., producer. 1985. *Snowstorm in the Jungle* (film). Atlanta: WTBS.

Daniels, P. 1983. *How to Grow Marijuana Hydroponically*. Seattle: Sun Magic Publishing.

Darth, C. 1977. *The Whole Drug Manufacturers Catalog*. Manhattan Beach, Calif.: Prophet Press.

Del Olmo, R. 1988. "The Attack on the Supreme Court of Colombia: A Case Study of Guerrilla and Government Violence." *Violence, Aggression, and Terrorism* 2:57–84.

Deutsch, K. 1978. "Paraphernalia." In *High Times Encyclopedia of Recreational Drugs*, 285–95. New York: Stonehill.

Drake, B. 1983. *Marijuana: The Cultivator's Handbook*. Berkeley: Wingbow Books.

Eddy, P., Sabogal, H., and Walden, S. 1988. *Cocaine Wars*. New York: W. W. Norton.

Feral, R. 1984. *How to Rip Off a Drug Dealer*. Boulder, Colo.: Paladin Press.

Frank, M., and Rosenthal, E. 1983. *Marijuana Grower's Guide*. Berkeley: And/Or Press.

Freedberg, S. P. 29 October 1986. "'Clean' Urine Clouds Drug Testing." *Miami Herald:* 1A, 15A.

Freemantle, B. 1986. *The Fix: Inside the World Drug Trade*. New York: Tom Doherty Associates.

Gentile, D. P. 1979. *Cocaine: Legal and Technical Defenses*. Houston: National College of Criminal Defense Lawyers and Public Defenders.

"Georgia Power: A Call a Day Keeps the Pushers at Bay." May 1987. *Drugs in the Workplace:* 1.

Gettman, J. B. 1986. *Marijuana in America—1986*. Washington, D.C.: National Organization for the Reform of Marijuana Laws.

———. September 1988. "The 1987 Crop Report." *High Times:* 23.

Godshaw, G., Koppel, R., and Pancoast, R. 1987. *Anti-Drug Law Enforcement Efforts and Their Impact*. Washington, D.C.: U.S. Government Printing Office.

Gonzales, L. April 1982. "The War on Drugs: A Special Report." *Playboy:* 134–37, 158, 200–16.

———. December 1985. "Why Drug Enforcement Doesn't Work." *Playboy:* 104–108, 238–49.

Goodwin, D. K. 1987. *The Fitzgeralds and the Kennedys: An American Saga*. New York: Simon & Schuster.

Gottlieb, A. 1973. *Basic Drug Manufacture*. Manhattan Beach, Calif.: Twentieth Century Alchemist.

———. 1979. *Legal Highs*. Manhattan Beach, Calif.: Twentieth Century Alchemist.

Greenhaw, W. 1984. *Flying High: Inside Big-Time Drug Smuggling*. New York: Dodd, Mead.

Griswold, W. S. 1972. *The Night the Revolution Began: The Boston Tea Party, 1773*. Brattleboro, Vt.: Stephen Greene Press.

Grubber, H. 1973. *Growing the Hallucinogens*. San Francisco: Twentieth Century Alchemist.

Hager, S. June 1987. "The Sauk City Shooting." *High Times:* 33–37, 64–67, 72.

———. September 1987. "S.S.S.C." *High Times:* 44–51.

Heller, J. D. March 1973. "The Attempt to Prevent Illicit Drug Supply." In *Appendix: Drug Use in America: Problem in Perspective. Vol. 3: The Legal System and Drug Control*. Technical Papers of 2d Report of the National Commission on Marihuana and Drug Abuse, 383–407. Washington, D.C.: U.S. Government Printing Office.

Himmelstein, J. L. 1983. *The Strange Career of Marihuana. Politics and Ideology of Drug Control in America*. Westport, Conn.: Greenwood Press.

"Issue of Using Motorized Battering Ram Comes Before Supreme Court." 8 September 1987. *Drug Enforcement Report* 3:6.

Jeri, F. R. 1984. "Coca-paste Smoking in Some Latin American Countries: A Severe and Unabated Form of Addiction." *Bulletin on Narcotics* 36:15–31.

Kamstra, J. 1974. *Weed: Adventures of a Dope Smuggler*. New York: Harper & Row.

Kaplan, J. 1970. *Marijuana—The New Prohibition*. New York: World Publishing Company.

———. 1983. *The Hardest Drug: Heroin and Public Policy*. Chicago: University of Chicago Press.

Kayo. 1982. *The Sinsemilla Technique.* San Francisco: Last Gasp.

Kearney, M. 1 March 1983. "Gerbils Start Secret Prison Work After Months-long Technical Delay." *The Journal.* 6.

King, R. 1972. *The Drug Hang-up.* New York: W. W. Norton.

Koretzky, S. December 1987. "Drug Abuse in the 80s: 'High Technology.'" *Street Pharmacologist* 12:1–2.

Lande, A. March 1973. "The International Drug Control System." In *Appendix: Drug Use in America: Problem in Perspective.* Vol. 3: *The Legal System and Drug Control.* Technical Papers of the 2d Report of the National Commission on Marihuana and Drug Abuse, 6–132. Washington, D.C.: U.S. Government Printing Office.

Lee, D. 1981. *Cocaine Handbook: An Essential Reference.* Berkeley: And/Or Press.

Leen, J. 22 September 1985. "Pot King's Savvy Finally Fails Him." *Miami Herald:* 1A, 10A.

———. 22 October 1985. "Drug Ring Called Area's Biggest: Alleged Leader Made Scarface His Role Model." *Miami Herald:* 1B–2B.

——— and Gugliotta, G. 5 February 1987. "Colombian Drug Lord Seized." *Miami Herald:* 1A, 4A.

Loccisano, A. 1983. "Combinations for Street Users." *Street Pharmacologist* 6:1, 3–4, 6.

MacDonald, J. M., and Kenndy, J. 1983. *Criminal Investigation of Drug Offenses: The Narc's Manual.* Springfield, Ill.: Charles C. Thomas.

Manuel. 1977. *The Coca Cultivator's Handbook.* Ukiah, Calif.: L'eaf Press.

Marshall, J., Scott, P. D., and Hunter, J. 1987. *The Iran Contra Connection: Secret Teams and Covert Operations in the Reagan Era.* Boston: South Bend Press.

McGraw, C. 4 June 1987. "Mother Held in Killing of Teenage Girl After Dispute Over Drug Use." *Los Angeles Times:* 1, 3.

McNicoll, A. 1983. *Drug Trafficking: A North-South Perspective.* Ottawa: North-South Institute.

Miami Herald Staff. 8–14 February 1987. "The World's Deadliest Criminals: The Medellin Cartel." *Miami Herald:* 1A ff.

Montalbano, W. D. 10 May 1987. "Colombia's Cocaine Boom Goes on Despite Crackdown, Kingpin's Arrest." *Los Angeles Times:* 6.

Mueller, G. O. W., and Adler, F. 1985. *Outlaws of the Ocean.* New York: Hearst Marine Books.

Murray, J. 13 February 1987. "Crack: A Horror That Comes Wrapped Like Candy." *Los Angeles Times,* part 3, 1, 16.

National Organization for the Reform of Marijuana Laws. 1978. *Legal Challenges to the Marijuana Laws.* Washington, D.C.: National Organization for the Reform of Marijuana Laws.

Nimble, J. B. 1986. *The Construction and Operation of Clandestine Drug Laboratories.* Port Townsend, Wash.: Loompanics.

"NORML Says Marijuana Is Number 2 Cash Crop for 1984." 23 January 1985. *Drug Enforcement Report* 1:7.

"O." 1979. *Opium Poppy Cultivation.* Seattle: Real Concepts.

Organized Crime Drug Enforcement Task Force. March 1985. *Annual Report of the Organized Crime Drug Enforcement Task Force Program.* Washington, D.C.: Office of the Attorney General.

"Organized Crime Starts to Move into Marijuana Growing." 23 September 1987. *Drug Enforcement Report* 3:1–3.

Oss, O. T., and Oeric, O. N. 1976. *Psilocybin: Magic Mushroom Grower's Guide: A Handbook for Psilocybin Enthusiasts.* Berkeley: And/Or Press.

Perry, D. C. 1977. "Street Drug Analysis and Drug Use Trends 1969–1975." Part 2. *The PharmChem Newsletter* 6:1–4, 9.

Petersen, J. R. April 1987. "The Social Costs of Drugs." *Playboy:* 41.

"Police Discover Crack in Tablet Form." 2 June 1987. *The Drug Abuse Report* 2:5.

"President Calls Drug Use a Matter of Rock 'n' Ruin." 4 August 1986. *Miami Herald:* 1A.

President's Commission on Organized Crime. 1986. *America's Habit: Drug Abuse, Drug Trafficking, and Organized Crime.* Washington, D.C.: Superintendent of Documents, U.S. Government Printing Office.

Pui-Nin Mo, B., and Way, E. L. 1966. "An Assessment of Inhalation as a Mode of Administration of Heroin by Addicts." *Journal of Pharmacology & Experimental Therapeutics* 154:142–51.

Raphael, R. 1985. *Cash Crop: An American Dream.* Mendocino, Calif.: Ridge Times Press.

Reuter, P. 8 November 1984. "Risks and Prices: The Economics of Drug Enforcement." Paper presented at Annual Conference of the American Society of Criminology, Cincinnati, Ohio.

———. February 1985. "Eternal Hope: America's International Narcotics Efforts." Santa Monica: Rand Corporation.

Rice, J. N. 1980. "A Chronicle of Federal Drug Law Enforcement." *Drug Enforcement* 7:2–65.

Sachs, S. 26 August 1984. "Drug Cash Getting Harder to Launder." *Miami Herald:* 1A, 4A.

Sapienza, F. 1984. "The Look-alike Problem." *Drug Enforcement* 11:25–30.

Select Committee on Narcotics Abuse and Control. 1985. *Annual Report for the Year 1984 of the Select Committee on Narcotics Abuse and Control.* House of Representatives Report 98–1199. Washington, D.C.: U.S. Government Printing Office.

Shannon, E. 1988. *Desperados: Latin Drug Lords, U.S. Lawmen, and the War America Can't Win.* New York: The Viking Press.

Shannon, P. 21 November 1986. "Motel Manager Latest 'Vigilante.'" *Miami Herald:* 1A, 3A.

"Shift in Poppy Seed Imports May Interfere with Urine Tests for Opiates." 1 September 1987. *Substance Abuse Report* 28:5.

Siegel, R. K. 1978. "Forensic Psychopharmacology: The Drug Abuse Expert in Court." *Drug Abuse and Alcoholism Review* 1:1, 13–20.

———. 1980. "Cocaine Substitutes." *New England Journal of Medicine* 302:817–18.

———. 1983. "Cocaine: New Issues for Defense and Prosecution." *Drug Law Report* 1:49–59.

———, Elsohly, M. A., Plowman, T., Rury, P. M., and Jones, R. T. 1986. "Cocaine Found in Herbal Tea." *Journal of the American Medical Association* 255:40.

Smart, R. G. 1976. "Effects of Legal Restraint on the Use of Drugs: A Review of Empirical Studies." *Bulletin on Narcotics* 28:55–65.

Smith, M. V. 1981. *Psychedelic Chemistry.* Mason, Mich.: Loompanics.

Sonnenreich, M. R., Roccograndi, A. J., and Bogomolny, R. L. March 1973. "Commentary on the Federal Controlled Substances Act." In *Appendix: Drug Use in America: Problem in Perspective.* Vol. 3: *The Legal System and Drug Control.* Technical Papers of the 2d Report of the National Commission on Marihuana and Drug Abuse, 169–239. Washington, D.C.: U.S. Government Printing Office.

Stamets, P., and Chilton, J. S. 1983. *The Mushroom Cultivator: A Practical Guide to Growing Mushrooms at Home.* Olympia, Wash.: Agarikon Press.

Stark, R. V. 1976. *Drug Manufacturers Bible.* Beverly Hills: Fifth Level of Consciousness.

Stevens, J., and Gee, R. 1978. *How to Identify and Grow Psilocybin Mushrooms.* Seattle: Sun Magic Publishing.

Stevens, M. 1979. *How to Grow the Finest Marijuana Indoors.* Seattle: Sun Magic Publishing.

Superweed, M. J. 1968. *The Marijuana Consumer's and Dealer's Guide.* San Francisco: Chthon Press.

———. 1969. *Drug Manufacturing for Fun and Profit.* San Francisco: Chthon Press.

Tomb, G. 16 February 1985. "We All Carry 'Drug Money,' Witness Says." *Miami Herald:* 1A.

"'Tough Love' Helps Parents of Drug-Using Children Be Tough." 15 April 1988. *Substance Abuse Report* 19:1–3.

Trager, L. 29 June 1987. "Cocaine Money: It's Almost Everywhere." *San Francisco Examiner:* A1, A11.

Trebach, A. S. 1987. *The Great Drug War.* New York: The Macmillan Company.

Wagman, B. 1 July 1988. "White House Conference Urges Stricter Anti-Drug Policies." *Criminal Justice Newsletter* 19:4–5.

Warner, R. 1986. *Invisible Hand: The Marijuana Business.* New York: William Morrow.

"White House Prescription for Drug Abuse: 'Social Censure' and Arrest." 1 November 1987. *Substance Abuse Report* 18:1–3.

Williams, N. B. 26 December 1986. "Opium-Plagued Thailand Fights New Problem: Pot." *Los Angeles Times:* 1, 12.

Wilson, J. R. 1985. *The Narc Book.* Boulder, Colo.: Paladin Press.

Wisotsky, S. 1983. "Exposing the War on Cocaine: The Futility and Destructiveness of Prohibition." *Wisconsin Law Review* 6:1305–1426.

———. 1986. *Breaking the Impasse in the War on Drugs.* Westport, Conn.: Greenwood Press.

Wynne, R. D., Blasinsky, M., Cook, P., Landry, L. A., and Murphy, S. 1980. *Community and Legal Responses to Drug Paraphernalia.* DHHS Pub. no. (ADM) 80–963. Washington, D.C.: U.S. Government Printing Office.

Zeese, K. B., and Meyers, P. H. 1983. *Ronald Reagan Wars on Drugs.* Washington, D.C.: National Organization for the Reform of Marijuana Laws.

Zimmerman, S. 1984. "A Windfall in Recovered Assets." *Drug Enforcement* 11:31–33.

14. WAKING DREAMS

Balandrin, M. F., Klocke, J. A., Wurtele, E. S., and Bollinger, W. H. 1985. "Natural Plant Chemicals: Sources of Industrial and Medicinal Materials." *Science* 228:1154–60.

Bezold, C., ed. 1983. *Pharmaceuticals in the Year 2000.* Alexandria, Va.: Institute for Alternative Futures.

Bingham, R., and Somers, L. M. 26 June 1981. "The Treatment of Active Rheumatoid Arthritis and Allied Inflammatory Diseases with Esterene." Paper presented at 15th International Congress of Rheumatology, Paris.

Brekhman, I. I., and Dardymov, I. V. 1969. "New Substances of Plant Origin Which Increase Nonspecific Resistance." *Annual Review of Pharmacology* 9:419–30.

"Care to Dance? Elderly Find Cocaine Helps Soothe Arthritis." 8 October 1983. *Arizona Republic.*

Church, G. J. 30 May 1988. "Should Drugs Be Made Legal? Thinking the Unthinkable." *Time.* 12–16, 18–19.

"Coca Tea from Peru Is Being Used in the Treatment of Cocaine Abuse." 9 July 1984. News release. San Francisco: National Addiction Research Foundation.

Efron, D. H., ed. 1967. *Ethnopharmacologic Search for Psychoactive Drugs.* Public Health Service Publication no. 1645. Washington, D.C.: Superintendent of Documents, U.S. Government Printing Office.

"Esterene in the Treatment of Rheumatoid Arthritis." April 1980. *Arthritis News Today* 2:1–5.

Evans, W. O., and Kline, N. S., eds. 1971. *Psychotropic Drugs in the Year 2000.* Springfield, Ill.: Charles C. Thomas.

Fedon, L. 16 January 1986. "Cocaine Scare Clears Tea from Store Shelves." *Centre Daily Times* [State College, Pennsylvania]: B1, B3.

Foldes, M. October 1976. "Does Lettuce Opium Get You Ripped?" *Rush:* 56–58, 66–67.

Fulder, S. 1980. *The Root of Being.* London: Hutchinson.

Grabowski, J. August 1984. "Profiles of Ideal Drugs for Therapeutic and Social Use." Paper presented to the 92nd Annual Convention, American Psychological Association.

Grinspoon, L, and Bakalar, J. B. 1981. "Coca and Cocaine as Medicines: An Historical Review." *Journal of Ethnopharmacology* 3:149–59.

Hiaasen, C. 13 January 1986. "'Cocaine' Tea Had Bitter Taste of Controversy." *Miami Herald:* 1B–2B.

Kaplan, J. 1970. *Marijuana: The New Prohibition.* New York: World Publishing Company.

———. 1983. *The Hardest Drug: Heroin and Public Policy.* Chicago: University of Chicago Press.

Kennedy, J. G. 1987. *The Flower of Paradise.* Dordrecht, Netherlands: D. Reidel Publishing Co.

Kolata, G. 1986. "New Drug Counters Alcohol Intoxication." *Science* 234:1198–99.

Lewis, W. H. 1986. "Ginseng: A Medical Enigma." In *Plants in Indigenous Medicine and Diet: Biobehavioral Approaches,* ed. N. L. Etkin, 290–305. Bedford Hills, N.Y.: Redgrave.

Lindesmith, A. R. 1947. *Opiate Addiction.* Evanston, Ill.: Principia Press.

Maloff, D., Becker, H. S., Fonaroff, A., and Rodin, J. 1982. "Informal Social Controls and Their Influence on Substance Use." In *Control Over Intoxicant Use,* ed. N. E. Zinberg and W. M. Harding, 53–76. New York: Human Sciences Press.

McGlothlin, W. H., ed. 1971. *Chemical Comforts of Man: The Future. Journal of Social Issues* 27(3).

Mule, S. J., ed. 1981. *Behavior in Excess: An Examination of the Volitional Disorders.* New York: Free Press.

National Research Council, Committee on Substance Abuse and Habitual Behavior. 1982. *An Analysis of Marijuana Policy.* Washington, D.C.: National Academy Press.

National Task Force on Cannabis Regulation. December 1982. *The Regulation and Taxation of Cannabis Commerce.* Washington, D.C.: NORML.

Pizano, E. S. 1980. *A Proposal to Legalize Marihuana.* Bogotá, Colombia: National Association of Financial Institutions.

Robins, L. N. 1979. "Addict Careers." In *Handbook on Drug Abuse*, ed. R. I. Dupont, A. Golstein, and J. O'Donnell, 325–36. Washington, D.C.: Superintendent of Documents, U.S. Government Printing Office.

——, Davis, D. H., and Goodwin, D. W. 1974. "Drug Use in U.S. Army Enlisted Men in Vietnam: A Follow-up on Their Return Home." *American Journal of Epidemiology* 99:235–49.

Siegel, R. K. 1979. "Ginseng Abuse Syndrome: Problems with the Panacea." *Journal of the American Medical Association* 241:1614–15.

——. 1985. "New Patterns of Cocaine Use: Changing Doses and Routes." In *Cocaine Use in America: Epidemiological and Clinical Perspectives*, ed. N. J. Kozel and E. H. Adams, 204–20. National Institute on Drug Abuse Research Monograph 61. DHHS Publication no. (ADM) 85–1414. Washington, D.C.: Superintendent of Documents, U.S. Government Printing Office.

——, Collings, P. R., and Diaz, J. L. 1977. "On the Use of *Tagetes lucida* as a Huichol Smoking Mixture: The Aztec 'Yahutli' with Suggestive Hallucinogenic Effects." *Economic Botany* 31:16–23.

——, Elsohly, M. A., Plowman, T., Rury, P. M., and Jones, R. T. 1986. "Cocaine Found in Herbal Tea." *Journal of the American Medical Association* 255:40.

Silverberg, R. 1975. *Drug Themes in Science Fiction*. DHEW Publication no. (ADM) 75–190. Rockville, Md.: National Institute on Drug Abuse.

Somers, L., Bingham, R., Myers, V. S., and Thorsen, C. 1981. "Cocaine Treatment of Rheumatoid Arthritis: A Neuromuscular Dysfunction." Unpublished manuscript.

Steinmetz, E. F. 1973. *Kava-kava: Famous Drug Plant of the South Sea Islands*. New York: High Times/Level Press.

Trebach, A. S. 1982. *The Heroin Solution*. New Haven: Yale University Press.

Tyler, V. E. 1986. "Plant Drugs in The Twenty-first Century." *Economic Botany* 40:279–88.

Weil, A. T. 1981. "The Therapeutic Value of Coca in Contemporary Medicine." *Journal of Ethnopharmacology* 3:367–76.

Whitefield, M. 10 December 1985. "Coca Researchers Seek New Uses for It." *Miami Herald*: 8A.

Zinberg, N. E. 1984. *Drug, Set, and Setting: The Basis for Controlled Intoxicant Use*. New Haven: Yale University Press.

—— and Harding, W. M., eds. 1982. *Control Over Intoxicant Use: Pharmacological, Psychological and Social Considerations*. New York: Human Sciences Press.

Index

forage plants, 28
Ford, Gerald, 276
Ford, Henry, 269
form of drug, 302
fourth drive, 10, 206–26,
    231, 312–13
    adaptability of, 278
    drugs medicating needs
    of, 309
    dynamics of, 222–25
    efforts to eliminate, 251,
    293
    principle of, 277
    universality of, 260
free base, 181, 224,
    306–7
Freud, Sigmund, 264
fungi, 24, 68

gangrenous ergotism, 69
*Garden of Worldly
    Delights* (Bosch),
    20
Gaston, Lucy, 269
Gautier, Théophile,
    146–47, 165
genetics, 62, 113, 115,
    193, 209
gerbils, 291–92
ginseng, 36, 308–9
girning, 163
glutethimide (Doriden),
    282
goats, 3, 15, 53, 54–55, 67
    and alcohol, 108
    and coffee, 209
    in discovery of poisons
    and intoxicants,
    37–39
    and plant drugs, 65, 100
goat's joy, 39
gods, 82, 83, 102–3, 126,
    173
Gogh, Vincent Van, 109
Golden Crescent, 285
Golden Triangle, 285
Gombe National Park
    (Tanzania), 89
Goodall, Jane, 67, 89
goose grass, 39
gorillas, 64, 90

government regulation of
    drug use, 9, 252,
    253, 266–70, 273,
    274
    failure of, 292–93
    response to, 274, 277,
    279–83
Grant, Ulysses S., 258,
    260–62
    memoirs, 261–62
grape vine, 101
grasses, 27, 69
grasshoppers, 30, 158–59,
    209
grazing, 48–49
green lily, 47
grubs, 23, 51
Guahibo Indians, 73, 77
guc-kand, 158
guinea pigs, 85, 110
guppies, 73, 194
gustation, 31
Gymnema sylvestre, 29
Gymnemic acid, 29
gymnosperms, 25, 27

habituation, 43–44, 215
hair analysis, 13, 125–26,
    290, 291
hallucinations, 21, 66,
    109, 220, 229,
    234–35
    in animals, 51, 63–65, 67
    with cocaine, 185
    and criminal behavior,
    239–41
    fixed patterns of, 227,
    232–35
    with hashish, 147, 233
    with peyote, 233
    reporting about, 14, 165,
    214
    in rodents, 151
    term, 72
    transformation of
    thoughts into visual
    imagery key to, 232,
    234
hallucinatory constants,
    231–32, 233–34
hallucingenia, 26

hallucinogens, 14, 24, 30,
    70–72, 161, 162, 209,
    211, 298
    accidents with, 55, 56–80
    animal use of, 14, 61–72
    and behavior change,
    193–200
    ceremonial, 54
    classification in
    Controlled Substances
    Act, 273
    controlled use of, 70–71
    dysfunctional behavior
    caused by, 72–75
    effects of, 74–75, 76
    intentional use with bad
    effects, 75–80
    as medicine, 309
    mental images created by,
    228–35
    risk of compulsion with,
    221–22
    safe, 297
Hammond, William, 259
hamsters, 86–87, 111
Hanks, Nancy, 257
Harding, Warren, 269
hare's-lettuce, 39
harman, 82
harmine, 64, 82
Harrison, William Henry,
    256
Harrison "Narcotics" Act,
    267–68, 273
Harvey, Gideon, 136
Harvey, William, 138
Hasan-ibn-Sabah, 159–60
hashish, 15, 145, 146–66,
    192, 278, 283, 284
    animal studies, 160–61
    as aphrodisiac, 158
    effects of, 147, 148–49,
    160, 165–66, 197, 202
    hallucinations in use of,
    233
hawkmoths, 23, 34, 83,
    132
Haydar (monk), 148
Hayes, Lucy, 263
Hayes, Rutherford B.,
    262–63